The Gospel for Buddhists
and the Dharma for Christians

The Gospel for Buddhists and the Dharma for Christians

DONOVAN ROEBERT

RESOURCE *Publications* · Eugene, Oregon

THE GOSPEL FOR BUDDHISTS AND THE DHARMA FOR CHRISTIANS

Copyright © 2009 Donovan Roebert. All rights reserved. Except for brief quotations in critical publications or reviews, no part of this book may be reproduced in any manner without prior written permission from the publisher. Write: Permissions, Wipf and Stock Publishers, 199 W. 8th Ave., Suite 3, Eugene, OR 97401.

Resource Publications
A Division of Wipf and Stock Publishers
199 W. 8th Ave., Suite 3
Eugene, OR 97401
www.wipfandstock.com

ISBN 13: 978-1-60608-040-5

Manufactured in the U.S.A.

Contents

Acknowledgments ix
Author's Preface xi
Foreword by Ven. Prof. Samdhong Rinpoche xv
Foreword by Prof. John W. de Gruchy xix
Introduction xxi

Part 1: Syncretism, Exclusivism and the Middle Way 1

Extreme Syncretism – Exclusive Conformism – Self, Relativity and the Absolute – Relative Selves, Relative Paths – A Middle Way – The Relative Nature of Self and Religion – Positively Open or Negatively Shut – Faith and Knowledge.

Part 2: The Teachers: Jesus Christ and the Buddha 17

Jesus in the Gospels – The Historical Jesus – The Teaching of Jesus – His life as Teaching – His Death and Resurrection – The Pattern of Christian growth – Evil Defeated – Christlike Sacrifice – Knowing God and His Kingdom – The Life of the Buddha – The Life of the Buddha as Teaching – The Buddha's Dharma: The First Noble Truth – The Second Noble Truth – The Third Noble Truth – The Fourth Noble Truth: The Eightfold Path – Other Teachings.

Part 3: The Saving Work of the Teachers 66

The Nature of the Teachers and the Nature of People – The Buddha as Universal Teacher – The Dharmakaya Emanation – Transcending Karma – A Buddhist View of Christ – Intellectual Analysis and Spirit – Other Complementary Truths – Fallenness: Eating The Fruit – Repentance and Renewal – Renewal in Buddhism – The Sense of Fallenness – In Christ – In the Three Jewels – A Pause to Look Back.

Contents

PART 4: OUTLINE HISTORIES OF CHRISTIANITY AND BUDDHISM 127

History, Diversity, Division and Authenticity – BRIEF HISTORY OF CHRISTIANITY – The First Century – Early Scriptures – Institution – Doctrine – Method and Practice – Summary of the First Period – The Second and Third Centuries – The Imperial Church – After Constantine – The Roman Church – The Later Byzantine Church – Schism – The Medieval Church – The Reformation – The Counter-Reformation – Protestantism – Later Developments – The Modern Church – Christian Diversity – The Christian Understanding of History – BRIEF HISTORY OF BUDDHISM – The Early Sects – Monasticism – The First Scholastic Splits – Early Buddhist Practice – Early Missions – The Mahayana – Developments in Mahayana Doctrine to 500 AD – The Hinayana in the Same Period – Later Buddhist Missions – The Tantrayana – The Later Spread of Buddhism – Chinese Buddhism – Japan – Tibet – Buddhism After 1000 AD – Revision and Diversity – History, Diversity and the Mean.

PART 5: THE PATHS AND THE GOALS 203

The Christian Goal in the World – Personal Will, Habits of Mind – Human Instinct – The Buddhist Goal in Samsara: Wisdom – Compassion – Comparative Comment – Christian Perseverance – Buddhist Determination – A Note on the Stages of the Path – Stages of the Christian Path – First Stage: The Path of Renewal – Second Stage: The Path of Awareness – Development of Self-View on the Path of Awareness – Other Aspects of Growth – Third Stage: The Path of Dying – Falling Away on the Path of Dying – Stability on the Path – Fourth Stage: The Path of Death – Purification – Completion – Fifth Stage: The Path of Resurrection – Two Approaches to the Christian Path – Obstacles on the Christian Path – Carnal Self-Centredness – Distraction – Doubt – Fear – Fear of Evil – Perfect Love as Antidote to Fear – Temptation – Actual Sin – Discouragement – Presumption – Despair – Summary: Mind on the Christian Path – Stages of the Buddhist Path – First Stage: The Path of Accumulation – Second stage: The Path of Preparation – Meditative Preparation – First Step: Cultivating Non-Distraction – Second Step: Identifying the Wrongly Perceived 'I' – Third Step: Reasoned Negation of the Inherent Existence of 'I' – Fourth Step: Cultivating Calm Abiding

(Shamatha) – Fifth Step: Single-Pointedness (Vipashyana) – Purpose – Mind and Modes of Consciousness – General Growth on the Path of Preparation – Third Stage: The Path of Seeing – Analytical Meditation on Emptiness – Alternating Meditation – Meditation on Emptiness – Attainments of Seeing – Meditation and Post-Meditation – Fourth Stage: The Path of Meditation – Wisdom-Compassion and the Perfections – Fifth Stage: No More Learning – Obstacles on the Eightfold Path – Wrong View of the Self – Wrong View of Others – Wrong View of Phenomena – Wrong View of Events – Wrong View of Dharma – Wrong Attitude to Self – Wrong Attitude to Others – Wrong Attitude to Phenomena – Wrong Attitude to Events – Wrong Attitude to Dharma – Distraction as Source of Obstacles on the Christian and Buddhist Paths – Overcoming Afflictions (Obstacles on the Christian Path in Buddhist Perspective) – Wrong Views and Attitudes (Obstacles on the Buddhist Path in Christian Perspective) – Self and the Inner Energy – Method – Empowerments – The Goal – Beyond Physical Death – The Christian View – The Buddhist View – Common Ground.

PART 6: CONCLUSION: AN INVITATION TO SPACIOUSNESS 309

The Essential Path – Doctrine – Spaciousness.

Acknowledgments

For instruction in the Christian and Buddhist paths I am indebted to the many teachers who have shared their insights with me me over the past thirty years. Foremost among them are Ven. Prof. Samdhong Rinpoche, an embodiment of Buddhadharma; and Fr Bernhard Wiederkehr OSSP, in whose life I saw most clearly the meaning of Christlikeness. To them this book is also dedicated.

For elucidation of some of the finer points of Buddhist doctrine, method, and practice, the following excellent guides have been consulted: Herbert V. Guenther, *Buddhist Philosophy in Theory and Practice*, Shambala Publications 1971; Jeffrey Hopkins, *Meditation on Emptiness*, Wisdom Publications 1996, and H.H. Dalai Lama, *A simple Path*, Harper Collins 1996. In the section on the life of the Buddha some utterances are quoted, with slight paraphrasing, from: *Buddha, His Life and Teachings*, Axiom Publishers 2003.

For quick consultation in Catholic and Protestant doctrine the following have been most helpful: Sebastian Bullough, *Roman Catholicism*, Penguin Books 1963, and Marvin Halverson & Arthur Cohen (ed.), *A Handbook of Christian Theology*, Meridian Books 1958. For source material in the development of Christian doctrine, theology, Christology, and method, as also for readings in Christian history, I have used with great profit Henry Scowcroft Bettenson (Ed.), *Documents of the Christian Church 2nd edn,* Oxford University Press 1963.

The books most handy and most often in use for my brief outlines of Christian and Buddhist history have been two: Paul Johnson, *History of Christianity*, Weidenfeld & Nicolson 1976, and the indispensible *Short History of Buddhism*, by Edward Conze, George Allen and Unwin Ltd 1980, whose elegant structure and amplitude of information are nowhere else available in such compact form. For readings in the history of the Eastern Orthodox churches, Dimitri Obolensky's *Byzantine Commonwealth*, Weiden & Nicolson Ltd 1971, has been an invaluable aid.

Acknowledgments

Warm thanks are also due to Prof. John de Gruchy, and again to my revered *kalyanamitra*, Samdhong Rinpoche, for providing forewords which, it is hoped, will encourage Christians and Buddhists alike to explore the enriching possibilities in Buddhist-Christian interaction.

To Bob Hill and Maarten Turkstra, and especially to my wife, Merriel, the kindest of critics, my thanks are due for critical readings of the work in progress.

Author's Preface

THIS BOOK IS INTENDED to encourage Christians and Buddhists to encounter one another with spacious minds. It is a plea for sharing religious truth at the most important level, that of our common humanity.

This was the chief motive for writing it, but it has other uses too.

Most Western Buddhists have come to the Dharma from Christianity, and this is often a cause for doubts and confusion. Even when this is not the case, the Western Buddhist practises in a largely Christian environment. In both cases there is a clear need for understanding how Buddhism stands in relation to Christianity, the Buddhist in relation to the Christian.

A further motivation was to provide for Buddhists with little or no knowledge of Christianity—Dharma teachers from non-Christian societies, for instance—some clearer insight into Christian spirituality. Christian teachings have too often been undervalued by those having only partial understanding of them.

The same holds good for Christians in their approach to Buddhism. All sorts of uninformed notions have been expressed by Christians who have barely scratched the surface of Dharma. In this regard the intention is not only to supply a fuller picture but also to show how much real benefit can be derived from it. The book is not meant for academic study. Its agenda is to bring Christians and Buddhists to authentic and fruitful dialogue and, beyond that, to a sharing of spiritual insights.

Buddhism and Christianity are vast subjects and my treatment of them can neither claim to be complete nor completely free from error. Behind the symbolism and allegory of all religions there is much room for diversity of interpretation, re-interpretation and, unfortunately, misinterpretation. But this essay does not want to be studied uncritically. Ideally it should both impart knowledge and challenge rigid thinking. Its best result would be to set in motion a vigorous and positive debate leading to a clearer understanding of what, fundamentally, Buddhists and Christians

Author's Preface

are about. They might find that they are closer to one another than they have traditionally supposed.

As for dealing with the varieties of doctrine and practice found within the many denominations of Christianity and schools of Buddhism, I have tried to stay on common ground. In my treatment of Christianity I have tried to remain in the broader scope of the *kerygma*, concentrating on the areas of faith and doctrine in which most Christians are united. In presenting Buddhism I have clearly favoured the Mahayana as inclusive of and developed from the earlier Hinayana. The Tantrayana has been dealt with only cursorily.

The five stages of the Buddhist Path (accumulation, preparation, seeing, meditation and no more learning) have been presented as if they were regularly accomplished within a single lifetime. This will no doubt amaze many Mahayanists. I have dealt with them in this way not only in the interests of comparison with the single-lifetime Christian Path but also because of my sense that most Western Buddhists are a little impatient with the idea of the 'countless lifetimes' needed to attain liberation, and also because liberation can be achieved in this very life. Still, I would be the first to acknowledge the unorthodoxy of this approach, as well as its simplistic character.

My treatment of the Christian Path may also raise some theological eyebrows (although, I hope, not temperatures). My analysis of mental aspects and processes involved in Christian spirituality may trouble some Christians. For one thing, the differentiation between 'mind', 'soul' and 'spirit' (*nous, psyche, pneuma*) traditional in Christianity has been a little softened here and the human spirit is, in some contexts, not presented as something fundamentally other than mind. But this has been done only for the sake of clarity and consistency. It does not reflect a doctrinal position. The Christian reader should easily discern where 'spirit' in the strict Christian sense is meant. It should be pointed out, on the other hand, that 'mind' as used in this essay is not to be understood only as the 'carnal mind'. What is meant, rather, is the total mental continuum of the person, of which the carnal mind and the spirit are aspects, energies or modes of mental experience.

My own Christian background is Roman Catholic, my Dharma is from Tibetan Buddhism. These personal elements have admittedly coloured my approach. I feel sure, however, that they will not prevent any Christian believer or Buddhist practitioner from finding an authentic reflection of their own spirituality in these pages. Indeed, my hope is that no one at all should consider themselves excluded from the message of this book.

Finally, there is the pernickety problem of the use in English of the masculine for the generic. It is a linguistic *fait accompli* which has so far only been overcome by the regular use of 'he or she', 'his and her' and 'him and her' whenever the singular pronoun has been needed. This solution seems as cumbersome and pedantic as the regular use of the plural 'they' eventually seems bizarre. The thing became so distracting that I was forced to settle for convention, albeit unhappily. In this case I must plead again the spirit of inclusiveness that is at the heart of this essay.

D. Roebert

Foreword

by Ven. Prof. Samdhong Rinpoche

WHATEVER 'TRUTH' IN ITSELF may be, it can never be plural or diverse. Anyone who sees it, sees it 'as it is' or in its 'suchness' (*tathata*). Yet, when the seer of truth tries to convey his or her experience of 'seeing,' the words used in describing it are bound to differ from person to person, although they have seen the same 'truth.' This is because language, which is a product of thought processes, has no direct relation with the thing being designated by words. For the sake of clear communication, people living in proximity to one another develop language by agreeing on definitive words for the naming of objects, but these words could easily be assigned to entirely different and even opposite objects by other communities with other languages. But the assigning of different words does not change the nature and identity of the objects to which they are assigned.

Enlightened persons who have perceived the absolute truth have revealed their perceptions of truth at different times, in different languages and terms, to people of different backgrounds. As a result, enormously different religious traditions have emerged and been developed. Only through these different means can the meaning of the absolute be brought to everyone, everywhere. If there were only one religious tradition and one explanation of truth, in one language, the message of truth would have remained only among a tiny minority of people, and may not even have developed into a tradition at all.

In the realm of relativity, diversity in everything is the beauty and richness of the universe. The diversity of spiritual traditions also is the beauty and richness of spirituality. Therefore, all spiritual traditions, as long as they maintain their own purity, can always supplement and enrich one another. But when spirituality decays, leaving only names and institutions to linger on without the essence of spiritual practice, division and conflicts emerge in the name of religion or spiritual traditions. Human individuals, void of spiritual mind, begin to fight against one another in the name of religion, bringing immense misery and destruction to spirituality, humanity, and to the earth with all its living creatures. It is unfortunate when humanity cannot differentiate between authentic religions and the mere institutions built in the name of religion, just as it is unfortunate when individuals having no authentically religious mind still claim to be followers of one or another religious tradition. For these reasons misnamed and misconceived 'religious intolerance' or 'religious fundamentalism' become common issues which lead to communal disharmony and conflict.

Human history has been sullied by its numerous accounts of so-called 'religious wars' or 'crusades.' In the twenty-first Century we claim to be living in a 'post-modern' civilization, yet we are still faced by the problems of fundamentalism and civilizational conflicts, and to a worse degree than ever before in history.

Conflicts in the name of religion have two basic causes. The first cause is not practising one's own religion in accordance with the methods and paths shown in the spiritual teachings; accumulating a large amount of information about religion through hearing or reading, and perpetuating it through mere thought processes, but having no authentic experience. The second cause is lack of information, or sheer misinformation, about other religious traditions. For these, or other reasons, disharmony can easily be caused among people 'belonging' to one of the great religious traditions, but having no experience whatsoever of that tradition's teachings. Unless and until the individual sincerely practises his or her religion, it is difficult to transmit experiential realization, and impossible to receive it. Even so, we can disseminate correct information about religion if we offer understandable and suitable language, and authentic explanation, to the reader.

Today, a great number of people in the world follow Christianity and Buddhism. During the previous century a great deal of interfaith dialogue and interaction took place among the various religions, and particularly between western Christianity and eastern Buddhism. This is a great revolution in the field of spirituality. Such dialogues have brought the spiritual traditions closer to one another and opened a new dimension for all spiritual communities to work together for the benefit of all sentient beings. In this process of Christian-Buddhist interaction, this book is a milestone effort.

Foreword by Ven. Prof. Samdhong Rinpoche

The book shows a deep understanding and experiential perception of both traditions, as well as a clear grasp of the modern mind. I have no doubt that it will be of enormous benefit to readers, both now and in the future. Its 'Middle-Way' approach, described in the first part, which recognizes the limitations of both Extreme Syncretism and Exclusive Conformism, is dynamic and appropriate in its view. The book proceeds to a discussion of the Teachers, which is the natural means for evaluating the teachings at first-hand, or from the source: the authenticity of the Teacher's life. It goes on to describe the teaching processes, their historical development and lineage, and finally extends to the paths and goals. This way of narration gives to the reader an holistic view of both traditions. The commentaries on Buddhist teachings, including the subtle philosophical tenets, are very authentic in the treatment of their subject and very powerful in their expression. The concluding 'invitation to spaciousness' succinctly sums up the teachings of both traditions, and extends a warm and touching invitation to the realm of awakening within the infinite space of unconditioned consciousness. This book will therefore be of equal benefit to both beginners and those more advanced in practice.

Owing to my present obligations I have not had time to write the fuller foreword I would have liked to. Thus, I stop here and leave it to the reader to evaluate the work. May all sentient beings be elevated to the state of happiness!

Samdhong Rinpoche
Former Director of the Tibetan Institute of Higher Studies
Kalon Tripa (Prime Minister) of the Tibetan-Govt-in-Exile

Foreword

by Prof. John W. de Gruchy

Donovan Roebert kindly asked me to contribute a foreword to his timely and thoughtful book. I am delighted to do so because I applaud what he has attempted to do. The Christian Gospel, or good news, centred in Jesus Christ, is not well understood by most Buddhists (or even by many Christians), and certainly Christians generally have little if any knowledge of the Buddhist Dharma. The need for better understanding of each other's deepest convictions and way of life is not only necessary in our contemporary pluralistic world, but it is also of importance for all of us who are engaged in the search for a truly human existence.

Understandings of both the Christian Gospel and the Buddhist Dharma vary considerably within their respective faith communities. My own understanding of Christianity is not always identical to that expressed by Donovan. But that is how it should be, for he brings to the discussion his own experience both as a Christian who has at various times explored Catholicism, Protestantism and the Charismatic movements, and his experience now as a Buddhist, yet one who is still exploring the boundaries of both traditions separately and in relation to each other. So this is a deeply personal account and as such it carries with it a note of authenticity that lends conviction to the discussion.

Genuine interfaith dialogue and understanding should never lead to a blurring of differences. Christianity and Buddhism are not the same, and their paths of salvation and enlightenment certainly differ and diverge at significant points. Donovan has shown this to be the case. But he has also pointed to many similarities, some of which may not occur without such a guide as he has provided. And that is essentially what his book does. It is a companion for those who are embarked on the journey of becoming more truly human and who, in doing so, believe that these (and other) great religious traditions have much to offer.

John W. de Gruchy
Emeritus Professor of Christian Studies
University of Cape Town

Introduction

CHRISTIANITY AND BUDDHISM HAVE much in common and, beyond the common insights which these two great paths share, there are perspectives unique to each which can be mutually helpful. There are approaches which can be complementary. It would not be going too far to say that they can illumine and enrich each other in fundamental ways.

In spite of these possibilities they have from time to time met only to draw away from each other at the crucial stage of interaction where they might have become open to genuine, transformative sharing. It is as though at that point both become fixated on the boundaries which separate them. They seem afraid that their respective identities and definitions might go lost in the transaction of open understanding. Ironically the same fear that keeps them from opening the gates with generosity of mind also keeps them in submission to their uncomfortable limitations.

It is questionable whether either would even acknowledge that such limitations exist. Each considers itself as containing the complete instruction to complete salvation, and there is a sense in which this attitude is valid. Both have developed doctrines and methods which enable the individual to find ultimate liberation from the limitations and delusions of self. Both hold out a final goal that is both desirable and achievable. Both proclaim the ultimate overcoming of suffering and death.

Yet followers of both paths are often afflicted by doubts, unanswered questions, confusion and fear. There is still much room for assurance, comforting, edification and clarity. There are areas where co-operative help is not only possible but needed.

Christianity today is not able to achieve even a healthy unity in diversity. The energy put into ecumenism has not resulted in complete openness between communions. Christians remain separated from Christians by points of doctrine and practice, by politics and history, and by simple pride or the habits of tradition. It is not that diversity of beliefs, practices and institutional structures is in itself bad. It is the intolerance of one

Introduction

another that is lamentable. The same is true of Buddhism, although the divergence of schools of Buddhist thought is much less forceful and there is greater tolerance. But since both religions have factionalism within their own belief systems and systems of logic, it becomes more difficult for them to open themselves to influence from systems outside their own divided folds.

Yet it is exactly such an act of spaciousness and confidence that might enable them to discover a basis for authentic unity in diversity within their own communions. By allowing the interpenetration of their peripheral boundaries, important lessons can be learned about the breaking of internal barriers.

It is even more relevant to remember the spiritual growth of individual people within these vast groups, to bear in mind how barriers between people cause anger, hatred, bigotry and many other miseries. So, while it is impossible to ignore the potential in formal or institutional openness and co-operation, the benefits for individuals within these formal religious structures are always more important. People being open and gracious to other people, people finding points of agreement and ties of commonality; these are the raw materials of real compassionate living. This is where fear is eroded and replaced by trust.

This book is written in the hope of generating trust and mutual confidence between Christians and Buddhists, both as people and as institutions, but as people first. There is no conversionist agenda and no attempt to demonstrate the superiority of one faith over the other. The aim is not to change what people believe, but to console and transform the areas of doubt, separation and confusion which cripple people's spirituality.

An essay with these aims cannot afford to be very complex or ultra-profound. The problems which discourage spiritual growth are mostly simple, immediate and quotidian, although painful. The central question must therefore be: how can Christianity and Buddhism work together to remedy each other's ailments? It is the answer to this question, rather than the belabouring of dogmatic intricacies, that is attempted here. Thus, a good deal of room must necessarily be left for doctrinal and interpretational disputes.

In searching for the complementary aspects of Christianity and Buddhism our real point of departure is not our religion but our shared humanity. All human beings have a general desire to live in a mental or spiritual atmosphere of inner contentment and to avoid as far as pos-

Introduction

sible unnecessary mental or physical suffering. In these facts, and in the fact that inner peace is possible to all people, we can clearly see our indisputable sameness. In terms of negative potential, all people share the same danger and fear of falling victim to neuroses and the other common miseries. These are the strongest reasons for generating the motivation to help one another, to understand one another, to make room within our minds for the other. Before we are followers of any religion, and even if we never practice a religion, these simple benefits can be fully realized. By focusing on them and carefully considering their value and truth, we are enabled to make the important shifts away from apathy or antipathy and towards sympathy and empathy.

We are also able, by considering our human sameness, to understand to what extent the practice of religion can divide people if they try to develop their own spirituality to the exclusion of the other. How can such a spiritual practice possibly bring benefit, either to the adherent or to others? The energy and flow of compassion are only possible when we make an effort to know the other not as this or that, but as a fellow human being.

The benefits of this kind of sympathetic interrelationship are obviously enormous. It widens the sense of community to eventually include not only all human beings, but all living beings. By consistently viewing others as the same as oneself, a real sense of universal responsibility can be achieved, and responsible actions ensue. In this way humanity can attain the fullest spiritual potential, and violence or harmfulness can be greatly reduced.

On the other hand, the effects of factionalism and division are self-evident. From the legitimized murder that is open warfare to the various forms of social, personal and inner conflict, these effects are experienced every day. Conflicts between spiritual groups are the most self-contradictory and self-defeating expressions of people's tendency to close ranks. All these forms of violence can be traced back to ignorance of our real nature, of our sameness, and of our potential. Openness, the willingness to engage with others, even with those who seem different, is the only way out of this fundamental blindness. The apparent differences between people and people are always superficial if closely examined.

The spirit of this book is a plea for healing by the exercise of commonsense. It is surprising how often spiritual endeavour and attempts at mental development are divorced from commonsense or 'groundedness'. This is not to imply that transcendence or even eccentricity have no place

Introduction

in spirituality, or that complex intellectual analysis is superfluous. All of these are also expressions of our humanity. But it is commonsense that ultimately keeps us sane. The destructive aspect of spirituality lies in the assumption of ignorant and neurotic views. The commonsense test of any view's validity is made on the basis of its violence or non-violence. And we need to understand that even a negative thought is violent.

Healing is not something we can only hope and pray for. It is something that is largely achieved through thoughts, words and deeds. Neither is it only an interpersonal dynamic. People need healing within themselves. Actually there is no effective way to bring about healing between people without first remedying the ills in individual minds. Those afflictions are not hard to identify: ill will, anger, desire, pride, fear and the like. Their source is always ignorance. We need to learn, and we can only take things in when we become open and relaxed. The same is true of our ability to pass things on, to give. There can be no authentic generosity of mind without calm clarity.

The hope for co-operation between various spiritual paths is not the same as the desire to encourage one world religion. Diversity is in the very nature of things. It will never be eradicated. That is one of the reasons why co-operation and trust are so necessary. The other vital reason is the need to create peace in the midst of ineradicable diversity. Since the fact of diversity will never change, we need to make peace with diversity itself. We need to learn from it and to use it as our medium for growth in love. Otherwise we will only love those whom we consider part of our own group. This seems a very restricted love, if it is love at all.

Part 1

Syncretism, Exclusivism and the Middle Way

EXTREME SYNCRETISM

Syncretism is sometimes described as a spiritual salad or a spiritual soup. The syncretist takes teachings from various religions and combines them into a new individualistic religious view. Syncretists are clearly open-minded, all embracing and tolerant. One of the problems of syncretism, however, is that the openness required to assimilate a syncretistic vision has its own personal and interpersonal dangers.

At a personal level syncretism might lead to excessive reliance on the imagination and, more specifically, the romance of the imagination. It can become irrational, inconsistent and flighty. It can lose truth in a sea of ritual, symbolism and over-absorption. This is a problem related to the function of mysticism, even in orthodox religious practice. The remedy in orthodox religion is generally to reign in, channel and rationalize mystical practice so that it does not lose touch with the common vision. In individualistic syncretism there are no controls.

Syncretistic expression can become distorted by personal neurosis, the more so as there is no doctrinal or institutional authority against which it can test itself. The temptations to self-delusion are manifold and powerful. Any system based only on belief has constantly to guard against the irrational tendencies of ego. When the belief system is unconstrainedly individualistic, the dangers of falling into neurotic self-expression disguised as spiritual expression are multiplied.

The elegance of doctrinal purity can also be lost, so that the syncretistic system becomes cumbersome and inconsistent. It is hard to deny that the most efficacious spiritual paths are essentially simple, no matter how much they might be complicated by intellectual development of the simple core. These developments are mostly transitory and always peripheral. For people in the struggle of worldly life, it is the elegance of a spiritual remedy that appeals and brings benefit. The basic creed should be compact enough to memorize and elegant enough to make sense easily. What cannot be remembered cannot be applied, and a teaching that makes no sense baffles belief. Although it is true that inner spiritual awakening is a constant reminder of how the spiritual person should conduct themselves in thought, word and deed, there are bound to be the dry periods when memory must be the guide. There must be a clear frame of reference.

Syncretism can also lead to moral crises because of its extreme tolerance and confusion of norms. Because there are no clear, fundamental points of reference, all things may become permissible. All things can be justified too. The 'free spirit' can be destroyed by the abuse of its freedom. This sort of abandonment of focus and centredness may lead to a quasi-religious 'acting out disorder'.

In essence, all the dangers of unrestrained syncretism are rooted in an insufficiency of wisdom. The pure light of wisdom is never overburdened with too much complexity. By its nature it is of course never dull or unreceptive. It has an answer to every question, but the answer is always close at hand. Wisdom does not need to seek out every possible answer from every possible source. Its answers are universal in the same way that thousands of different words in thousands of languages mean the same thing. If syncretism fails to generate the wisdom that is near to all people, it will also fail to generate compassion and inner contentment.

Much can be said about the hazards of the syncretistic path and everyone should contemplate them in order to avoid them. We will confine ourselves here to the possibilities sketched above: irrational departure from reality, neurotic and egotistical distortion, doctrinal incoherence and moral degeneration. The syncretist who can avoid all these might well attain to wisdom, but will have travelled by an unnecessarily long and tricky path to get there.

With regard to interpersonal relations and the consolations of communion, syncretism envinces a long list of negative possibilities, both from the side of the syncretist and from the side of the religious community. The syncretist is a non-conforming personality and the religious community is at least conformed around its pivotal creed and within its traditional sphere of religious experience.

Syncretism, Exclusivism and the Middle Way

Conformity is not always narrow and bigoted. In its best form it derives from a mindset which values unity and consensus. Within a particular religious communion it is a relative expression of agreement, providing a basis for unconflicted communication and, more importantly, establishing the crux from which the communal wisdom arises and towards which it tends. This tension ensures that the shared wisdom does not develop into sophistry, hypocrisy or folly.

The non-conformist threatens the stability and the bonds of agreement in any conformed and united fellowship. The refusal to conform is a rejection of the teachings, spirit and other unifying factors within a particular spiritual communion. This is not simply a matter of conflict between assenting and dissenting people. The factors around which the assenting group is gathered in unanimous fellowship cannot be made vulnerable to please the taste of the non-conformist. Both weak- and strong-minded people share the same central religious system. The weaker members need a firm foundation of reference and refuge. Stronger members have a duty to uphold the tradition, not only for the sake of the weaker members, but to protect the fundamental system from falling into confusion. The non-conformist cannot expect to be admitted.

It is unlikely that a syncretist would want to be admitted to a conformist fellowship, but this leaves the syncretist in a lonely environment, both psychologically and spiritually. Both the ego aspect and the spiritual essence of the person must walk a lonely path. Syncretists also cannot have full religious communion among themselves, because the central dogma is always individualistic. There must be a mutual exclusivity, however subtle.

The conformist group may not always practise, but always values humility. Humility is the authentic spirit of conformity, and it does not necessarily imply dumb submission. One expression of humility is the openhearted willingness to conform for the sake of others. By its nature, syncretism cannot allow that kind of humility. Syncretism must have two faces, one of openness and the other of divisiveness. In that case humility can only go so far, and must be accompanied by a limited wisdom and a limited compassion.

The argument that syncretism allows all people a communion or unity through their freedom to believe what they want to believe is not ultimately valid. If it were valid, it would be tantamount to admitting that all religious systems, including orthodox and conformed systems, are of equal spiritual value. That being so, the syncretist should have no objections to becoming conformed, if only for the sake of others.

Whatever the stated position may be, it is hard to argue against the opinion that non-conformists and conformists must co-exist uncomfortably, and more probably in a state of conflict and suspicion. Of course, neither can benefit from such a relationship. The conformist group cannot remedy the problem by becoming non-conformist in the syncretistic sense, because that would imply dissolution into an increasingly individualistic or antinomian interaction which would guarantee heightened possibilities for division. So another way has to be found if there is to be true communion between spiritual people of all religions.

EXCLUSIVE CONFORMISM

When conformism functions as the opposite extreme of syncretism, it is perhaps even more divisive, unwise and uncompassionate than unconstrained individual religious freedom. It becomes closed, rigid and exclusive. It is compelled by its own rigidity to advocate the salvation or liberation of the 'few'. This means that its members are the only people in possession of the truth. All others are lost.

Such groups always couple their teaching with an ultimatum: join us or perish. The remainder of humanity and its diverse religious quests are written off as worthless and pitiable. There are no points of contact with other communions, only two isolated groups remain: the chosen few and the lost many.

Whereas the syncretist claims that all paths are valid, the exclusivist holds that only one path can lead to liberation. There is a blank refusal even to consider that religious diversity is inevitable and good.

It worth pausing to examine how and why people create and choose to belong to these exclusivist institutions. Again there are many complex factors at play, and we can only look at those which are central in terms of human psychology, spirituality and community.

The ordinary or ego mind is driven by anxiety to seek out a pattern of security. This anxiety is not the wholesome spiritual discomfort which recognizes human shortcomings in relation to absolute truth and purity, and motivates the person to remedy his ignorance and failure. It is the ordinary anxiety which cannot cope with the ordinary human problem of loneliness, separation, failure and so forth. It drives the ego-mind towards any place which promises ultimate security, even if that security is achieved at the cost of universal responsibility and compassion. The frightened individual can huddle together with the few, and that is enough. This dynamic is the most basic component of psychological exclusivism. Once having joined the few, the only anxiety the person need consider is the fear of excommunication or ostracision. Otherwise, liberation and salvation are assured.

From a developmental vantage point the exclusivist goal is purity or holiness attained by concentrating intently on the particular doctrines, practices and experience in the isolated communion. Generally, this kind of determined focus is useful for spiritual growth. It becomes self-defeating, however, when it turns its back on all people outside of the narrow communion and when it abandons the generosity even to admit the possibility that other paths can lead to truth and enlightenment. The wider scope of human spirituality, both historically and in terms of present diversity, is simply shut out, as is the fact that other exclusivist groups believe with equal fervor that only their communion is chosen for salvation. If all the exclusivist groups in the world could agree to debate on logical grounds which one of them was actually the sole possessor of truth, there would have to be a collapse into absurdity.

Logical approaches cannot have a place among exclusivists, because logic would always prove them wrong. It would always tend to prove that the vast area of common ground between people extends most markedly to their spirituality. That is why real fruitful love arises from a recognition of human sameness based on commonsense research. We cannot love only because we are commanded to love. We need to see that others, no matter how apparently different, are always exactly what we are. In this recognition, all basis for judgment is destroyed. Exclusivism, on the other hand, cannot exist without judgment of the other, or else it must cease to be exclusive.

The exclusivist community functions as one mind. There is no room for unity in diversity because diversity means dissent and the dissenter must be excluded. It is impossible that groups functioning in this way can be held together in complete absence of fear. Even where that fear plays an unconscious or unperceived role, it must be present. Thus, the channels of compassion must be restricted.

Usually exclusivist fellowships are united under one strong individual who claims the sanctity of revelation without the breadth of spirit to love all people equally. The leader is the focal point, the sole representative of saving truth. The disciples are manipulated by fear and the prospect of special salvation. Their contentment and consolation are found in their inclusion into the special group and its teaching.

There can be no discussion around the exclusivist group in its spiritual relation to the total human community. The rest of humanity with its diversity of spiritual paths is already excluded. Any act of inclusion, other than by conversion, is a contradiction in terms and would alter the exclusive nature of these groups.

The exclusivist is harder to reach than the syncretist because the syncretist is at least open to every possibility. The exclusivist group settles doggedly around the set of doctrinal emphases which it has chosen as its own field of truth and endeavour. As an individual, the exclusivist can seldom be approached without reference to the group. This only becomes possible once doubts have arisen in the individual mind. In the best cases, these doubts will arise because of a dearth of love in the practices of the exclusivist group.

SELF, RELATIVITY, AND THE ABSOLUTE

Between the two extremes of syncretism and exclusivism there are varying shades of non-conformism and conformism, and in the middle a broad band of more or less tolerant, open-spirited religious practitioners and communions. The most mature of these strike a healthy balance in the tension between receptivity and guardedness or between unlimited acceptance and unrelenting rejection.

Sometimes the reason for tolerance may just be apathy or agnosticism: nothing is ultimately valid, so an attitude of tolerance is inevitable and rational. Or the reasons may be completely intellectual, based on the perception of the unspiritual ego-mind. Since there is such a variety of diverging philosophies, the reasoning goes in this case, everything can be argued into validity. There is no spiritual groundedness discriminating between mere intellectual analysis and spiritual wisdom. In all cases of apathetic agnosticism and intellectual lassitude, wisdom and compassion arise rather stuntedly from an insufficiency of spiritual energy and effort.

We need to discover an open, tolerant way that is wholesome and conducive to spiritual growth and sustained friendship between different religious groups, rather than a way of openness that is merely passive, uncritical and unreflecting. This kind of way cannot produce an energized heart-meeting between spiritual people on different paths. It is coming out of a surrender to partial understanding and so can only ever yield a partial or incomplete result. Any institution or person having lost spiritual energy and clarity will run down into a state of resignation. The acceptance of others coming out of resignation to doubts and failures is the same as acceptance of spiritual defeat. It is not a useful, creative meeting ground.

In trying to find a way forward to a positive and spiritually vibrant arena of sharing and growing, we must begin by looking at two central questions involved in our spirituality: the question of selfhood or identity, and that of relativity or interdependence. We need to contrast them, not with their opposites, but with that which is found in their absence: when self and relativity are absent, what is there in their stead? We must then go on to relate the extremes of syncretism, exclusivism and the wholesome middle way to these factors. Then we have to find out how self, relativity, and the absolute which is revealed in their absence, influence wisdom, compassion and salvation or enlightenment. In this section we will deal with these questions in a general way rather than examining their dynamics in the specific spheres of Christianity and Buddhism. We want to consider what is common to all people first.

'Self' is the main problem in all authentic spiritual practice. Untransformed or untranscended self is recognized as the chief obstacle to spiritual growth and spiritual expression in wisdom and compassion. In a more ultimate sense, the ordinary or relative self cannot be liberated, saved or enlightened. In its relative nature it cannot survive or evolve to attain to Absolute Truth. It must overcome its relative self-view in order to discover its absolute nature on the path to Truth because Final Truth and the experience of Final Truth are in the absolute category.

RELATIVE SELVES, RELATIVE PATHS

The relativity of self can be explained on three fundamental grounds. First, the relative self or ego is naturally impermanent, conditioned and subject to change. If this were not so, nobody would be able to make new choices or arrive at a new understanding. Something that is absolute cannot change. The Absolute is not something which can evolve into something else. It is what it is, and remains exactly what it is. If the relative self were actually absolute, it would have to ask itself what has happened to the relative self of yesterday, of last month, or of twenty years ago? Why is it no longer present as it was then?

Second, the relative self is clearly something that has been produced, whereas something absolute cannot be produced. If it could be produced, it would exist in dependence on that which produced it, and something absolute can by its nature never exist in dependence on other things. Neither is the relative self only initially produced. It is being produced second by second, so to speak. It is arising from psychological principles and dynamics that are not themselves the relative self. The Absolute, on the other hand, is always self-sufficient.

Third, the relative or worldly self is subject to suffering; it is passible at every point. We speak with Hamlet of the 'thousand shocks that flesh is heir to.' Everybody experiences these shocks in the course of life in the world. The relative self has its unavoidable growth pains, its struggles, regrets, hopes and fears. Something absolute however, cannot experience these alternating periods of pain and happiness because the absolute has no need of growth-inducing episodes, nor can it regress. It is always the same.

We need go no further than this to establish that the worldly self is relative and therefore limited in what it can achieve. The Absolute need not achieve anything because it already is everything it can be. Thinking about this, we can clearly understand the relative nature of self and the nature of relativity itself.

When the relative self is absent, its Absolute Nature is present. In the absence of all relative things, all the people, creatures and phenomena that make up our world and our realms, only the Absolute remains. Without any specific definitions, we must agree that, in a general way, our spiritual search is a quest by relative beings for discovering their Absolute Essence. If we do not discover our Absolute Essence we must forever remain limited, dependent, changeable and inclined to failure and suffering, since these tendencies are inherent in the relative mode of existence.

It is not possible for a relative being, a relative self, to walk on an absolute path. An absolute path is a contradiction in terms. A religious path implies a journey towards a destination, and nothing that is absolute can function as a gradual path of progress. The destination, which is absolute, is not the same as the path which leads to it. The path is a progressive way which is always leading to something beyond itself. Therefore the path is necessarily relative.

Syncretism, Exclusivism and the Middle Way

Where the self is completely overcome or transcended, to be fulfilled in its Absolute Essence, there is no need of a path to follow because the Absolute Nature has 'arrived'. The fact that it can arrive shows that there is no unbridgeable divide between our relative world and its Absolute Essence or Source. Our relative existence derives from the Absolute and can return to the Absolute.

But our personal selves and our religious paths are still relative. That is why there is so much room for disagreement, for differing views, doctrines, practices and methods among relative personal selves and among the varieties of religious paths.

Since paths cannot be absolute, there can be no absolute paths. If there were an absolute 'path' there would be no need for religious method, practices, doctrines and belief, for these are all relative instruments which guide and motivate people towards the goal.

These small examinations represent only a fraction of the arguments available for demonstrating the relative nature of our selves and of our religious paths. At first these arguments may seem daunting or unconvincing. They need to be contemplated with diligence and sincerity if we are to be loosened from the conviction that our own path is absolutely self-sufficient and unable to accommodate helpful truths from other religious systems. Besides, the realization of our relative situation is useful for cultivating humility and kindness and, in the end, a wisdom that is adaptable and inviting.

A MIDDLE WAY

There are right and wrong ways of dealing with the knowledge that we and our religious paths are relative. The fact that selves and paths are relative does not mean that they are to be despised. They have an inherent value as tools for getting at the truth and for helping others to do the same. They are exciting, pliable and full of potential for positive usefulness.

In the hands of the syncretist the relativity of our nature is taken too far. Relativity does not mean that anything goes. It does not mean that eclectic mental passivity is the way towards Final Truth. In this case the person is allowing himself to live at the mercy of sheer relativism, to be subjected to a choiceless experience in terms of which everything is believable and acceptable.

The exclusivist, on the other hand, completely fails to see or acknowledge the fact of relativity. In the exclusivist world-view a few chosen relative selves and relative doctrines are consecrated as absolutes. Everything else may be naturally relative, but these things are not. So a double folly is committed. Some relative things are absolutized while the rest are cursorally dismissed. By these acts exclusivists change some tools into holy objects and simply discard others. There is not much left to work with.

A moderate middle-way recognizes the inherent usefulness of the fact of relative selfhood and of relative religious systems. It sees relative reality not as a cosmic theatre of confusion, but as a pliable and workable medium in which can be found a set of useful, complementary tools. It also does not view natural relativity as excluding the Absolute, but as an interdependently functioning mechanism for attaining liberation in oneness with the Absolute.

By making wise, compassionate decisions we can harness our relative reality to our quest for a saving truth. Not all things are useful and many aspects of our relative being may be harmful. Only wisdom can discern these factors. That same wisdom, working in concert with openness and lovingkindness, never dismisses any truth by which it can be enriched and empowered. All things are tested, and the good is retained. Nobody is discarded or judged only on the basis of their personal convictions. Ultimately there are only two kinds of people: those enslaved by their refusal or inability to reach beyond the relative, and those who are using various relative tools to achieve spiritual wholeness. The former are in need of compassionate help and the latter of compassionate fellowship and encouragement.

By contrast, if the relative nature of self and of religious paths is not recognized as relative, it can be of little or no use. All that can be done is to consider some relative truths and some aspects of the relative self to be absolute, unchangeable and final. This switch can only be achieved by a system and mindset based solely on belief. The problem here is that anything has been and can be believed by people. Blind belief is a huge part of the reason why people are so divided and caught up in cycles of conflict.

THE RELATIVE NATURE OF SELF AND RELIGION

The relative self has an innately intuitive sense of its Absolute Source. This intuitive clue as to their real nature causes in people a yearning for spiritual awakening, for union with the Divine. That is always the beginning of the spiritual path. The obverse of this yearning is a fear of going lost in the negative patterns of selfhood and selfishness. This is the beginning of wisdom. The beginning of wisdom occurs in the relative domain and one of the first steps in acquiring spiritual wisdom is the search for a religious path. This search, too, is conducted by a relative self looking among relative options. In making a choice, tradition, the predominant religion of the society, and the varieties of individual predisposition play the most determinative roles. Having chosen a path, the spiritual practitioner uses the tools and methods provided by that path to draw closer to the Absolute Source. In some cases the tools and methods may not be sufficient to help the practitioner at certain crucial points, or the practitioner may lack the skill to use the tools and methods properly. In this case, rather than making spiritual shipwreck, it is reasonable to bring other tools and methods into the path. In the final analysis what one believes or conceives is not of ultimate importance. The important thing is that the self find a passable route to Final Truth and to the inner contentment which Truth supplies.

The relative self can only practise genuine compassion to the extent that it has cultivated wisdom. There is a long distance between the practice of relative compassion, which is derived from the reasoning processes and the emotions, to Absolute Compassion which is spiritual and without limit or judgement. On this road no helpful tools and methods can be despised, because compassion expressed in wisdom is the greatest good people can do for one another.

Although this subject will be dealt with in more detail in later chapters, it is worth noting here that all of the functions of relative selfhood are carried out by means of the ordinary reasoning mind and the ordinary emotions. Of course there are strong possibilities for using these faculties in negative ways or, even worse, for being used by them. A person is particularly vulnerable to the pressures of ego when ego is viewed as a final or absolute self which asserts that 'This is I. This is what I am. This is all I am.' The same is true of relative religious paths: 'This is the only path. This is my path. There is no other path.' Many opportunities for healthy development and skilful spiritual practice are lost because of this very common error.

In relation to salvation or enlightenment the understanding of relativity can demonstrate two fundamental truths. In the first place it teaches people that the relative self, even the positive or good aspects of the relative self, cannot be brought to final liberation. It can only walk the path, and hopefully walk it skilfully, to the Absolute Source of self, wisdom, and compassion. At the point of authentic meeting with the Absolute, the relative self becomes little more than an instrument of expression. It is no longer driven by its mundane desires, aversions, ignorance and other neuroses. It no longer acts out of its reasonings or emotions, whether positive or negative. The liberated self simply expresses the Absolute Wisdom-Love-Compassion in relative modes that are helpful and comprehensible to other relative selves.

(It is as well at this point to explain the use of the rather cumbersomely hyphenated term 'Wisdom-Love-Compassion.' It is being used here to describe the highest ideal of both Buddhism and Christianity. In Buddhism, 'compassion' is defined as 'the wish to liberate all sentient beings from suffering' while 'love' is defined as 'the wish to establish all sentient beings in highest happiness.' Compassion, in this differentiation, is that which recognizes suffering and works to eliminate it, while love looks at the potential for happiness in others and encourages its growth. In Christianity, 'love' in the highest sense is perfected spiritual love or *agape*. It is the kind of developed love which is free from all self-interest and respect of persons. Christianity does not much use the term 'compassion' because the idea of compassion is implicit in *agape*. In later passages the ideals of Christianity and Buddhism are defined respectively as 'Wisdom-Love' and 'Wisdom-Compassion' in order to reflect the traditional language of the two paths. But this usage neither implies that compassion is absent from the Christian ideal, nor that love is absent from that of Buddhism).

The relative religious path has no absolute qualities until it reaches the goal of Salvation or Enlightenment. At that point, the path and the goal become one. When the path and the goal become one, the person on the path has arrived at the goal, which is absolute. Thus, at that blissful meeting ground, the path, the person, and the Final Truth, expressed in Absolute Wisdom-Love-Compassion, are united into one energy of Life-Love-Truth.

It is always beneficial to have companions and guides on any path. It is foolish to dismiss wisdom and beneficial instruction, not to speak of the joys of sharing, only because the person who is wise and able to benefit one is not on the same path as oneself. Wisdom is drawn to wisdom wherever it is found, and the same is true of compassion and love.

Syncretism, Exclusivism and the Middle Way

This deep, genuine affinity should never be discredited because reason or emotion exclude it on one or another merely relative religious basis.

POSITIVELY OPEN OR NEGATIVELY SHUT

If the previous paragraphs on the relativity of selfhood and its religious paths are meant to loosen, if only a little, the habitual sense of fixity and absoluteness, the next lines are intended to summarize in a clear and simple way what has been said above.

Regarding the relative person or relative self, we can say that it has no life-in-itself. Its life is derived from the Absolute Source and in the absence of that Source no relative self could arise. The relative self is, in a conventional sense, neither completely evil nor completely good, but it experiences a longing to know and to be united with the Absolute Source. The wholesome way forward is to make an effort to acknowledge this innate longing and to follow where it leads. The first step towards achieving this is training the relative self to cultivate and express its positive potential in thought, feeling, word and deed. This is like constructing a ladder to climb up to a higher place. If the positive potential is not cultivated, the negative potential must predominate and the mind becomes a useless instrument, a broken ladder that cannot be used to ascend.

A relative religious path is not only a course along which the relative self moves towards true spirituality. It is also taken up into the relative self as components of knowledge and faith leading to wisdom and compassion. If it is a beneficial path, it will encourage and establish the positive qualities needed to attain to Absolute Wisdom-Love-Compassion. But it remains a relative path and a relative guide for a relative self. It is not closed and fixed, which is why it can influence the relative self and be taken up into that self. Since it is not closed and fixed, there is no reason why it cannot learn from and be enriched by other paths, if those paths are also wholesome and beneficial.

Finally, an inadequate or bad path will lead the relative self to its destruction if it is not abandoned in favour of a good path. It is like a poor road on which people always stumble, hurt themselves and lose their way. To a great extent, then, the quality of a particular path can be judged by the qualities of the people moving on it.

All relative paths which are able to lead people to the Absolute, expressed in people as spiritual wisdom and boundless love-compassion, are related to one another. They produce people of like quality. Therefore it is eminently reasonable to conclude that these relative paths and the relative selves moving on them can greatly benefit one another. How much more, then, can the spiritually realized people on these various but complementary paths help struggling others to become realized at the Absolute Source.

FAITH AND KNOWLEDGE

A relative religious path is bounded at the beginning by faith and knowledge which together constitute a religious view. At the end the path is bounded by the Absolute Source. So, before embarking on a religious path, certain elements of faith and knowledge must be internalized by the relative self. To a large extent, the initial acquisition of faith and knowledge, and the elements of that faith and knowledge, determine the methods and tools, the practices and conduct, which are required of the adherent on the path. We need to consider to what extent the prerequisite initial faith and knowledge are relative and whether they are at all absolute.

When faith is equated simply with a belief system, that system can easily be viewed and held as something absolute because it need not be referred to logic or commonsense. A person can believe that paradise is in the heavens or that it is in the heart, or both. Nobody can contest this belief on analytical grounds because it is a subjective conviction based on subjective teachings. Yet there is a sense in which faith can be shown to be relative. This argument can be pursued on two grounds.

First, faith as belief is subject to doubt in ways that objective knowledge is not. Doubt can lessen such faith or overwhelm it. Even when belief is not hampered by doubt, the possibility that doubt may arise is always there. Faith as mere belief is thus dependent on an absence of doubt, and as it is dependent on something, even on the absence or inactivity of something other than itself, it must be a relative mindstate.

Second, faith-belief grows, diminishes or in various ways alters its character as the relative self pursues its quest for the Absolute on the relative path. What a person fervently believes today is always changed or even eradicated and replaced by something else as the changeable person grows in understanding. No one believes at fifty what they believed at fifteen or twenty years old. There are bound to be changes and switches which happen naturally as the person matures or regresses. This is a sure sign that, however set in stone the dogma may be, the nature of faith itself is changeable and therefore relative.

There is another experience of faith which is not a matter only of believing in one or another doctrine. This sort of faith comes by an awareness of inner Presence. It is a mindstate-energy of unshakeable trust in the guidance provided by that Presence, and in the trustworthiness of the Presence itself. It is to this experience of faith which the writer of Hebrews refers when he writes that 'faith is the substance of things hoped for, the evidence of things unseen.' So far from being only a matter of human belief, this energy of conviction is experienced by Christians and practitioners of other religions as the sustaining Energy of Truth itself. Yet it, too, can be assailed by doubt. For instance, it can be viewed as a type of brain function developed in the individual mind by continuous suggestion.

A more trustworthy experience of faith is that which is frankly ascribed to mental conditioning. The person accepts that what he knows by the mind of faith, and sees through the eyes of faith, is the product of his own mental-spiritual development. When doubts arise, they are not despised or feared as evil attacks on faith, but as contrary insights driving the person to a deeper and clearer faith-informed vision of Truth.

So, whenever faith is considered in this book, it will be useful to bear in mind these distinctions between the various levels and experiences of faith-as-belief, faith-as-energy and faith-as-insight.

Knowledge is more obviously relative. It is related not only to the development of the individual, but to that of humanity as a whole. For thousands of years it was 'known' that the sun and planets revolved around the earth, and much later it was 'known' that the cosmos functioned in a deterministic way. Both views have since been falsified. It is the same with religious knowledge. That is why doctrines and methods evolve through the ages. They become refined and in some cases are abandoned. Thus, it is impossible to deny that knowledge is also a relative tool.

The acceptance of our relative nature and of the relativity of our religious paths, methods, practices, faith and knowledge, sets us free. We become liberated to use these factors for growth towards the Absolute. Indeed, we are only able to use them because they are relative and because we ourselves are enabled by our own relative natures to make choices. We should rejoice in the fact of our relativity and the relativity of our physical and mental domain because these are our means *par excellence* for developing into spiritual beings. We can relax in the way it is and extend our openness to others.

In the search for common ground ecumenism and interreligious movements repeatedly come up against relative issues which have mistakenly been made into absolutes. The walls and strongholds which divide people are very often mental creations, having no real value as divisive imperatives. Nevertheless, it is important to distinguish right from wrong motives in ecumenism and interreligious ventures. The aim should never be to subsume all religious paths under one global institution. Diversity is natural and good. The less diversity there is, the more unnatural and controlled people become. Discouraging diversity is to deny the fact of our relativity. The right motive is to encourage sincere, compassionate sharing of wisdom precisely because we acknowledge our relative natures. There should be a real respect for the varieties of religions and the people who practice them. On such middle ground real reconciliation, encouragement and enrichment can take place.

Part 2

The Teachers: Jesus Christ and the Buddha

In this section brief and simple accounts of the lives and teachings of Jesus Christ and the Buddha, based on canonical scriptures, are provided for those with little or no knowledge of one or the other. No attempt at critical examination of the scriptural accounts has been made, the intention being to stay close to the original *mythos*. It is in the unelaborated myth, after all, that the deepest resources for personal spiritual development and subjective diversity of experience and interpretation are to be found. Of course, these simple outlines cannot pretend to supply to the reader the fulness of the poetry and insight found in the Gospels, the Sutras and other scriptural sources.

JESUS IN THE GOSPELS

According to the Gospels Jesus was born in Bethlehem, having been miraculously conceived by God in the human body of Mary, a virgin. In this way he was born true God and true man. That is why he is able to save human beings by re-uniting them with his Father in Heaven. As the Son of God he was also born without the taint of original sin, and is therefore able to save sinners by his own sinless merit.

At the time of his birth there were several auspicious events and signs. Wise men or *magi* from the east recognized a star which guided them to his birthplace in the barn of an inn in Bethlehem. Angels appeared to nearby shepherds to announce the good news of the birth of the Saviour. John, later to become the Baptist, leapt with joy in the womb of his mother, Elizabeth, Mary's cousin.

But there were also some who were distressed at the news of the birth of the Messiah or Anointed One. Herod, king of Judaea, deployed soldiers to murder every newborn son in the region so as to avert this threat to his reign. The persecution was so fierce that an angel commanded Jesus' parents to take the infant to safety in Egypt. Many of the religious authorities in Jerusalem were shaken by the prospect of a Messiah lessening or taking away their positions of eminence.

From an early age Jesus showed precocious spiritual insight and capacity. The Gospels relate how, at the age of twelve, he was separated from his mother and was later found debating with the elders and scribes. When Mary rebuked him for absconding he replied that she should know that he would be found in his Father's house. He thus revealed from his childhood on that he was aware of his Divine nature and purpose.

When he was thirty years old, he went into the desert where John the Baptist was preaching repentance and baptizing penitents in the river Jordan. John was accustomed to telling his followers that, while he was preparing the way for the Lord and baptizing with water, one greater than himself was to come, who would baptize in the Holy Spirit and with Fire. When Jesus entered the water to be baptized by John, the Baptist was perturbed. 'I should be baptized by you,' he said. 'And do you come to me?' For John had always taught that One was to come, the latchets of whose sandals he was not worthy to untie. And as he entered the water, John recognised that Jesus was this Anointed One, the Christ. While he was being baptized, a dove appeared above him and the Father spoke. Those standing by heard the voice which said, 'This is my Son, in whom I am well pleased. Listen to him.'

Then Jesus was taken into the wilderness where he was tempted in various ways by Satan, the deceiver and destroyer of souls. When at the last he tried to tempt Jesus to bow down and worship him in exchange for all the kingdoms of the world, the Lord dismissed him with the rebuke that only God was to be worshipped and obeyed. The temptation and fast had lasted forty days.

After this Jesus began teaching and gathering disciples to himself. He chose ordinary people from all walks of life: fishermen, a tax collector, and other people of low standing, and even some who were despised and cast out by the community. There are many stories which testify that the Lord did not make appeals to those who took pride in their own righteousness. On the contrary, his stated purpose was to teach, heal and save those who were lost, broken and humiliated. He had come to set captives free and to call sinners to repentance.

The Teachers: Jesus Christ and the Buddha

Jesus' teaching and presence had great authority. He summoned his disciples with a word, and they left off what they were doing to follow him immediately. In fact, they simply abandoned the whole of their earlier lives and livelihood to walk with him. Jesus showed his authority in other ways too, by casting out demons, healing the diseased, bringing the dead to life and performing many other miracles and wonders. His teaching had the power to completely transform his hearers.

He was regularly in conflict with the religious teachers and leaders of Israel because he taught in ways that went beyond religious law to the heart of human understanding and divine love. He demonstrated that the religious laws should be transcended and even transgressed when they went against spontaneous compassion and commonsense. He saw to the core of human nature, easily refuting the legalism of the religious structures of the time, and confounding the cunning of religious leaders who attempted to trap him in his words. Jesus displayed intense contempt for hypocrisy and legalistic pettiness.

At the same time he did not claim any glory for himself. He pointed out that he did nothing from his own strength, but that his words and actions proceeded only from what was taught him by the Father. He taught that all people with sufficient faith could do the things that he was doing, and even greater things. As the Master, he made himself into a servant. As the Son of God, he made himself the humblest of men. Because of this emptying of himself, he had access to a higher power: he was never at a loss in either mundane or spiritual things.

His closest disciples, later to be known as the apostles, were taught in a different way from his other followers. In addition to receiving deeper spiritual truth, they were the first to whom Jesus revealed the Glory of his Divine nature and unique Divine sonship. It was the Apostle Simon who recognized and acknowledged the Divinity of Christ before any of the other apostles clearly saw it. For this reason Jesus gave him the name Peter, the Rock on which his Church would be founded. In Jesus' own words, Peter did not receive this revelation from flesh and blood, but directly from the Father in Heaven.

The close disciples were also taught in other ways, through example and by events. They saw Jesus walking on water and calming a storm on the sea of Galilee, demonstrating the power of faith. When Simon Peter attempted to walk on the water to his Lord, he began to sink. Jesus instantly rescued him and rebuked him for his lack of faith. At the Epiphany the Lord appeared to James, John and Peter in a Divine manifestation. In these and other ways he showed them the meaning of his person.

Although he himself described his work as being for the lost sheep of Israel, he demonstrated that his healing and salvation were for all people everywhere. He showed this by healing the child of a Roman centurion, whom he also praised as having greater faith than anyone in Israel. He cured a non-Jewish woman of haemorrage after testing her humility. He revealed his salvific nature to a Samaritan woman who had given him water to drink, and who marvelled that a Jew should accept help from any Samaritan, because Samaritans were despised by all Jews. In the parable of the Good Samaritan he made it clear that the value of any person lies not in their race or culture but in their capacity for love and compassion.

As his influence in Israel grew, many secular and religious authorities became concerned and hostile. His teaching and example exposed their pedantry, hypocrisy and corruption. In their turn they began to plot against him and to slander and accuse him. They wanted to humiliate him publicly in order to break his authority with the people. But Jesus steadfastly revealed their malice in the face of his own innocence.

In the three years of his public ministry he lived the life of a homeless itinerant teacher and prophet. During this time he continuously showed his Glory to the people of Israel and, in a special way, to his close disciples. Even among the religious leaders and people of influence, there were those who became convinced that Jesus was sent by God. The majority, however, were of the opinion that he was a public danger. Owing to his uncompromising holiness, extreme feelings and opinions were aroused. Moderate voices advised that he be left to teach: if he was of God his teaching would endure, if not it would soon disappear. As time passed, it became clear that he was not an ephemeral charismatic figure. The people were hailing him as their Messiah and Saviour.

Seeing what was to come, and knowing that the messianic prophecies were to be fulfilled in him, he began to tell his disciples about the death he was to die. Simon Peter remonstrated with him, but the Lord rebuked him sharply. He knew that he must suffer and die for the sake of many. He foretold his suffering, death and resurrection in cryptic language which the apostles only fully understood once he had risen from the dead.

At the time of the Passover, in his thirty-third year, Jesus went to Jerusalem to celebrate the feast commemorating how God had saved the Jews from death and slavery in Egypt (the Passover). This Divine histori-

The Teachers: Jesus Christ and the Buddha

cal act of redemption from slavery was about to become the first symbol for Jesus' great work of universal salvation.

He entered Jerusalem in triumph and to the ecstatic acclaims of the people, who hailed him as the King of the Jews and the Son of David, the greatest and most revered of all the kings of Israel. This popular exuberance so disturbed the leaders in Jerusalem that they decided to devise a way to have Jesus put to death. They did not realize that they were destined to play a terrible role in God's eternal plan for salvation. Those who sought to obstruct, silence or destroy the Lord were put to shame in a tragically ironic manner.

In Jerusalem, Jesus ate the Passover with his apostles in the meal later known as the Last Supper. Before the Passover meal he had foretold what was to happen to him. The apostles were deeply grieved, not understanding that he would fully reveal his Glory through his death and resurrection. At the supper Jesus broke bread, gave it to his disciples and said, 'Take this, all of you, and eat it. This is my body.' He poured wine into a cup and said, 'Drink of it. This is my blood which will be given for many.' By these means he began to reveal the deep meaning and mystery of his life, death and rising from the dead.

Later, in the garden of Gethsemane, Jesus prayed fervently, in preparation for his suffering. Because he was both true man and true God, his human nature was tormented and oppressed while in his Godly nature he was utterly submissive to his Divine mission. In great sorrow he prayed, 'take this cup away from me. Nevertheless, not my will but Your Will be done.' In this extreme hour even his closest friends were not able to stay awake and watch with him.

At the Last Supper Jesus had plainly told Judas Iscariot that he was about to betray his Lord, and had commanded him, 'What you are about to do, do it quickly.' Judas, disillusioned with the spiritual nature of Jesus' kingship, had offered to betray him and hand him over to the authorities who desired his death. Now he had led a group of soldiers to the Lord as he was praying in Gethsemane. With a kiss, he identified Jesus to his enemies. Jesus said, 'Judas, do you betray me with a kiss?' Then he was arrested and taken before an assembly of the chief priests and elders of the people.

Their case against him had been prepared. It did not matter how transparently malicious it was, so long as it would serve the purpose of having him sentenced to death. He was tried on the charge of blasphemy, in that he confessed himself to be the Son of God. Jesus then asserted before this malevolent assembly that he was indeed the Christ. With a great show of outrage the high priest condemned him. Then they spat in his face, beat him, and mocked his claims.

Peter, who had followed at a distance, was accosted in a courtyard by a maid who told him that she recognized him as one of Jesus' followers. As he tried to leave, another girl recognized him, and finally the crowd also told him that they knew him as one of the disciples. Three times Peter denied it, claiming with an oath that he did not know the Lord. Then he went out and wept bitterly, remembering how Jesus had predicted that he would deny him thrice before the cock crowed.

In the morning the chief priests and elders put Jesus in chains and led him to the Roman governor, Pontius Pilate, so that Pilate should pronounce the death sentence. But he was reluctant to do so, realizing that Jesus was innocent of any crime deserving death. He knew that it was all a plot concocted by the religious leaders.

So he had Jesus sent to Herod for trial. Herod, king of Judaea, was both delighted and amused. In his view the Lord was a curiosity, a wandering miracle-worker and insignificant prophet. He pressed Jesus to perform a miracle and attempted to question him, but the Lord did not respond. After mocking him, Herod had him escorted back to Pilate.

Pilate questioned him 'Are you the King of the Jews? Do you not hear all the evidence that the chief priests and elders have brought against you?' But Jesus made no reply, much to Pilate's astonishment. The governor was reluctant to punish Jesus, because his wife had had a dream about his innocence. The Jewish leaders, however, continued to press for the death sentence.

Pilate then tried to bargain with the people, 'Whom shall I set free, Bar-Abbas or Jesus called the Christ?' The crowd, persuaded to it by the chief priests and elders, called for the release of Bar-Abbas, a known murderer, and the condemnation of Jesus. 'What am I to do with Jesus?' Pilate asked them. 'Crucify him!' they shouted. Pilate asked, 'Why, what harm has he done?' But the mob only called more loudly for Jesus' death. Then Pilate had a bowl of water brought and washed his hands. 'I am innocent of this man's blood,' he said. The crowd retorted, 'Let his blood be on us and on our children.' So Pilate had Jesus flogged and gave him over to be crucified.

By this time Judas the traitor had hanged himself in remorse for his treacherous deed. He had returned to the chief priests and elders to give them back the thirty pieces of silver which they had paid to him to betray his Lord. He told them that he had betrayed innocent blood, but they would hear nothing. So Judas, seeing that Jesus was condemned, committed suicide.

After being handed over to them, Jesus was mocked and abused by the Roman soldiers. They dressed him in a scarlet mantle, gave him a staff, and placed a crown of thorns on his head, hailing him as King of the Jews. They spat on him and beat him on the head. Then, having flogged him, they led him away to be crucified.

At a place called Golgotha, Place of the Skull, the soldiers crucified him, dividing his clothes among themselves by lot. Over his head they placed an inscription which read: 'Jesus of Nazareth, King of the Jews.' Later the chief priests complained to Pilate that the inscription should not read 'King of the Jews' but rather 'He claimed to be King of the Jews.' Pilate replied, 'What I have written, I have written.'

As Jesus hung dying on the cross, the people and their religious leaders jeered at and insulted him. 'If you are the son of God, come down from the cross and save yourself. Then we will believe in you.' Jesus prayed: 'Father, forgive them. They do not know what they are doing.' Jesus hung for hours in intense suffering. Then darkness fell, between midday and three in the afternoon. At about this time Jesus cried out, 'My God, my God, why have you forsaken me?' Then, having committed his spirit to the Father, Jesus died.

At the moment of his death the curtain in the Hebrew temple was torn in two and there was an earthquake which split rocks and opened graves. Subsequently many holy people came back to life and were seen in Jerusalem after Jesus had risen from the dead. When the Roman soldiers saw what was happening as the Lord died, they believed that he was indeed the Son of God.

In the evening Joseph of Aramathea, a righteous man and a follower of Jesus, approached Pilate and asked him for Jesus' body. He took the body, wrapped it in a clean linen sheet and placed it in his own tomb, rolling a big stone across the entrance to seal it.

The next morning the chief priests and Pharisees went to Pilate to request that a guard be posted around the tomb to prevent the disciples from stealing the body and claiming that the Lord had risen from the dead. Pilate agreed. So they sealed the tomb and had soldiers stationed to guard the entrance.

Jesus had been crucified on Friday and lay in Joseph's tomb on Saturday, the Jewish sabbath. On Sunday morning Mary of Magdala and Mary, the Mother of the Lord, came to inspect the grave, but they found only the linen sheet. Confused and distressed, they began to cry. Then an angel appeared. He told them that Jesus had risen from the dead as had been foretold, and he commanded them to go quickly and tell the disciples.

After this Jesus appeared to his close disciples and followers several times. He showed them the marks in his hands and feet, where the nails had pierced them, fastening him to the cross. He showed them the wound in his side where a soldier had pierced it with a spear to the heart to ensure his death. He ate with them and spoke with them, assuaging their doubts and fears.

Before being raised into Heaven, he commissioned them to make disciples in all the nations, baptizing them in the name of the Father, the Son and the Holy Spirit, and to teach them all his teachings. And he assured them that he would be with all believers, even to the end of time. Then Jesus ascended to sit at the right hand of his Father in his Kingdom.

This is the story of Jesus as recorded in the Gospels. Many other things are written about him in those books, which are not told here. At the end of his Gospel, John says: 'If all the things that Jesus did were to be written down, I suppose that the whole world could not contain the books that would have to be written.'

THE HISTORICAL JESUS

The Gospels present the life and teachings of Jesus the Christ as told by some of the earliest followers of the Lord, two of them apostles. Further teachings and elaborations on the deeper meaning of his death and resurrection are given in the Book of Acts, the Epistles, and the Book of Revelations, which deals with eschatological or 'end-time' themes.

Over the last hundred and fifty years or so many scholars have attempted to reconstruct a life of the 'historical Jesus.' The aim of these endeavours is to find the real historical person and events behind the scriptural myth or *mythos*. This term is not to be misunderstood as denoting mere imaginative mythical fabrication. The myth, in this context, is the story of Jesus presented in the language of faith and spiritual meaning.

Central to demythologizing the story of the Christ are the questions surrounding his birth and resurrection. This is an endeavour of great importance to Christians who believe in the message of Christ but are unable to accept a literal approach to the scriptures, particularly with regard to the miraculous and the supernatural events recorded in them.

In accordance with this need alternative ways of understanding and interpreting the Gospels have been established. One method is to understand the mind of people of the first few centuries after Christ, especially the Christian mind, and to reinterpret that mind in terms acceptable to the modern mentality. Thus, when Mathew, Mark, Luke and John say so and so, they actually mean this and that. They are speaking symbolically, not literally. They are communicating in the language of faith rather than recording real events only.

These scholarly approaches and conclusions are often difficult to refute. At best, what they achieve is to make people more aware of the importance of critical study without allowing it to dominate the life of faith.

Another method is to find material for a life of Jesus outside of the Holy Scriptures. This is done not only because of intolerance of the supernatural, but also because there are inconsistencies in the Gospels themselves. Scholars point out things like the differing genealogies given by Mathew and Luke, the inconsistencies with regard to Jesus' dying words, and general discrepancies in a good number of recorded events. These and other factors are certainly a valid stimulus for attempting to discover or establish a more consistent record.

Unfortunately non-biblical references to Jesus are very scant indeed and some of them, such as a description of Jesus' activities in Josephus' 'Jewish Wars', are now known to have been later insertions, in this case by Byzantine Christians. Otherwise Josephus mentions the stoning of 'James, the brother of Jesus who was called Christ.' There is a reference to Jesus' birth in the Talmudic tradition, which describes him as being the illegitimate son of a Roman soldier called Panther. But this assertion seems of very doubtful validity, considering the inimical response to Jesus by the Jewish religious establishment of the time. There are minor references in the Roman historians Tacitus and Suetonius: in the former case confirming his crucifixion under Pilate, in the latter speaking of the persecution of his followers. Thus there is really not much to go on.

Other 'lives of Jesus' written by popular authors are highly conjectural. In them we have speculative ideas ranging from Jesus having travelled to India to study Buddhism, to his having survived the attempt to crucify him and subsequently fleeing to Gaul. These pseudo-histories are not much more than controversial speculations.

In spite of the unavoidable inconclusiveness of even the scholarly researches, many modern theologians have reacted selectively towards them. In the light of them, they have attempted to construct a number of new Christologies and doctrinal evaluations. Many of these new formulations offer a somewhat confusing blend of intellectualism and religious sentiment, resulting in materialistic, psychological and sociological religious visions which fail to do justice to traditional and authentic Christian faith and experience.

Still, serious scholarly study into the life of Christ and its meanings at various levels of human experience is not to be dismissed as misguided research. These enquiries are a search for truth in the context of the modern mindset. As such they are valid and legitimate, even though they are often offensive to devout traditional Christians and are capable of breaking down faith. The point is not whether they are good or bad or whether or not their conclusions are authentic. Ultimately they cannot replace the central and ancient *mythos* itself, to which the adherent must always return for his own authentic understanding and experience of spiritual truth.

THE TEACHING OF JESUS

The teachings of Jesus can conveniently be divided into two categories: those teachings which derive directly from the story his birth, life, death and resurrection, and those spoken by him during his public ministry. The first category of teaching provides the essential meaning of Christian Truth while the second expounds the way in which Christians should live in order to conform to that meaning, and to be transformed by the experience of divine revelation.

The mere fact of the birth of Jesus, as well as the manner of it, are significant in several aspects. It marks the beginning of the full revelation and accomplishment of the Father's will for humanity. 'According to the flesh' or in terms of his humanity, Jesus is born in the line of David, fulfilling the prophecy that the Christ or Anointed One would be of davidic descent.

According to the spirit he is born of God, as the Only Begotten Son. In this divine endowment he mirrors Adam, the first human being, who was directly created by God and into whom the Spirit of God was breathed. But, unlike Adam, Jesus is not marred by sin. He is born without the taint of inherited sinfulness and does not succumb to temptation. For this reason he is able to save people from their sinful predisposition, as well as from the eternal consequences of their sinful deeds, so long as they repent and become obedient to God.

Jesus is born the perfect human being, fully human and yet fully divine. Through his birth he reveals the pattern of what people really are meant to be. At the same time, as the unique Son of God, he is always more than other people. He is the way through which they can be redeemed and raised to their own divine destiny in him. His birth as a human being is also the greatest sign of the Father's love for humanity and for the whole of nature, since all people and all of nature are redeemed in him. As the sign of God's love, he shows the kindness and compassion of the Father in that he is born a lowly person and is sent to sinners. It is God being born in the humblest of circumstances to extend forgiveness and the opportunity for reconciliation to all people everywhere.

HIS LIFE AS TEACHING

In his life, and particularly in the three years of his public ministry, Jesus showed his followers how to live their lives in obedience to God. The submission to the will of the Father which he exemplified in himself has several foundational aspects.

The first is obedience to the intuitive spiritual laws of God rather than to the legalistic religious injunctions and practices of the time. He stressed that the Law is a living, sanctifying and directing force in people's hearts rather than a vast collection of precepts. People are to submit, moment by moment, to the divine voice in their hearts and minds, and not to their own fixed and general legal references, even if these legalities have traditionally been understood as deriving from God. Jesus made it clear that God examines the motives and attitudes of the heart, and not outward deeds done only in obedience to a set of precepts.

He stressed that people should walk in faith, opening themselves to the unseen life of the spirit. They should place their complete trust in him, who came from the Father, for all that is needed in both the mundane and the spiritual life. He repeatedly demonstrated that the sufferings, failures and despair of humanity are due to lack of faith. If people will only believe, all things are possible to them.

Throughout his ministry, Jesus manifested the deep and holy love of God. The Father had sent him in an eternal act of love, and he himself loved humanity beyond measure. He taught his followers to do the same, to the extent that the faithful are to be known by this sign: that they love one another. But he went further than this, insisting that they love their enemies too. The love of which he spoke was not the ordinary kind, that which is only experienced as a feeling or a sense of obligation. His love is informed and saturated by divine power and wisdom. It is spiritual, unfailing love.

Simplicity was also to be practiced and honoured. Jesus taught through his own example that the way to the Father is simple, not relying on intellectual formulas or intricate religious systems. This does not mean that Jesus advocated deliberate simplemindedness. He exemplified godly simplicity coupled with godly authority in his inner being, as also in his words and actions. By this holy simplicity he was able to instruct all people and to rebuke or refute his detractors. His life, too, was simple; neither cluttered by unneeded possessions nor complicated by superfluous activity.

In his social dealings as well as in his ministry, the Lord was no respecter of persons. Because he was able to see into the hearts of people, he was always able to discriminate between the persona and the real human being. He repeatedly displayed his contempt for hypocrisy and self-righteousness or self-importance. He judged people only by their faith, humility and willingness to turn to the Father in repentance.

Most importantly, he demonstrated in himself the fruits of a life lived in full communion with God. He assured others that they too could attain to the stature of Christlikeness, possessing through their own obedience the authentic results of knowing the Father in a deeply subjective and personal way. He proved that it was possible for all people to live in the direct presence of the Divine.

In these and other ways Jesus walked as the perfect servant of God, providing for people a perfected example of the spiritual life of humanity. He showed not only how this kind of life should be lived, but also that it is possible to all people. In these ways he brought to them the sure hope of salvation.

In his divine nature as the Son of God his life is a revelation of the Father's love for all people. The surest proof of his love is demonstrated in that he sent Jesus to minister to, to teach and to redeem those who were lost, afflicted and without hope. It was a love from grace to grace, poured out richly on those who had not in any way merited it; a love searching for the lost children of the Father, a love that called them home to their eternal destiny.

Jesus revealed the true nature of the Father, which until his coming had been largely misunderstood. Religious leaders and teachers had, through their focus on the Law, caused God to be viewed more as the power of divine justice than of divine mercy and lovingkindness. The result was that many practised religion out of fear, or just abandoned it, keeping only the outward show of service to God.

The Lord was himself the remedy to this religious ignorance. He came as the messenger, the authentic voice of the Father, to call such religion-weary people to the refreshing and life-giving service of God in Spirit and in Truth. Through him the Father revealed his love, grace, mercy and power. Knowing Jesus became the real way of knowing God; seeing the Son, it was possible to see the Father.

HIS DEATH AND RESURRECTION

His death, like his life, was an act of obedience. It was the supreme salvific act in which Jesus took on himself the sin and sinfulness of humanity, redeeming people for God and saving them from everlasting death or hell. In the Old Testament God had saved the Jews from death in Egypt by having them paint their lintels with the blood of a sacrificed lamb, so that the angel of death would pass over their houses. Now, at the time of the Passover feast, Jesus became the blood-sacrifice for all people, to save them from eternal death.

In his human nature he suffered the agonies of death. He died the death of an ordinary sinful man, but on behalf of all men. It was because he died in his fully human nature, and bearing the sin of the whole world, that he cried out: '*Eli, Eli, lama sabachtani?*' or 'My God, My God, why have you forsaken me?' for sinful humanity cannot be in the Presence of God, neither in life nor in death. This cry of the Lord seems to show that he laid aside his divine nature at the time of his dying.

That is why the sacrifice of Jesus is so great and so unparalleled. Not only did he suffer indignity and torture at the hands of violent men, and the most agonizing of deaths, but he put aside his divine power and purity in order to suffer and die as an ordinary person for the salvation of all people. The Father had sent his only Son to pay the blood price for the redemption of the lost. At the death of Jesus, the veil in the Hebrew temple was torn in two, signifying that the Holy of Holies, the place of God's Presence, was now open to all who wanted to know God.

Having died as a man to save all people, the Lord was raised from the dead through the mighty working of the Father, who would not allow the body of his Son to see corruption. In the lapse between his death on the cross and his resurrection, Jesus descended to the dead, where he preached and set captive spirits free. But on the third day he rose from the dead to take his place at the right hand of the Father. In this he showed his eternal glory and proved that he was indeed the Word which was with God from the beginning, the Divine Reason through which all things seen and unseen where created.

For his followers the resurrection was the irrefutable proof of the glorious salvation which Jesus had accomplished for the world. It made clear to them their own destiny in Christ, the fulfilment of the promise of eternal life. The one who had come into the world for the salvation of humanity was now lifted into the heavens, eternally redeeming every person who would believe in him. Having been made man, died, and been raised again to eternal union with the Father, Jesus had made it possible for all people to enter into personal relationship with God. Shortly after he was raised from the dead, the Holy Spirit was poured out on the disciples, empowering them as children and servants of the Lord.

THE PATTERN OF CHRISTIAN GROWTH

The birth, life, death and resurrection of the Lord, besides being a teaching about who Jesus is, also constitute an allegory which reveals the pattern of Christian growth and life. They are symbols of the stages through which a believer passes on the way to complete personal fellowship with God, through the Holy Spirit, in Christ.

When Christians are born anew through the Spirit of God, they are born directly of the Father just as Jesus was born of him. Although they are children of Adam in their human nature, tainted by the adamic fall into sinfulness and separation from the Divine, they become through their spiritual rebirth children and heirs of God in his kingdom.

Living their lives through the power and guidance of the Holy Spirit, they are made holy as Jesus is holy, and are changed from glory to glory as they walk in Christ's nature. The life they live is not in the flesh but in the spirit, because the experience of being born anew is actually preceded by the death of their human nature. This sinful nature or carnal person has been crucified with Christ. Thus Jesus' death is mirrored in the Christian's death to the carnal self.

The new birth in the Spirit is at the same time a resurrection from a condition of spiritual death. The old carnal person has always been dead to the life of the spirit, but alive to the sinful, guilty and condemned life of the flesh. When the carnal person submits to co-crucifixion with Jesus, the old person dies and, through the power of Christ, the person is raised to life again as a spiritual being, at one and at peace with the Father. In the process of being raised to a spiritual life in Christ, the Christian is born a child of God. From this time on the Christian, like Jesus himself, lives in direct communion with the Father.

EVIL DEFEATED

The birth, life, death and resurrection of Jesus also have definitive meaning in relation to evil, expressed in the Christian Faith as the nature and works of Satan, the prince of this world. We have already seen how the coming of Christ provided a way for overcoming the carnal person or self or flesh, a way which is an individual path of faith and obedience. In the wider, ontological-metaphysical sense, the way of the world under the dominion of the devil was also overcome by Jesus.

His birth signified the approaching end of Satan's power over the world and over the minds of people. Jesus came into the world to destroy the power of evil in the world. That is why the attempts by Herod and others to put the infant Christ to death can be interpreted as being inspired by Satan, the angel of light who fell from glory because he desired to usurp the throne of God. It was he who tempted Adam in the beginning, and brought about the fall of humanity from divine communion. Thus Jesus, as the spotless Son of God, in coming to redeem people from slavery to evil, must destroy the power of the principle of evil itself.

At the start of his public ministry Jesus was forty days in the wilderness, fasting, praying and being tempted by Satan. The devil tried by various means to corrupt the very essence of who Jesus was. He appealed to Jesus to use his miraculous powers to prove his Divinity. When these tactics failed, he attempted to bribe the Lord by offering him the rule of earth's kingdoms if he would worship the tempter. Throughout these trials Jesus stood steadfast. So Satan went away to await other opportunities for destroying Jesus.

Throughout his life and public ministry, Jesus was regularly hounded by Satan. He used people to try to obstruct and frustrate the Lord's work. He worked through the ignorance and arrogance of the leaders, and played on their personal fears and prejudices, to rouse them to destroy the Lord. Satan was present even while Jesus agonized in Gethsemane. Yet Jesus was not overcome. He was able to discern the work of Satan in the lives of people, and demonstrated his authority over Satan's kingdom by expelling demons with a word and undoing the works of evil in many other ways. His life was a complete triumph over the prince of this world.

The death of Jesus was the moment of the utter defeat of all evil. Fully human and yet fully submitted to the Father's purpose, he triumphed on behalf of all people over the works of the devil in the minds of people and in the collective worldly mind. That is why one of the utterances attributed to the Lord at the time of his death on the cross was: 'It is accomplished.' By willingly becoming the sacrificial Lamb of God, he made it possible for all people to begin anew, through belief in his person and his sacrifice, as acceptable and cleansed children of God. It was not that Satan would no longer work in the world and in the minds of individuals, but that people, from now on, would find a perfect refuge from all evil influence in the sacrificial death of the Lord, and in the person of the risen Christ.

Through his resurrection Jesus made an open display of his victory over all evil, and over the prince of this world and his demonic cohorts. By rising from the dead he made clear once for all that the power of death over humanity had been broken. Death, brought into the world by the works of the devil, was itself transformed into eternal life through Jesus Christ.

CHRISTLIKE SACRIFICE

We have discussed the way in which the birth, life, death and resurrection of Jesus reveal a pattern of the Christian's spiritual development. In becoming spiritually identified with these aspects of the Lord's work, Christians grow into the stature of Christlikeness.

But Jesus' work is also an example of what Christians should do in the world for the sake of others. Because of their identification with Christ, they are, as he was, in the world but not of the world. In him they have overcome the world, and through him they continue to do his work in the world. They continue to show forth the love of Christ and the glory of Christ in the world.

Although it is true that the work of Jesus is complete and final, it is also true that the same work is always being carried out by faithful Christians in the world today, as it has been carried out for more than 2000 years. Jesus gave to his disciples the authority to do the works he had done and instructed them to carry on these labours of mercy, kindness and power.

Thus the fully formed Christian is empowered, through co-crucifixion and co-resurrection in Christ, to heal the sick, cast out demons, bring sinners to repentance, tear down the works of evil, and establish the Kingdom of God in human hearts. Likewise, mature Christians are expected to sacrifice themselves for the sake of others, to love their enemies, and to lay down their lives if need be. The Christian may be called on to suffer and even to die for the sake of Christ and the children of God, just as Jesus suffered and died for the sake of the whole world. So, for Christians, the birth, life, death and resurrection of the Lord are not only symbols of their own individual spiritual progress, but, having been born of God themselves, they may have to share in the actual works and sufferings of Jesus in order to share in his glory.

KNOWING GOD AND HIS KINGDOM

Like Socrates and the Buddha, the Lord Jesus Christ himself left no written record of his teachings. He taught orally only, and for many years after his death and resurrection his teachings were orally transmitted. Yet, in spite of the relative lateness of the written Gospels, there are no discrepancies with regard to the sense of the Lord's spoken teachings. From the Gospel accounts we can also safely conclude that these lessons, observations, parables and instructions were uttered with an immediacy of spiritual authority that touched the hearer in a challenging and transforming manner. The teachings of Christ are further elaborated and interpreted in the Epistles or letters of some of the earliest disciples, and these will be considered later.

The groundnote of Jesus' teaching was that the Kingdom of God is near and is, in fact, already come. But Jesus did not mean this only in a temporal sense. While it is true that God's kingdom or the reign of God in the human heart was brought to people at a given time in the person of Christ, he was mainly concerned with opening people's minds to the truth that the Divine Kingdom was now near to their own hearts. All they had to do was repent, to change and to open their minds and hearts to the truth that it was now possible for everyone to commune with God in a profoundly personal way.

The Lord spoke several times in parables about the Kingdom of Heaven, likening it to a mustard seed from which, although so minute, a large tree grows in which birds can nest, and again, to a woman who places yeast into three measures of flour until the yeast has been spread through all the dough. Thus the Kingdom of God in an individual life and in the life of a community is a spiritual experience which begins with repentance and then grows into fulness and completion.

In view of the accessibility of God's kingdom, Jesus taught that there was no need to be anxious about one's needs, ailments and sufferings. God, who sustains all of creation, would not leave the righteous person in want. Neither was it necessary to fear evil in life and in the world, for the spiritual life more abundant was given to humanity and the Lord had overcome the world, its corruption and the dominion of the devil. Jesus often instructed his listeners and disciples not to fear and not to let their hearts be troubled.

But he also made clear the way to achieving the personal experience of God and the resultant banishment of all anxiety. This way is based on overcoming self. He taught that it is impossible to know God unless the self-centred carnal mind is overcome, denied or put to death. His exhortation to the disciples was that they should deny themselves, take up their cross and follow him. Since one does not take up one's cross unless to be crucified, his injunction points clearly to the death of self. Following Christ means both imitating his example in the conduct of one's life and being willing to share in his crucifixion.

Jesus taught love of God, love of one's neighbour and love of one's enemies. To love God is to put him first and to seek his counsel in every thought, word and deed. Loving God is made real by constant and authentic awareness of his Presence and by complete submission and obedience to his will. Loving one's neighbour is summed up as doing to others what one would have them do to oneself. But Jesus went further than this: if someone compels you to walk one mile with him, walk two; if someone strikes you on one cheek, turn the other to him. In other words, render more than you are forced to render, and do not repay evil with evil. Kindness is always both the right action and the right reaction. Love of enemies is evidenced in forgiving all harm done and praying for the wrongdoer. It is this kind of unfailing love that leads to spiritual perfection. The love which Jesus' disciples practise should reveal the love of God whose pattern Jesus described in the parable of the prodigal son who squandered his inheritance and ended up living in a pigsty, sharing swill with the swine. When he could no longer bear his degradation, he returned to his father's house, asking to be treated only as a servant. But the father, overjoyed at his son's return to his true home, ordered that he be dressed in fine robes, a ring be put on his finger, and a feast be held in celebration of his return.

But Jesus did not teach divine love and forgiveness as spiritual principles to be abused. He insisted on authentic repentance and a way of life worthy of God's children. He admonished his disciples to be perfect, just as their Father in Heaven is perfect. Forgiveness is in the nature of God, but must be reciprocated by the believer in a life of purity, faith and obedience.

The love which Jesus advocated was also practical. It is not good enough only to express and experience divine love in attitude and speech or in refraining from unloving conduct. The love which God engenders is also generous, concerned and sacrificial. Jesus taught liberality, hospitality and sincere charitability as the inevitable result of a godly love which is enthusiastic and warm.

He taught faith as a foundational principle leading to calm trust in God and reliance on him in all circumstances. Through the exercise of unswerving faith, all things are possible to those who believe. Jesus many times rebuked his disciples for lack of faith. Wherever he found unhesitating faith he held it up as an example to them.

Essential to a life of submission to God, expressed in repentance, love and faith, is a turning away from the passing pleasures and rewards of this world. From his disciples he demanded a way of life based on renunciation of the mundane. However, this renunciation did not extend to civil disobedience or the neglect of the demands of worldly leaders and laws. Although the religious and civil leaders of the time suspected that the Lord was advocating civil strife, and used this premise as a means to trap him in his words, Jesus replied that it is right to render to Caesar that which is due to Caesar, and to God that which is due to God. But with regard to worldly gain or prominence, he asked: what does it profit people to gain the whole world at the cost of losing their inner spiritual life?

He advocated humility and meekness in attitude and conduct, as well as the assumption of a reconciliatory stance towards all people. Lack of arrogance and considering oneself as the least, or putting the self last, are praised as virtues which will have their reward. At the same time these virtues are not to be practised at the expense of righteousness. The child of God does not compromise righteousness for the sake of peace, although he seeks to make peace in every situation of strife. In the same spirit he made it clear that, while righteousness is discerning, it does not judge or condemn others. Nor does it seek vengeance or recompense. Judgement and repayment are the exclusive province of God; only he can see into people's hearts and fully understand their motives. Therefore only he can judge with full insight and repay every person not only according to their visible deeds, but also in the light of the motives and intentions of the inner person.

Jesus invited people to come into the light, to desist from hiding themselves in darkness where their hearts, minds and actions could be kept out of sight. In any case, there is no way to hide from God's scrutiny and no place, however dark and hidden, that cannot be penetrated by his light, love or judgement. Therefore it is reasonable and desirable to walk in the light, to live openly without hypocrisy or dissimulation.

But the light to which Jesus referred is also the Light of God's infinite wisdom and compassion. In this sense his summoning people into the light is a call to becoming open to receiving the Light of God's truth. By being illumined in this way people are enabled to walk in spontaneous love and righteousness. They are set free from the letter of the law in order to live in accordance with the inspired laws of God's Spirit. Here again Jesus taught that the righteousness of human institutions is like filthy rags in comparison to the righteousness which the Spirit of God can instil in the human heart and mind.

It is true to say that Jesus sought to bring to people all the common virtues, but in an exalted form. Lovingkindness, mercy, a forgiving spirit, modesty, self-denial, piety, wisdom, righteousness: all of these, in their most powerful, consistent and effective dynamic are gifts of the Father. If practised superficially or legalistically they can only go so far. It is when they are quickened by the Spirit of God that they are raised far above the level of moral convention and are transformed into potent means for transforming the believer and for touching the lives of others.

These spiritual virtues, Jesus taught, are to shine forth from the disciple. They are to be displayed, not as self-righteous or hypocritical accomplishments, but as light from Light. The Light of God, illumining the heart and mind, should be held out to others as the saving Light which can draw them to salvation by making visible God's Light in the lives and conduct of his children.

The Lord's teachings also included several severe warnings. He warned that the uncompromising life of faith and obedience to God would bring dissension and division between people, turning children against parents and brother against brother. There is no way to live the radical spiritual life without causing offence, perhaps even to members of one's own family and one's closest friends. He also said that only a few are destined to find the way that leads to eternal life, because the gateway is constraining and the path is narrow beyond the perserverance and capacity of most people. Yet it is necessary to find and walk this path because failure to do so results in eternal separation from God.

But the love and mercy of God, and the saving power of God, are greater than the most stringent tests, dire failures, doubts and weaknesses common to all people. Through faith in Jesus Christ the world and the principle of worldliness in people can be overcome. Thus there is no need to fear or to become disouraged. The saving grace of Jesus is full of lovingkindness and the desire to rescue all people everywhere. Through the strength he imparts all things are posssible.

Jesus taught the sacraments of baptism and the sharing in his body and blood in the sacrament of Holy Communion. He also stressed the sacred nature and the indissolubility of the bond of marriage, so that, at least implicitly, the sacrament of marriage had his blessing. Baptism is the rite in which the sinner, through immersion in water, shows his repentance and intention to live a new life in Christ. Holy Communion is a re-enactment of the supper which Jesus ate with his disciples on the night before he was arrested and condemned. This was the meal at which he broke the bread, gave it to his disciples and said, 'Take. Eat. This is my body.' Likewise, he shared the cup of wine with them saying, 'This is my blood.' These were signs of the suffering and death he was about to undergo for the salvation of humanity. He instructed his disciples to continue to re-enact this holy meal in memory of him and of his sacrifice.

It was also a symbolical injunction to believers to sacrifice themselves for the sake of others.

By recognizing and emphasising the sacrament of matrimony, Jesus was also illustrating the indissoluble and pure nature of the believer's walk with God. Jesus taught that he was the bridegroom and his followers the collective bride. This relationship was to be spotless and without adultery.

The Lord declared openly that he would return as the Judge of all people, separating the sheep from the goats, the children of God from the unrepentant. It would be a great and terrible day, since he would return on that day no longer offering salvation, but only to pronounce judgement. It would be well for the servant to be found about his work on that day. He admonished his followers to be alert, faithful and prepared for his coming.

Having taught them all these things and others besides, he was betrayed and crucified. After his resurrection he instructed his disciples to go and make disciples among all the nations, baptizing them in the name of the Father, Son and Holy Spirit, and he promised to be with them until the end of the world. Then he ascended to his place at the right hand of the Father.

THE LIFE OF THE BUDDHA

Although some attempts have been made to discover the historical Buddha, this kind of research has not been as important to Buddhists and Buddhist scholars as the search for the historical Jesus has been to Christian intellectuals. Buddhists seem to accept that the lives of great spiritual teachers must be composed of a mixture of fact and myth and that there is no need, in the interests of spiritual Truth, to make any critical discrimination between the two.

Siddharta Gautama was born about 563 BC. He was a prince of the Sakyans, the rulers of a kingdom in the border regions of India and Nepal. His father was King Suddhodana and his mother the Queen Mahamaya. While she was carrying the infant, Mahamaya had a dream in which a pure, radiant white elephant entered her womb. An assembly of wise men interpreted this dream as meaning that her son would be either a great worldly monarch or would attain Supreme Enlightenment.

Siddhartha was born while Mahamaya was undertaking a journey. She gave birth to the child in the park called Lumbini, in a white enclosure erected for this purpose. At the time of Siddhartha's birth, Asita, a seer and

The Teachers: Jesus Christ and the Buddha

spiritual counsellor to Suddhodana, saw in meditation that the devas were celebrating with great joy. When he asked them why they were so filled with ecstacy, they replied that a Being was about to enter the world, who would achieve full and complete Enlightenment. Asita then wept, realizing that he, already very advanced in age, would not live to see the fulness of the Buddha. Then Asita and Suddhodana worshipped the child.

It was also understood that the Buddha was being born into this world after countless lifetimes of preparation as a bodhisattva, a compassionate being on the path to Final Enlightenment. In his many lifetimes of preparation he had fully realized or manifested the Ten Perfections: the *paramitas* of generosity, morality, renunciation, wisdom, effort, patience, truth, determination, great compassion, and equanimity. By various auspicious marks on his body, the infant was recognized as the incarnation of a great spiritual master. On the fifth day after his birth, at the naming ceremony, he was given the name Siddhartha which means 'The one who achieves his aims.' Seven days after his birth his mother died, and he was put under the care of her sister who was Suddhodana's second consort.

Because the most learned and accomplished Brahmins had foretold that the child would either become a great king or achieve Ultimate Enlightenment, his father took care to keep him secluded from mundane miseries, and to indulge him with every pleasure. Suddhodana knew that, if Siddhartha were to go forth to seek Enlightenment, he would have to leave the palace to live the life of a wandering ascetic. The king did not want this life of deprivation for his son, and for this reason kept him close in the luxurious palace environs.

In spite of his misgivings, Suddhodana was compelled to acknowledge the karmic destiny of the child Siddhartha a second time. This happened when the young boy, attending a plowing festival with the royal family and common farmers, was left alone in his tent under a jambu tree. The nurses returned to find the boy in deep meditative absoption, and reported this to his father. The king, seeing his son deeply absorbed and in the posture of an accomplished yogin (an advanced practitioner of meditation), then worshipped him.

Yet the king persisted in trying to nurture his son away from the homeless life of an ascetic seeker. The Buddha later spoke of this sheltered life of luxury: 'Monks, I lived in utmost refinement, complete refinement. My father had lotus ponds made in our palace, where red lotuses, white lotuses, and blue lotuses bloomed, only for my sake. A white sunshade was held over me day and night to protect me from cold, heat, dust, dirt and dew. I had three palaces: one for the winter, one for the summer, one for the monsoon.'

At sixteen Siddhartha was married to the Princess Yasodhara, his cousin. Throughout these years his father the king continued to provide the prince with every comfort and entertainment, and with every reason to remain in the palace and take up the splendid role of royalty. But Siddhartha was preoccupied with deeper matters, with questions that were not put to sleep by his pampered lifestyle. He pondered illness and death, realizing that all his regal privileges could not save him from these, and that in this regard he was no different from any ordinary person.

At the age of twenty-nine, he drove out into the city with Channa, his charioteer. On three separate occasions he witnessed respectively a very old and infirm man, a man so ill that he had fallen into his own excrement, and a corpse. His charioteer explained to him that all these were conditions common to humanity. All people grow old and weak, all suffer illness, and all must eventually die. On the fourth occasion he saw a wanderer with a serene expression, wearing the ochre robes of the ascetic. Wanting to know how such serenity could be attained in a world so full of horror and misery, he decided to renounce the palace life and to set out to find the peace and wisdom of Ultimate Truth. Having seen and understood the inevitable suffering of all beings, he desired to find a way out of suffering on their behalf. Motivated by compassion and the yearning for wisdom, he decided to go out into the life of homelessness, to search out the Truth beyond visible reality.

On his return to the palace, after having encountered the ochre-robed ascetic, Siddhartha was told that a son had been born to him. In spite of this news, he made the great renunciation, abandoning his life of regal luxury and taking up the way of the ascetic. He left the palace at night, accompanied by his charioteer, and riding his favourite horse. Crossing the Anoma River in the early morning, he gave all his princely garb and jewelry to Channa, sending him back to the palace with Kanthaka, the prince's prized horse. Then Siddhartha went out as a wandering seeker.

He travelled south to the places where spiritual teaching and practice were highly developed. Going forth into homelessness, he avoided evil deeds in body, speech and mind, and sought only to purify himself. He went first to Rajagaha, the citadel of Magadha, where he lived by begging for alms, although endowed with all the marks of spiritual greatness.

The Teachers: Jesus Christ and the Buddha

King Bimbisara of Magadha, looking out from his palace, noticed him and, impressed by his regal and stately demeanour, sent messengers to inquire about this princely monk.

When he discovered who Siddhartha was, the king went out to speak with him, inviting him to remain at the palace and share his kingdom. But Siddhartha declined the offer, re-stating his firm intention to live the ascetic life until he should attain Enlightenment. Since his mind was set on the search for Truth, he could not take up again those comforts and distractions which he had solemnly renounced.

He then left Rajagaha, seeking teachers who could help him on the path to Truth. He first sought out Alara Kalama, a wise teacher of great renown, and asked to be his student. Gautama was accepted by Alara, and soon became adept at all the spiritual teaching of his master. In the school of Alara the highest attainment was to the 'realm of no-thing', and Gautama soon achieved this insight, becoming equal with his teacher. Alara invited him to teach this way as a master together with himself, but Gautama was not satisfied with having attained this high level of insight, for it revealed only a partial understanding of reality. He, however, was seeking Highest Absolute Truth, the state of Nirvana, so he left Alara.

Gautama said: 'Alara Kalama placed me on the same level with himself and paid me great honour. But I thought, this dharma does not lead to disenchantment, to dispassion, to cessation of suffering, to stilling, to direct insight, to awakening, nor to Nirvana, but only to appearing again in the realm of nothingness. Unsatisfied by that dharma, I left.'

He next went to receive teaching from the sage Uddaka Ramaputta and quickly learned this doctrine, a spiritual insight higher than that taught by Alara Kalama. Uddaka taught and disclosed the realm or dimension of 'neither perception nor non-perception.' But again Siddhartha was dissatisfied with abiding in this incomplete knowledge. Again he declared that this dharma did not result in disenchantment, dispassion, cessation, stilling, direct knowledge, awakening or Nirvana. So, once again, he left.

From this time on he decided to subject himself to extreme austerities and deprivation in order to discover whether these practices might lead his mind to Ultimate Truth. He found a beautiful grove with a river nearby, close to a village called Senanigama. Here five other ascetics came to practise with him, including Kondana, the Brahmin who had foretold that Siddhartha would certainly achieve Ultimate Enlightenment.

In this forest near Senanigama and Uruvela he practised extreme forms of self-mortification and deprivation for a period of six years. Of these practices he later recounted: 'Clenching my teeth and pressing my tongue to my palate, I overwhelmed and crushed my mind with pure awareness, as a strong man seizes a weak man to overwhelm and constrain him. Sweat trickled from my armpits. Even though clear awareness arose, my body was not calm because of the agonizing effort. But the agony did not enter my mind or remain there.

'Then I thought, what if I were to become lost in the deep meditation of non-breathing? I prevented inbreathing and outbreathing through my nose and mouth. There was a loud roaring of winds expelled from my earholes. Powerful energies cut through my head and terrible energies dissected my stomach, as if a butcher were slicing up the stomach of an ox. On seeing me, the devas were not sure whether I was dead or dying.

'Then I considered taking only minute portions of nourishment, a spoonful of soup. My body became completely emaciated. My limbs were like segments of vine or bamboo stems, my buttocks like the hoof of a camel, my spine projected like a string of beads, my ribs stuck out like rafters, my eyes were sunk deep in their sockets like a gleam of water in a deep well, my scalp shrivelled like a gourd, my belly cleaved to my spine; if I urinated or defecated I fell prostrate, and my hair fell from my body as I rubbed it. I thought that no agony could be worse than mine, but through these austerities I had not attained any higher state, nor any noble knowledge or vision. It seemed to me that there must be another way to Illumination.

'I lived in terrifying places such as forest shrines and tree shrines. Wild animals came, or a twig would fall, or there would be a rustling of leaves. When terror and anxiety came, I decided to overcome them rather than only wait for them. If fear came while I was pacing to and fro, I refused to stand or sit or lie down. I continued pacing until I had overcome that fear. If terror came while I was standing, I would stand until I had overcome it. When terror came while I was lying down, I would not sit up, nor stand nor walk. I would remain lying down until I had overcome that terror.'

Although these austerities may have had a provisional value, they could not bring Gautama to the Ultimate Enlightenment which he was seeking. Realizing this, he decided to abandon these practices of self-mortification, and to restore his physical health by taking proper nourishment. As a result the five ascetics who had joined him in the belief that he would show them the way to Enlightenment became disappointed and abandoned him. But Gautama, continuing to regain his strength, was resolved to continue the search alone.

One morning during this time Sujata, daughter of the landlord of Senanigama, brought some food to Gautama. It was his last meal before he would realize his Enlightenment. Having spent the rest of the day in a grove, he went towards evening to sit in meditation beneath the Bodhi Tree. He now determined not to rise from this meditation until Enlightenment had been attained.

His first encounter in meditation was with the evil tempter, Mara, the destroyer of purity and lord of the sensuous desires, who had come accompanied by his demonic host to discourage Gautama and to prevent him from gaining the realization of Full Enlightenment. But Gautama sat fearless in calm meditation, strengthened by his full attainment of the Ten Perfections: compassion, virtue, renunciation, wisdom, effort, patience, truth, boundless love, strong determination and equanimity. Through these Mara was conquered.

This was his second meeting with Mara, who had also appeared to him while he was practising severe austerities in Uruvela. In that encounter Mara had pointed out that Siddhartha was close to death, and feigned sympathy with him, pleading with him to choose life instead. But Siddhartha had sharply rebuked him, reciting the ten evil deeds which were Mara's means for destroying both worldy people and spiritual aspirants: lust, aversion to higher attainment, hunger and thirst, craving, sloth, cowardice, doubt, hypocrisy, false renown and pride, resulting in contempt for others.

Mara having been overcome under the Bodhi Tree, Gautama remained there the entire night in profound meditation. In the first watch he achieved knowledge of his previous lifetimes. In the second or middle watch he gained the wisdom to see how the death and rebirth of all beings occurs. In the final watch he concentrated his mind on the insight which enables the overcoming of all impurities, the wisdom by which the ego-mind attains to direct understanding of its true Absolute Nature, and he understood the Four Noble Truths. Thus, clearly perceiving the principles of cause and effect which lead to suffering and the cycle of birth and death, of fortune and misfortune, and the principles which lead to the cessation of this cycle and the awakening of undying bliss, he discerned that for him birth was ended, the task completed. Ignorance was destroyed, knowledge took its place. Darkness was dispelled and Light shone. His mind was freed from craving. Gautama was thirty-five years old when he attained the Supreme Enlightenment. Thus, during the full moon period of the *Wesak* month (May), he attained to full Buddhahood.

Then the Buddha spent seven weeks in Uruvela, meditating on all the aspects of the Dharma which he had realized. In particular, he meditated deeply on the truth of dependant origination which distinguishes the relative mode of existence from the absolute.

When he had completely and thoroughly formulated his Dharma in all its aspects, he asked himself whether other people would be able to understand it, because it is 'deep, hard to see, difficult to comprehend.' The darkness in which most people lived their lives would render this profound and subtle Dharma even more difficult to grasp and accept. Having considered these problems, the Buddha realized, however, that people are of various levels of spiritual growth and ability, and that at least some of them would see this truth. He decided to teach it first to the five disciples who had abandoned him and were now living at Varanasi. So he went to them and set in motion the wheel of Dharma. This was his first teaching.

In the first turning of the wheel of Dharma the Buddha taught the avoidance of the extremes of self-indulgence and self-mortification. He taught the middle-way which leads to calmness of mind, to understanding, to seeing, to realization and to bliss. In Varanasi he first expounded the heart of his realization which is expressed in the Four Noble Truths.

The first Noble Truth is that all ordinary existence lived in the ego-mind is filled with dissatisfaction, stress and suffering. It reveals that life lived in the ego-mind can never bring genuine, lasting happiness and inner wholeness. The ordinary, unenlightened mind is incapable of finding equilibrium, detachment and final peace. This is known as the truth of suffering.

The second Noble Truth is the truth of the causes of suffering. The Buddha taught that all suffering is caused by ignorance of the real nature of one's mind and being, and that this ignorance traps the ordinary mind in the cycle of attachment and aversion. Because people are centred in the ordinary mind they are always subject to craving and dislike. The most painful craving is the desire either to establish the ego-mind as the final 'I' or, in despair, to desire complete annihilation, of which neither are possible to the ego, and of which absolute non-existence is not possible at all.

Only the middle-way between these extremes is achievable, and will lead in the end to complete liberation from the causes of suffering.

The third Noble Truth is the truth of cessation. Here the Buddha showed that suffering can be made to cease if certain conditions are met in the mind and lifestyle of the spiritual aspirant. By determinedly practising the right path the aspirant can attain to Full Enlightenment or Buddhahood.

The fourth Noble Truth is the truth of the Path to Enlightenment. The Buddha expounded an eightfold way leading to cessation of stress and misery. The eight aspects of the path are: right action, right speech, right living (these have to do with morality), right concentration, right effort, right attentiveness (having to do with mental development), right thinking and right understanding (having to do with wisdom).

The Four Noble Truths are the essence of the Lord Buddha's Teaching. Within their framework all the developments and multifaceted aspects of the Dharma are included. These, together with other general teachings of the Enlightened One, will be discussed in more detail a little later.

From the time of attaining Full Enlightenment the Lord Buddha became the *Tathagatha*, one who acts fully in accordance with what he knows and teaches, and who teaches only what is consistent with all that he knows and does. He is the overcomer, the unvanquished, the all-seeing. Therefore his teachings are worthy of acceptance and veneration. And though all people can achieve the same Full Enlightenment, the Buddha was set apart as the one who went before, who was the first to realize the Path to Nirvana. By this fact he would always be greater than the greatest of his followers.

When he ended his first teaching in Varanasi, the five monks were admitted as bikkhus. They were the first members of the fellowship of buddhist adherents, the Sangha. Some days later the Buddha gave teachings on *anatman* (not-self) or the absence of inherent selfhood, at the end of which these first five disciples became perfected ones or *arahants*.

The Buddha remained in Varanasi about three months, during which time he made sixty disciples, all of whom took refuge in the Three Jewels: the Buddha, the Dharma and the Sangha. By taking refuge in the teacher, the teachings and the fellowship of practitioners they made their first steps in renouncing the mundane life, the delusory and unsatisfying realm of Samsara.

These sixty disciples were sent by the Buddha to teach the Dharma to the world. He instructed them to convey to people in the darkness of ignorance all the lasting benefits of a life lived in Wisdom-Compassion. They were each to go out in separate directions in order to reach as many people as possible. The Tathagatha himself went to Uruvela. On this journey he made thirty more disciples who also became arahants, and he taught the well-known 'Fire Sermon' which warns that the unenlightened are being consumed by the fires of craving, hatred and delusion.

After this the Buddha went to Rajagaha where he visited King Bimbisara in fulfilment of his promise. Here Sariputta and Mozellana joined the order. These two ascetics, followers of Brahmanism, became in time the two most important early disciples and teachers in the Buddhist fellowship. Again, in Rajagaha, many new disciples were made, including king Bimbisara himself, who gave his private park to the Buddha for the construction of a monastery.

The Enlightened Prince of the Sakyan clan next returned to Kapilavastu together with many of his disciples. Here, in the Sakyan kingdom, he went about begging for food. His father, king Suddhodana, was distressed at hearing this. But when he was convinced to accept that this was the inevitable way of all the Enlightened Ones, he invited the Lord and his followers to eat a meal at the palace.

In the course of this visit the Buddha's father, his wife Yasodhara, his half-brother Nanda and his son Rahula, in addition to many other members of the Sakyan clan, became his followers. These things were achieved by the enlightened radiance of the Blessed One.

He made countless other disciples and had followers among all classes of people. His great compassion and illumined insight made no distinction between the various ranks and conditions of people. He taught the Dharma to rich and poor, to the exalted and the lowly, to lepers, evildoers, murderers, and to the righteous and the unrighteous alike. He treated all people with the kindness and respect which flowed from his great compassion. Men and women were received equally into the order, becoming bikkhus and bikkhunis, and many of them achieved arahantship through his liberating teachings. The Blessed One was the 'arouser of the unarisen path, the creator of the uncreated path, the teacher of the untaught path, the knower of the path, the one who understood the path thoroughly and expertly.' His Dharma was 'good in the beginning, good in the middle and good in the end.' And, because he had fully realized this Dharma, he was able to hold converse also with celestial beings.

Throughout his life he travelled widely, continuing to live the life of a simple itinerant monk and giving teaching to any person willing to listen. He taught the Dharma in many different ways according to the capacity of his hearers, more or less profoundly as the occasion demanded, so that all might benefit to the fullest extent and none remain confused. His ministry was marked by endurance, patience, kindness, tolerance and unfailing goodwill. He was so deeply loved and respected by all his adherents that kings wondered why he had more authority over his followers than they had over their subjects.

When he was eighty years old, the Buddha, having travelled and taught widely and constantly, and having fashioned upright and wise disciples, set out on his last journey from Rajagaha to Vesali. In the nearby village of Ambapali he came close to dying but revived himself through strong determination in order to prepare his followers for the time when he would no longer be present in the world. Once recovered, he admonished the bikkhus to take refuge in their own capacity for seeing Truth, and in the Dharma. He emphasized that it was not his own person which was important, but the Truth of the Way It Is which he had consistently taught.

Then he journeyed with his followers to Pava, where he stayed in the gardens owned by Cunda, a goldsmith by trade and a close disciple of the Buddha. Here he became very ill and suffered much pain, but he did not complain. The venerable Ananda entreated him to remain in this world, but the Buddha replied that it was now too late for such a request. Ananda was very grieved.

In Cunda's park the Blessed One gave his last teaching: 'Learn, develop and conscientiously practise the teaching which I have given to you through my direct insight into the Truth, so that a pure life may arise and remain for the benefit of many, out of compassion for the world, and for the wellbeing of gods and people. All compound and conditioned things are transient. Work diligently to achieve your goal.'

This was the Lord Buddha's final exhortation. The Tathagatha died, and his body was cremated a week afterwards. At the time of his death there was a great and terrifying earthquake, accompanied by thunder.

THE GOSPEL FOR BUDDHISTS AND THE DHARMA FOR CHRISTIANS

THE LIFE OF THE BUDDHA AS TEACHING

As with the life of the Lord Jesus Christ, the life of the Tathagatha is also a significant teaching about the way to Absolute Truth. Although it is understood in a very different way in the Buddhist context, the birth, life and death of the Buddha have the aspect of divine intervention into the world of darkened and stumbling humanity. Speaking of himself, the Buddha said: 'When a Bodhisattva or Enlightened Being of infinite Wisdom-Compassion comes down from Heaven, the world is lit by a splendid Light which surpasses the glory of the strongest glow; and all the dark areas which lie beyond the boundaries of the world are illuminated by this Light'.

Thus the Buddha was and remains the greatest of all the bodhisattvas who have come to the aid of people. A bodhisattva prepares himself or herself over countless lifetimes by diligent purification, profound meditation and the determined cultivation of enlightened qualities and realizations in order to come to the salvation of humanity. At the right time the bodhisattva appears in the world to demonstrate the Path to Enlightenment. And, while it is true that there are multitudes of bodhisattvas, the Tathagatha is pre-eminent among them.

The Buddha fully identified himself with the Truth or Dharma which he taught. Those who see the Buddha but not the Dharma remain in the dark. Those who revere the Buddha without embracing the Dharma are far from him. But even if a monk or lay-practitioner should live far from the Buddha, the Buddha will be seen wherever the Dharma is practised. He said, 'The one who sees Dharma, sees me.'

He is uniquely qualified to help people to Enlightenment because he knows Absolute Truth and the realm of Absolute Truth, the way to the realm of Absolute Truth, and the practice by which the realm of Absolute Truth can be found. This is because the Enlightened One comes from that realm and knows it directly. He walked the difficult path to Full Enlightenment in this world in order to make manifest to people the way of liberation. The Buddha comes from the Light of *Dharmakaya*, the Absolute Enlightenment, and shows to all who can hear and see the way back to it.

It is clear, then, that the birth of the Buddha is no ordinary birth. He is born a human being like all other people, yet he is intrinsically pre-eminent. Although he is not to be worshipped as though he were God, he is worthy of all reverence and homage. Although the state of Buddhahood can be achieved by all people, it is through the Tathagatha that the perfect teaching has come. More especially, the bodhisattva chooses to be born into this world in order to liberate beings, whereas those who have not attained Enlightenment are cast into this world involuntarily, by the forces of karma which lead to rebirth in this, the desire realm.

That the Blessed One is different from ordinary people is evidenced in the experience of sufficiently advanced spiritual practitioners who can see his exalted Buddha-Body. On the soles of his feet are thousand-spoked wheels. His complexion is golden. He has a sonorous voice reminiscent of heaven. His eyes are of a deep blue colour. His head is like a royal headdress. On one occasion Ananda placed golden robes on the Lord's body, and the robes seemed to grow dull. Ananda then declared, 'It is wonderful how bright the Lord's skin appears. It is brighter even than the golden robes which clothe it.' Every person is like the Buddha in their potential to realize Enlightenment, but not in their present state of actual realization.

The Tathagatha's life is a teaching in unrelenting perseverance in the search for Absolute Truth. But he does not persevere only for his own sake. In his bodhisattva aspect he has come to reveal Truth to all other sentient beings. Therefore his life is also a teaching in perfect compassion.

His Path is the path of renunciation for the sake of Truth, and for others. Not only does he leave the palace with all its comfort and pleasures, not only does he renounce the happy bonds of royal kinship and his own close family, but he is willing to face the evil one and death itself in order to uncover Dharma for the sake of others. It is clear that the Buddha intends this to be an example in endeavour for all who can follow him in this way.

He is also a magnificent example of kindness and mercy. He was always willing to stop and listen to those who sought his counsel. He abandoned all distinctions based on rank and class, an extremely dangerous and unpopular attitude in the caste-conscious brahminic culture of his time. But he was obedient to his inner humility.

Through his life he revealed the all-important difference between ordinary knowledge and the knowledge which has been developed into realization, which comes by an inner revelation and makes the Dharma Truth real in the total experience of the spiritual practitioner.

In short, the Enlightened One is the manifestation of humanity made perfect. He has no more obstacles to overcome, nothing more to learn and nothing more to achieve. He abides in unhindered bliss and dispenses treasures of Wisdom-Compassion to all people.

His death is the final teaching of human transience. Even the Buddha, having obtained by choice a human body, was subject to sickness, suffering, decay and death. In this relative realm there can be no escape from this cycle. 'Like an old chariot,' he told his followers shortly before his death, 'the body which has aged cannot go on without constant repairs.' But he showed that the Enlightened Mind lives on beyond mere physical death.

THE BUDDHA'S DHARMA: THE FIRST NOBLE TRUTH

The Buddha's central teaching can be summarized formally in the context of the Four Noble Truths. Indeed, the Noble Truths are the framework containing the entire vast body of the Dharma.

The first Noble Truth, the truth that all mundane life is suffering, may seem at first unreasonably morbid. It may be considered that all life, even life in the ordinary, uninspired mind, is not suffering. It is a mixture of pleasure and suffering, at least. This is true, but only in a qualified way. To fully understand suffering it is necessary to understand the real nature or dharma of worldly pleasure: it is a pleasure which invariably fades and changes into boredom, discomfort or misery.

If the inherent nature of worldly pleasure were indeed pleasure, then we should find such pleasure always increasing. But we do not. Sitting in the sun may be pleasurable, but it soon becomes uncomfortable. The same is true of eating, drinking, walking, talking and so forth. None of our pleasurable activities renders pleasure indefinitely. But the inherent nature of worldly suffering is not like this. Suffering does not of itself eventuate in pleasure; it can increase indefinitely to the point of unconsciousness or insanity or death. It is this dynamic; the inherence of suffering and the transience and mutability of worldly pleasure, that make life in this relativistic, worldly realm stressful and unsatisfactory. The only genuine route to liberation is by the spiritual path away from the relative and towards the Absolute. Only that path is continuously rewarding.

The chief cause of our suffering is that we mistake the relative for the Absolute, or that we try to transform our relative experience into something absolute by holding on to it, clinging to it and struggling to make it permanent when it is by its very nature inescapably transient. We want good experiences to endure and bad experiences not to arise. More crucially, we want our relative selves, our ordinary personalities, our everyday modes of consciousness and experience, to last forever, to endure as something absolute. Nobody is pleased to know that their ego-self is naturally impermanent, decaying, conditioned and provisional. This is a great cause of suffering.

The whole of the Buddha's doctrine can be said to centre in the question how to view and manage the self in order to progress towards Enlightenment. With his last breath he reiterated the truth that all conditioned phenomena are transient. But the Buddha's full teaching on compound, conditioned (or, relative) phenomena is that they are in their nature impermanent, subject to suffering and void of self-entity. Only by fully and experientially realizing this truth and acting on it can people begin to escape samsaric suffering, stress or discontent.

While it is of course very relevant to understand why and how all compound, relative phenomena are impermanent, are suffering and are not-self, such an understanding is actually meant primarily to prepare people for the liberating insight pertaining to the ego-self: that this self is a compound, relative phenomenon and is therefore, together with all other worldly things, impermanent, suffering and not-self. It is only through the direct insight into this truth that Enlightenment can be achieved.

The quality of impermanence is perhaps the easiest to understand. No mundane thing, including the mundane self, has any sort of permanence. This statement is not hard to prove by simply pointing at common human experience. Mundane things and mundane selves are always fading. Even those things and persons which appear to be enduring are in truth always subtly and imperceptibly degenerating. Over extended periods of time this is easier to perceive. Where is the person that anybody was ten years ago? Where are the solid pyramids that stood in Giza four thousand years ago? At the microphysical level the inescapable principle of transience is an observable and measurable law.

The second quality, that of inevitable suffering, is harder to accept as it requires a little more insight. We have already discussed the suffering or stress of people in the desire-realm that is this world. In the light of transience we can more readily understand the truth of suffering as a passive imperative. Everything that exists relatively, that is conditioned and compounded, is always being acted upon by a number of forces, and acted upon in such ways that it suffers diminishment, damage or fatigue in one way or another. Thus 'suffering' is not always a conscious or unconscious experience in the minds of sentient beings. Inanimate phenomena 'suffer' diminishment, reduction or destruction. By grasping the suffering nature of all worldly phenomena without exception, people can assent with a wider understanding to the truth that the worldly self partakes of the same suffering by its very nature. Everyone suffers under the knowledge that they are gradually and inevitably passing away.

The third quality, that of not-self or *anatman* is the most difficult to understand and the most difficult to accept even when it is understood. The Buddha taught that the selves which people habitually experience, perceive and accept as being their own fixed selves, are not in fact their selves. 'That self which you call yourself; that is not yourself.' If it were oneself, one would have no prospect of liberation from self, for in being liberated from the only self that one can ever be, one would have to be liberated into mere nothingness. As it is, however, the Dharma of Enlightenment is not a Dharma of nihilism. If people attaining Full Enlightenment were to lapse into nothingness there could be no Buddhas. Besides this obvious point, if Enlightenment were to be the simple extinguishing of all awareness, it would be more beneficial to remain unenlightened.

But if the perceptible and conscious ordinary self is not the real self, and if the realization of not-self does not tilt over into nothingness, then what is the 'not-self-mind' which is realized by the Enlightened Mind and what is the Enlightened Mind which is realizing the not-self-mind? For the Buddha clearly taught that no 'self' can ever be brought to Enlightenment. This question and other questions relating to it will be discussed together with the third Noble Truth, the truth of cessation from suffering.

In the meantime it is important to add that the three characteristics of existence; impermanence, suffering and not-self, are not only negatives acting to cause or intensify much of our suffering. Properly understood, they are also the very factors which enable people to embark on the way to Enlightenment.

The characteristic of impermanence or transience does not only have to do with the inevitable diminishment and extinction of the relative self, but is also the quality which permits positive change, the development of a different view, the modification of attitude and conduct, and other beneficial switches in the course of people's lives.

Suffering as an inherent quality of conditioned existence encourages renunciation of the delusory pleasures of this world by pointing to the truth that the samsaric realm is not our 'natural medium.' If it were our true abode we would not be so prone to suffering and dissatisfaction in it, and we would not always be moving towards decay and extinction in it.

Realizing this, we know that our true home is to be looked for elsewhere, in our spiritual nature.

When we clearly grasp that our ordinary selves are not our 'Absolute Selfness,' we naturally begin to move forward on the path to Enlightenment. Knowing that we can discover neither the truth about ourselves nor any genuine, lasting happiness in the provisional, conditioned self, we are driven to seek out the unconditioned mindstate where there is calm, peace and bliss.

Besides understanding the first Noble Truth existentially, we should also consider the simple everyday forms of suffering which afflict people. Sickness, old age and death cause obvious misery and anxiety, and we are not able to overcome them. And there are all the other manifestations of suffering and stress which afflict us: our negative emotions and mental stresses together with all the physical pain and discomfort which we experience in the course of a lifetime. So far from resigning ourselves to these, we should try to find ways to reduce and finally to be liberated from them.

Lastly, we should understand that the Noble Truths are truths seen from the vantage point of the Noble Ones or *Aryas*. They are able to see the vast suffering of people in ways that ordinary people cannot see. In other words, most people simply cannot see that the provisional pleasures and happiness which they enjoy in Samsara are actually sufferings. The noble view is perhaps analagous with that of adults looking back on childish or immature pleasures and realizing that these things can no longer bring happiness.

THE SECOND NOBLE TRUTH

The Buddha disclosed the fundamental causes of suffering, which are the substance of the second Noble Truth. The truth of the causes of suffering lists three negative qualities of the ordinary mind: ignorance, attachment and aversion.

Attachment and aversion are the essential negative qualities associated with the mental experience of the desire-realm. Attachment is the inability to let go of the things we treasure and which give us provisional pleasure, ease and security. People want to hang on to them, to make them last as long as possible. At a deeper level, people are attached to their sense of selfhood; they want to embellish, project and sustain their ordinary personalities as much as they can. In the process they develop habitual defence tactics, stratagems of power and control, and aggression. Attachment is of course inseparable from the sense of possession which must always eventuate in one or another form of violence, even if that violence is confined to speech and thought. In this way attachment is a root cause of suffering for the relative self and for others. It obstructs the path to spiritual development by keeping the relative mind concentrated on the very things that hold people back from genuine spirituality.

As much as the ordinary mind attaches itself to its comforts, it is more or less intensely averse to all adversity, pain and misery. In addition to innate aversions which are common to all people, aversions are also fostered on the basis of acquired habits, views and personality traits. People dislike other people for this or that reason, and this dynamic extends to whole societies and cultures, becoming manifest in racism, contempt for other cultures and the establishment of social divides.

Taken together, attachment and aversion are powerful causes of all subtle and gross forms of violence. In fact, one should not view them separately as discrete causes of suffering since they are actually dual aspects of a single process: aversion arises from attachment just as attachment arises from aversion. This conditioned cycle causes anger, frustration, fear and a host of related negative emotions and thought patterns. Out of this negative mental cycle come great suffering and the afflictions which hold people back on the way to liberation.

Attachment and aversion spring from the profound root cause of all suffering, which is ignorance. The whole of the Tathagatha's teaching is aimed at shining the light of Truth into the darkness of not-knowing (*avidya*). The way out of suffering as taught by the Buddha is essentially a way out of the confining straits of ignorance. One could say that ignorance is suffering.

People are ignorant of the real nature of the reality in which they live, of the real nature of their own minds and of Mind itself. People do not know where they are, what they are, how they came to be in this reality and how this reality is situated in relation to all Reality. This being the case, how can they expect to find meaning, purpose and joy in life unless they can find a way out of the severe limitations imposed on them by *avidya*?

In relation to the spiritual path, ignorance is the prime stumbling block. It is owing to ignorance that people do not know how to react to their dissatisfaction with worldly life and to the impulse or yearning which drives them towards the relief of a spiritual vision. One result of this is that, knowing themselves to be in search of happiness, they try to fulfil this natural urge by indulging in the various kinds of provisional pleasure which inevitably result in disappointment and increase of misery.

Because they have a very limited insight into the way things really are with them and with their world, they lack the skill to use the tools present in their own relative experience for achieving liberation into Absolute Truth. In fact, they do not even know the difference between the relative and the Absolute, the conditioned and the Unconditioned, the constrained and the Free. So they keep themselves attached to the ordinary cycle.

To begin to understand ignorance and the way out of ignorance it is necessary to gain insight into the nature and functioning of karma and rebirth. All living beings endowed with awareness (sentient beings) are subject to countless rebirths in samsaric realms until they are liberated from this cycle of suffering by the attainment of Enlightenment. It is owing to the forces of karma that samsaric beings are trapped in the cycle of rebirth, samsaric life, and death. And the only way out of ignorance and misery is by discovering the wisdom that leads beyond rebirth and perpetual becoming.

At the simplest level, karma is the law of action and the results of action; thus it is the force behind the law of becoming. All our activities have a karmic result and in consequence of these results people are always changing, becoming something different than they were before. So there is a perpetual flux of the processes which make up our world and our humanness, our reality and our mental perception of that reality. What interests us today bores us tomorrow, what pleases us now annoys us at another time, and so forth. We are obviously not static.

Only by relating karma to our mental processes can we understand its working more insightfully. Karma is not a law which applies only to our external conduct. Indeed, it cannot apply only to our outward conduct because all our conduct is determined and qualified by mental factors. The karmic fruit of an action depends on the motivation and the degree of insight which the acting person holds. An action which seems only bad may have been inspired by a good intention or a sincerely benevolent motive, and vice versa. A deed committed by a person who does not know what he is doing will not invite the same type of karmic effect as the same action done by someone acting in full understanding of either the negative or the positive consequences. There are also degrees of completion of the action itself: a negative action may not be brought to completion; it may be abandoned on account of the conscience. Its karmic consequences will not be as negative as those of a bad action knowingly carried through to the end. Similarly, remorse after committing a bad deed will lessen the negative karmic results. The same principle holds good for positive actions: the motivation, degree of completion and the subsequent mindstate, perhaps pride or modesty, will qualify the nature of the karmic effect.

But the working of karma must also be understood at a much more fundamental level, at the level of our conventional being in this samsaric realm. Whatever we humans conventionally are is the result of our collective karma. The way we perceive our environment is also determined by karmic forces. Our perception of ourselves and of the reality in which we find ourselves is determined by the karmic calibration of our minds. This does not apply only to our individual characters and dispositions but to our collective experience as a species. All sentient beings are karmically calibrated. Dogs live in a dog reality, horses in a horse reality, people in a human reality, and the various spirit-beings in Samsara are also calibrated by their respective karmic conditioning. Our instincts and faculties, the way our ordinary minds and senses funtion, and the way our physiology is put together to make us function as humans specifically, are all factors which are the result of our collective karma. The way to Enlightenment is therefore a path which must lead us to an escape from the collective conditioning of our human karma.

The Buddha taught that our karmic conditioning has resulted in the composite bases of conventional being and perceiving, called the *skandhas*, or aggregates. These bases are called aggregates because they are themselves composed of a myriad interdependent factors. The Buddha demonstrated the composite nature of the five skandhas by placing five heaps of rice before his followers. These skandhas are: form, sentience, perception, mental formation and conciousness. Everything we perceive ourselves and our reality to be arises from these interrelated bases.

The skandhas function interdependently, and from their interdependent functioning arises the illusory sense that I am what I appear to be, and that reality truly is what it appears to be. On the basis of the five skandhas people take for granted that everything in existence conforms exactly to its appearance. Of course, in a relative realm things are exactly as they seem provisionally to be. But this relative experience tells us nothing about their ultimate or absolute nature. We can understand this by a simple consideration of the quality of solidity. We know from scientific conclusions that matter is not really solid, yet we perceive and interact with it as though it were. What it is in its own nature, however, we cannot say because of our adaptively conditioned calibration.

Our experience of selfness also arises from the five skandhas. This is one of the main arguments used by the Buddha to show the absence of an inherently existent self. Since the relatively existing self, or sense of self, arises in dependence on the skandhas, it cannot have an inherent existence or an existence from its own side. Nothing which exists absolutely and therefore permanently can come into existence in dependence on factors other than itself.

But as regards the generation and our experience of our relative, conscious 'selves', these are based on the operation of the skandhas. Our reality has the aspect of form or corporeality. We have a certain mode and range of feeling-awareness. Our modes of perception are channeled by a set of senses related to interpretative mental mechanisms. Our human mental formation gives rise to specific instincts, natural drives and biases of will. Our human consciousness is constrained by certain parameters so that we are unable to grasp or realize the Absolute unless we train our minds through spiritual practice. If our collective karma were different, we would perceive and experience reality differently. If our collective karma were nobler or more spiritual, we would be born with skandhas enabling us to see all things in a nobler, more spiritual light. If our karma were coarser, we would experience all things more coarsely.

We are born into ignorance, however, because of the skandhas we have inherited as a result of the karma we have collectively generated. That is why our only way out of ignorance is by transforming our karma through right understanding and by practising the other 'right' aspects of the Eightfold Path. Ultimately, by transcending karma altogether, we can escape the conditioning and limitations imposed on us by the operation of our specific skandhas. We can attain to Supreme Enlightenment..

THE THIRD NOBLE TRUTH

The third Noble Truth is the truth of the cessation of suffering. The Buddha demonstrated in his own life and death that suffering could be made to cease. This does not mean that all samsaric suffering will cease while the spiritual practitioner is still on the path in this world; but it will cease completely when, having attained Supreme Enlightenment, the practitioner dies, never to return again into samsaric realms. He or she will have attained Buddhahood. Still, even in samsaric realms suffering can be greatly diminished through right understanding and spiritual practice. People can reduce their own suffering as well as the suffering they cause to other people and to other sentient beings.

The cessation of suffering is achieved gradually, and the way to cessation is by first transforming the ordinary mind so that it views selfness and samsaric reality in a more accurate light. Once the correct view has been established, the ordinary mind must be transcended so that the transcendent mindstate can exercise direct insight into and direct realization of Ultimate Reality, the truth about reality which is normally veiled by the appearances of the conventional world. Then, when the mind is developed and stabilized in the Ultimate View, it experiences deep liberation, peace, compassion and happiness.

The path to cessation runs concurrent with a progressively deepening insight into the three characteristics of ordinary existence: impermanence, suffering and not-self. A penetrative understanding and acceptance of impermanence as an intrinsic quality of samsaric experience engenders renunciation in the mind of the aspirant. People who have clearly seen and acknowledged the transience of everything, including the ordinary self, naturally become less grasping. Knowing that nothing, including the ordinary self, can be held onto indefinitely, they begin to let go. As they learn not to cling to self and its preferences they become more relaxed, more open and more generous.

Something has already been said about suffering as the first of the Four Noble Truths. As an intrinsic quality of mundane life it must in the first place be recognized for what it is. People who cannot recognize suffering as suffering are far from liberation. It may be that they are not able to see that the endless chase after worldly pleasures leads to eventual meaninglessness and misery, jadedness and shallowness. Or they might find contentment in their worldly labours and pursuits, not recognizing that these should be used as a means to gaining deeper spiritual insight. In short, they may refuse to accept the truth that suffering is all-pervasive. They are looking at life from a strictly human point of view, and that is enough for them. For such people the teachings of the Buddha have nothing to offer until they awaken to the truth of suffering.

The teaching of not-self as an intrinsic quality of samsaric existence is of central importance to eventually attaining complete cessation from suffering. It is a difficult doctrine but one which the aspirant must master both cognitively and experientially in order to make progress towards liberation. The analytical explanation of not-self is usually presented in the context of 'dependent origination,' which explains how phenomena come into being and are impermanently sustained in dependence on a range of factors external to themselves. This analytical approach is called the king of reasonings.

The aim of the teaching of dependent origination is to bring people to understand that no worldly phenomenon exists in and of itself. Because worldly phenomena are neither self-generated nor self-sufficient they cannot be said to exist inherently; their existence is always provisional by the fact of their existential dependence on factors other than themselves. This teaching, although applicable to all phenomena, has a special bearing on the conventionally perceived human self or ego-self.

A fundamental help in understanding non-inherent, relative existence is to gain some clarity into the nature of absolute, inherent existence and to attempt to define it. All absolute things, including absolute selfness, must have certain qualities which logically differentiate them from all relative phenomena. In saying this, however, we must bear in mind that the Absolute exists independently of any logical definition we may attempt: if it depended for its perceptibility on anything we said about it, it could for that reason no longer be called absolute. So, we are merely trying to describe it, using limited mental tools, in order to increase our understanding of the relative. We can say nothing absolute about the Absolute because we have only relative tools of thinking and expressing at our disposal.

The first and most telling thing that we can say about something absolute is that it exists causelessly. Like mere or brute existence itself, it simply is. It has not come into existence as a result of factors working together to bring it into being. Now if it exists in this way, independently of any causes or principles of causation, then it must always have existed and must always continue to exist. Since it exists without causes, it must exist in and of itself and must be self-sustaining. It has no need of anything other than itself to continue existing. And because it exists causelessly, it cannot be made up of component parts, for it would then depend for its existence on its parts. It is not affected by attachment or aversion, not limited by ignorance. It is permanent. It does not suffer. None of these characteristics of relative existence apply to it. In the teaching of the Buddha this causelessly existing entity is pure awareness, the Absolute Nature of Mind.

It is easy to see that one's relative self is not like this; neither are other relative selves and all the relative phenomena in Samsara. All of these depend for their existence on various causes. Therefore they are qualified by impermanence, suffering and not-selfness.

This teaching is important not only as mere philosophical or psychological theory. The Buddha's teaching always had a very practical aim. The practical aim of the wisdom-insight into the nature of the ordinary or relative self is to help people escape from the delusion that they are inescapably identified with their ordinary selves. By getting free from the sense that they are only and finally that which they ordinarily experience themselves to be, they can begin to aspire towards their Absolute Nature. By becoming loosened from the conditioned mental experience of intrinsically *being* their relative selves, they can stand apart from the relative self, no longer to be used by it. On the contrary, they can now begin to use the faculties of relative selfhood as a set of tools for achieving Enlightenment. By using them skilfully they can return to their Absolute Nature which is uncaused, self-existent, permanent and free of suffering.

But what do we find when we discover and realize the Absolute Nature of our being? Can we speak of it as being in any way a 'self'? The most accurate thing we can say about it from our relative point of view is that it is that which manifests when the relative, provisional ego-self has been abandoned. We can describe it as pure awareness but we cannot know what that means until we have experienced it.

In order to progress towards an understanding of the Absolute Nature of Mind, the pure awareness from which all relative selfness arises, we need to consider the most fundamental quality of the ordinary self and of all ordinary phenomena. The Buddha characterized this quality as 'emptiness' or 'voidness' (*shunyata*). All relative selves and phenomena exist in an 'empty' mode. This characterization of the self as empty or void is used to negate the *inherent existence* of self, and of all relative phenomena. This being so, it is necessary to understand what exactly is meant by 'emptiness' as a way of existing. And it is important to discern eaxctly what it is about something, including the self, that is being negated when we describe it as being 'empty', or, as existing in an empty mode.

The Teachers: Jesus Christ and the Buddha

In the teachings on emptiness the Buddha demonstrated that samsaric phenomena are, from an absolute point of view, delusory or dreamlike. We can illustrate this sense of delusion by looking at a phenomenon such as a piece of music. The music we hear depends for its existence on numerous factors or bases. There is the musical score set down on paper; there are musicians, musical instruments, the activity of playing the instruments, and the faculty of hearing on the part of both the musicians and the audience. From the interdependent interaction of all these factors the music arises and is heard or experienced. However, if we look for the music outside of all the aforegoing bases and without the faculty of hearing, we will fail to find it. It is nowhere to be found outside of the factors or bases from which it arises. From this we can know that it is devoid of inherent existence. It is empty; it is *shunya*.

But this does not mean that the music does not exist in any way at all. Through the understanding of emptiness we are not negating that the music exists in a relative or conventional mode. Speaking conventionally, it certainly exists for us. In its provisional, relative nature it definitely exists. But it does not exist in and of itself: therefore it is said to be 'empty' of inherent existence. In the same way all phenomena and all selfness in Samsara are empty.

The teaching of emptiness is crucial to spiritual development because it loosens the grip of the ordinary self on the aspirant. When we know that the ego-self is only a projection arising from its bases, the five aggregates or skandhas, its power over us begins to wane. By realizing the emptiness of self in a direct way, through sustained meditative practices, we become able to transcend self completely. Then we can experience the bliss and freedom of our inherent nature, the Absolute Nature of our minds which is pure and spotless, free and undeluded from 'beginningless time'. On the basis of this wisdom we are enabled to exercise boundless compassion, achieving Enlightenment and having the skill to lead others to liberation.

Thus we can say that, unlike the ordinary self, the Absolute Nature of 'self' or 'mind' is not empty. It exists in and of itself, unchanging and unblemished, without beginning or end. It is the primeval Energy of Mind which has the potential and the impulse to become individuated into a myriad relative selves. The relative self which arises from the Absolute Nature of Mind is not evil in itself. But it becomes a cause of ignorance and suffering when it is not seen for what it is, is held onto for its own sake, and allowed to degenerate into selfishness.

THE FOURTH NOBLE TRUTH

Since our suffering is based on ignorance about the real nature of the relative self, and since this ignorance derives from the collective karmic conditioning which has resulted in our specific skandhas, the way of liberation must be a path which can undo our enslavement to our karma. It must be a process which first alters our karma by refining our awareness. Then, ultimately, it must be a path leading us beyond the reach of the cycle of collective and individual karmic forces.

The fourth Noble Truth is the truth of the Eightfold Path which leads to cessation from suffering. The Eightfold Path is divided into the three developmental components of morality, mental development and wisdom. These three aspects, and the eight facets of the Eightfold Path, are tightly interrelated and, although they can be practised separately in the early stages, they must eventually find spontaneous expression as a unified way of knowing and doing.

The cultivation of morality is a practical necessity for developing the mind towards Final Wisdom. People engaged in harmful deeds, living and speech cannot make progress in the subtler areas of mental development and the attainment of wisdom. By imposing the discipline of outward morality on themselves, people learn to control their minds and to persevere on the Path. By purifying the grosser aspects of their self-expression, they gain a clearer insight into themselves.

The three moral components of the Eightfold Path are: right speech, right conduct and right living. The minimum qualities of right speech are: abstaining from lying, from slander, from harsh speaking, and from idle conversation. It is easy to see how these abstentions can channel not only our speech but also our thinking into clearer and purer expression.

The fundamental laws of right conduct are: abstaining from killing, from stealing and from sexual immorality. Again, these are obviously the minimal aspects of right conduct. Essentially, right conduct consists in the refusal to harm other people and all other living beings, but killing, stealing and sexual immorality are the coarsest acts of harmfulness. They are also the most extreme typifications of the categories of harmful or violent conduct which they represent. Thus, the practitioner knows that under these coarser examples many subtler forms of interpersonal violence are included. For example, depriving someone else of their living is a form of both murder and theft, and the sexual desire for someone else's spouse or betrothed is a form of sexual immorality. By practising the restraints of right conduct, people become less confused and more discerning, and the suffering of guilt diminishes as an obstacle to their inner spiritual development.

Right living or right livelihood refers to the ways in which people sustain themselves and their dependants. Right living is not only directly related to the work we do to earn our living, but also to how we treat others in the course of doing our work or conducting our business. The spirit of right living is that it should be completely non-harmful to the environment, to other people and to all other beings. At a deeper level this means that we are placing our innate survival instincts under moral constraints. It is a much more difficult discipline than it seems at first glance to be. It teaches people to behave more selflessly in an area of activity that is by its very nature a matter of self-preservation.

The sphere of mental development encompasses right effort, right mindfulness and right concentration. Right effort is practising with determination to avoid unwholesome thoughts, feelings and mental images and to overcome them if they arise in the mind, but also to encourage and develop wholesome thoughts, feelings and mental images, and to maintain them in the mind once they have arisen. Clearly this is a practice in the purification and ongoing renewal of the mental domain. By practising right effort the mind becomes equipped to act and react positively, and is expanded to receive more wisdom.

Right mindfulness is of four kinds: mindfulness of the body, of feelings, of thoughts and of the objects of the mind or mental images. This is a practice which enables the practitioner to pay ever-increasing attention to the coarse and subtle motions of body and mind, and to cultivate a heightened and continuous awareness with regard to them. The results of right mindfulness are increased and keener self-knowledge and the ability to view mental and corporeal events objectively, thus aiding the person to take distance from the ego-self by separating more sharply the observing and the observed aspects of selfhood. It also awakens the kind of intense and clear consciousness that is required for fine discernment and for the skilful practise of meditation.

Right concentration refers to the correct practice and application of meditation. In the first stage it is fixing the mind tightly to a single mental object so that the mind becomes 'tethered' to one place. By this practice the ordinary mind learns to control the garrulous flux of thoughts and feelings in order to become able to see beyond them into calmer and clearer mental regions. Indeed, the developed ability to hold the mind steadily to one object, and one object only, rapidly leads the meditator to a state of calm accompanied by intense mental clarity or luminosity. In this state it becomes possible, after determined and regular practice, to experience the equanimity and detachment which are qualities of the Enlightened Mind. (More will be said about meditative practices in later chapters).

The wisdom aspect of the Eightfold Path comprehends right thinking and right understanding. Right thinking is the absence of lust, of ill will and of cruelty in all thoughts. Thoughts which are purified of inordinate desire for pleasure, free from malicious or vengeful notions and harbouring no elements of gross or subtle violence, are right thinking. The practice of right thinking brings inner peace and happiness, as well as situational wisdom to the mind of the aspirant. Right thinking prepares the mind to receive the profound insights of right understanding.

Right understanding is the clear and undivided knowledge of Emptiness (*Shunyata*). It is the understanding which penetrates to the clear differentiation between relative and absolute being, the thorough perception of the provisional nature of conventional individuality and the exact mode in which the ego-self exists. Right understanding, cultivated and perfected by contemplation and meditation, and by the determined practice of the other aspects of the Eightfold Path, sees through self, others and all phenomena, penetrating to the ground of their being and liberating the mind from the delusory acceptance of appearances as reality.

The diligent study and practice of the Eightfold Path reveal how every one of the eight aspects or steps is connected to and latent in every other. As the aspirant advances, the Eightfold Path reveals itself as one composite and spontaneous expression of right being, or living in conformity with the Way It Really Is. The Buddha taught that the Eightfold Path can be practised in either a mundane or a supramundane way. In the worldly way of practice, the Eightfold Path brings success and contentment in this life. When it is practised with spiritual determination, renunciation and perseverance, it is the path to deathlessness, the path that leads people to discriminate in experience between what is impermanent and conditional and what is causeless and undying in the mental domain.

OTHER TEACHINGS

The Four Noble Truths constitute the central teaching of the Buddha, although he also taught on other matters concerning spiritual growth and spiritual decay. The canon of the Buddha's sayings and discussions is vast and multifaceted, yet most of this material is an elaboration of the central teaching, a hammering home in a variety of practical ways all aspects of the Noble Truths.

What remains to be noted are his teachings on the unprofitable questions, those intellectual curiosities which can find no final answers, except as articles of faith. Foremost among these are the questions around 'I.' Will some form of 'I' exist eternally? Will everything that we think of as 'I' be annihilated at death? What is the 'I' that is being observed by the observing 'I,' and what is the observing 'I.' And which of these am I? These the Buddha considered foolish speculations which can do nothing to alleviate misery.

In the same vein he remained silent when questioned about the existence of a Deity. In his teachings there is no reference to a supreme Divinity, either impersonal or personal. His teaching about mere existence is that it has existed from beginningless time, being what it is in itself, uncaused and eternal. It just is. There is nothing more that we can say or discover about it. So far as the relative or 'created' world is concerned, this the Buddha viewed as coming into and going out of existence by the operations of a collective karmic force. All the various sentient beings that inhabit a particular realm have brought that realm into being on the basis of their interdependent and interoperative karma. Their realms indeed exist as they perceive them to exist, but the perceptual potentialities and modes have been shaped by their karma.

To illustrate the vanity and the obstructive dangers of the unprofitable questions, the Buddha used the metaphor of a man having been struck by a poisoned arrow. It would be foolish for someone in that predicament to question what type of wood the arrow was made from, or who shot the arrow at him, or what type of bow it was released from. The most useful thing to do would be to get the arrow removed as quickly as possible so that the process of healing could begin. Such is the practical aim, philosophy and nature of the Tathagatha's wisdom and compassion

Part 3

The Saving Work of the Teachers

BOTH JESUS AND THE Buddha came to rescue people from the ongoing predicament of the unfulfilled mundane life. They came to show people what is essentially wrong with the way they think and act, what has caused them to think and act as they do, and how they can be liberated from wrong-mindedness and wrong action, and from the consequences of these. In the case of both these great teachers the relative world and its inhabitants, especially its human inhabitants, are being addressed from the perspective of an absolute vision. We can say that Jesus and the Buddha came from the Absolute into the relative domain in order to rescue the relative world and its beings from sliding into the nihilism of ultra-relativity. Their way of doing this was to lead people along relative paths back towards Absolute Truth.

In exercising his ministry of leading people towards the Absolute, neither teacher is condemning the relative world in itself. Neither is saying that the relative realms are an evil in themselves. They are saying that ignorance and wickedness abound in the relative world when the relative world is wrongly perceived as an end in itself, as an absolute theatre of being and doing.

The relative is always only an expression of the Absolute and is never self-sufficient. On the other hand, the Absolute always expresses itself through some relative manifestation. When the Absolute expresses itself, relative minds and relative domains appear. If there is another way in which the Absolute expresses itself, we cannot know about it. The relative world, therefore, should not be condemned. It is, to our knowledge, the only tangible means through which the Absolute (or, the absolute fact of being-in-itself) is expressed. Only if the Absolute were no longer to express itself would the relative reality cease to be.

The Saving Work of the Teachers

In Christian terminology the Word of God is Absolute Expression manifested in relative reality. The negatively polarized mindset of ultra-relativity comes by a corrupt understanding of Absolute Expression. It is understanding the relative mind and realm, not as expressions of the Absolute, but as ultimate ends in themselves, as existing by their own power and on their own terms. Naturally, the relative world can only be made a place of ignorance and wickedness when the sentient beings, especially human beings, who live in it, allow their minds to decay into the unspiritual conditions of ignorance and wickedness. But this is not the end of hope. The suffering brought on by evil and darkened understanding is not irremediable. People's minds can be saved from the death of ultra-relativity by a return to the Absolute.

But what do these teachers mean when they teach a return to the Absolute? In the first place they seek to persuade people that, although they now exist provisionally in this relative world, they are not in any final sense *of* this *world*. This world is not their true or ultimate home. It is the unsatisfying home they have made for themselves by abandoning their spiritual nature.

By having allowed their own minds to become coarsened, they have corrupted the relative world which they inhabit. So, there can be no condemnation of relative realms in general—relative realms will exist relatively as long as Mind exists—but our realm is tainted by the corruption of ignorant relative minds. The way back to Absolute Truth is not by attempting to recreate or renew the relative realm in which people live, but by transforming the corrupted relative mindset which has left our world in its fallen state, because its fallen state is a reflection of our own fall.

The relative world, according to the *mythos*, was not always a place of misery. There was an epoch when our world was good because the minds of the beings inhabiting it were uncorrupted by wrong understanding. These uncorrupted minds were open to the Absolute, knew the Absolute and lived in constant communion with the Absolute, although in a relative world. Their relative minds being permeated by the Absolute, the realm they inhabited was likewise filled with absolute rightness, balance, bliss and love. But people's ordinary minds became corrupted by grasping at unrighteous possibilities for self-expression, for unspiritual ways of self-fulfilment and selfishness offered by the relative realm; and they began increasingly to seek only the mundane possibilities available in the relative world, and the mode of existence of the relative world itself, as ends in themselves.

A necessary consequence of this development was an altered and corrupted self-view. The ordinary or ego-self also was turned into an end in itself. Its interests, its gratifications, its aversions, its manifold provisional tendencies were nurtured outside of communion with the Absolute. The human mind progressively closed its consciousness to penetration by the Illumination of the Absolute. People began to turn from and to hide from the influence of the Absolute in order to become ever more immersed in the flux of the relative mind and its relative domain. From the Christian point of view they abandoned their God. In the Buddhist view they became ignorant of the true nature of their minds. In either case they could be likened to actors in a play who have become so neurotically absorbed by the drama in which they are acting that they can no longer distinguish between these unreal preoccupations and the actual reality offstage.

The way of liberation is not a reverse abandonment of the relative world and the relative self in order to become lost in the Absolute, and to pretend that the relative aspect of existence is simply no existence at all. In Christian terminology the remedy is that the relative self should be indwelt by the Spirit of God, and the pervasive Presence of God be realized in the relative domain. The Buddhist exhortation is that the ordinary self should become fully aware of its Absolute Nature. By these means, suffering, ignorance and lovelessness can be eliminated. It becomes possible for people to enter into the Kingdom of Heaven or into the Buddha realms. In these realms or kingdoms there is not complete absence of identity, but identity is subtly transformed so that the relative aspect becomes a perfect instrument for expressing its Absolute Nature.

Beyond this the ordinary mind can neither imagine nor rationalize. What it means to be utterly translated into the Absolute is something which people cannot grasp in a formulable manner. Neither Jesus nor the Buddha spoke of the individual going utterly lost in the Absolute, but only of the experience of deepening awareness and increasing union with the Absolute Source and Absolute Nature of the individual being. Thus, renunciation is not renunciation of the relative world and the relative self per se, but of the relative world and the relative self insofar as these are uninformed by and unconformed to the imperatives of their Absolute Nature.

Jesus and the Buddha demonstrated the truth of their teachings in their own lives. From the time their respective ministries began they did not conduct themselves in the manner of ordinary people. Their understanding, thoughts, speech and conduct were so permeated by and so referred to Absolute Truth that they acted in ways which must be described as superhuman. Yet they assured their followers that this way of life was within reach of all people.

THE NATURE OF THE TEACHERS AND THE NATURE OF PEOPLE

The lives of both teachers show that they came to people from a realm higher than that which people ordinarily inhabit. Jesus came from Heaven as the Son of God, the creative Word of God made flesh. The Buddha achieved Full Enlightenment across countless lifetimes and returned of his own will as a Bodhisattva. Both came to the world to demonstrate and teach the way of salvation by the way they lived their own human lives.

Both emptied themselves for the sake of those they had come to teach and to rescue. Jesus is God consenting to be made man. The Buddha is an Enlightened Being choosing to become a human being. Although their appearance among ordinary people is a very real self-humbling, there is also no way that the Absolute can express itself to people unless it takes on a relative form. Their humility lies in their choice to express the Absolute for the benefit of people who have chosen against God or against their true nature. Jesus and the Buddha have set aside their glory, the glory of absolute self-sufficiency, to minister to relative minds gone astray.

They also set aside their royal heritage in order to walk among ordinary people. Jesus becomes a man despised by the authorities of his day, although he is of the royal lineage of David. Siddhartha relinquishes his royal heritage as Prince of the Sakyans to become a mendicant ascetic. They descend from a holy place into a defiled realm, defiled because the minds which live in it and are aware of it have cut all ties with their Absolute Nature, to rebel against the royal or ruling stature of that nature. So these compassionate kings become 'commoners' in order to bring commoners back to a right perspective. Yet these royal teachers, having become 'common men', are nevertheless greater than common men: greater because they live and act not as ordinary people, but as perfect people. In this way they retain the authority of their royalty and the purity of their absolute heritage. Their lives are a constant revelation of the fulness of being human; that is, the relative expression of the Absolute which fully expresses the Absolute in full submission to the Absolute.

There are nevertheless very marked differences in the way these two teachers appear in the world, in the means by which they descend to live among people. Jesus comes as the only Son of God, born of a virgin. His mother conceives him by the Spirit of God. It is necessary that he be born directly of God so that he will not inherit the original sin and sinfulness of Adam, the first and disobedient man, through whose disobedience all people are rendered impure and unable to commune directly with God. The Saviour of people cannot be tainted with the impurity of people, or else he cannot save them. Neither can he walk among them both as true God and as true man.

The Buddha is very decidedly the son of King Suddhodana, royal but human. His ministry is to rescue and liberate people, not, as in the case of the Son of God, by his death and resurrection, not by taking on himself the sinfulness of the world, but by teaching and demonstrating to people the power of the Dharma. The Son of God comes to reconcile humanity to God by paying in himself the price of human wickedness, by suffering and dying on behalf of all people. Through his self-sacrifice people obtain forgiveness of their sin and are redeemed for communion with God the Father. Siddhartha also sacrifices the bliss of the Enlightened Realms, as well as the privileged earthly life to which he is by birth entitled, but he cannot by these, or any other sacrifices, pay the price of ignorance on behalf of others. He cannot alter people's collective or individual karma. The most he can do is show people the way out of ignorance and towards transcending the karmic forces which bind them to the cycle of samsaric existence. Unlike Jesus, while the Buddha is a Fully Enlightened Being, he is not the Son of God, or God in human form. He has all the authority of the perfected human being, but not the omnipotence of the Creator.

From the point of view of an ordinary human being there is no use putting any faith in the divinity of the Buddha because the Buddha is not divine. Not only is he not divine, but he also does not recognize the existence of a personal Divinity. Nor does the Buddha put much store by faith, either in himself or in his teachings. He exhorts his followers to test his teachings for themselves and only after experiencing their benefits to believe in their liberating force. The only form of faith which the Buddha asks of his disciples is that they believe in their own potential to attain Full Enlightenment. He asks them to believe that they too can become what he has become. Thus, while the Christian must believe that Jesus is God made man, the Buddhist must believe that the Buddha, the Fully Enlightened One, was also once an ordinary man like any other.

Again, as God made man, Jesus is also the Lord of all creation, the King of Kings, worthy of the worship of all created beings, and particularly of human beings, for whose sake he was born, crucified and resurrected. The Fully Enlightened One, although worthy of the highest respect and devotion, does not and cannot ask to be worshipped, for he is neither the creator nor the king of creation. He is fully conversant with the Absolute and with the glorious power of the Absolute, but he is not himself the Absolute. This relative world did not come into being as the result of the Buddha expressing himself, nor is it sustained in consequence of his self-expression. But Jesus, as the creative Word of God, brought all created things into being and keeps them in existence. He is both Son of God and Word of God. He is the expression of the Absolute which manifests as the whole of the relative creation. From this perspective, the Christian perspective, the *Tathagatha* must be understood as having been created by Jesus, the Word of God. For through the Word of God all things, including all sentient beings, came into being.

Neither the Buddha, nor any Buddhist practitioner, admits to this. The Buddha arose spontaneously from the Absolute Nature of Mind, as did all sentient beings. In common with all relative beings, he arose first as a perfect expression of the Absolute, a relative being fully expressing the Absolute. But together with all relative beings he fell into ignorance in the course of countless lifetimes. Then, as rebirth followed rebirth, he, like many other relative beings, applied himself to a dedicated search for the Absolute and eventually attained Full Enlightenment. Taking the Path of the Bodhisattva, the Enlightened Being of Boundless Compassion, he delayed passing into the Final Nirvana, the highest state of relative being, in order to return to this realm of desire for the sake of ordinary suffering humanity, to show them the way out of the cycle of misery.

Thus the Buddha, like all other people, comes from the Absolute, as an expression of the Absolute. This being the case, he is entitled, together with all other people, to call himself a 'son of the Absolute' or, if the Absolute is understood as a personal Deity, to call himself a 'son of God.' In the same way all people can correctly call themselves sons or daughters of the Absolute (or of God) if they fully express and are fully submitted to the Absolute (or to God, if they conceive of the Absolute as a personal creative Deity). However, the Buddha does not use the terminology of kinship. He does not refer to the Absolute as God or the Father, or to himself as a son of God, because he does not conceive of the Absolute as in any way personal. But even if he did, he would not claim to be the only begotten Son of God because he sees all people, in their potential, as being exactly what he is. All people, together with himself, and together with all enlightened and unenlightened beings, are equally and collectively the only begotten sons and daughters of God, the only sentient, relative expressions of the Absolute.

So, from the Christian standpoint, Jesus is greater than the Buddha to the extent that he actually created him. A Buddhist, on the other hand, would argue that Jesus, if he really became a man, must be co-equal with all of humanity and, indeed, with all sentient beings in their potential to become just like him. In their view, Jesus, as an expression of the Absolute, must himself have been a 'created' being, or else he could not have existed as a relative being in a relative realm. To go a step further: in the Mind of Christ, the Buddha is one of the beings created and sustained by him. In the Mind of the Buddha, however, Jesus is a fully Enlightened Being, a fellow Bodhisattva who teaches people the path to liberation, but uses different symbols and methods, including the sacrifice of his earthly life.

Christologists would point out that Jesus is *begotten, not made*. Jesus is not created by God, but is born of God's seed. It is hard to see how this could be a physical seed since such a birth would make of Jesus something other than a human being, yet the teaching is that he is fully human, suffering and being tempted at all points, like all common people. It seems more in keeping with what we know about Jesus that the seed of which he was born is a spiritual essence. It would be the same seed to which he obliquely refers when he tells Nicodemus that he must be born again. And he goes on to say, 'What is of the flesh is flesh, what is of the Spirit is spirit.' So it seems more fruitful to conclude that Jesus is spiritually born of the Father, or else the hope of the very same spiritual birth could not be held out to humanity by him. And it is certainly possible that all people can experience a spiritual birth. This is fundamental to both Christianity and Buddhism.

A Buddhist would not see any significant difference between the terms *begotten* and *created*. If the Absolute were to express itself in the production of human seed, that would still be an act of *production* or *creation*. The only question would be whether what is produced, created, or, in Buddhist terms, *caused*, were in all respects a human being or not. If Jesus is fully human, there can be no structural differences in the biological seed which produced him. However, if in his spiritual nature he has come to the world from the Divine or Absolute Realm; that is, from a realm much more permeated by and conscious of the Divine, then it could certainly be said that he is 'begotten of the Father.' He has inherited the spiritual attributes, always relatively expressed, of the Father, or, in Buddhist language, of the Absolute Nature of Mind.

But a Christian would still be left with the difficulty of the inescapable doctrine of the virgin birth. Every Christian has to solve this problem for himself, and most would consider it best left to stand as something eternally miraculous and incomprehensible to the mere human mind. And there is no reason why it should not stand since it is a matter of faith. No harm can be caused by Christians believing that the Saviour was born of the Virgin Mary. Only, it should not be used as an obstacle to communion with people who do not or cannot see that this article of faith is indispensable.

From the Buddhist angle, there is no good reason why any practitioner of Buddhism should be unwilling to acknowledge that Jesus was begotten of the Father. The virgin birth may surprise Buddhist logic, but there are several areas of Buddhist belief, aspects of doctrine which Buddhists take for granted, which are equally surprising. For instance, there is no proof, other than mystical 'proof', to justify a belief in physical rebirth. It is not that these articles of faith are irrelevant, but only that they need not be erected as barriers between people who are sincerely following different spiritual paths.

From the doctrine of the virgin birth, Buddhists can learn much about the transformation of their own ordinary minds. They can understand more deeply their own inextricable relationship to the 'Father,' and they can do this in the first place by drawing parallels between the birth of Jesus and that of the Tathagatha. In Buddhism it is said that the Buddha is an emanation, a relative representation of the *Dharmakaya* or the Absolute Nature of Enlightened Being. In the teaching of the virgin birth, the relationship between the Teacher and the Absolute Nature of Being is presented in a powerful symbol. By not inheriting the human weaknesses, impurity and ignorance of a worldly father, the Teacher is immediately liberated from bondage to moral frailty, and this liberation is understood in terms of his Enlightened Mind. For all wickedness proceeds from the mind. There is no sinful or ignorant desire of the body that cannot be overcome by the enlightened mind. By the virgin birth the Teacher demonstrates the way of salvation or liberation: people who wish to attain Enlightenment must be born again; having been born as human beings after the flesh, they must be reborn as children of God after the spirit. That part of mind which communes with God or with the Absolute Nature of Mind, and which is submitted to that nature, is called spirit. The teaching unfolding in the pattern of Jesus' birth is that we are all born of a Virgin Mother and a Divine Father, but our ignorance prevents us from knowing and experiencing ourselves in this light. Our 'virgin-born' aspect is our carnal nature which, though it is tainted by sin, is not in its original nature designed to sin. Our divinely-born aspect is the enlightened consciousness which comes to know this, as Jesus knew it and as the Buddha knew it.

Conversely, the Christian can gain more insight into the nature of Jesus' virgin birth by examining it in the light of the Buddhist view of the Teacher as being an emanation of the *Dharmakaya*. By this principle the 'superhuman' nature of Jesus can be more clearly understood. By understanding himself to be an emanation of the *Dharmakaya*, or 'begotten of the Father,' Jesus was able to accomplish his marvellous saving work. The Light of the *Dharmakaya* was the seed which produced his Enlightened Mind or Spirit and, by extension, his physical body. For all relative phenomena, including physical bodies, are produced as an expression of the minds of sentient beings. People who understand their minds to be an emanation of the *Dharmakaya* will produce physical bodies capable of pure speech and conduct and even, as is believed, of miraculous feats. On the other hand, people who are ignorant of the origin and nature of their minds will produce bodies prone to frailty. In this regard, what our bodies are and how they conduct themselves, are factors determined by our authentic self-view. Jesus knew himself to be the Son of God and the Buddha knew himself to be an emanation of the *Dharmakaya*, and as a result both were able to devise means for setting people free from ignorance about their own true natures. Understood in this way, there seems to be no final reason why Buddhists should not acknowledge Jesus as the Son of God or why Christians should not view the Buddha as an emanation of the *Dharmakaya*. Then both teachers can become valuable to followers of both religious paths.

However, the problem posed by the Christian belief that Jesus is the first and only begotten Son of God still remains, as does the doctrine that he is the creative Word of God, from whom all created (or relative) phenomena proceed. Of course, these articles of faith are not problems for the Christians who believe them, but in themselves these doctrines immediately make all other religious paths subservient or secondary to the Christian faith, or else they simply render all other faiths invalid.

There are yet more unique qualities which set Jesus apart from other religious teachers generally, and from the Buddha in particular. In the Christian belief Jesus is the one great mediator between humanity and God. 'I am the Way, the Truth and the Life,' he said. 'No man comes to the Father but by me.' He also is the only Universal Sacrifice by means of which people can be reconciled with the Father. He has paid, in his own blood, the necessary price of human sinfulness, which is death. By taking on himself the wickedness of humanity, he has redeemed them. Henceforth they may freely approach the Father in Jesus Christ, having been cleansed and purified by his sacrificial work. The sacrificial death of Jesus is followed by his resurrection from the dead and ascension into heaven to take his place at 'the right hand of the Father.' In this way Jesus is identified with God, as one of the Three Persons of the Triune Godhead. Speaking to the religious leaders of his day, he says: 'Before Abraham was, I am.' By this statement he identifies himself fully with the Eternal Father who, speaking to Moses, referred to himself as 'I am that I am.'

In these cases too, the most useful interpretation by non-Christian faiths would be to see in them general or collective truths expressed in the individual person of the Christ. The idea of the first-born son could then be taken to refer to all people through the personal insight of Jesus. He sees himself as the first-born Son of God, and he speaks of himself in these terms because, unlike other people, he is not ignorant of this truth about his humanity. People who do not see themselves as first-born children of God are blind to an essential truth about themselves. As the highest or most conscious relative form-beings expressed by the Absolute 'Father' in this realm and in this world, people, among all other sentient beings, may well consider themselves to be the 'first born' children of God. They are able, at least in their own estimation, to seek, to know, and to commune with God, and to express their God-Nature or Absolute Nature in ways not possible (or at least not observed) in other species of living beings. And also in an evolutionary or historical sense people might view themselves as the first-born children of God. They, more than any other living beings, are the first to appear in this world with the full capacity to express the Absolute, to demonstrate their resemblance to their Absolute 'Father.' But they have lost their inner knowledge of these things. Then Jesus, fully knowing them, expresses them again on behalf of those who have forgotten their 'first-born nature.' For the Buddhist, then, he might be seen as the skilful Teacher who shows people what they really are by pointing to his own enlightened self-view.

Jesus as the creative Word of God can be reinterpreted by the same sort of extension from the Illumined Teacher to the ignorant mass. The creative Word can be understood to be the dynamic which translates the Absolute into the relative at the point at which the Absolute expresses itself. In Buddhism this dynamic is seen as a function of the minds of those beings which inhabit a particular samsaric realm. Their collective karma predisposes their collective mindset to interpretatively project the qualities of the phenomena perceived in their relative realm. Two beings from two distinct relative realms would each view a phenomenon such as water in quite different ways. This projected interpretation of the outer environment is clearly a creative function and, more than that, it is a function in which the Word (*Logos*, or *meaningful, reasonable principle*) is present. The act of creation is at one and the same time an act of imbuing the created realm with meaning, purpose and interrelationship. The karmically predisposed 'creative-*logos*' mind is always projecting and interpreting its relative environment, even without knowing it. But anyone with the same degree of self-knowledge as that possessed by Jesus could see themselves as creative word of God; that is, as the relative mental channel through which the Absolute is being expressed both as subject and object, or, as creative-perceiving *self* and created-perceived *environment*.

In the same way all people can be seen to share in the mediatorship of Christ. In the internalized sense—a sense very characteristic of Buddhism—the mediator between relative human mind and Absolute Nature of Mind is the 'Christ within.' The inner mediator is that aspect of the relative mind which is able to conceive of the Absolute, and which yearns to know it and to commune with it. It is the mental channel by which the ordinary mind becomes transformed through an ever-increasing realization of its Absolute Nature. Thus, Christ is the mediator between all people and the Father, but to non-Christians this can only be understood to refer to a Christ-principle within themselves, of which Jesus is an external, human symbol. Searching in their own deep mind, all earnest spiritual seekers, and all Buddhist practitioners, will recognize that part of their mind which calls to them, 'I am the Way, the Truth and the Life. No person attains to Enlightenment, but through me.'

The sacrificial crucifixion of Jesus Christ is, from a Christian vantage point, central to the problem of human sinfulness or human failure; and here again the sacrificial work of Christ is seen as unique and universal. No other religious leader has died to redeem his followers, and in the Christian view no person can be redeemed unless they put their faith in the sacrificial work of Christ. No other religious teacher has paid or can pay the price of sin on behalf of his followers because only Jesus is God made man. He alone is God in human form redeeming human beings. But why is Jesus uniquely qualified to accomplish this sacrificial work, and how is it accomplished? He is qualified in that he alone is the Perfect Man, without sin and fully obedient to the Father. For this reason his is the only sacrifice on humanity's behalf which can be acceptable to God. It is also uniquely efficacious for redeeming people. He alone is able to pay the price of sin, which is death, without being overcome by death. Having died for the sins of the world, he can be raised from the dead because he is pure and sinless within himself. He alone is able to pay the price for others because he does not have to pay it in his own behalf.

The sacrifice is accomplished by the death of his body and spirit on the cross. His body dies by crucifixion and his spirit 'dies' through being defiled by the sin of the whole world. That is why he cries out, 'My God, my God, why have you forsaken me?' It is the indication of the spiritual death or complete separation from God which he is experiencing as he dies, having taken upon himself the sin of all people. For spiritual death is the complete loss of the awareness of God. And with regard to Jesus' physical death, the sacrifice of his body, we must bear in mind that it is a human body born of a virgin. It is a physical body untainted by any lapse into sinfulness, a body neither predisposed to, nor corrupted by, sin.

This is the only sacrifice acceptable to God because it is God sacrificing himself in the form of a perfect human being. It is a sacrifice efficacious for all people who put their faith in the sacrificial work of Christ and become conformed to the pattern of human living which he exemplifies in himself. Any person who does not put their faith in Jesus' sacrifice has no alternative means of redemption, for there is no other perfect sacrificial victim. Here again all other religious paths, from a Christian point of view, are at a loss, for none of them have access to the only acceptable sacrifice.

The Gospel for Buddhists and the Dharma for Christians

But to Christians, the sacrifice of Jesus has both an outer and an internal aspect. By the outer, historical event of Christ's crucifixion their sins are forgiven and they are redeemed to commune anew with God. In the internal sense, the crucifixion denotes an inner sacrificial death by which the person becomes conformed to Christ.

Christians are exhorted to identify themselves with Jesus in his death and resurrection. By becoming one with Jesus in his death they are empowered to put to death their own ungodly selves and to be resurrected in Christ as children of the Father. By becoming identified with Jesus, by being one with him in his death and resurrection, they are sanctified and liberated to reassume their rightful status as God's sons and daughters. It is the mystical identification with Jesus that is all-important in this spiritual practice. And this identification with Christ is not a function of the imagination: it is considered to be a living inner oneness, although a mystery. Practitioners of other religious paths cannot achieve this identification, unless they become Christians, or, put in another way: people who achieve this identification with Jesus have by that act become Christians.

The internalization of the death and resurrection of Christ as a pattern of spiritual transformation is not, in a more general sense, a pattern exclusive to Christianity. Overcoming or putting to death the ultra-relative self—the self which lives outside of communion with God, or in ignorance of its own essential Absolute Nature—is one way of symbolizing Buddhist self-transcendence. In Buddhism, however, the 'death of self' is accomplished through special insight, by knowing the relative self for what it is: empty of inherent existence, but replete as an expression of the Absolute. By arriving at this insight the practitioner 'dies' and is 'resurrected' as a relative self growing more and more into conformity with its Absolute Nature, and becoming increasingly accustomed to knowing itself as an expression of its Absolute Nature of Being. For the Buddhist, of course, the inner pattern of death and resurrection is not related to Jesus Christ but to the teaching of the Buddha which is *Dharma*: the Way it Is. It is a spiritual commonplace that death and resurrection, understood allegorically, are essential aspects of the Path to the Absolute.

As to the external, historical death and resurrection of Jesus; the Buddhist cannot relate to them by faith in, nor by identification with, the Son of God. The Buddhist can and does put his faith in an authentic teacher. Buddhists view all authentic teachers as Enlightened Beings, as the Buddha himself. But not as God. First, Buddhism does not admit to a personal Deity. Second, Buddhists can view a teacher or master as fully representative of the Absolute Nature of Mind, but not as being identical with it in a complete sense. A relative appearance which, so far from only representing it, actually *is* the infinite and eternal Absolute, is a logical contradiction in terms.

The identification with the teacher is understood and practised in Buddhism as a merging one's own mind with the mind of the guru. This practice has both an imaginative and a mystical dimension. The identification with the teacher is more than an internal notion; it is an internal fact. However, in becoming identified with the teacher, the Buddhist achieves union with an Enlightened Mind and not with a Deity claiming to be the unique vessel of salvation. Still, this kind of identification, known as *Guru Yoga*, has great similarities with the Christian practice. And it is far from impossible that Buddhists might practice *Guru Yoga* in relation to Jesus as an Enlightened Teacher.

But Buddhists cannot depend for their salvation on the sacrifice of Christ because Buddhism holds that all beings must save themselves by understanding and practising the Dharma. In Buddhism the teacher can save aspirants by inspiring them through example and by teaching them the way. The teacher can illumine the Path to Enlightenment but cannot achieve Enlightenment on behalf of others. This would violate the laws of karma. No amount of faith placed in the teacher can save the faithful follower. It is a matter of attaining Enlightenment by persevering on the Path, which includes the mystical practices in the various forms of meditation, such as *Guru Yoga*.

So, for Buddhists, the sacrifice of Christ must remain, in its external aspect, a great and profound teaching on the love-relationship between the Teacher and the aspirant. It is something to be imitated rather than accepted as a vicarious means of liberation. The meditative practice of *Tonglen* (giving and receiving) is the method which seems most appropriate for comparing the Buddhist attitude in this regard.

Tonglen involves making a mental exchange of whatever is good and wholesome in one's own experience for the suffering of others. It is practised on the in- and outbreath. Breathing out, one sends all beneficial thoughts and feelings to others; breathing in, one takes into oneself all the pain, darkness and misery of others. The practice is expanded to include all sentient beings caught up in suffering. Finally, in the fully developed phase, the practitioner is taking the suffering of all beings into his own heart-centre, and sending out to all of them healing and beneficence.

Although Buddhism believes in the real efficacy of such mental practices, *Tonglen* and other similar practices are also intended to prepare the practitioner for bearing the suffering of others in more tangible ways. The practice of *Tonglen* has the purpose of gradually and thoroughly transforming the mindset or 'heart-attitude' of the practitioner into a willingness to sacrifice what is good and take up what is painful for the sake of others.

The Buddhist is schooled in many other ways to take on himself what is negative in others in exchange for what is positive in himself. In dealing with various sources of mundane gratification and aversion, the practitioner is taught to exchange praise for blame, gain for loss, and so forth. Still, while all these practices result in a strong attitude of self-sacrifice on behalf of the other, they cannot pay the price of sin or ignorance on the other's behalf. Indeed, the very idea of restitutive sacrifice is foreign to Buddhism. So, while Buddhists can certainly revere the attitude and act of sacrifice exemplified in Jesus, they cannot by faith depend on these for their own salvation or liberation from Samsara.

Neither can they depend on the intercessory work of Christ which follows on his resurrection. Buddhism can no doubt comprehend the internalization of the symbol of rising from the dead into spiritual rebirth, but again, no one can accomplish this on behalf of another. Nor would Buddhists understand either the significance of or the need for a resurrection of the physical body into a glorified body. This would only be understood as an exchange, through death, of the relative human body for the Buddha-body of the Enlightened Realms. The physical body cannot itself be resurrected and glorified. There is in Tibetan Buddhism the tradition of the 'rainbow body.' In this tradition the physical bodies of very advanced practitioners are dissolved into a light-energy after death, leaving behind only the hair and nails. But this is not at all what is understood by Christian faith as the resurrection of the body.

To sum up, Buddhists can learn much from the life, death and resurrection of Jesus Christ, but only as powerful and authentic symbols of the spiritual development of mind from ignorance to Enlightenment. Every aspect of Jesus' life, death and resurrection affords insightful teachings on the spiritual Path common to all humanity. But, while Buddhists can with great profit contemplate the teachings inherent in the life of Jesus, they cannot put their faith in his person as a universal sacrifice. This would nullify the principles of individual and collective karmic responsibility in terms of which people as individuals and as a race in Samsara are required to practise with diligence what is needful for their own liberation.

THE BUDDHA AS A UNIVERSAL TEACHER

The Buddha's appearance among people should be considered both in its relative and in its absolute contexts, or in its conventional and its mystical dimensions. Buddhism is not averse to viewing the Buddha from only one or the other angle, or from both, or from any other perspective which is useful for the mental development of the practitioner. The Buddha is an historical, a mystical and a mythical figure, all combined to make for fulness of teaching.

This lassitude of interpretation makes the Buddha easily accessible to people of non-Buddhist faiths, and there seems no good reason why Christians should not allow themselves to develop their own spiritual insight by studying the life and teachings of Siddhartha Gautama. As a spiritual teacher the Buddha does not intrude into those areas of faith and worship which, in Christianity, belong to Jesus Christ only.

In conventional terms Siddhartha appears in the world as a human being who, dismayed by the forms of suffering which afflict people, makes a determined effort to overcome the miseries common to everyone. He does this in two ways: he develops his understanding of the human condition through contemplation and meditative exercises, and the study of the spiritual traditions of his time, and he applies what he has learnt to the way he conducts himself in thought, word and deed.

Having exhausted every available avenue of meditation and practice taught by the gurus of his day, he adopts the middle-way between the extremes of asceticism and luxury, and determines to discover the insight necessary to liberation by a profound meditative research into his own mind. His mind having been prepared through many years of arduous practice, he is able to penetrate meditatively into the fundamental truths about human existence. Then he goes out to teach these to others.

In order to walk his path of realization he has had to make many sacrifices. He has sacrificed his royal inheritance with all that it implies of wealth, pleasure, power and security. He has given up worldly status and gone forth as a begging ascetic, depending completely on the generosity of others for his subsistence. He has relinquished his home and his family. In short, he goes out utterly alone and unsupported to search for his Truth.

After attaining his Enlightenment, he becomes a revered Teacher whose spiritual understanding is transmitted not only to his close adherents, but throughout his country and even further afield. People of all ranks, from the most exalted to the most despised, recognize in his Dharma the means to their own self-understanding and final liberation. He lives a long life, teaching and exhorting, and dies as an acknowledged Buddha, an Enlightened One.

The essential teaching here is surely that of single-minded perseverance. This is a first principle of spiritual attainment in both Buddhism and Christianity. In the latter it is 'he who perseveres to the end' that will be saved. Half-measures are the means, not to spiritual mediocrity, but to spiritual failure. The search must be wholehearted to the extent that it willingly incorporates severe renunciation of mundane distractions. Like Jesus, and like the great apostles, the Buddha walked in full compliance with the extreme demands made on the aspirant who is motivated to achieve full understanding, full conformity to transcendent Truth, and Final Enlightenment.

As such, the Buddha is a teacher for whom Christians who know the rigours of the spiritual quest should easily feel a sympathetic reverence and from whom they can learn the renunciate determination necessary for spiritual attainment. The Buddha, moreover, pursued this Path five hundred years before the advent of Christ, when the person and message of Christ were not known to the world. So, no Christian can claim that the Tathagatha has taught a spiritual Path which detracts from the person and teachings of Jesus. As an ordinary, albeit royal and gifted human being, he followed the promptings and yearnings of the profound areas of the human mind, and discovered a way of consolation and liberation for himself and others. Every person, and every Christian, can, through an act of sincere introspection, recognize the mental type of the Buddha within themselves, in those aspects of their own minds which resonate with the Buddha's motivation. Through the contemplation of his struggle and final victory they might find in the Buddha not an alien threat to their worship of Christ, but a human being who has fully realized his spiritual potential. There is no question of Christians worshipping the Buddha. There is no question of anyone, even Buddhists, worshipping him. The point is to find the grounds of commonality with him and then to learn from him.

The Saving Work of the Teachers

Of course, Christians might argue that they have no need of spiritual examples outside of Jesus Christ, who is God made man. Yet Christians do look to the great saints and teachers of the Church for examples in the practical spheres of spiritual practice, expression and conduct. Even if they view the Buddha, as they do the saints, as less than Christ (because the Buddha and the saints are not themselves divine), they can learn a great deal from his person and path.

Buddhists, on the other hand, might protest that in their view the Buddha, as a teacher and as an Enlightened Being, is equal with Jesus in spiritual stature. But Buddhists do not see the Enlightened One as God in human form, nor do they believe in the existence of a personal Deity. Bearing these considerations in mind, it should not be difficult for them to grasp why Christians have no choice but to ascribe the greater authority to Jesus. For if a personal God exists, as he certainly does for Christians, and if Jesus is himself that personal God, which again he certainly is for Christians, then Jesus, for Christians, must be the greatest among all human beings.

Viewed as a human being developing his human potential and capacity, the great lesson taught by the Buddha is that this potential and this capacity are present in all people. Attaining the full expression of the Absolute Nature of Mind in his human nature, he invites all people to do the same. For all people it is a vitally important teaching about what is actually in people.

There is in people a yearning to rise above the slough of mundane human failure, and this must be particularly true of sincere Christians. This yearning grows into an inner pressure and, if acknowledged as authentic rather than kept suppressed, it develops into the motivation to seek out Truth. In the first place this truth is always the truth about what, in himself, the person really is. The more the yearning is considered, the more it reveals itself as a longing for inner fulfilment, for liberation or relief from the existential sense of human dissatisfaction. Then the pressure becomes the motivation to find that fulfilment. But it cannot be found without first understanding what tools or qualities are available in the human mind, and in what domain the source of fulfilment is to be discovered.

The Buddha found in himself the qualities of humility, perseverance, intelligence, discrimination and honesty. In his humility he did not scorn to place himself under the guidance of any teacher who might help him in his search. Nor was he too proud to admit his lack of self-knowledge or to make the sacrifices needed to acquire it. About his perseverance we have already spoken. Without this quality he would have become discouraged and resigned to the ordinary human experience of ignorance and suffering. His intelligence enabled him to accept what was useful in all the teachings he received and in all the experiences he underwent as he progressed along his Path. The tool of discrimination was used to put aside those teachings which were not beneficial and to renounce the temptations of mundane experience. The light of his honesty supplied him with the wisdom to know that he was still unsatisfied, and to act on that knowledge, again with perseverance, until he should find the Supreme Illumination, the Satisfying Bliss.

These seemingly simple qualities are indispensable to the attainment of authentic spiritual illumination. Everyone needs them in order to reach the goal. As an essential type of humanity, the Buddha demonstrated the fortunate fact that everyone possesses them. No one who searches with determination will fail to find in their own minds the same tools which the Buddha found and used.

The Tathagatha also demonstrated how to use these tools skilfully. If not used skilfully, they can degenerate into the means for settling into the sham of self-deception, or they might be used positively, but incompletely, for mundane ends. These great spiritual gifts can be misapplied or underapplied. Humility can become a false modesty which settles for spiritual failure or half-measures with the excuse that the person lacks the other qualities which are needed for greater spiritual growth. If the Buddha is the measure of the qualities available to all people, then such self-deception arising from distorted humility is exposed as false.

Perseverance can be misapplied to the pursuit of wrong spiritual goals, the dogged persistence in fostering delusory spiritual achievements and experiences; what Christians would call the way of the 'false prophet.' This occurs when perseverance, practised purely in the ego realm, is divorced from the tools of humility, intelligence, discrimination and honesty.

The tool of intelligence can be used to aspire to an inflated 'spiritualized' intellectualism, usually contentious, self-satisfied and proud. Again, this happens when one of the five qualities is used without the balancing and tempering functions of all the others. The quality of discrimination may be misapplied to arrive at the conclusion that all spiritual teaching and all spirituality are false, incapable of leading people to liberation and ultimately futile. The chief cause of this sort of conclusion is the failure to cultivate and sustain the qualities of honesty and perseverance, and the misuse of innate intelligence. Even honesty can become corrupted into the mere willingness to admit complete spiritual failure, and to settle down in it. False humility, the lack of perseverance, and misuse of intelligence and discrimination are the causes of a self-deluded honesty.

So the Buddha demonstrates, first of all, that all people possess the necessary qualities in equal measure, but that it is up to them to discover and nurture these for spiritual ends. Next, he shows that they are to be used wisely, with skill, for spiritual purposes. And finally, he provides an example of how they should be applied in relation to one another, with balance, each reinforcing the other to help the practitioner to spiritual maturity. In this way he reveals to people their common capacity for self-transcendence, and how it is to be applied.

So far as the limits of human potential are concerned, the Buddha provides a worthy example of the human capacity for Full Enlightenment, which is the proper end towards which all these powerful human possibilities are to be employed. Had the Buddha not demonstrated the human potential for achieving full realization of the Absolute Nature of Mind, people would be justified in using their positive mental endowments for lesser ends. But since the human potential for Enlightenment, for realizing the Buddha-Nature in all its fulness, is clearly demonstrated in the life of the Tathagatha, people can know that these mental tools are worth far more than is apparent from their ordinary mundane applications.

Still, even if they are used only as tools for managing their mundane lives, people can benefit one another by applying them in this way. The conscientious use of humility, perseverance, intelligence, discrimination and honesty in worldly affairs must lead to a more harmonious, more compassionate community. By strengthening these qualities in themselves and by becoming good examples for others, people bring the flavour of their Absolute Nature into the world, even if they do not realize it themselves.

In the aspect of his humanity, then, it should not be problematic for Christians to accept the Buddha as a highly developed and exemplary Brother in Christ. Since, for Christians, Jesus is the *Logos* from whom all created beings proceed and in whom they are sustained, the Buddha must be included in Christ. Since he brought an authentic spiritual Path to people before the advent of Christ, he might well be seen as one who partakes in the work of Christ. By carefully considering these things rather than avoiding them through anxiety or religious exclusivity, Christians can be brought to see to a much greater extent the inclusiveness of the Christian and Buddhist Paths, and the necessary expansion of spaciousness and tolerance which these considerations demand of them.

In his mystical aspect the Buddha is revealed as the Enlightened Bodhisattva who delays entering into Final Nirvana in order to return to samsaric realms to help all sentient beings towards Enlightenment. Motivated by his Great Compassion (*Maha Karuna*) for all beings caught up in the cycle of ignorance and suffering, the Bodhisattva returns to bring the gift of Cessation. He has walked a very long path, through countless lifetimes, to acquire the wisdom, compassion and skilful powers of the bodhisattva. Therefore he is fully able to teach and to rescue sentient beings by a variety of skilful means. Just as Jesus did, the Buddha teaches people in accordance with their individual capacity to hear and to understand. He leads individuals to Enlightenment in a variety of appropriate ways designed to awaken each person at the level of his or her own karmically determined receptivity. The work of the Buddha was the work of the bodhisattva.

As a Bodhisattva, the Buddha has no need of developing his human qualities to realize his potential for Supreme Enlightenment because he has already attained that Enlightenment in previous lifetimes. But he puts his attainment aside, as Jesus did, to become for people a fully human teacher and a fully human example. He becomes like people for the sake of people. Then, in the presence of people, he shows the way to spiritual realization. He re-enacts what he has actually already achieved. Thus, in his Bodhisattva Nature, the Buddha's work is self-sacrificing, salvific and perfect.

It is self-sacrificing because he has delayed his entrance into Final Nirvana, the realm of perfect bliss. Ordinary people cannot adequately grasp the deep implications of the sacrifice, because they cannot conceive what delaying the passing into Final Bliss experientially means. It can only be inadequately imagined as involving vast sacrificial intent of the kind which turns aside from the quenching of unendurable existential thirst, a kind that finds its parallel in the Gethsemane experience of Jesus, if it be understood that the cup from which Jesus so agonizingly recoiled was the cup of sinfulness and not the prospect of crucifixion.

It is salvific because the returning Bodhisattva is equipped to liberate beings from suffering, ignorance and their entrapment in the wheel of samsaric life. He returns to people as something greater than ordinary people and is therefore full of the authoritative means for saving them. For ordinary people cannot save ordinary people, just as the blind cannot lead the blind.

The Buddha is perfected, having attained all the accomplishments of the bodhisattva. Together they are summed up as the Perfection of Wisdom and Compassion.

By the wisdom aspect the bodhisattva sees clearly and penetratively into the way beings really exist, as opposed to their ignorant acceptance of existence at face value. He understands the nature of the absolute and the relative realms, and how sentient beings, and especially human beings, have become trapped in the provisional reality which is called the desire realm. He has attained omniscience through the refinement, expansion and liberation of his mind. Therefore all his teaching is reliable, whether expressed in his words or in his conduct.

In the compassion aspect lies the powerful and unfailing motivation of the bodhisattva to save all beings. His compassion is not restricted or distorted by selectivity or respect of persons, nor by an inclination to condemn. All living beings, even those in the hell realms, are objects of his compassionate endeavour. Then, through the perfection of his skilful means, he brings many beings to liberation.

Yet he accomplishes all these works as a human being, undergoing the sufferings, anxieties and temptations known to common people. He triumphs over all of these to show to people the triumphant potential inherent in all people. Then he dies as all people must, but unlike ordinary people unliberated from their karma, he passes into his Bliss. The power of his teaching, however, remains, not for decades or for centuries, but for millennia. This is surely one of the most undeniable signs that a great Bodhisattva has been among us.

It should not be hard for thinking Christians to recognize the parallels between the coming of the Lord Buddha as a great Bodhisattva and the advent of the Lord Jesus Christ as the Saviour. The only differences, as has been shown, are to be found in their respective self-views, in the manner in which those self-views have been interpreted and believed in by adherents and believers, by the symbols which express them, by the life events of these two Teachers, and by the total cosmology or religious background into which Christians and Buddhists are respectively born. Yet, even though the acknowledgement of these parallels is instructive, and a useful aid for cultivating openness and mutual sharing, the differences are not to be argued away on the simplistic grounds that a different set of events and symbols are being used by Christianity and Buddhism to say the same things about their Teachers or their teachings. Still, by removing, through careful consideration and a relaxed, unanxious openness, the spurious grounds for treating these very real differences as solid barriers, generous room can be made for acquiring very beneficial cross-referenced insights into the nature of the Teachers, their utterances, and our own human minds or spirits.

THE DHARMAKAYA EMANATION

We must now consider what it means to view the Buddha as a relative expression of the Absolute Ground of Enlightened Being; that is, in Buddhist terms, as an emanation of the *Dharmakaya*. What the *Dharmakaya* is in itself we cannot conceive with our ordinary minds. Even in the most refined, most profound meditation we can only experience the Absolute within the limitations of the relative channels that we are. Of course we can vastly expand our mental capacities to increase and concentrate that experience, but *we cannot be it in itself*. We cannot be it in itself because that would imply a total annihilation of our relative existence. If we can decrease our ignorance to the point where our minds can be penetrated and suffused by the vision of Absolute Truth, we will still always know it in and through our relative selves, and we will know our relative selves to be existing in it. In that way we become reunited with it, conscious of it and one with it, but we are not utterly lost or annihilated in it. Even when people say, as some mystics do, that they are lost in it, this does not mean that they are annihilated in it, or else there could be nothing remaining to enable them to know the experience of being lost in it. No matter how close or complete one's union with the Absolute or the Divine may be, something relative always remains. For without the relative, the Absolute abides unexpressed. This is essential to an understanding of the communion-in-love that is called the Love of God by Christians and Absolute Bodhicitta by Buddhists (*bodhicitta* meaning 'the Enlightenment Thought' or 'Enlightenment expressed in wisdom-compassion').

As an emanation of the *Dharmakaya* the Buddha may be expressed in many modes or in many 'bodies.' These bodies or vehicles *(not to be understood as form-entities only)* are subtler or coarser depending on their 'nearness' to the Absolute Source of expression. Still, no matter how subtle, they remain relative expressions of their Absolute Nature. The Buddha can assume a variety of 'bodies' or modes of existing, or even several bodies simultaneously. So, while abiding in Equipoise in the subtlest body, the Buddha can simultaneously manifest in human form and carry out his compassionate works. He can appear now as this teacher and at another time and place as another, while his subtlest body remains in Equipoise. He is able to manifest in these ways because, fully knowing the nature of the Absolute and how the Absolute is expressed in a relative vehicle, however subtle or course, he is able to bring these manifestations into relative existence at will. This is one of the fruits of his liberation from the ignorance which keeps ordinary beings attached to their coarsest relative forms.

We can use an analogy from the creative sphere of the arts to better grasp this notion. In his work the artist is expressing something about himself in a chosen medium such as painting, music or poetry. If the artist were to attempt to express the same idea in all three media, they would come out looking and sounding quite different from one another. The painting, the musical composition and the poem, although completely different in their various structures, forms, expressive potential and way of existing, would nevertheless still be expressions of the same idea arising from the same mind. At the other extreme, if the artist chose not to express himself, there would be nothing on whose basis the mind or the very existence of the artist could be imputed.

From this analogy we can also gain some insight into the relationship or relatedness between the Absolute Source and its relative expression, about how near or far they may be in relation to each other, and about how obscurely or purely the Absolute may be manifested in the relative expression. Although such an analogy can be illuminating, we should make the perfunctory note that all analogies only work to a very limited extent, and all become absurd or break down if used carelessly or too enthusiastically. So we proceed with caution.

For instance, we cannot infer, from the existence of relative phenomena and beings, the existence of the Absolute Source which expresses them in quite the same way as we can infer from a work of art the existence and expression of the artist. At a much cruder level, we cannot use the analogy as an indication that the Absolute Source is personal and creative in the same way that the artist is. An analogy is always only an inadequate illustration, helpful perhaps, but not fully representative.

It can give us a sense of the truth which it is trying to clarify, but it is never a proof of that truth. Indeed, one of the most problematic distortions in religion occurs when spiritual analogies are treated as literal truth.

In arguing for the existence of the Uncaused Absolute, we might begin by asserting that 'existence exists without cause.' (By 'existence' we do not mean all the phenomena and beings in existence; we are speaking of existence as separate from existing things, as mere existence: the potential for and fact of existence by virtue of which all existent things exist). Not only the fact, but the dynamic or the energy of existence just exists. If we were to contend that the fact and energy of existence must have their causes too, we would simply be pushing the conceptual boundaries back to another fact and energy of existence which would again pose the problem whether they are caused, and so on ad infinitum. It is in that area, the area beyond our conceptual reach, that we speak about the Uncaused Absolute.

The problem here is that it is postulable but not explicable by logic. It is something other than logic which verifies for us the existence of the Absolute. It is the odd sense of awe which may arise when we contemplate the way in which the fact and energy of existence itself *just are*. In a curious way we are as unable to deny them as we are to explain them. They are in the domain of the spiritual mysteries.

On the other hand, we can argue that relative phenomena and beings are simply expressions of themselves. They are what they express, and everything that exists exists relatively: The conventional, relative, interrelated and interdependent processes of cause and effect are, in terms of this view, the Essence of existence.

In this case we would have to pursue the processes of cause and effect along a continuum of infinite historicity, only to discover that there can be no cause for causality if causality occurs infinitely. Contemplating causelessness we would find in our minds the same inability either to deny or to explain it. For, if cause and effect operate infinitely, there can be neither beginning nor end to the relative realm. And if the relative realm has no beginning (and no end), we are again in the presence of the Uncaused from which causality proceeds, because Uncaused Causality would then be the nature of existence. Or, if the working of cause and effect does not begin at a given point, its operation must be uncaused. And we have arrived back at the paradox of the Uncaused.

If the nature of relative existence is uncaused, then causelessness is its First Cause. And causelessness itself must be uncaused. So we are back at the Uncaused First Cause. We are again up against the causeless from which causality proceeds or in the domain of which it operates.

We can see from these considerations how very qualified the analogy between the Absolute expressing itself in the relative, and the artist expressing himself in the work of art, must be. We have used it here to gain a sense of how the Buddha can exist and appear in various 'bodies' as an expression of the Absolute Nature of Being or of Mind. We must speak of 'being' and of 'mind' as interchangeable because, as conscious beings, the Absolute exists for us both as Uncaused Being (the first principle of existence) and as Uncaused Awareness (the first principle of mind), or as 'pure existence' and 'pure awareness.'

The Absolute is expressed through us in these two fundamental ways: in the fact of our relative existence and in the fact of our relative awareness. Thus we infer that the Absolute exists absolutely and is Absolute Awareness. We infer that it exists because relative existence cannot derive from absolute non-existence. And we infer that it is awareness because relative awareness cannot arise from absolute unawareness. If we are expressions of the Absolute, the Absolute can be neither non-existent nor unaware. Therefore we can describe the Absolute simply as 'pure awareness', understanding that Absolute Being is implied in the notion of Absolute Awareness. The artist in our analogy is thus pure awareness, and the Buddha is the manifestation of that pure awareness in a variety of relative forms.

It should also be clear that, although the Buddha can manifest in a variety of expressions of pure awareness, he cannot be that Pure Awareness itself. The work of art is not the artist. It is a manifestation of the artist's expression. And yet, in a curious way, it is the artist too. Perhaps we unconsciously express this sort of suggestion when, speaking of a piece of music, we say, 'It is Beethoven,' or, of a painting, 'It is a Picasso.'

The nature of pure awareness may find expression more purely or more obscurely as the case may be. The artist's idea can be expressed more or less successfully, or even unsuccessfully. This depends on the skill of the artist and on the pliability of the medium, of its capacity to yield to the artist's expressive force. So the work might be clearer or subtler, or more obscure or coarser. It is, however, never divorced from the artist in any final way. It remains the artist's expression, whether successfully or unsuccessfully manifesting.

As relative expressions of the Absolute, how is it, then, that people can be expressed as 'successful,' 'less successful,' or 'unsuccessful' manifestations? What has gone right and what has gone wrong? Is it possible that the Absolute can be 'skilful,' 'less skilful' or 'unskilful', as in the case of the artist? Or is skill and the lack of it all on the side of people?

From one point of view we may say that there could be no impure or distorted expressions of the Absolute if the Absolute were incapable of impure or distorted expression. But we would immediately have to relate this statement to the single mode of Absolute Expression, which is always relative. Since the Absolute is only ever expressed in relative manifestations, the possibility of imperfect or 'unsuccessful' expression can never be excluded, or else the relative would have to become absolute in itself. The artist's medium would have to lose its pliability, and the result would be stasis, the absence of expressive dynamism. So, the potential for failure is inherent in the very nature of the medium for expression. And the medium for its expression, relative existence, arises from the Absolute. There is nothing moral or immoral, nothing good or bad, about this. It is just the Dharma of existence, the Way It Is. Neither the Absolute nor the relative are inherently flawed, they just are what they are.

This being the way it is, it is clear that the onus is on the relative manifestation, the sentient being, the human being, to conform itself to its Absolute Nature, to become a purer channel for the expression of the Absolute. For it is the manifestation of pure awareness which, because of its relative nature, can exercise choice, move from ignorance to Enlightenment, and shift itself along various continuums of negative and positive possibilities. That is in the nature of its relative mode of existence. The Absolute, by definition, cannot change 'for better or for worse.'

No matter where we are along these relative continuums, we can never detach ourselves from our Absolute Source, nor can the Absolute detach itself from us. Yet we can regress into a condition of ultra-relativity, of the ignorance and pride which mistake the relative for the Absolute, the relative self for the Absolute Not-Self, and the relative or ordinary mind for the Absolute Nature of Mind. We can become ignorant enough to view our impure expression of mind as the final expression of mind. Still, even this degree of failure does not separate us from our Absolute Source.

We are its expression, however distorted, and its nature is to express itself continuously. This is the sort of inseparability which Christians call

The Saving Work of the Teachers

Divine Love. For the Buddhist it means that all beings must be destined eventually to attain Enlightenment.

Having purified his mind in the course of countless lifetimes, the Buddha was able to become, as a relative being, an extremely subtle relative being, the purest expression of the *Dharmakaya*. As that *Dharmakaya* emanation he obtains an extremely subtle 'Buddha- body.' In his other manifestations of the Absolute he takes on other 'bodies,' coarser than the 'Buddha-body,' yet he is always the purest expression of the Absolute that can be manifested in any specific 'body,' including the much coarser human body.

And these purest manifestations of the *Dharmakaya*, expressed through our mere humanness, are possible to all people. Everyone can use his or her earthly life to achieve increasing development towards the pure manifestation of the Absolute Nature of Mind. As they move through the cycle of birth, death and rebirth, all people are able to ascend towards Final Enlightenment, the perfectly pure expression of the *Dharmakaya*.

TRANSCENDING KARMA

In this final state of Enlightenment, which the Buddha has achieved, karma has been completely transcended. We need to understand what this statement means. We cannot accept it without clarifying it because it implies that a relative being, perfected and pure in its expression of the Absolute, is no longer present to the relative laws of cause and effect, and of becoming. One might argue that this cannot be true of any relative being, however perfect and pure, because only the Absolute exists non-karmically, or beyond the reach of the forces of karma.

So in what way can the Buddha be said to have transcended his karma while continuing to exist in a relative mode? We can begin by stating that he has transcended them in the sense that he has attained the perfection of relative existence, the purest, subtlest form into which a relative being can develop.

As the purest expression of the *Dharmakaya*, he abides in the perfect mental Equipoise which denotes complete absence of distraction, desire, regression or progress. It is the relative mind developed to its purest capacity for expression of the Absolute. All the obscurations beneath which the Absolute has been veiled have been removed. In the state of Perfect Equipoise there is no more becoming; there is nothing more to achieve. As the perfect and final 'effort', the Supreme Equipoise is beyond the operation of causality, just as nothing can be added to or taken away from the perfect work of art, the perfected expression of the artist's original idea.

And there is no possibility of degeneration or retrogression precisely because the work has been perfected. That which has attained perfection has by that fact crossed a threshold beyond regression. Thus, as the perfect manifestation of the *Dharmakaya*, the Buddha abides in unchanging, impassible Equipoise, the highest state of bliss and the perfected relative expression of the Absolute.

In the case of such a fully Enlightened Being, cyclic existence with its karmic forces has been transcended. The same relative realm, by virtue of whose nature and dynamics failure and distortion are possible, allows, by virtue of the same relative nature and dynamics, for the attainment of the perfection which places the Enlightened Being beyond the operation of karma. The happy inference here is that perfection is always the final state whereas failure never is.

In his perfection, the Buddha has transcended Samsara, the cyclic realm of birth, death and rebirth, and of suffering. He has transcended it by cultivating a non-cyclic mind, a mind in Perfect Equipoise. Abiding in the highest relative state beyond the reach of the operation of the samsaric cycle, he can be expressed in the relative domain without being subjected to its forces. That is why his symbol is the lotus flower which rises from the murky water without being defiled by it.

This is a very simplistic way of describing Buddhahood. We can add to the idea of abiding in Perfect Equipoise by saying that the Wisdom of Perfect Equipoise becomes a 'body.' At that point it is both the Enlightened Mindstate and the vehicle or carrier of that Mindstate. Thus it is no longer a 'self' or 'person' as we ordinarily understand these to be. But it continues to exist as a sentient being.

We might go on to say, for the sake of knowledgeable Buddhists, that it abides in non-duality, beyond the distinction of subject and object; that it is a rediscovery of the pure state of its non-inherent existence which has existed from 'beginningless time;' that it is uncaused and spontaneously manifesting, and therefore partakes of the nature of the Absolute; that it is relative in its expression; that it is unconditioned and therefore omniscient; that it abides beyond existence and non-existence—but these insights are mostly meaningless to the new inquirer and do not have a direct bearing on what is being said here.

The Saving Work of the Teachers

At least at some points, then, we have shown in this simple analysis of the Buddha's modes of existence how the relative realm, as an expression of the Absolute, must allow for possibilities ranging from the highest to the lowest and from the purest to the most distorted. Buddhism regularly speaks in terms of developments from the gross to the subtle, from the coarse to the refined, from ignorance to realization, and from darkness to light. At the highest level of attainment there is the unassailable Equipoise of Bliss; at the lowest, that of man at his most retrograde, there is always the potential for ascent.

A BUDDHIST VIEW OF CHRIST

We can see in the light of the above how Buddhists would view the person and attainments of the Lord Jesus Christ. Certainly he would be acknowledged as a great Bodhisattva, the study of whose life and teachings must be hugely beneficial for making spiritual progress. He would be seen as a Perfected One.

His Divine Sonship would be understood rather differently than it is by Christians. The notion of Sonship would be taken to mean that Jesus is a true or 'just' manifestation of the Absolute Expression, in that he perfectly resembles and reflects the 'Father'. The Father is present in him, as all fathers can be said to be present in their sons and to have a fatherly authority over them. More than this, Jesus directly receives and communicates the qualities of the Father. Through his own person he projects these qualities, in a relative expression, into the relative world. The father-son relationship would be seen as a personified symbol of the perfected relationship, exemplified in Christ, between the absolute and relative mindstates..

Buddhism has no mindset for accepting the personhood of the Absolute Nature of Mind. If the Absolute were in any way a personal God, having all the attributes of a Divine Personality, having attributes such as love, justice, righteousness and so forth, such a God could not be understood as being absolute. He would no longer be able to say, 'I Am that I Am,' because the 'I Am' would have to be predicated by relative qualities such as 'loving, just' and whatever other qualities God is believed to possess. In short, such a God would have to be a relative being.

In the Buddhist view it is people who attribute these qualities or characteristics to the (Divine) Nature of Mind. They are personalizing

God because they can understand him only in the context of their own relative personhood. Put more boldly, they are projecting their relative personhood on to the Absolute. Even the Buddhist description of the Absolute as 'pure awareness' refers only to the subjective relative experience of Absolute Mind. That is why Buddhists prefer the term 'the Nature of the Mind' as their designation of the Absolute. This expression means simply 'that which Mind intrinsically is.' For in Buddhism the Absolute is experienced as Mind.

Jesus, then, is the perfect relative expression of the Absolute. It is not only that the Father has chosen to express himself through Jesus, or that Jesus has chosen to become the perfect expression of the Father. There is no other way, but through the relative medium, in which the Father does express himself. Of course, we cannot dogmatically say that there is no alternative way in which the Absolute can ever express itself, but that is another argument entirely. For us, in our relative realm, the Absolute is always expressed in a relative mode. As the perfect expression of the Father, the Son is completely conformed and submitted to the Father's expression.

In this we can see how closely related to the Father Jesus is. But at the same time, from the Buddhist perspective, we would have to question what is meant by the uniqueness or 'onliness' of his sonship. For, although the Absolute Father is expressed perfectly in him, he cannot, in the Buddhist view, be fully expressed *only* in him. The conclusion would have to be, as has been said, that Jesus, within the spiritual tradition of his time and place, was the first and only person who correctly saw himself as a son of God and correctly understood that God is expressed only in relative beings. So the Buddhist would interpret the claim to exclusive begotten sonship as follows: 'Jesus is the Only (person in this time and place to have become fully aware, through self-transcendence, that he is a) begotten Son of God.'

We can also attempt to clarify, by using the Buddhist model, how Jesus is untainted by original sin and sinfulness, how he has overcome death and how his kingdom and his person are not of this world.

Both the taint of original sin and the predisposition to sinful conduct are products of collective and individual karmic forces which operate in the context of relativity. In the highest state of Perfect Equipoise, the Perfect One, though still existing within the karmic field, is no longer subject to either collective or individual karmic force. Original sin can be interpreted as humanity's collective karmic inheritance. By its force all people are held in the grip of ignorance and suffering. But Jesus has developed beyond that impure condition. None of the degenerate 'fallen' qualities associated with original sin, with collective ignorance and suffering, pertain to the Lord. In Christian terms, he has no need of forgiveness or renewal at the hands of the Father because he is beyond collective guilt.

It is the same with the predisposition to sinfulness. Sinful conduct is the result of the pressures of cause and effect. In the web or interplay of the myriad collective causal possibilities and conditions it is inevitable that ordinary minds will succumb to temptation; to thoughts, feelings and actions which proceed from ignorance as to their true nature. Again, in the state of Perfect Equipoise, Jesus is beyond the reach of these forces.

Jesus has overcome death because he has developed beyond the influence of the samsaric cycle of birth, death and rebirth. His mind abides in Perfect Equipoise, no longer cyclic in its propensities. Other than by the attainment of Perfect Equipoise, the only liberation from cyclic existence would be by annihilation of personhood in the Absolute. The Perfected One, however, has achieved that Perfect Equipoise of which the relative mind is ultimately capable, and therefore abides eternally alive. For death, too, is a product of the karmic conditioning of the relative mind.

The glorified resurrected body of Christ must be, to Buddhists, that most subtle of all possible relative 'bodies.' The way relative beings perceive their bodies is also due to karmic conditioning of their collective and individual mindstate. It is worth briefly considering here what will be dealt with at greater length later: how the relative mind derives its self-view and its view of phenomena from karmic conditioning.

In Buddhism there is a school of thought (the *Chittamatrins*) which holds that self-view and views of phenomena, the way we perceive ourselves and our realm, are all projections of the relative mind. This view is not the same as simple idealism in the technical language of Western philosophy, but we need not enter into these subtle distinctions here. The much more widely-held Buddhist view is that the Absolute Nature of Mind expresses itself in the relative realm as both subject and object, as both *this* (the perceiving subject) and *that* (the perceived object). But the perceived object, the phenomenon in the external environment, is perceived very differently by various types of karmically conditioned relative minds. A crude illustration of this notion might be the ways in which the same phenomena are variously perceived by bats and by elephants, or, closer to home, by sane and insane people. Buddhists illustrate this principle in the teaching that hell-beings and human beings perceive water in completely in different ways. Hell-beings are said to experience water as a scorching fiery substance.

It is owing to the same karmic conditioning that people perceive themselves as people and bodhisattvas perceive themselves as bodhisattvas, each manifesting in their respective bodies. The highest subtle body, perceived by the perfectly pure Mind of Enlightenment abiding in Perfect Equipoise, is beyond destruction by death just as it is beyond being affected by either collective or individual karmic forces and conditioning. As the mind of the Perfect One is perfected in purity, so is the correspondingly subtle relative body projected by that mind.

These are the terms in which Buddhists would understand the Christian teachings about Jesus as the glorified Son of God. They are derived from the quintessential Buddhist view that everything that exists, and the multiplicity of possible manifestations of everything in existence, are products of Mind and occur in the realm of Mind. This is not the same as mere idealism. There is something 'out there,' but it, together with the relative mind, is at one and the same time an expression of the Absolute Nature of Mind.

Of course, Buddhists cannot expect Christians to explain the glorification of the Lord Jesus in the same way used by Buddhists to understand the Lord Buddha's state of Supreme Enlightenment. Christians traditionally do not attempt to search out meanings which deviate from those presented in the Holy Scriptures. They are content to accept that Jesus is the Son of God who was born among people as a person, died as a person, and was resurrected in his glorified body. What these things actually mean is generally considered to lie outside of the human capacity to comprehend. Christians accept them as spiritual mysteries, the full understanding of which will only occur when they themselves rise from the dead to see their risen Lord face to face. And, however much Buddhists have developed concepts and insights to explain the perfected state, we have to admit that its transcendent mystery still remains. Or else we ourselves would have to be perfected.

INTELLECTUAL ANALYSIS AND SPIRIT

In developing insights, formulations and keen logical and mystical apprehension, refined by meditative practices, Buddhists have never sought to pull spiritual mystery down to the level of the mundane. However intricate and elegant their religious theories of Mind may be, they do not study, meditate and practise for mundane ends.

The popular notion that Buddhism is a way of life rather than a spiritual Path, or a set of philosophical tenets rather than a great mystical tradition, is simply false. In Buddhism all the powers of the relative mind, whether cognitive, affective, intuitive or mystical, are brought to bear on the great spiritual questions. In attempting to answer these questions by logical analysis their profound achievement has been not to formulate a 'spirituality' which conforms, hugely truncated and deprived of its authority, to the mindset of a world given over to a materialist doctrine. If anything, by their determination to explain what lies beneath the symbols of spirituality, they have managed to place their spiritual insights permanently beyond the possibility of a decline into facile psychological and social reinterpretation.

Christians have achieved the same resistance to decline into the mundane by holding fast to the *mythos* symbols which constitute the mystery of their faith. Although countless attempts at secularisation or psychological reinterpretation have been made, the story of Jesus, the power and authority of Jesus, and the glory of Jesus have been rendered untouchable. They will never be brought down to the level of psychosocial mythology or social doctrine. Such is the faithfulness of Christ's Church on earth.

OTHER COMPLEMENTARY TRUTHS

Beyond the consistent parallels between the teachings of Jesus and those of the Buddha, there are a number of central truths which, although presented rather differently by these two teachers, can become more instructive if approached as complementary rather than as mutually exclusive doctrines.

This is not to say that they ought only to be approached in this way, as though the two religious paths ought to be amalgamated into one. The aim should not be to establish a broader, more inclusive doctrine, but rather to accept the elucidation which each of the two presentations can bring to the other, and this is always more a matter for the individual than for the institution.

The Gospel for Buddhists and the Dharma for Christians

The body of teachings itself is vast and ramifying: it addresses every important aspect of human life and understanding, and is given in a variety of forms and spoken into a multiplicity of situations. There are teachings which are derived from the context of miraculous deeds performed, or from sermons delivered to individuals and assembled groups, or in the course of a number of real events as they develop, or in a number of other circumstances. So it becomes necessary to identify the universal problem to which, in their diversity and fulness, they are all intended to apply. That universal problem is, of course, the human condition, not of a particular time, but of all times.

Both teachers saw the essential condition of people as one of suffering and unfulfilment. Both gave teachings on the causes of these miseries, and on their remedies. They instructed and concerned themselves with people out of a motivation of great compassion and from a wellspring of inclusive wisdom. The remedies they sought to bring were not provisional but transcendent. They did not offer recourse to one or another religious or philosophical system but to a latent spirituality that is immanent and alive in all people. Thus, although their teachings speak to all the layers of the mind, they are ultimately addressed as authoritative and authentic inspirations to the deepest mind or spirit of people. And they are planted there as living, transformative words: seeds that will bear fruit.

Jesus begins his teaching with the two inseparable pronouncements that the Kingdom of God is near and that people should prepare themselves, by repentance, to receive it. They need to repent because they are fallen. They are in an unfit state to receive the grace of God's Kingdom within them. For, although it is to be received as a gift, it cannot be discovered without preparation, effort and search.

For Jesus, the Kingdom of God (or of Heaven) is both an abode and a spiritual condition. As an abode it is both an external spiritual realm in which the saints abide in God's Presence, and an area or aspect of the human mind, the human spirit, in which God's Presence abides in people. It is this second abode, the internalised Kingdom of Heaven, which leads people on earth into the condition of holiness, the condition of being separated out to live and grow under the experience of God's direct inspiration, his love, his forgiveness and his guidance. This Kingdom or *kingship* of God is near to all people and is their rightful heritage if they will be purified to receive it.

The Saving Work of the Teachers

The Buddha comes from the Bodhi Tree teaching that the Absolute Nature of Mind can be fully expressed in and through all people. Indeed, it is already present within them, just as it is in all other sentient beings, but they are separated from it by mental defilements and obscurities. They can uncover and discover their true nature by identifying the encrustations of ignorance and by removing these through study and practice. By these means people can attain to Supreme Enlightenment, an Enlightenment which is again both a realm and a mindstate.

The Enlightened or Buddha Realms are spiritual realms projected by the enlightened minds of Enlightened Beings, and in these realms they abide in Perfect Equipoise, 'close to' the Absolute Source of expression. Their final mindstate is one of perfect wisdom and perfect bliss, which derive from perfect conformity to the expression of the Nature of Mind.

In this general picture the parallels are quite clear. But the specific symbols and ideas behind the general pattern are somewhat different. On the one hand there is the perfect personal God, on the other, the perfect Nature of Mind, alive with the quality of absolute pure awareness, but without personhood. These differences in interpretation of the Absolute are naturally reflected in the respective Christian and Buddhist notions of fallenness and ignorance, and of repentance and the development of motivation. There are also differences in the understanding of how the Absolute is near to people and in what way people are near to the Absolute.

We might begin by asking ourselves how these two very different visions, that of a personal God by Christians and that of the Absolute Nature of Mind as pure awareness by Buddhists, can be mutually complementary. Certainly they cannot be reconciled. We cannot begin searching for mutually beneficial ground by trying to discover which of the two views is right and which wrong, and how the wrong view can nevertheless be used to clarify the right, or how the right can be used to correct the wrong. We have to find a means by which we can conclude that both are right.

Firstly, both are correct when considered in the context of their own respective doctrines. Without a personal God the teachings of Jesus would make no sense. The Buddha's teachings, on the other hand, would suffer a crippling flaw if a personal God were admitted.

Second, they are both right because each is confirmed in the experience of the respective teachers and their adherents. The point here is that all religious doctrine finds its final confirmation only in subjective spiritual experience. For the atheist, the idea of 'no God' or 'no Absolute' is right, but only if the atheist is genuinely experiencing it as right. Otherwise it is wrong. A Buddhist who experiences the presence of a personal God would be wrong to cling to the notion of the impersonal Nature of Mind. A Christian who sincerely perceives God as Absolute Pure Awareness would be wrong to exchange a sincere view for an inauthentic one only because the latter is the orthodox view.

This brings us to the third point, which is that both are right because both (and also other views) are possible. They are both possible because both can be sincerely experienced and subjectively inferred. They are both 'not wrong' because neither can be proven by any form of relative theorizing. If either (or any other) could finally be proven, all people would be converted, not by faith, but by indisputable fact.

Buddhism and Christianity can be considered complementary on three fundamental grounds. Neither religious system is atheistic; neither holds that there is simply nothing outside of the relative domain. Both view the Absolute as Mind, though the one ascribes personhood to Mind while the other does not. They are, rather, prevented from being mutually exclusive by the fact that they do not worship mutually exclusive gods. Buddhists have no god to worship because their 'God' is without personhood, and people cannot validly worship an entity that is not a person, for there can be no personal relationship. For the same reason Christians cannot assert that Buddhists are worshipping a false god. At most, Christians might argue that Buddhists believe in the same God whom Christians worship, but have an incomplete understanding or experience of their God. Buddhists, on the other hand, might say that Christians have gone a step too far in imputing personhood to the Absolute Nature of Mind. Yet it is precisely because of these differences that an understanding of the other's vision can increase the insights of each

Before moving on to a consideration of the qualities attributed to the personal Christian God, we need to clarify some relevant provisions. The Christian God is Trinitarian, one God expressed in Three Persons: Father, Son and Holy Spirit. In this section we are dealing with the personhood of the Father.

We need to note also that there is no final agreement among all Christians as to the essential nature of the Father's Person. In many respects the personhood of the Father remains for Christians a mystery, a matter of faith, and of varieties of individual faith. There are among Christians more or less traditional, more or less philosophical, and more

The Saving Work of the Teachers

or less sophisticated interpretations; and these are not matters of contention within the wider church. But the broad idea that the Father is a Person is fundamental. (And here we must bear in mind that by 'person' we mean an entity with which the believer can enter into a personal, inter-responsive relationship; that is, we are not confusing the use of the term with its more technical meanings, derived from the *Personae* of the Latin Trinitarian formulations).

Traditionally the Father is seen as possessing certain faculties: He wills, feels, thinks, speaks and acts. He has certain characteristics: he is loving, merciful, righteous, unchanging, all-wise, holy and so forth. He has inherent qualities: he is omniscient, omnipotent and omnipresent. He is all these things and yet, in his Divine Glory, he is inexhaustibly, indescribably and infinitely more, for he transcends the human capacity for description.

Viewing the Father in this way, it is clear that we must come up against many internal contradictions. As has been pointed out, we are attributing relative qualities to an Absolute Entity. If, for instance, the Father's will is eternally bound to be loving and just, it follows that his will must be limited, which detracts from his omnipotence. If his nature is eternally unchanging, we have to think of his will as something completely different to our relative conception of volition. Again, virtues such as loving-kindness, mercy and righteousness are necessarily bound up with their negative opposites, as well as with relative modes of expression.

Love is an act of will which tends away from a relative pole of non-love. In addition, it is expressed and experienced in a relative range of feelings and urges, and in patterns of thought, speech and conduct. We have to conclude that the Father's love is something we can only know and give a name to once we have experienced it in our relative selfhood. And selfhood itself arises from a flux of relative processes. So, as there can be no personhood without selfhood, the personhood of the Father would have to depend on the same relative processes, and the Father would have to be a relative being.

The only way to make sense of all this is to approach it from the only perspective in which it does make sense: from the point of view of our own relative personhood. We can make an analogy of something as apparently simple as fire to demonstrate what is meant. If fire were to be considered as a symbol for the Absolute Father, we might begin by asserting that, essentially, 'fire is what it is' (I am that which I am). We might then attribute qualities to fire in dependence on our various experiences of fire. When it warmed us we would say it was loving. When it burned us we would say it was wrathful or just. When it gave us light we would say it was wise. And because we could say all these things about fire, we would attribute personhood to fire. But, outside of our personal experience of fire, we would be unable to say what fire was in itself.

So, if fire were absolute, there would be only two ways in which people could interpret it. On the basis of their experience of it they might ascribe personhood to it. On the basis of their thinking about it apart from experience, they would have to conclude that 'it is what it is,' ultimately unknowable.

The Buddhist view of the Absolute is that 'it is what it is,' and, because Buddhist thinking cannot conceive of mind as arising from anything that is not mind, whereas it can conceive of phenomena as arising from mind, it concludes that the Absolute, the Uncaused First Cause, is Mind. But to Absolute Mind it does not ascribe personhood because it understands that personhood exists (non-inherently) by virtue of relative causes and conditions.

The Christian view of the Absolute Father is formulated by human experience on the one hand and by abstract thinking on the other. Christians acknowledge that their understanding of his personhood is provisional and limited. They also admit the limitations of their abstract notions about the Father. For Christians the personhood of the Father has found its full expression in the person of Jesus Christ. For them that expression suffices. But as to the personhood of the Absolute Father, this is for them a Holy Mystery.

One of the great benefits of understanding and experiencing the Absolute as a personal Father is that Divine Love comes to stand as the eternal source of Christian life and living. The nearness of God to people, as taught by Jesus, is an intensely loving nearness. The Father loves all people and yearns to receive them into his loving Presence. More than this, he yearns to dwell in their hearts, to exist in pure union with his creatures.

In order to accomplish this end he sent his Son to live among people and to reveal to them his eternal love. That love is fully expressed in and through Jesus who can say: 'If you see me, you see the Father.' The Father's nearness to people is seen in the love which he expresses in and through his Son, Jesus. The Kingdom of God is near to people because Jesus, the

Way to the Kingdom, has appeared among people. Thus Jesus both announces and is in himself the nearness of God's Kingdom.

On the one hand God's nearness to people is seen in his redeeming love for people demonstrated in Christ. On the other hand it is seen in the actual redemption of people in Christ. In Christ, then, the nearness dissolves into union. Through Christ the nearness of God to people is both announced and demonstrated. And then, in Christ, the union of God and people is fulfilled.

This, again, is a mystery. People's being in Christ also entails Christ's being in people, and people being in union with the Father in Christ, and the Father being in union with people in Christ. The nearness of God is concluded in spiritual union only through this process of inclusion in and identification with Christ. And for Christians there is no other way to progress from nearness to union because Jesus has said, 'I am the Way, the Truth and the Life; no one comes to the Father except through me.' We can see then how personal and how rooted in love this process is. For Christians are not being included into and identified with an Absolute Principle, but with the Persons of the Divine Trinity, which indwell them as they abide in Christ, and as Christ abides in them.

For Buddhists the nearness to the Absolute Nature of Mind has not to do with Divine Love and their response to Divine Love, but with the Way It Is. The Nature of Mind is already present in the total reaches of the human mental continuum, but is hidden from experience by the darkness of ignorance. It is near but it is not sensed, and so abides unrealized. Yet, in the sense that all people and all sentient beings are ultimately inseparable from it, however inadequately they may be expressing it, it can be spoken of as a relationship of 'love.'

So the Nature of Mind is near to them because it is the essential element, even though they have not yet realized it, of their total nature. But their route to full union with and full expression of the Nature of Mind is not by a faith-inclusion in the saving work of the Buddha, but by following the path laid out for them in the Buddha's teaching. The Buddha's teaching is the Way which leads them back to the Way It Is.

Personhood is found not in the Nature of Mind but in the Buddha. And there is a way in which Buddhists are included in the person of the Buddha and become identified with him. They are included in the Buddha and the Buddha in them because all are together partakers of the same Nature of Mind.

So the Buddhist can begin his path in the knowledge of this inclusion. But identification with the Buddha is a gradual process. The practitioner becomes, so to speak, more and more identified with the Buddha as he develops towards Final Enlightenment. At the attainment of Enlightenment one might speak of full identification. For all Buddhas are the same.

Looked at mystically, we might even reinterpet this notion of identification as being a oneness rather than a sameness by considering how, in the state of Perfect Equipoise, the gross distinctions of personality have been transcended, leaving only the very subtle traces of self-experience, which must remain even at that level of purity. Self-experience in that state is so subtle that there may well be potential for interpenetration and complete inter-identification, yet without annihilation of the subtle, enlightened individual 'bodies.'

Buddhists can love the Nature of Mind as expressed through the Buddha, and they can love the Buddha as the lovable and loving expression of the Nature of Mind. Therefore, in this sense, the nearness of the Nature of Mind can be experienced as a loving nearness. But Buddhists, practical and determined followers of the Dharma, the Way It Is, are more disposed to experience this nearness as an existential insight: they are suffering because they are not conformed to the way things actually are, and to the way they themselves actually are, and their unconformedness is due to ignorance. But their 'redemption' is near; just beyond the barrier of ignorance.

And the Father's yearning for communion with his creature might be interpreted by the Buddhist as the deep inner knowledge of personal alienation from the Absolute Source. The presence of the Nature of Mind in people, although obscured by the ignorance of the ordinary mind, is nevertheless sensed as the spiritual home which 'calls to people,' and to which many people feel themselves subtly drawn.

Perhaps the most obvious lessons to be learned from these two different visions have more to do with common human experience than with mutually informing religious elements, although the latter are clearly discernible.

With regard to their common spirituality, both Buddhists and Christians begin their paths with the sense of an unfulfilled selfhood, a condition of personal 'wrongness' that is nevertheless aware, in some deep area, that 'rightness' is possible. There is the sense of a much greater experience of being, whose exact nature and potential are unknown, but which seems to promise release from the limitations of provisional knowing, moral failure and the isolation of self. These yearnings and subtle perceptions, alive in the minds of people, are always near. And the accompanying question, whether conscious or unconscious, must always be: can people yearn for and perceive modes of existence, even exalted existence, that are altogether outside of their human capacity to achieve? To answer in the negative is never to know; a complete failure of human motivation. The only alternative is to take hold of the natural intuitions which inform us that our lives and minds are stunted by our own ignorance and doubt. Having taken that step, we may experience the nearness of our salvation.

Then, if we do discover what we call God or the Absolute in ourselves, and ourselves in God or in the Absolute, we can only truly know this experience, this Absolute Being, in ourselves. Our experience of ourselves conditions the way in which we perceive or know God. The more we cling to coarse personality, the more coarsely personal our God will be. The more keenly aware we are of the personhood of our selves, the more God in us will seem to reflect that personhood. But if we move closer to mindstates of pure awareness, our experience of God will change as the grip of personal selfhood on us loosens. After all, these ways of knowing God or the Absolute are familiar to Christian and Buddhist contemplatives alike.

FALLENNESS: EATING THE FRUIT

When God is expressed as a Person as He is expressed in Jesus and in Jesus' teachings, the idea of the fallenness of people can only be understood in the dynamic of personal relationship: the relationship between people and God. The fall of humankind must come by an act of disobedience to God.

It is told in the story of Adam and Eve, the first human beings created by God in the image of God. In the primeval Garden of Eden where they live in familiar union with God, Adam and Eve are seduced by Satan to eat the fruit of the Tree of the Knowledge of Good and Evil, the tree from which, alone among all the trees in the garden, God has forbidden them to eat.

As long as they do not eat from the Tree of the Knowledge of Good and Evil they may eat from the tree of Life. But they are barred from the Tree of Life once they have disobeyed God's command and eaten of the forbidden fruit. Then, having eaten of the Tree of the Knowledge of Good and

Evil, they are fallen and cursed, and all subsequent generations of people partake in their fallenness. Their intimate personal union with God is severed and henceforth they can no longer live by the intuitive ethics of the spirit, but become subject to an external Law against which, in their fallen frailty, they are bound to transgress. From now on the most urgent need in people is to be reunited with God. And God desires their redemption.

But how is it that people can be separated from God by merely becoming familiar with the knowledge of good and evil? Without this knowledge they would, after all, be less than human. Good and evil are fruits of the same forbidden tree; they spring up, so to speak, from the same root. They are polar opposites on a relative continuum. Without knowing evil, people cannot know good.

At first glance it would seem that people become separated from God by the mere fact of their relative nature, by whose principles they cannot but develop the capacity for knowing good and evil. If they were unable to discern between good and evil, they would also be unable to discern between every kind of polar opposite: up and down, backwards and forwards, sorrow and happiness, love and fear, and so forth. Conversely, if they are able to discern between other polar opposites, they must *ipso facto* possess the capacity to know the difference between good and evil. And without this capacity to distinguish polar opposites, they would lose their bearings in their relative realm.

It would then seem, absurdly enough, that what separates people from God is not only their acquired ability to discriminate between good and evil, but their total predisposition to experience life in a relative mode of existing, the very mode in which the Absolute inevitably expresses itself.

This point is rendered more problematic in that good and evil stand as the essential problem necessarily associated with spirituality expressed in the context of relative existence, because the potential for evil in people must separate them from a God whose nature is wholly good. Yet, without possessing the potential for both good and evil, people could not exist in the relative mode, the only mode in which God can be expressed in and for people.

Looked at in this way it is easy to be misled into concluding that the flaw is inevitably inbuilt: people cannot be people unless they are fallen people. There is a sense in which this is obviously true, but only if we hold the view that people can never escape their fallenness, that they cannot spiritually evolve into something other than and higher than people.

The Saving Work of the Teachers

Christians, however, believe that people can grow into 'Christlikeness' and beyond that into the glorified resurrected state when the human body and the human condition are left behind in death.

But even in these spiritually developed states the purified person, however subtle and refined and expressive of the Father, must still exist in a relative mode. So, in order to escape from the separating principle of moral opposites inherent in the fact of relativity, there must be a condition of relative existence which does not partake of the potential for good and evil. There must be a way to transcend relativity while remaining subtly relative.

That way, as we have seen, is by the attainment of Perfect Equipoise. And so we must conclude that the fallenness of people is not an inevitable consequence of their existing as relative beings, but of their having lost the relative mindstate of Perfect Equipoise. But can this Buddhist notion be described in Christian terms?

In a vital way it is of course expressed in the human person of Jesus Christ, and especially in the resurrected Person. The person of Jesus in the Gospels marvellously demonstrates this Equipoise expressed in his humanness. Jesus is never out of communion with the Father, except when he takes upon himself the sinfulness of all people and pays the price for sin in his death. He is always spiritually in one place, we might say. His expression of the Father is never compromised. He is always able to walk the middle-way, the way of Equipoise, remaining in the exact place where the Father finds His fullest expression in the human mind or spirit. It is hard not to conclude that, in his humanity, he is exactly what Adam and Eve were before they fell from Equipoise, losing the full harmony of their will with the will of the Father.

For the Christian, this Buddhist concept of Equipoise is translated as 'holiness', and holiness means being set apart from the world for God's purposes. The holiness of people comes by the submission of their individual wills to the Will of the Father.

So, eating from the Tree of the Knowledge of Good and Evil is not the same as merely knowing , in oneself, the potential for both good and evil; a potential which, after all, is an inherent and inescapable aspect of the relative mode of existing. The fall comes by the eating, not by the knowing only. And the eating is the exercise of will which claims the right to practise either good or evil as opposed to only knowing them; the right to depart from the equipoise of will in which the Father's Will is only and continually expressed. Thus, in the Christian view, the fall of Adam and Eve was possible, but not inevitable. It came by an exercise of human volition, independent of and contrary to the Father's Will.

People were not estranged from God by the mere fact of their capacity to discern between good and evil, or by knowing that both good and evil actions were possible to them, but by their assuming the right to choose for evil, to exist in the ultra-relative mode.

By this act of rebellious wilfulness they were separated from the Tree of Life. This symbol can be understood in many ways, even by Christians. Perhaps the most relevant way of understanding it in the context of human fallenness is that people are deprived of the potential for growing 'from holiness to holiness' into the 'life more abundant.' They are barred from experiencing the spiritual bliss of abiding in holiness in the loving Presence of the Father.

With the Fall, the Father's beautiful, subtle creatures immediately become coarse, much more restricted and determined by the laws of their relative humanness. The beings created for eternal existence in a subtly relative 'body' become subject to death, trapped in 'this body of death.' They can no longer live by the spontaneous wisdom of the Spirit, but are subjected to a coarsely externalised law of conduct. Yet, having fallen into a coarser inner state, they cannot but break these crude external laws. Their fallenness is perpetually expressed in their sinfulness.

They now find themselves in a ceaseless struggle against the evil being who seduced them in the Garden of Eden, for they have fallen under his dominion. Some surrender and give themselves over to wickedness. But, whether they struggle against or finally submit to Satan, their lives are rendered miserable.

In Christianity the first principle of evil is embodied in the person of Satan, the supreme Angel of Light who fell from the Kingdom of Heaven by his pride. As the Light Bearer or 'Lucifer,' the highest and most beautiful of all the angels, he rebelled against the authority of the Father, desiring to 'set his throne above the Throne of God.'

Although many Christians believe that this event actually occurred in the hierarchy of Heaven, there is also a symbolism by which the rebellion and fall of Satan can be used to illustrate human fallenness.

The keynote of the symbol is the problem of pride, the Sin of Pride, which is expressed in orthodox Christianity as the *non serviam*: 'I will not serve.' The primeval sin, then, is the refusal to serve the Father, and from

The Saving Work of the Teachers

this refusal all other sins and sinfulness follow. The fall comes by a forcefully negative act of will, not by mere weakness or helpless error. Through this identification of people with the sin of Satan, people and their world are made subject to Satan who, after the fall, is called the 'Prince of this World.'

The consideration of these truths and these symbols leaves Christians with the obvious question: how is it that the omniscient and omnipotent Father has allowed evil to enter his creation, has allowed the devil entry into the Garden of Eden, thus giving him access to the holy human creature?

And how is it that the angels themselves were created with the capacity to choose between serving and refusing God? For if God is omnipotent, could he not have created a realm in which evil has no place? And the crux of these questions is this one: why did the infinitely holy, infinitely loving Father create the living principle of evil?

Once again, the question can only be answered satisfactorily in the context of the inherent nature of the relative and the absolute modes of existence; by the insight that the Absolute is always expressed in and through the relative. Only when this is understood as an existential law, as the way it inevitably is, can the presence and operation of evil in our realm be explained without injury to the Christian understanding of the Father of creation.

In a relative realm there can be no question of the complete absence of the principle of evil, whether or not it is personified. The central problem and its answer are therefore not to found in discussing alternative ways in which God might have fashioned his creation, but in knowing how living beings, especially human beings, can overcome evil. And the problem is complicated by the condition of human fallenness. Evil is no longer only a principle or potential in the face of which people must retain their holiness; it is a disease of the will by which they have been infected. It is to heal this disease that Jesus comes with the remedies of repentance and salvation. By becoming identified with Jesus and his saving work, people are restored to personal fellowship with the Father.

REPENTANCE AND RENEWAL

The basis of Jesus' teaching is 'Repent, for the Kingdom of God is near.' The idea of Christian repentance as expressed in the Greek *metanoia* is that of a change of heart and of the deep mind. The transformation implied is a shift from the self-view of fallenness to the self-view of restoration.

Because the Kingdom of God is near and the love of God is reaching out to people, they have a real basis for hope. Not only is the Father inviting them to a restored fellowship, but he has given them the means of restoration in Christ Jesus. Repentance therefore means, in the first place, opening the heart and mind to receive this Truth.

Its reception engenders a new aspiration in the mind of the recipient. Once people begin to grasp the depth of God's love for them, the fear of judgement and the shame of separation are replaced by the comfort of forgiveness, because God in Christ is forgiving all who sincerely repent.

People habitually try to hide from God, to banish him from their awareness, because of their own anxious sense of impurity. Because they perceive their fallenness as irremediable they are continuously prone to impure conduct in thought, word and deed, and this dynamic increases their sense of guilty anxiety and intensifies the urge to keep God out of their field of consciousness.

By an act of repentance human separation from the Father is ended. As people begin to experience and to grow in the love of the Father, their will becomes submitted to his; their heart-attitude is transformed from the *non serviam* to that of willing and loving service. They are being conformed to the Nature of God expressed in Jesus.

Of course, Christian repentance presupposes a belief in and an experiential sense of the personhood of God. Because the person is separated from the Father by adamic sinfulness and rebellious wilfulness, there is often a strong sense of the wrath of God, which rouses fear in the believer. On the other hand, a sense of God's love gives rise to feelings of contrition, and the sense of God's holiness to feelings of shame.

All these feelings and others involved in the living patterns of broken relationship bring personal and interpersonal authenticity to the act of repentance, which is crucially an interaction between the mind of the penitent and the Personal Mind of God. It is a restoration of relationship between creature and Creator.

Because repentance is a spiritual act, the emotional experiences associated with Christian repentance are not of the same order as those felt in the reconciliation between people and people. Reconciliation between people and the Divine Father is a spiritual event, and the emotions accompanying it signify parallel and deeper events of a spiritual order. A spiritual awakening is occurring. The *metanoia* undergone by the penitent is more than only a personal act of will: it is an act of will initiated by

The Saving Work of the Teachers

the informing and transforming power of a living, personal God. It is God working in and through the person, a relatedness involving intimate inner cooperation with the Spirit of God.

Besides the restoration of their personal relationship with the Father, there is in Christian repentance also the aspect of people's rediscovery of their original created state. In Christ they are to be reconformed to the unfallen adamic nature, and repentance signifies personal assent to this process. Through repentance people come to know that, veiled behind the truth of their fallenness, the more fundamental truth of their union with God is discoverable. That union is expressed in the truth of the primeval state of human holiness; of being, before the fall, the pure and subtle relative expression of the Mind of the Father. In this respect, repentance is the beginning of a rediscovery of the original spiritual pattern of the human mind. It is the reawakening to a Truth that has always been present, but hidden behind the obscurations of sin, shame and fear.

This Truth of the original spiritual pattern is attained by 'death to self', and by being 'born again.' In accordance with these mystical symbols of spiritual transformation, repentance is also the point at which the Christian 'puts to death' the 'old man,' the carnally centred and corrupted self, in order to be reborn as a child of God. The outward sign of this inward event is the sacrament of baptism. The penitent is baptized in water as a sign of putting away his past life of corruption by a symbolic act of cleansing and burial. Rising from the waters of baptism, the penitent stands before God purified and re-created. Henceforth his life will be an expression of the life of God in Christ within his own deep mind.

RENEWAL IN BUDDHISM

Although Buddhists do not speak of fallenness and repentance, there is in Buddhism a parallel central idea of regression, corruption and renewal. The process of the degeneration of humanity is linked to the forces of karma and the functioning of the skandhas. Through ignorant choices which have influenced the interdependent operation of karmic forces and the skandhas, the minds of the various forms of relative living beings have become increasingly coarsened by a gradual aggregation of negative causes and conditions.

This coarsening of minds is reflected in the relative realm itself, because these coarsened minds have projected aspects of function and meaning onto the objective 'stuff' of 'mind-reality.' It is worth recalling here that, in the Buddhist view, the Absolute Nature of Mind is expressed into the relative domain both as subject and object (or, the person and his world).

But phenomenal reality is not simple idealist projection, as in a dream. Buddhists hold that an ultimately amorphous or indeterminate 'mind-matter' is being expressed by the Absolute as an objective externality, but this external raw material is given form, function and meaning by the subjective minds which perceive it in accordance with their own karmic and skandhic conditioning. So the qualities of their external realm are continuously being determined by the qualities of the conditioned subjective minds perceiving their realm, even though the mere objective reality of the external realm is not projected by the subject.

The fallenness of people has come about as a result of the adoption of a fatally mistaken idea about self and the development of a mistaken experience of how self exists: the ignorant belief that self exists inherently, having an independent existence from its own side, rather than only a conventional existence which is imputed on the basis of several interdependently functioning causes and conditions.

Immediately the self is perceived in this mistaken way, as an entity which *is* the entity which is perceiving it, instead of what it actually is (a flux of ongoing mental events), the perceiving aspect of the subjective mind grasps at its personhood, at its identity, at its individuality. Then the flux of mental events which the subjective relative mind actually is, seeks to redefine itself as being an independent entity, an 'I am this,' 'this is myself,' 'this is mine.' And this act of grasping at self-existence is the first step of the decline into ignorance, into falling away from being the natural and spontaneous expression of the Absolute in the relative mindstate. The increasingly ignorant relative being, originally subtle and luminous in its expression of the Absolute, declines into ultra-relativity: the deluded establishment of an inherently existing self, seeking only to express its own relative 'selfhood.' Once this process has ripened, its fruits are craving, aversion and stubborn ignorance; a self-centred abiding in self-delusion about self.

As it is perpetuated with ever-increasing ignorance through countless lifetimes, the deluded perception of self becomes entrenched. The results are attitudes of self-defence, self-will, self-centredness, and so forth, served and sustained by a self-preserving violence of mind. The subtle, luminous relative expression of the Absolute has become a degenerate expression of 'itself.'

In this process of decline into entrenched delusion there is in Buddhism no question of culpability, for it is not primarily due to an act of wilful rebellion or disobedience on the part of the person. And the Absolute Nature of Mind is itself not a personal entity against which the human person, or any other sentient being, can sin. The fall into course humanness is owing to the natural intrusion into the subjective and relative mental domain of a false sense of self, leading to a wrong interpretation of that false sense of stable, circumscribed personhood. The inaccurate apprehension of self occurs the more easily because there actually is a certain mode of self-experience, very subtle and difficult to define, behind the falsely identified self. It would perhaps be easier if 'self' and 'not-self' were simply a matter of existence versus non-existence: the notion that the sense of self is delusory because there is in truth no self at all.

But this is not the case in Buddhism. To completely negate the existence of the conventional self is to fall into another extreme of delusion. So the crucial distinction lies in knowing what it is about self that is to be negated. We cannot simply say that the self does not exist because, clearly, we know that ourselves and other sentient selves are conventionally present and functioning. What is to be negated is the way in which these selves are commonly but wrongly perceived to exist ultimately.

(To restate: The existence of the conventional self can only be inferred from the subjective experience of self which arises in consequence of the interactive functioning of the five aggregates: form, feeling [or, sentience], perception, mental formation and consciousness. Because we directly experience the 'self' which arises from these aggregates, we designate and define that complex self-experience which arises as 'myself.' Yet, if we were to search among the factors from which the sense of self arises, we would not be able to discover any inherently existing self. This problem is akin to that of an optical illusion which arises from a given juxtaposition of a group of visual objects. Because the objects are arranged in a particular way, and because our visual faculties are calibrated in a certain manner, and then focused in ways determined by their a priori calibration, the optical illusion appears, and we designate it as a tree, an elephant, or whatever else. To get behind the truth of the illusion we would have to understand the principles by which it arises. Only then are we able to understand its true nature, even while we continue to perceive it as illusion. We then perceive the illusion penetratively. It exists, we perceive its existence, but we also understand the 'emptiness' of its way of existing. We are no longer in its thrall, no longer convinced by it: we are liberated from its convincing power over us).

So guilt, fear, shame and contrition do not play much of a role in the Buddhist recognition of human fallenness. This is not to say that they are altogether absent. From a moral point of view, from the point of view of human harmfulness, these emotions are part of the fallen experience. But they are not related to a wrathful or loving personal God. They are felt only in relation to other sentient beings. The primal lapse into delusion about self is more likely to find in the Buddhist mind a reaction of dumbstruck or doleful humour, and a determination to cultivate a correct perspective

The recognition of personal fallenness is thus not a great emotional crisis for Buddhists. There is not much emotional dwelling on it or much chance of becoming psychologically immobilised by it since it is approached as a largely practical problem to which the human mind, with sufficient training, is able to find a clear and lasting solution. Rather than concentrating on the dangers of their decline into ultra-relativity, Buddhists are likely to be relieved at having penetrated to an understanding of the first cause of human suffering.

It is easy to see why the prime motive of Buddhist 'repentance' is the possibility of finding the way out of suffering. The imperative is not in the first place a matter of obedience to what the Absolute demands of people. The person turning to Dharma is expressing an intelligent assent to becoming conformed to the principles of the Way It Is and to the most beneficial way of being human. That the person is in this process reconciling himself with an Absolute Imperative is acknowledged, but what is of central importance here is that the human way to Enlightenment has been found.

There is no cause for standing repentant before the Nature of Mind because the Nature of Mind is in no way personally related to the human mind. It is the energy-source of the human mind, but it in no way condemns or approves any human thought, feeling, act of will or action. The 'penitent' in no way conceives of any harm done to a divine relationship; he recognises instead the harm he has done to himself and to others.

The motives associated with turning to Dharma have more to do with coming to one's senses than with being re-created or reconciled. There is a reawakening to an aboriginal self-understanding and not an awakening in relationship to a Divinity. The practitioner is coming fully to know *himself* rather than renewing his knowledge of the Absolute. The Absolute is not seen as possessing any attributes other than those attributed to it by the subjective experience of the person. For what the Nature of Mind is *in itself* cannot be known, except through subjective inference.

Turning to Dharma is therefore, at bottom, the regeneration or re-discovery of a profound common-sense. Even so, Buddhism remains a religion rather than only a philosophy. The common-sense to which the practitioner returns is more than a dry intellectualism: it is a spiritual energy, the Nature of Mind Itself. In this Energy the practitioner takes refuge. In mystical language he takes refuge in the Three Jewels (*Triratna*): the Buddha, the Dharma, and the Sangha.

This is the starting point of the Buddhist change or re-education of mind. Refuge is being taken from one's own deluded interpretation of self, of others and of the phenomenal world, and refuge is being taken from the distractions, suffering, craving and aversion active in the ordinary mind and in the ordinary world.

In taking refuge in the Buddha, the practitioner is seeking shelter in three aspects of the Buddha: the historical human manifestation, the Enlightened Manifestation, and the Absolute Nature of Enlightenment (*Dharmakaya*) embodied in the Buddha. It is a statement of heart-attitude and intent.

Taking refuge in the Buddha's human manifestation means seeking to conform oneself to the perfect example given by him of the human journey from ignorance to Enlightenment. Refuge in the Enlightened Manifestation means preparing and opening the mind to discover the same Wisdom-Energy which the Buddha awakened in himself; and refuge in the *Dharmakaya* means stating one's determined intention to become a pure expression of the Absolute Nature of Enlightened Mind. At the same time this refuge of threefold depth is an aligning oneself with the energies of each level, a mental assent to and invocation of these powerful mental forces which ultimately proceed from the Absolute Nature of Mind.

Taking refuge in the Dharma is also accomplished at these three levels. At the relative level, the Dharma is the teaching of the Buddha as set forth in the canon, and refuge is taken in its aspect as cognitively and intuitively apprehensible truth. At a deeper level it is the Wisdom-Energy behind the Teaching and from which the Teaching proceeds. At the deepest level it is the Absolute Truth of the Way It Is, the Truth which finds its relative expression at the first and second levels respectively as verbal Dharma and as subjectively experienced Wisdom-Energy.

The same principles apply to taking refuge in the Sangha: at the first level the Sangha is the fellowship of human practitioners and teachers helping each other towards higher attainment, at the second it is the Enlightened Sangha with its emanating collective Wisdom-Energy; at the deepest level it is the one expression of Enlightened Mind in which the entire Sangha partakes, and which it manifests with varying degrees of purity.

Taking refuge in the Three Jewels is a first step on the Way to Enlightenment, but is also a continuous act of renewal in and devotion to the energies of Ultimate Wisdom. It is a daily renewal of the intention to attain Supreme Enlightenment by using all the methods, energies and truths involved in spiritual development. It is akin to the Christian's daily renewal of faith in the proclamation of Jesus: 'I am the Way, the Truth and the Life,' if these are interpreted as Teaching, Absolute Truth and Spiritual Energy respectively.

THE SENSE OF FALLENNESS

The sense of fallenness elicits strong psychological and spiritual reactions. In the ordinary mind thoughts and feelings testify to experiences of impurity, delusion, confusion and inadequacy. People feel burdened and lost in a world in which they are not ultimately at home. This may, however, not be true of all people. There are those who claim not to be at all troubled by any notion of fallenness. These are the worldlings: in Christianity they are 'the dead', in Buddhism 'the ignorant'. They seem to live in reasonable contentment and enjoyment of the mundane life, experiencing its vicissitudes at face value. But for the fallen who know that they are fallen, there is suffering and search.

Those who turn to Christianity are immediately confronted with their own intrinsic sinfulness. They are brought to stand before a loving and just God, and if their focus is on themselves, it is only on themselves in relation to God's love and justice. The first motive for their repentance is to satisfy the Divine Imperative, for they have sinned, in the first place, against God.

In contrast, Buddhists are encouraged to consider in the first place their own liberation from the delusions of the ordinary mind. They are standing before no other judge than their own intelligence, informed by their experience of the frustrations of the mundane life. They have both the right and the duty to seek genuine, lasting happiness because no living being desires suffering for its own sake. Seeking one's own spiritual happiness is an intelligent and natural form of 'selfishness,' quite different to the mundane selfishness which keeps people enslaved to misery. But this 'spiritual selfishness,' though viewed as the first sign of an awakening deep intelligence, is not seen as the highest or final motive for practice.

The highest motive is that of the bodhisattva, who generates the compassionate motivation to liberate himself in order to bring others to the same liberation. No one who is not himself liberated, or at least on the path to liberation, can help another. The blind cannot lead the blind. Therefore liberation from self must be the first attainment. In this case the 'selfish' motive is considered to be not only legitimate but noble, because it aims ultimately to bring the highest benefit to others.

Negative emotions such as guilt or self-loathing are not considered very useful, except as manifestations of suffering, compelling the practitioner towards liberation from self and helping him to generate compassion by the empathetic realization that others are experiencing the same inner misery. None of these emotions are seen as sanctifying in themselves. They are merely the natural result of a life lived in ignorance, craving and aversion.

Thus Buddhists, having experienced these negative emotions and the sense of helplessness while in their grip, would not condemn worldly people who are suffering the same miseries. The suffering worldly other would be seen as a victim of delusion in need not of judgement but of succour and wisdom. This same insight is expressed by Jesus in his injunction to his followers not to judge others.

So in Buddhism the highest motivation is to come into conformity with the Way It Is in order to be an example and a helper to others. In Christianity this same motive, although secondary in this case, is shared in the Christian's desire to come into fellowship with God in order to shine his Light into the lives of those still living in sin and misery under the dominion of the prince of this world. But the primary and highest Christian motivation is to please God by becoming reconciled to him in Christ.

The love of God has as its corollary the righteous judgement of God. Those who do not accept the gift of salvation in Christ Jesus remain under God's condemnation. In Buddhism the pressure of Divine Judgement is wholly absent. It being absent, there is no possibilty of the sanctified person standing together with God in condemnation of the stubbornly unliberated other. There can only be compassionate and intelligent concern for the rescue of the suffering other. It is this sort of non-judgemental and universal concern that both Jesus and the Buddha so perfectly exemplify.

IN CHRIST

At repentance the Christian penitent has acknowledged his sinfulness and failure, his separation from God, and his powerlessness to be redeemed outside of God's merciful intervention. He stands in need of a vehicle in which to make the journey of faith, and of spiritual equipment for overcoming the many obstacles to faith which will arise. He is confronted by spiritual adversaries, forces which will constantly work against his spiritual growth. There are carnal forces within the mundane self (the 'flesh'), and within the world, and there is the destructive work of Satan and his demons.

Christians cannot prevail against these forces unless they abide 'in Christ.' Christ alone is the safe vessel in which the spiritual journey can be accomplished. Jesus, as the Way, the Truth and the Life, is everything needful for salvation. The Christian must abide in Christ in order that Christ abide in him. It is an intimate union of faith and the empowerment that comes by faith. For, if the Christian abides in Christ and Christ in him, he is daily being transformed into the likeness of Christ. In Christ, with Christ, through Christ, he is becoming spiritually unassailable. And spiritual adversaries are being overcome by the power of Christ operating within him.

All of this is given him undeservedly, by the Grace of God. God has loved him first, even while he was still unredeemed in Christ. God has loved him, not because he has in any way merited being loved, but only because of the merit gained in his behalf by the perfect obedience of Jesus Christ.

The Christian need not struggle to earn God's acceptance by his own performance. There is nothing he can do to increase the fulness of God's love in Christ for him and for all people. Whatever good he does in thought, word and deed can only be acceptable to God if it is done 'in Christ,' through the power of the indwelling Spirit of Christ. Good conduct carried out 'in the flesh' is of no spiritual value because it is never wholly free from the taint of fallenness and selfishness. Nevertheless, good works remain indispensable because faith without good works is a dead faith. Good works, then, are the natural consequence and manifestation of the same faith which has come by grace into the life of the believer. God initiates and God fulfills: the believer is only able to submit to God because of the faith which God, by grace, has given him in Christ.

For the Christian is no longer under the Law, but under Grace, so long as he walks 'after the Spirit' and not 'after the flesh.' This means living in an authentic consciousness of the presence of God's Spirit within the regenerated spirit of the believer.

The Spirit of God, the Holy Spirit, is the Third Person of the Triune Godhead: Father, Son and Holy Spirit. The Holy Spirit is called the Comforter (*Paraclete*), and is the Inner Presence, within the spirit-mind of the believer, which makes known to him his unity with the Father in Christ, the Son. By this consciousness faith is perpetually being strengthened, the love of God increasingly manifested and the fruits of a spiritual life continually expressed in thought, word and deed. In this way the believer is sheltered in Christ as in a refuge, carried by Christ as in a vessel, and equipped by God in Christ.

Outside of Jesus Christ there is no way to experience this union with and transformation by God. This is a doctrine fundamental to Christianity. Some Christians today find it a difficult or untenable point, but most accept it as a radical truth. Some believe there are many ways to God, others do not. Most believe that people ignorant of salvation in Christ will be treated mercifully by the loving Father because, never having heard the Gospel of Christ, they have had no opportunity to put their faith in it. Yet others believe that all who are outside of Christ, whether knowingly or unknowingly, are condemned; for these believers also hold that certain people have been predestined by God to find salvation in Christ, while others are not chosen.

IN THE THREE JEWELS

From the outset Buddhism does not see itself as the only path to Enlightenment. People are Buddhists because their particular mindset finds an accord with Buddhist teaching and method. Other people with other mindsets follow other paths. If they follow their own paths sincerely they will discover Truth. The only proviso is that the Path itself must be authentically representative of the Way It Is. Authentic religions may employ differing symbols, teachings and methods, but if they lead to liberation from suffering by the energies of Wisdom-Compassion they are valid. The Buddha likened the spiritually ignorant to children playing obsessively with their toys in a burning house. The religions he likened to toy wagons which the father of the house brought to the scene to lure the children out.

As has been described, the Buddhist at the beginning of his path takes refuge in the Three Jewels, Buddha, Dharma, and Sangha, and at the three levels of form (or cognition), wisdom-energy, and Absolute Truth. But Buddhists also take refuge in the immediate teacher (*guru*) and in the pliable and illuminable mind within themselves.

The immediate teacher is regarded as the kindest and most compassionate of friends, who is rightfully to be revered as the Buddha himself. The teacher stands in the Buddha's stead, directly guiding and training the practitioner, using a variety of skilful means to bring him to Enlightenment. Ultimately, the external teacher will awaken the Inner Teacher, the authentic guiding energy within the mind of the student. The *guru* is therefore indispensable. The highest spiritual knowledge has always been transmitted along a lineage of teachers from the time of the Buddha down to the present. Much of this knowledge is dangerous and tending to delusion if transmitted by corrupt or unskilled 'teachers', or if transmitted to practitioners who are not yet ready to receive it. Only the authentic teacher knows the uncorrupted knowledge, and how and when it can be usefully relayed to the developing student. In this way the tradition of the highest teachings is perpetuated without becoming vitiated or diluted as it would be in minds not subtle and pure enough to properly contain and expound it. So the authentic energy of the Dharma is prevented from degenerating into set of mere precepts.

From the time they enter into the Path, Buddhists are taught that human life is precious because it is, among all the expressions of sentient existence in Samsara, the one most suited to practising the Dharma of liberation. It is a fortunate birth, an opportunity to be seized with gratitude, joy and determination. For, although our suffering humanness is the result of an accumulation of negative karma over countless lifetimes, there is nevertheless in the human mind a unique capacity to travel the path to Enlightenment. Moreover, to have been reborn as a human being and then to have come within the influence of Dharma is especially rare and fortunate. Not many people have such an opportunity: it is the result of a particularly auspicious karma. Having come this far after so many lifetimes, the aspirant should seize the opportunity offered by the Dharma, and seize it with a confident faith in his ability to make spiritual progress. For, if the potential for spiritual development were not present in the aspirant, he would not have been attracted to Dharma by karmic forces. The Buddhist can therefore take refuge in this optimistic truth about his own readiness.

The nature of Buddhist faith is related to this insight. It is a faith which is generated by recognizing the results of the operation of karmic forces, a rational confidence in the just and inevitable workings of cause and effect. By employing this sort of faith-insight the aspirant can know his position in relation to the Way It Is, and can put his trust in methods which, through the operations of cause and effect, can bring him into conformity with the patterns of a liberated way of being.

Buddhists, knowing that they have come to Dharma by the sure operations of cause and effect, and not randomly, know also that their practice of Dharma will not be without due result. Thus, despite the difficulties and obstacles, they can walk the Path confidently. There is also an incremental effect as their practice yields it results. As the Buddha taught, confidence in the just operation of cause and effect becomes finally valid when borne out by experience. As the practitioner grows in openness, inner peace, wisdom and compassion, his faith in cause and effect is strengthened.

Like the Christian penitent entering, in Christ, upon the Way, the Buddhist neophyte has his corresponding vehicle in the Three Jewels, his help in the immediate teacher and his initial impulse in an optimistic faith. Both these initiates into Truth are well-equipped to walk the arduous path to liberation. It could be argued that the Christian has more because the Living God indwells, strengthens and guides him directly. There is also the strong emotional and spiritual impetus of the experienced love of God and the sense of full security in Jesus Christ.

But Buddhists, too, are permeated by the sense of the Buddha's great compassion, experienced directly in the presence of the immediate teacher who is compassionately and skillfully concerned with the acolyte's development towards the attainment of Wisdom-Compassion.

Christians also have their teachers, pastors, priests, prophets and counsellors, who carry out the ministries of Christ, and these ministries guide the infant Christian towards greater understanding of his faith, and must continue to guide him until the Inner Teacher, the Holy Spirit, is experienced as a living, indwelling Power. Perhaps this is not the same as the awakening of the Inner Teacher in the deep mind of the Buddhist practitioner, but both Christians and Buddhists can and do walk their paths with full assurance and authority once the Inner Teacher is revealed. In both cases the ordinary or carnal mind is in the process of being transcended, the treacherous enticements of the self are being renounced, as are the worldly life and all the powers of wickedness and deception. Such renunciation is a spiritual, not a legalistic, attitude of mind. It implies partaking of the wholesome aspects of the world without becoming attached to them. It also means being able to live fully in the impure and ignorant world with all its craving, hatred and violence, yet without becoming defiled by these.

For the world is always present to people; even to people who withdraw into monastic life or other types of solitary living. Spiritual renunciation is an inner withdrawal and detachment in which the pure mind is kept in Equipoise as the pure expression of the Absolute, which abides eternally uncontaminated. Whether striving towards this experience or, having attained it, simply abiding in it, Christians and Buddhists share the same fundamental path and goal, at least in terms of what their inner religious experience aims at and achieves.

The differences, nevertheless, have to be acknowledged. Once again there is the difference between the personal and impersonal apprehensions of God or the Absolute Nature of Mind. In Buddhist practice the impersonal view results in greater detachment in the stance towards the other, and in a sense of the inevitability of the Absolute rather than in any attitude of worship or personal obedience. Perhaps this attitude renders Buddhists less likely to crises of faith and crises of relationship. Many Christians arrive at these sorts of crises in the faith-relationship with the Triune God. Yet there are many others who, clearly understanding the inevitability of God's love, abide steadfastly in it. The key for both Buddhists and Christians is to keep a sincere mind, seeking its purification with determination.

A further apparent difference might be found in the degree of responsibility which Christians and Buddhists take for their own liberation or salvation. Because Christians believe that their salvation is wholly in Christ and in his saving power, they might be inclined to make little of their own efforts and righteous deeds. On this matter there are differing schools of thought within Christianity. Some teach that salvation is only by faith in Christ, others that good works can gain merit for the believer. Jesus himself taught that the way is narrow and arduous, and he encouraged his followers

The Saving Work of the Teachers

to do good works. This is taught throughout the Christian Church. As has been said, however, many Christians rely on Christ within them to initiate and sanctify the expression of their faith in good works, and this reliance can be problematic in the face of moral failure.

Buddhists, on the other hand, must take full responsibility for all their conduct on the Path, the more so as they understand the principles of karma. It follows that they must also take full responsibility for their failures. A crucial difference here is to be found in the Christian teaching of Divine forgiveness for which there is no equivalent in Buddhism. At repentance the Christian initiate is forgiven all his past sins and, as he grows in Christ towards his sanctification, he will continue to find forgiveness for sins, weaknesses and failures, as long as he is 'walking after the Spirit'; that is, continually maintaining a faith-consciousness of the indwelling Spirit and striving to submit in all things to the Will of God. This can be a very painful and disappointing process. But the rewards are vastly disproportionate to the sufferings of failure: eternal life with God after physical death, and the bliss of abiding in God's Presence in this life.

For Buddhists the inner sense of the Absolute Nature of Mind (or, the Buddha Nature) is comforting both in its inevitability and in its impersonality: it is pure awareness without judgement. If the Buddhist fails, the only intelligent reaction is to get up and go on practising. Christians, also, having brought their failures to God in Christ, must recover and persevere. The Buddhist perseveres in transforming negative into positive karma, and in strengthening the positive; the Christian perseveres in walking after the Spirit, taking each defeat as a lesson, obtaining God's forgiveness, and walking on.

As they continue to grow spiritually, both Christians and Buddhists must refine their moral sensitivity and conduct. They must purify their minds and bodies as they grow in holiness and spiritual nobility. They must grow in wisdom and love so that their presence and labours are always for the benefit of others. They must deal with their failures. Central to all these aspects of development is the imperative to overcome the mundane self, the crucial obstacle to spiritual growth. For the final goal of their spiritual practice is to be fully transformed from ignorant worldlings into pure channels for the expression of the Absolute: the Triune Living God, or the Absolute Nature of Mind.

To this end they have been equipped at repentance or at the time of awakening with vehicles, empowerments and spiritual-mental tools.

These will accompany them along their paths, providing refuge, protection, comfort and skill. And, as they progress, they will acquire new and more specific methods and skills enabling them to reach still higher ground and, having reached it, to stand firmly on it.

A PAUSE TO LOOK BACK

Before going on to review these aspects of growth and their methods, tools and skills, we must now turn to a brief consideration of the history and development of Christianity and Buddhism from the times of the earliest disciples to the present day. We must do this because the process of historical development naturally brought with it both consolidation and reformulation of doctrines, as well as schism and the establishment of diverse communions.

New ways of practice were discovered and disseminated. Thus, there are some institutions and doctrines in Christianity today that would not be recognised by the earliest adherents of the faith, and the same is true of Buddhism. Having a clear understanding of these developments will help us better to grasp the modern mindsets of these religious paths, and to see how diversity in creed and method evolved.

Then, bearing in mind the historically evolved diversity in both religious systems, we can go on with a broader understanding to discuss the Christian and Buddhist Paths as they are presented and practised today.

Part 4

Outline Histories of Christianity and Buddhism

HISTORY, DIVERSITY, DIVISION, AND AUTHENTICITY

It is stating the obvious to say that the history of anything, including the history of religions, unfolds in a relative realm. Historicity is only possible in a relative realm where the tenses of time, past, present and future, exist in interdependence on each other. Conversely, non-historicity is an impossibility in a relative realm because the absence of historicity is transcendent stasis.

But history is not only the passage of time: it is also the processes of mind active in time, and it is verbal and physical activity resulting from mental processes. Historicity combined with historical activity is a process of ongoing cause and effect. It is cause and effect ultimately proceeding from the Uncaused First Cause. History in all its dimensions, those of mental and physical activity, of cause and effect, and of diversification through evolution, is the expression of the Absolute Fact Of Existence unfolding across time. In our realm it is Absolute Expression made coarse by a decline into the impurity of ignorance: an impure ultra-relative expression which, by reason of its impurity, holds potential also for negative, erroneous, distorted expression.

Diversity is an inevitable outflow of historical processes implicit in the historicity of our realm. Historical processes are extremely complex cycles of interdependent activity which cannot but manifest in diversity. Diversity, for us, is part of the way it is. We can neither prevent it nor put an end to it. When we do try by artificial means to prevent diversification the result is an artificial construct, a thing of no life.

As with all historical processes, the principle of inevitable diversity also holds good for the historical development of religious systems. No religion exists which has not been diversified in time. Diversity in religion is not a problem any more than natural diversity is a problem. To be intolerant of religious diversity is to be in conflict with an inescapable principle of relative existence. Diversity is to be understood rather than vainly struggled against or condemned.

Every diversification in a religious system comes by a set of causes which may be positive, negative or neutral; or the set of causes may embody a combination of positive, negative and neutral influences. Causes are themselves as complicated as their effects. For one thing, causes of diversification in religious sytems are primarily related to mental activity, either of the ordinary or of the deep mind or spirit. All the complex factors and processes of the human mind: reason, emotions, volition, beliefs, and so forth, are present in the causes of which religious diversity is the effect. So diversity in religion should not surprise us at all. We should rather be surprised if we found that religions were tending to homogeneity of expression. This would mean either that humankind was approaching a state of collective spiritual equipoise or that something artificial was being compelled into existence.

In understanding diversity in religious patterns we need also to exercise discernment because, as systems striving to express Absolute Truth, religions can be either authentic or deluded. (As we have noted, diversification in our coarsened realm can also manifest in ultra-relative distortion). In discriminating between these we need to find just and reliable criteria. What qualities make a religious system either authentic or deluded, beneficial or harmful, valid or invalid, true or false?

The most directly authentic criteria can only be found in our common human experience, in those things which we know to be true about ourselves and about all people (and, also, about all sentient beings). The most obvious of these is our common desire to escape from suffering. We know, of course, that we can never be completely rid of suffering in this world. The most we can do is reduce it as much as possible and ascribe meaning to whatever suffering is unavoidable. Then suffering becomes bearable, and we may even find healthy grounds for rejoicing in it. So far as our spirituality goes, we know that it will not rid us of every form of suffering in our world. But we do rely on our spiritual practice for the reduction of inner suffering, mental suffering, in particular. Our spirituality should bring us inner peace, harmony, security and contentment.

But we know also that spiritual awakening is not only a matter of our own release from anguish. The energies of spiritual life are directed against the entire principle of suffering in this realm. Thus our religious practice cannot be an activity for gaining our own inner peace by causing harm to others, or by leaving others to suffer without succour. We know that spirituality means human communion and, indeed, the communion of all living beings. To use our spirituality exclusively for our own comfort is simple ordinary selfishness. Valid spirituality is universally responsible: it takes universal suffering into account. There is really no authentically spiritual means of easing our own suffering while ignoring the suffering of others. Whatever inner peace we find in this way will not be complete, nor will it endure. So we know, if we are spiritually awake, that release from suffering comes by ceasing from harmful behaviour and, more than this, from practising conduct which actually benefits others. It comes not by the feeling of love, but by the practice of love.

So the most fundamental distinction we can make between valid and invalid religious systems rests on the question whether or not they are functioning against universal suffering by the practice of love. Spiritual wisdom is essentially love relieving universal suffering in all its forms, including the suffering of ignorance. If love is not relieving universal suffering, it is love without wisdom, and wisdomless love is not spiritual love.

Any religious system which effectively relieves universal suffering by the energies of Wisdom-Love is valid, for it is confessing the interdependent unity of all living beings as the complex yet single living expression of the Absolute.

In authentic spirituality, Wisdom-Love relieves suffering by removing the causes of suffering. It reduces suffering by shining the light of compassionate understanding into the darkness of suffering. It deals with the roots of suffering rather than only alleviating the symptoms by one or another form of escapism. It operates not only to make people feel better, but to make them well. It does this by helping people to understand what they are in relation to everything that is. It makes them see what they actually are behind the veil of what they only seem to be. It shows them ways to come into conformity with the truth about themselves so that they can escape the suffering which is the total result of their deluded understanding of themselves. So Wisdom-Love is always urging people to understand and overcome their mundane selves, and providing methods for achieving this. It is always leading people out of ignorance about themselves because this ignorance is the greatest cause of their miseries. For, to the extent that the deluded self is understood and overcome, Wisdom-Love is the more completely expressed.

Thus valid religions show the way to understanding and transcending self because there is no other way to eradicate suffering: they recognize that the prime cause of suffering lies in a deluded understanding and experience of self.

But valid religion does not seek to 'transcend' self by any form of psychological escapism such as emotionalism, sentimentalism or trance. That would be to attempt to remedy delusion by increasing delusion. Valid religion moves from delusion to Truth: it confronts the adherent with transcendent reality by revealing the ultimate nature of self. It reconciles the relative being with its Absolute Nature, and with Absolute Truth itself.

Lastly, and coming full circle, valid religions agree that the Absolute is authentically expressed only in Wisdom-Love. It asserts that suffering can only be radically removed when people come into conformity with the Absolute Truth whose sign in our relative world is Wisdom-Love. No matter how diverse their relative interpretations and symbols of Absolute Truth may be, or whether it is revealed to them by revelation, intuition or logic, valid religions always insist that the authentic human expression of the Absolute is seen in the energies and practice of Wisdom-Love.

The Absolute is bound to be diversely formulated because it cannot be truly known except as a subjective experience within the mind of the person. We can only formulate it in terms of our spiritual experience of it. If we were to describe it as finding authentic expression in ignorance, wickedness and suffering, we would have to conclude that there can be no escape from these negative dynamics, except by some form of delusory escapism. Authentic religion would then absurdly be concerned either with bringing people into perfect conformity with evil as a natural expression of the Absolute (if truth were its first concern), or with discovering the most effective form of escapism (if relieving suffering were its first motive). It could not advance Truth as the way out of suffering.

We can only draw back with horror from the thought of such a religious path. It does not square with what we know in our deepest nature. Neither does it find confirmation in our sanity. It is also refutable by logic. So, although we may disagree as to our formulations of the Absolute; for instance, as to whether it is personal or impersonal, we must agree that it finds its just expression in Wisdom-Love. We cannot admit that an evil Absolute is a valid diversification of the interpretation of Truth.

Interpretation involves skill, refinement, subtlety and insight. Religious symbols may be more or less apt, profound or revelatory. Methods may be more or less efficient. Doctrines may be more or less accurate and insightful. Institutions and polity may be more or less spontaneous, restrictive, and so forth. A myriad causes lead to these inevitable diversifications, and they should not be cause for distress. Insofar as diverse religious groups are centred in Wisdom-Love, they remain diverse expressions of a single Truth. Insofar as they depart from Wisdom-Love, there is no longer only diversity; there is division.

Such division, when it occurs between Truth and untruth, is natural and spontaneous, not artificial. It does not arise from differing formulations of Truth but from a departure from Truth on the one side. Even so, when division occurs, spiritual people whose mindset is permeated by Wisdom-Compassion recognize the suffering of people caught up in a mindset which rejects Wisdom-Love. Their motive is not to condemn or to reject, but to rescue. How much more, then, should their motive be to enrich and be enriched by spiritual paths which share their fundamental mindset of Wisdom-Love while differing in doctrinal details.

It is in this context that we should understand the histories and development of Christianity and Buddhism. We should try to understand with penetrative insight how one aboriginal spiritual impulse becomes in the complex chain of cause and effect a variety of diverse expressions. And we should carefully investigate which of these expressions are valid and which are not, realizing that mere traditions and prejudices cannot speak for us here, because they are qualities of the ordinary mind and not of the spirit or deep mind

In the ensuing brief treatment of the histories of Christianity and Buddhism we will mainly consider the development and diversification of institutional forms, religious symbols, doctrinal formulations and methods of practice. These are the elements most likely to prove sources of artificial divisions between religious practitioners, and we should try to discover how such divisions can be overcome, if not in the sphere of institutionalized religion, at least in the spaciousness of our individual minds.

BRIEF HISTORY OF CHRISTIANITY

The First Century

In about the year 30, Jesus Christ was crucified on charges of political sedition and blasphemy. The main force behind these trumped up charges were the Pharisees, one of the two leading sects (the others were the Sadducees) of Hebrew religion at that time. Jesus' message was a fundamental danger to their status and teaching. He had made himself co-equal with God, had preached against rigid and pedantic observance of the Jewish religious laws and had often embarrassed the teachers and expounders of the Law (the scribes) by exposing the futility and lovelessness of many of their rules.

It was a dangerous time in Palestine, with conflict and rebellion occurring everywhere. During the reign of the Roman Emperor Tiberius the governors were placed under extreme pressure to keep firm control over the seething situation in the Palestinian colony. The Jews, on the other hand, were desperate to throw off the Roman yoke or, at the very least, to ensure that their religious traditions and status as God's chosen people would not be vitiated by the oppressive presence of their Gentile rulers. It was a period in which extremism in religion and politics were resorted to by the Jews in order to preserve their unique identity. In the religious sphere, Jewish exclusivist intolerance was at odds with tolerant Roman religious views. In politics subversive groups, especially the Zealots, sought to drive the Romans out. There was a popular expectation that a Messiah would arise, who would lead the Jews to victory over their conquerors.

Jesus, claiming to be that Messiah (Greek: *Christos*; Anointed One), contradicted every Hebrew notion of what the Messiah should be like. He broke many of the ceremonial laws and yet claimed to have come to fulfil them. Instead of leading the Jews in revolt, he taught love of the enemy. He made claims about his person which far exceeded their idea of the anointed Priest-King who was to come. Yet his charismatic popularity was threatening to tear the Jewish establishment apart. Essentially, by flouting the religious laws, by associating with 'unclean' races and individuals, and by teaching a universal love and acceptance beyond all religious strictures, his admonishments seemed aimed more at the dissolution of Jewish religion and racial barriers than at purifying and more zealously maintaining them. At a time of such religious and socio-political crisis this could not be allowed.

But the expedient of putting him to death as a revolutionary and blasphemer, and of publicly shaming him on the cross, could not put an end to his divine work. Jesus rose from the dead and appeared to many of his disciples before ascending to the right hand of the Father. Then, on the day of Pentecost, the Hebrew commemoration of Moses' receiving the Law from God, the Holy Spirit descended on the disciples gathered in hiding in an upper room in Jerusalem.

This was a crucial event in the history of the Christian Church. It demonstrated, by experience, that the Church of Christ did not come by the philosophical precepts of a mundane religious mind. While the apostles were praying together a sound like a strong wind blowing was heard in the room, and tongues of flame appeared above their heads. They were filled with the cleansing and exalting inner Presence of the Spirit of God, and began to prophesy in languages which they had not previously known. This new spiritual energy enabled them to preach boldly in the Name of Jesus and empowered them to perform miraculous deeds. They were no longer afraid of the religious leaders who had put Jesus to death because, gripped by the joy and power of God's Spirit within them, they lost all fear of persecution and of death itself. They were living and teaching daily in the direct Presence of God, transformed by the indwelling power of the Holy Spirit. The Christian Church was born in the Divine Fire, with believers daily experiencing the prophetic and the miraculous.

After the experience of Pentecost the first people to whom the apostles preached the Gospel were their fellow Jews in Jerusalem. Though they were arrested, harassed and beaten by the religious leaders, the apostles continued undaunted. Within a short time a large group of converts had been established. These consisted of Jews both local and from the diaspora in the Greek colonies, who had returned to settle in Jerusalem. Living renewed in the Holy Spirit, they sold their estates and lived in community, sharing all they had with one another. Their number was increased every day as people, witnessing their joy, love and purity of life, were converted to The Way.

But they were not left to practise their faith free from persecution. The religious leaders were anxious to destroy any remnant of Jesus' teaching, especially since the apostles were claiming that he had risen from the dead and was indeed the Son of God. This belief made of Jesus something even more dangerous to traditional Judaism than he had been in his lifetime because, if he had indeed been resurrected by the power of God, their own guilt would be ineradicable and their law fatally compromised. So, when Stephen, a Greek Jew from the dispersion, began boldly to preach the new spiritual dispensation, rebuking the religious teachers for their stubborn resistance to Jesus, he was put to death by stoning. Then severe persecution of the believers followed, largely instigated and organized by Saul of Tarsus, who had given his approval to the stoning of Stephen, and who was later to become one of the greatest of Jesus' apostles.

Within the new fellowship a problem of critical importance was now also emerging; critical because its outcome would establish the universality of Christianity for all time. In its severest form the problem posed the question whether non-Jews (Gentiles) should be allowed into the fellowship at all. If the Messiah had come in accordance with the prophecies of the Jewish scriptures with their emphatic doctrine of the Jews as God's only chosen people, then Jesus must also have come exclusively for the Jews. Indeed, early Jewish Christians combined the new faith with a strict observance of the ancient religious laws. Allowing Gentiles access to their Messiah would mean an adulteration not only of God's race-specific revelation but also of the purity of the Hebrew religious observances.

Less rigid Jewish believers, mostly those from the Hellenist dispersion, advocated the admission of Gentiles on condition that they observe the religious laws, including the prerequisite rite of circumcision. Essentially then, any Gentile wishing to convert from paganism to Christianity would first have to be made into a Jew. These questions were debated with some acrimony, even among the apostles. Finally a compromise was reached: Gentile believers were to be asked only to submit to Hebrew food laws. But still there remained Jewish Christians who insisted on full judaization of Gentile converts.

The Gentile problem was to be solved in a dramatic way by the miraculous conversion of Saul of Tarsus, the zealous Pharisee and persecutor of the Christians. Saul was converted while travelling at the head of an entourage leading Christian prisoners in chains to Damascus. While he was on the way a bright Light appeared to him, and he was blinded, falling from his horse. The voice of Jesus spoke to him from the Light, 'Saul, Saul, why are you persecuting me?' Saul asked, 'Who are you, Lord?' The voice replied, 'I am Jesus, Whom you are persecuting.' From this time Saul of

Tarsus became an indefatigable missionary for Christ, and his name was changed to Paul (indicating smallness of stature).

Subsequently Paul always claimed that he had received his revelation of the Gospel directly from the risen Lord and not from any of the apostles at Jerusalem. His revelation was that the salvation of Christ was for all people. While it was true that this salvation was 'of the Jews', it was intended by God in Christ that all people everywhere were to be blessed through them. They were not to appropriate it for themselves only. Paul boldly challenged the narrowness and hypocrisy of the Jewish Christians, and even of the apostle Peter who was considered their leader. With a zealous love for Christ, with a keen and scholarly mind, and full of the Holy Spirit, he brought the Gospel to the Gentiles throughout the hellenized world, preaching and teaching in Syria, Asia Minor, Greece and, finally, in Rome, the most powerful city in the world.

Through his insight into both the Hebrew and Hellenistic traditions he was able to communicate the Gospel to the Gentiles in ways directly relevant to them. Although he at first preached through and to the Hebrew congregations of the diaspora, he later taught the Gentiles directly. He founded numerous Christian communities which he confirmed in the Faith by visits, exhortations and letters of teaching. It was these letters (the Epistles), lucid and elegant in doctrine and full of burning love, which would later make up the larger part of the Christian New Testament scriptures. More than any other single person Paul, the erstwhile murderer of Christians and self-styled 'Hebrew of Hebrews' worked to establish the Gentile churches and to confirm them in a coherent spiritual doctrine. So great was his contribution to the development of Christianity that no other Christian saint has ever equalled it.

Paul's missionary activity took place between AD 46–60. Although there are no scriptural allusions to his martyrdom, it is a certainty that he was put to death in Rome during the reign of the vicious emperor Nero, sometime between AD 60–68. Thus the period which embraces his initial persecution of the Christians, his conversion and his ministry extends from about AD 32 to 68.

During this same period the other apostles were carrying out missionary activities in Judaea, Samaria and other areas of Palestine, as well as in Syria, Egypt and Ethiopia. Among them, Peter was the only apostle specifically concerned with Gentile Christians. After some dissension with the Jewish fellowship, Peter left Jerusalem and probably preached in Syrian Antioch, Corinth and Rome. According to the Letter to the Corinthians written by Clement of Rome (c. 96) Peter was also martyred in the imperial capital during Nero's reign.

Early Scriptures

By the end of the first century all of the scriptures of the Christian New Testament had probably been written, but were not yet collected into a single sacred book. Writings other than the Gospels and apostolic Epistles were also regularly used for instruction and worship. Chief among these were the Hebrew scriptures (Old Testament) which had been translated into Greek around BC 250. This translation, used by the Greek-speaking Jews of the dispersion, was known as the Septuagint. Jews who had embraced Christianity studied and interpreted these scriptures as allegories prophesying and prefiguring the coming of Christ. Because Gentile Christians of the first century saw themselves as 'grafted onto' the Hebrew tradition through Christ, they were keen to study the old Hebrew scriptures in order to increase their spiritual insight and deepen their worship of God. At this time, and for decades to come, however, there was no thought of gathering the various scriptures into a single canonical work. Teachings and traditions of the Faith were kept current largely by oral transmission.

Institution

As an institution in the latter half of the first century, the Church saw itself as the universal body of Christ, with the risen Lord as the Head. In the communities established by Paul and the other apostles there were two forms of gathering together. Jewish Christians attended the synagogue on Saturdays in accordance with the Sabbath Law and then met together in private houses on Sundays (the Lord's Day). Gentiles met for fellowship only on Sundays. During these gatherings there were readings from both the Septuagint and the new Christian writings. Hymns and prayers preceded the Holy Eucharist and Holy Communion (the ritual sharing of bread and wine, signifying the Body and Blood of Christ which were sacrificed for the forgiveness of sins and the salvation of the believers). Meetings were led by an overseer assisted by a deacon. There would also be some prophesy and praying in tongues.

Paul mentions several ministries in the early church, and lists them in order of importance: apostles, prophets, teachers, miracle-workers and healers, general helpers, administrators, and those with the spiritual gift of 'speaking in tongues'—a prophetic spiritual utterance in which a message would be spoken and interpreted during the meeting. These ministries were exercised within the administrative structure of the group: an overseer at the head, elders to deal with problems in the community, to give counsel and to punish or excommunicate incorrigibles, and deacons who assisted in regulating the gatherings and performed charitable works. The highest authorities were the apostles themselves, and their position was later accorded to their successors, the apostolic fathers and the patriarchs.

Doctrine

Church doctrine was exclusively that taught by the apostles. Christians were exhorted to put their faith in one God, the Father of all, and in his revelation and salvation in Jesus Christ, his Son. At this stage there was not yet a clear doctrine of the Holy Spirit, although believers were baptized in the Name of the Father, the Son and the Holy Spirit.

After being baptized they were to live in faith, love and pure virtue, offending none. They were to lead holy lives in expectation of the imminent return of Jesus, who would come again to judge all people, gathering the righteous to himself and rejecting the sinful. It was expected that no one should commit any sin after being baptized.

There were also a number of apostolic, especially Pauline, precepts for conducting family life and life in the world generally. Two heresies were to be guarded against in the Gentile churches: the Jews' demand that Christians conform to the Judaic religious law, and the teachings of the gnostics, who promulgated mystical and esoteric doctrines of various forms, none of them acceptable to Christian leaders. Some gnostics taught, for instance, that sinful conduct was inconsequential, since the spirit was entirely unrelated to the body.

On the whole, Christian doctrine of the first century had been formulated by Paul, who explained the traditional Hebrew scriptures as prophesying, through types, allegories and symbols, the advent of Christ Jesus the Saviour. The remainder of the details of Christian belief were to be developed over the next three centuries.

The Gospel for Buddhists and the Dharma for Christians

Method and Practice

Christians were baptized in water after a period of preparatory teaching and the recital of a simple profession of faith. Some time after baptism they received the gift of the indwelling Holy Spirit through the imposition of hands (hands laid on the head of the new believer). They were then expected to attend the regular gathering of believers, especially for the celebration of the Eucharist. They were to study, pray and perform good works, and to fast regularly in order to to encourage self-denial and increase personal purity. They were to refrain from all wickedness in thought, word and deed, and to exercise the Gifts of the Spirit for the edification of the community. Their guide in all conduct should be Christ revealed in them by the Holy Spirit.

Although the first Christians were taught to obey scrupulously the worldly authorities, this did not save them from vigorous harassment. Persecution came from two sides: from non-Christian Jews of the diaspora, who incited opposition to the Christians because they considered them blasphemers, and from the pagan religions of the Roman world, which saw the new teaching as a threat to the survival of the old ways. Christians refused, for instance, to worship the Roman emperor as a god. For these and other reasons many Christians suffered torture and martyrdom.

The first church was established in a time of great spiritual power and awareness. The Spirit of God was directly present to the believers, and was manifested in prophesy, miracles, visions, exorcism and demonstrations of extraordinary zeal. Believers saw themselves as engaged in spiritual warfare against demonic wickedness 'in high places.' Their goal was to bring the world to renewed subjection to God's Truth and Power.

Summary of the First Period

In the Church of the first century we see the initial spiritual outpouring following on the resurrection of Jesus, in all its spontaneous and powerful expressions, being channeled and given simple doctrinal form by the apostles and other leaders. A balance is being sought between authentic and false or antinomian spiritual expressions.

At the same time, authentic spiritual spontaneity is being given a concrete symbolic shape in order to foster unity of belief, practice and conduct. Individuals possessing various spiritual gifts are likened by Paul to different parts of a single body which are to function to preserve and edify the whole. Spontaneous expression in prophesy, tongues and so forth are regulated in Christian gatherings in order to prevent egotism and disorder. A coherent doctrine is superimposed on spontaneous expressions to protect the growing church from extreme individualism and unsound interpretations. Essentially, a balance is being struck between spontaneity and formalism. This early striving for balance is to set the pattern for the development of Christianity over the next two millennia.

Indeed, the central problem of the earliest Church is the struggle between strict legalism and the spiritual liberty introduced by Jesus. The Faith was born in an environment of unbending and intricate legalism and prescriptive practice. It was a threat to Judaic legalism from the outset. And, since it was only to be fully understood in the context of the Hebrew tradition, new interpretations of the role of Judaism had to be found. The Hebrew scriptures had to be reinterpreted as constituting a religious message whose fulfilment lay in the spontaneity of the new faith. More than this, the religious laws embodied in the Septuagint were to be understood as provisional, as applicable only to the period before the advent of Christ, who brought into the world the 'Law of the Spirit.' Religious legalism was now only for the 'dead'; the reborn person, spiritually alive in Christ, was to conform to a spontaneous righteousness which flowed from the indwelling Holy Spirit. But this Living Law, inscribed on the heart, was not to be misunderstood or abused as an excuse for indulging in unholy or erratic emotional behaviour. On the other hand, there should not be a regression into lifeless legalism.

Spiritual freedom was to be harmonized with religious conformity in all aspects of Christian life and practice. In the church institution individual spiritual liberty was to be regulated by a structure of overseership. Free worship was to be contained within a formal structure and expressed through a simple liturgy. A doctrinal framework was created to contain all the elements of religious experience. Yet none of these steps detracted from the individual and collective liberty of the Church as a living spiritual organism open to further growth and revelation, and poised for diversification.

The Second and Third Centuries

By the time all the apostles had died, the Church was being administered by bishops, presbyters and deacons. By the second century a general structure of the Church was in existence. Until the conversion of the Roman

Emperor Constantine in 312, the Church suffered repeated episodes of suppression and persecution, with destruction of property and burning of scriptures. From about the year 70 until the accession of Constantine it was expanding, carrying out missionary activities and developing doctrine and polity. It was challenged by new heresies which were probably the single most important reason for the relatively rapid consolidation of orthodox doctrine. During this time, as well, the canon of scripture was largely settled. The Church also had to formulate a stance towards the Judaic tradition on the one hand and Hellenist philosophy, particularly neoplatonism, on the other.

The earliest Christian leaders to deal with these issues were the Apostolic Fathers, so called because they were the last surviving churchmen to have had direct contact with the apostles or their associates. They dealt chiefly with questions of church organization and hierarchy, with some emergent theological points, and with the reassessment of the relationship between Judaism and the new faith.

Their work reflects the entrenchment of the bishop-presbyter-deacon hierarchy and the beginnings of the vesting of ultimate authority for settling disputes in an assembly of bishops. The primacy of the Roman Church and Bishop of Rome also began to be asserted on the basis that Rome was the capital of the empire and, more importantly for Christians, that the Bishop of Rome could claim to derive his authority from Peter, the chief apostle of Jesus. Thus Rome was considered to have the right to regulate affairs throughout the universal (catholic) Church.

Theological work concentrated on the reinterpretation of the Judaic scriptures to suit the developing Christian doctrine. In some cases there was severe criticism of the Hebrew tradition, and it was sometimes considered obsolete. The Fathers were also responsible for some writings which came close to being included in the New Testament canon. 'The Shepherd of Hermas', 'The Epistle of Barnabas', and the 'Didache' were widely used for instruction throughout the growing Church.

The gnostic teachings were the main object of concern for the leaders of the second century Church. Gnosticism was a pervasive heresy which drew many adherents. Its central teachings were that the God of the Judaic tradition was not the supreme God, that Jesus was a spirit-being whose human body was not of flesh, that the world of matter was entirely delusory and evil in itself, that salvation could only be gained through secret knowledge discoverable in the deep mind, and that people were divided into two basic types: those capable of spiritual attainment and those lesser beings who could only advance at the psychological and material levels. All of these ideas were repugnant to the Fathers of the Church. Even though the Hebrew scriptures were being reinterpreted along Christian lines, it was accepted that the God of the Old Testament was the One True God and Father of Jesus. And Christian teaching insisted that Jesus, although divinely conceived, was also fully human. The material world, although fallen, had been created by God, was essentially good, and was being redeemed for God in Christ. Knowledge of Truth came through Jesus and not by the uncovering of an innate spiritual energy-wisdom. The Gospel was not for a spiritual elite only, but for all people.

Marcion, not to be fully identified with the gnostics, broke with the Roman Church in 144 and established his own following. The basis of his teaching was that the inconsistent and often cruel God of the Hebrew scriptures was not the Christian God of love revealed in Jesus. He excluded all Judaic elements from his version of Christianity.

Montanus (c.157) was another teacher considered heretical by the early church leaders, although his teachings were widely accepted by the laity. He was a strong proponent of antinomian practice and prophetic revelation, who claimed that the Holy Spirit uttered Truth through him. His view was that there could not be a closed and defined Christian doctrine because God, speaking through his prophets, would continually be revealing new and deeper teachings to his Church.

These sorts of teaching, considered heretical by the church authorities, compelled the Church to define more clearly its belief system and determine a canon of sacred scripture. It began more frequently to use the tool of excommunication to cast out heretics and, in so doing, to preserve unity and purity of communion. It now began also to assume a defensive stance.

The Christian apologists of the second and third centuries were occupied not only in defending the Church against heresy but also in establishing a definitive Christian position towards Judaism and the pagan religions and philosophies of the Hellenized world. Towards Judaism the apologists displayed a new assurance, signifying a departure from the ealier close association with, and even dependence on, the Hebrew tradition. The tendency of the Church was now to assert that it, rather than the Jews, had the correct interpretation and revelation in Christ of the allegorical readings of the Old Testament, and that Hebrew literalism was the result of ignorance.

The Gospel for Buddhists and the Dharma for Christians

The response to Greek philosophy was at first unsure and divided. Justin Martyr (martyred in Rome c. 165) had a positive approach whereas his pupil Tatian completely rejected Graeco-Roman culture. The final response, however, was the reworking and absorption of pagan philosophy into Christian theology. This was justified largely on the basis that God in Christ was the bringer of all that is good, noble and true in human thinking, including the good in non-Christian philosophies. Working from this premise the Church was able to use many of the concepts and technical terms of Greek philosophy in the formulation of its belief system. Most notable among these borrowings is the use of the Greek idea of the *Logos* (the rational, creative principle pervading the universe) as constituting the essential nature of Jesus, The Word or *Logos* of God.

Christian thinking also began to appropriate the ideas of the neoplatonic philosophers and mystics. Neoplatonism was derived, as its name implies, from the philosophy of Plato which advances the notion of a realm of ideal forms, imperfectly and partially expressed in the material world. By the second century neoplatonism had evolved into a mystical path seeking unity with the highest transcendent Source; 'The One' or 'The Good' which is beyond all categories and about which nothing can be predicated. The ascent towards Absolute Truth or 'The One Good' was achieved by passing gradually through progressively higher spiritual states. It was inevitable that the Church should find parallels in neoplatonism with the Christian idea of ascent in Christ to the Father.

Whereas Christianity could come to terms with pagan philosophy and even absorb many of its ideas, the Church could not be reconciled with pagan religion, its pantheon of gods, its magical rites and its often sensual practices. Since traditional Roman religion was also the religion of the imperial state, Christians were bound to be viewed as rebels against the emperor and the Roman traditions and laws. Many spurious charges were brought against the Church, including the charge of cannibalism, on account of a malicicious misrepresentation of the sacrament of Holy Communion. Christians were also charged with promiscuity and corruption of Roman citizens.

From its side, pagan philosophy was often not content to find accord with Christian doctrine. Many Hellenist thinkers were offended by such irrational doctrines as the virgin birth of Christ and the resurrection of the body. Their philosophical training led them to view these teachings as primitive and superstitious. On the other hand, those practising pagan religion blamed Christianity for social misfortunes and calamities, believing that the pagan gods were punishing them for tolerating the Christian Faith in their midst. Thus the Church was besieged on several fronts: the religious, the political and the philosophical.

In spite of these difficulties many important doctrinal and organizational advances were made. Clement of Alexandria developed the idea of Jesus as the *Logos*, and an orthodox version of the moral and spiritual ascent of believers to God along neoplatonist lines. Origen reinterpreted the scriptures in expansively allegorical fashion. He also took a poll of the scriptures in use by the various local communities in order to establish a canon of sacred writing, proclaimed the neoplatonist idea of the pre-existence of souls, and sought to define the Trinity. Latin writers, including Novatian and Cyprian (both c. 200–258) defended Christian beliefs about Jesus as the Son of God against the heresies of Marcion, those of the Docetists, who taught that Jesus was a human being only in appearance, and of Sabellianism which denied distinction of persons in the Triune Godhead. They also wrote on morals.

The conditions of persecution and harassment of the Church continued until the end of the reign of the self-proclaimed 'emperor-god' Diocletian in 306. With the accession of the next emperor, Constantine, Christianity was to undergo a radical change in its development.

Summary of the Second and Third Centuries

Having, in the apostolic era and the three decades thereafter, settled its internal problems, those of finding balance between spiritual liberty and legalism, and formulating liturgy and polity, and, having established itself as a religion in its own right, no longer closely dependent on Hebrew tradition, the Church of the second and third centuries, embattled socially and intellectually, takes on the task of defending itself. It finds its place in the total milieu by absorbing into itself what is socially, morally, philosophically and spiritually acceptable, and rejecting what is not. It begins to define itself in relation to its time and its world, and in what it can tolerate. Its leaders and adherents are willing to face martyrdom rather than allow their faith to be diluted or compromised. Its only weapons of defense are its spirituality, morality and intellectual strength. It has no other power in society. Its truth is asserted by means of spiritual authority, moral purity and intellectual coherence.

The Gospel for Buddhists and the Dharma for Christians

Embattled as it is, its search from the outset is for cohesion and unity of belief and practice. The Pauline teaching that the Church is 'one body in Christ Jesus' is a strong factor in the disallowance of deviation and diversification. Yet there are incipient schisms, as evidenced by Tertullian's break with the Roman Church in favour of the Montanist teachings. Still, there is room for divergent ideas about the nature of the Father, of Christ and of the Holy Spirit in their relation to the Triune Godhead. There is also diversity in the interpretation of scripture and in the stance towards Hellenism and Judaism. The liturgy and rites are fairly well established, as is the consensus regarding the canon of scripture. Although well-advanced, the search for a final definitive doctrine is not yet over. Various approaches in typology, symbology and allegory in aspects of faith (particularly as revealed in scripture) are still being tested. The institutional hierarchy has become more centralized, its authority vested in the college of bishops with a degree of primacy afforded to the Bishop of Rome. Christian practice is, on the whole, uniform, but new mystical methods related to neoplatonism are being explored. So strong is the compulsion to unity in all these areas that all significant deviation is branded as heresy and carries the penalty of excommunication. Doctrine is refined in response to heresy, and there is debate and apologetic writing. The Church has not yet attained the power that will later permit it simply to outlaw or destroy those it condemns as heretics.

What the early Church considered heretical provides insight into the doctrines which it considered inviolable; those points at which diversification must go over into division. All teachings which sought to diminish or to do away with the God of the Judaic tradition were rejected. Doctrines which sought to modify or to deny the full divinity and full humanity of Jesus were opposed. Among the other intolerable teachings were: any views of Jesus as only a universal type of the authetically spiritual person, rather than as the unique universal Saviour, or, God made man for the salvation of humanity; any dualistic views expounding the inherent evil of the God-created material world; and any idea of a spiritual elite which had exclusive access to God in Christ. Lastly, as demonstrated in the case of Montanism, the early Church did not accept any claim by a believer to be a prophet of ongoing divine revelation unregulated and untested by the scriptures and the authority of the Church. All acceptable diversification in the early Church must take place within these bounds. Thus, in the most general sense, the early Church continued to uphold the apostolic tradition. All valid diversification must, finally, be tested against the teaching of the apostles. What is not apostolic is heresy.

Individual and communal practice were also derived from the apostolic tradition. In the Didache or 'Teaching of the Twelve Apostles,' a church document from the second century, instructions for practice and living are set out in sixteen brief chapters. Other writings also stress the apostolicity of church practice. The so-called 'Clementine Liturgy', although written in 390, probably reflects practices current in the pre-Constantine Church.

Christian neophytes would not be admitted to baptism without a twofold preparation: first they would have to prove the sincerity of their intent by changing all aspects of their life not yet in harmony with Christian principles; only then would they receive instruction in doctrine and morals. Baptism was not easily permitted. Pre-baptismal preparation and scrutiny were necessary for safeguarding the purity of the communion, as well as to impress upon the neophyte the widely held belief that no sin committed after baptism could be forgiven by God. The second coming of Jesus was thought to be imminent, and he was expected to come in judgement of the world. It was in this urgent expectation that Christians practised their faith. It was customary to pray that the Lord delay his return so that more people might be brought to repentance before that terrible day of judgement. Only when thoroughly prepared would the new believer receive baptism in the Name of the Father, Son and Holy Spirit, after having rejected Satan and his works, and having recited a simple credo.

Believers were required to live in great purity, love and devotion. There were clear rules regarding the conduct of evangelists, teachers, prophets and other itinerants. No one was to profit by Christian ministry or to live idly in the community. Itinerant teachers should not stay longer than two days, a Christian wayfarer should not expect hospitality for longer than three.

Within the broader hierachy of bishops, priests, deacons and sub-deacons, those with special spiritual gifts could carry out their ministries only in submission to the authority of the bishop or the priest. Prophets, exorcists, those praying in tongues and those with gifts of healing were submitted to a guiding authority. Gatherings were orderly. Believers fasted twice weekly. A set liturgical rite, including the rite of the Eucharist, was practised in gatherings on 'the Lord's Day' (Sunday). There were readings from the Septuagint and the new Christian writings, and formal prayers were recited.

In individual religious experience the life of the indwelling Spirit was the source of all other religious practice. This inner life testifying to the gift of eternal life in Christ was the basis and substance of the believer's faith. From it flowed righteousness and love. It was not a cold faith. It had to be vital and powerful enough to sustain the believer in the face of persecution, and even martyrdom.

Although apostolic doctrine had to some extent been elaborated, many important details had not yet been worked into a final form. There was still debate over the doctrine of original sin, an idea with which Origen, for instance, did not concur. The exhortation to sinless perfection, expressed as the disallowance of sin after baptism, was slowly being softened into something more realistic. Doctrines of the Divine Trinity were still being developed. The inner spiritual experience of the Christian was still in the process of becoming translated into categories and formulas.

The Imperial Church

From the year 312 the Church was in many ways profoundly altered. When the would-be emperor Constantine had a dream in which he was commanded to inscribe the monogram of Christ on his shield, and was told , 'By this sign conquer', and subsequently won the crucial battle of the Milvian bridge, the battle which raised him to the imperial throne, Christianity became the state religion of the Roman Empire. By Constantine's Edict of Milan Christianity was raised to a position of religious pre-eminence and dominance. Church and state were henceforth to be inextricably linked.

In the Roman religious scenario the tables were suddenly turned. The pagan religions soon became the objects of Christian persecution, and the power of the secular authority was used against them. The Church itself became, in the final analysis, an arm of the state, with the emperor as its de facto head. Christian belief, practice and lifestyle were made into articles of imperial law, so that to break a Christian precept was to be guilty of a civil offence. This arrangement, by and large a comfortable one, was to endure in one form or another until the Reformation in the fifteenth century.

In order to cement the relationship between church and state, and to give it legal and institutional form, the first general council of the universal Christian Church was convoked by Constantine in 325 in Nicaea. By this time the emperor was constructing the new imperial capital at first called New Rome, but later to be known as Constantinople. Old Rome, however, was to continue to play an authoritative and determinative role in church affairs.

The Council of Nicaea was presided over by Constantine. This was the first time that the deliberations of the Church were, at least nominally, subjected to a secular authority. But Constantine does not seem to have dominated the churchmen. He acted as an advisor, more interested in achieving uniformity within the Church for the maintenance of imperial order than in influencing doctrine. No doubt many church leaders viewed this cooperation between church and empire as the beginning of the establishment of God's kingdom on earth.

One of the chief reasons for calling this first ecumenical council was to settle the question of the Eastern Christians who followed the teaching of Arius of Alexandria that Jesus was a created and not a divine being; a human being who had been 'adopted' into divine sonship on account of his holy conduct, and was for that reason an acceptable sacrifice for the sins of the world. This view was rejected as heresy, and the Nicene Creed was formulated to state the orthodox position on this and other contentious questions. Formulated by the bishops and made into an imperial decree by Constantine, the Nicene Creed became the first universal Christian statement of belief.

It reads:

'I believe in one God the Father Almighty; maker of heaven and earth, and of all things visible and invisible.

'And in one Lord Jesus Christ, the only-begotten Son of God, begotten of the Father before all worlds, [God of God], Light of Light, very God of very God, begotten, not made, being of one substance [essence] with the Father; by whom all things were made; who, for us men and for our salvation, came down from heaven, and was incarnate by the Holy Spirit of the Virgin Mary, and was made man; and was crucified also for us under Pontius Pilate; he suffered, died and was buried; and on the third day he rose again, according to the scriptures; and ascended into heaven, and sits on the right hand of the Father; and he shall come again, with glory, to judge both the living and the dead; and his kingdoim shall have no end.

'And [I believe] in the Holy Spirit, the Lord and Giver of Life; who proceeds from the Father [and the Son]; who together with the Father and the Son is worshipped and glorified; who spoke through the prophets. And [I believe] in one Holy Catholic and Apostolic Church. I acknowledge one baptism for the remission of sins; and I look for the resurrection of the dead, and the life of the world to come. Amen.'

(Words in square brackets are later additions by the Western or Roman Church).

Here then was the formula for Christian faith, which had several uses in the imperial Church: it would unite all believers in a single essential confession, it provided a means for determining heresy, and it could be imposed on all bishops and churches. All Christians, including church leaders and teachers, could find assurance and security within its framework.

After Constantine

The late fourth and early fifth centuries saw, under Theodosius I (emperor 378–395) the destruction and closure of pagan temples and a rise in anti-Jewish activities. This was largely a reaction to the attempts by Julian ('the Apostate', emperor 361–363) to re-establish paganism as the official religion of the empire. Some fifty years after the Council of Nicaea, the Church had radically departed from the religious tolerance of the Constantinian era and now took a position of stern and harsh authoritarianism. Christians guilty of grave sin or heresy were punished by a variety of tortures or put to death. Factionalism was bitter and often violent. The Orthodox Church was asserting its right to exist above criticism and beyond the influence of divisive doctrines. It should be single, pervasive and dominant in the pattern of the imperial state with which it was so intimately associated.

This period also marks the beginning of an enduring division between the Western Church under Rome and the Eastern or Byzantine Patriarchates of Constantinople, Alexandria, Antioch and Jerusalem. With the advent of the Western emperors in 395, during the papacy of Damasus, the Roman See began to consolidate its own church-state relationship and to follow a line of development separate from the Byzantine Church. The issue of Roman primacy was also repeatedly raised. The Byzantines, however, while willing to accord to the Bishop of Rome a position of honour, would not accept outright Roman leadership. In their view decisions on all aspects of church life could only validly be made by a general council of the five Patriarchates, including. but not dominated by, the Roman Papacy. In time this dispute would lead to a final schism between the Eastern and Western churches.

The Roman Church

While the Byzantine Church continued to bicker and to convoke councils over incipient heresies and hairsplitting points of doctrine, the Roman Church was steadily consolidating itself. In the persons of Ambrose of Milan, Jerome, and Augustine of Hippo, it was laying strong foundations for institutional, scriptural and doctrinal unity, and establishing its catholic authority.

Ambrose was a convincing proponent of the pre-eminence of divinely ordained ecclesiastical authority over that of the secular state. When the emperor Theodosius attacked the church at Thessalonica for destroying a synagogue, Ambrose had him excommunicated. The emperor was only allowed back into communion after a humbling act of penance. Bishops began to exercise civil authority and to control the social and charitable institutions in their dioceses. The line between secular and ecclesiastical power was often blurred. The imperial government, by now completely christianized, did not resist this development. It recognized that bishops generally had greater insight into the problems of their communities, and commanded more respect than their secular counterparts.

Jerome, the irascible and pious scholar, brought scriptural uniformity to the Roman Church by his Latin translations of the Old and New Testaments, which came to be known as the Vulgate. As the standard replacement of predominantly poor and inaccurate Latin translations, it provided a basis for sound doctrine. Jerome was also much occupied with the exaltation of the monastic life. He had lived as a desert monk for two years before being ordained a priest at Antioch in 377. In the mid-fourth century monastcism was still unorganized and often fanatically antinomian and eccentrically ascetic. Indeed, it was the one aspect of the Christian community not yet brought under orthodox control, and was confined mainly to the Egyptian desert around the Nile. Owing perhaps to Jerome's idealized 'Life of Paul', the Church turned its attention to regularizing monastic life. Gradually, through the work of bishops of both the Roman and Byzantine churches, monasteries and nunneries became incorporated into the orthodox body.

The Gospel for Buddhists and the Dharma for Christians

Augustine, Bishop of Hippo (354–430), had a hugely consolidating effect on the Roman Church. Having been converted from Manicheanism to Christianity, he became the great advocate of Roman imperial orthodoxy. His vision of the divinely ordained imperial Church with its interrelated ecclesiastical and secular powers became the model for Western Christianity until the Reformation. He worked tirelessly to oppose and punish heresy and to compel heretical movements into the orthodox mainstream by force of state law and church authority. He formulated a definitive Trinitarian doctrine and was responsible for the teaching that no one could be saved outside of the Divine Grace operating exclusively in the Orthodox Church. His writings abound with the personal experience of God's holy love, and stress the inability of people to please God without the empowerment of the indwelling Holy Spirit. In Augustine there is the sacred and stern combination of authentic spiritual experience coupled with a rigid orthodoxy constraining the believer into a single divine path within the one Catholic Church.

The heresies dealt with in the late fourth and early fifth centuries were not as dangerous to orthodoxy as the earlier gnostic teachings had been. They were really only minor variations on orthodox belief and practice. Yet, under the new and stricter church authority, bolstered by imperial legislation, they were harshly opposed. Heresies such as Donatism, Nestorianism and Pelagianism brought down on themselves persecution, excommunication, violence and state punishment. The Church was enforcing uniformity and submission.

It had by this time grown into an impressive, elevated and dominant institution. Architecturally imposing edifices, richly adorned and filled with ceremonial splendour, displayed to people the grand authority of God's kingdom on earth. Ecclesiastical vestments reflected the grandeur of aristocratic imperial dress. Refined and scholarly minds debated and wrote on all aspects of Christian life. The spirtual mystery of Christ was imprinted on the public mind by elaborate and awe-inspiring rituals and liturgy. And these displays of authority were upheld by the power and vigour of the church-state civil administration. It was up to authentic spirituality to survive this outward triumphalism and the overwhelming inner structures of the authoritarian Church.

The Roman Church was now as solidly entrenched as the Byzantine. Even the sacking of Rome by Alaric in 410, though it caused upheaval and consternation among believers, who supposed it to be the immediate prelude to the return of Christ, did not seriously affect church structure. Although some of the conquering Gothic tribes were Arian Christians, they succumbed with time to Roman orthodoxy and accepted Roman overseership as being more capable. They were also drawn to the benefits of christianized Roman law.

The Later Byzantine Church

In the Byzantine Church relations with the state were rendered more closely interdependent with the accession of Justinian (emperor 527–565) who saw himself as divinely elected to the extent that he was 'divinity walking on earth.' His motto was 'One empire, One Law, One Church', and departures from orthodoxy were treated with renewed severity. Jews and pagans were persecuted. Hellenist intellectualism was no longer tolerated. The famous academy at Athens was closed in 529. Imperial laws were scrutinized and reshaped to bring them into closer conformity with Christian doctrines and morals.

Justinian also claimed a new degree of authority over church affairs. He enjoined the clergy to live morally exemplary lives and barred them from gaming and the theatre. He elected and dismissed important bishops and even patriarchs. In his view the Church was an organ of the state, charged with the spiritual and moral wellbeing of the populace. So long as the Church conducted itself in ways pleasing to God the empire would thrive. He built new monasteries, churches and the magnificent Cathedral of the Holy Wisdom, the *Hagia Sophia*.

The dominant heresy of the sixth century Byzantine Church was that of the Monophysites who asserted that Christ, although derived *from* two natures (divine and human), had from that dual derivation a single indivisible nature. The orthodox view, upheld by the Council of Chalcedon in 451, was that Christ existed *in* two natures, the one fully divine and the other fully human. These subtle differentiations were a cause of sharp and violent division in the Church, leading to rioting and murder. The Monophysites prevailed in the Syrian and Egyptian churches, and threatened to weaken the empire which, by the mid-seventh century, after Justinian's reign, came under increasing threat of Muslim invasion.

The Council of Trullo in 692, convened in the reign of Justinian II, reflected a growing concern with codifying and solidifying the unity of church and state in an empire by that time severely shrunken by Muslim territorial gains. Egypt and Syria had been lost and Jihad bases were being set up in Asia Minor. Although Christianity was tolerated by the Muslim rulers in the conquered areas, the Church was divested of much of its secular power and of the influence it had enjoyed within the boundaries of the empire. The Council of Trullo, which was not attended by legates from Rome (and was thus not considered a fully ecumenical council), laid down strict norms for the conduct of both the clergy and laity. The clergy should live irreproachable lives. The laity were to be less conspicuous and more submitted to the clergy. Monastic life was also more strictly legislated. Details of liturgy and of theology were revisited and embodied in canons.

The council reflected a new unease and self-revision of the Church and empire under the pressure of the Muslim advances. Why was God allowing such loss and suffering to the Christian Empire? In the first half of the eighth century, under Leo III, the idea was proposed that God's wrath might be ascribed to the Church's 'idolatrous' use of icons.

Leo's son, Constantine V (emperor 741–745) was a rigorous iconoclast. By his decree anyone making, revering or hiding an icon 'shall, whether layman or monk, be anathematized and deemed guilty under the law of the empire as a foe of God's commands and an enemy of the patristic doctrines.' By now the christianized state was almost in complete control of the Church. After the Council of Hieria in 754, Constantine V proclaimed by edict that all heretics would be punished as rebels against the state. Church icons were destroyed under state and ecclesiastical supervision. For a century there followed a series of reversals and counter-reversals, with the veneration of icons being blamed whenever the empire came under threat or suffered defeat. Finally, in 843, under the Empress Theodora, the use of icons was permanently reinstated.

The close relationship between church and state was to continue for as long as the empire endured, with the emperor's power over the Church fluctuating according to the relative strength, prosperity and stability of his reign. His divine privilege was, however, never doubted by the Church. He was, together with the clergy, 'the upholder of the Orthodox Faith and of Christ.'

Until the fall of Constantinople to the Turks in 1453, the Byzantine Church-State and its culture became increasingly self-conscious and complacent. The entire system was in the main preoccupied with its own preservation and the maintenance of religious, intellectual and social harmony within the imperial boundaries and the broader Byzantine commonwealth. Although the Orthodox Church was successfully established in Russia, Bulgaria, Serbia and even Moravia, the 'lesser breeds without the law' did not much occupy the minds of Byzantine officialdom.

The Church of Constantinople, splendidly triumphant and comfortably integrated into the machinery of the Byzantine commonwealth, could never seriously entertain the claim to Roman primacy, voiced with increasing conviction by the Pope, the Bishop of Old Rome, the ancient imperial capital, and seat of both Peter and Paul. This problem would come to a dramatic head in the mid-eleventh century.

Schism

Between the sack of Rome in 410 and the first schism in the Christian Church (in 1054), the Western Church, although flourishing and, like its eastern counterpart, enjoying a close-knit relationship with the state, had its own challenges to overcome. The Western Empire in the fifth and sixth centuries suffered a series of invasions by barbarian tribes. By the end of the sixth century the Western emperors had been vanquished and the Roman Church had to forge new relationships with the tribal chieftains now ruling Europe. Those of the tribes which had previously been christianized were of the Arian heresy, and had to be persuaded into orthodoxy, while heathen tribes became the objects of missionary activity. Under Pope Gregory the Great, Roman orthodoxy was spread as far afield as Britain. The Germanic peoples were, in their turn, converted by English and Irish missionaries.

By the ninth and tenth centuries the Roman Church had re-established orthodoxy throughout Western Europe. For ecclesiastical as well as political reasons the Western Church began to press the issue of papal primacy in the Universal Church. The Byzantine Church would, however, not be dissuaded from the view that final authority in church affairs was vested in the five traditional Patriarchates, with the Bishop of Rome being accorded a place of honour, but not the highest authority.

In 1054 the papal legates under Humbert visited Constantinople to argue for submission to the Pope. When the Byzantine Church refused to submit, Humbert placed a bull of excommunication on the main altar of the Hagia Sophia. Four days later, on July 20, 1054, the Patriarch of Constantinople, Michael Celularius, issued a counter-excommunication of the Roman See. The Universal Church was split in two. These mutual excommunications were lifted only in 1965. For the intervening 900 years the Western and Eastern churches lay under a reciprocal anathema.

From the time of the great ecumenical councils (the last was the Council of Nicaea in 787) until the start of the Reformation in the sixteenth century, the Church underwent no radical doctrinal or institutional changes. The Eastern church-state entity continued to function until Byzantium was overthrown by Islam in 1453. Under Muslim rule many Eastern Christians converted to Islam, while the Patriarchates declined in power. Orthodox practice, however, continued unchanged although the Church no longer existed in the grandeur of its imperial days. Although tolerated by the Turks, the Church was deprived of all civil influence or privilege.

The Western Church, however, continued to grow in power in its relationships with the emperors and kings of medieval Europe. It held its own councils and, although undergoing some internal struggles and minor schisms, retained its unity, centralized under the Papacy. As the unopposed, official religion of the West, Roman Catholicism had become much more a socio-political institution than a vital spirituality.

The Medieval Church

By the early middle-ages the Christian Church was a consolidated and closed entity. In both the Eastern and Western churches there was not much room for spontaneous spiritual renewal. The institution was set in a fixed hierarchy and was able to manage all aspects of social and civil life, from the highest mundane authority to the daily problems of the humblest members of the laity. It had made of itself an indispensable, all-pervasive, authoritative influence in every sphere of endeavour. More than this, it had become imposing and oppressive, intolerant of all other religions and apparently even less tolerant of departures from orthodoxy within its own fold. It was an inescapable controlling force. Its polity was based on the imperial system, kind to the compliant but ruthless towards dissent. It was the voice and power of God on earth.

But the focus of its teachings was not on love. Its chief concern was with orthodoxy. Authentic spirituality was secondary to right belief. The major emphasis was on conformity and obedience. Besides ecclesiastical punishments, eternal hell awaited all who did not believe and practise according to the precepts of the Church. Purity of life and love of God and neighbour were stressed to the laity but were seldom observable in the clergy. Priests were often ignorant; the higher clergy corrupt. There was great display of wealth and pomp. Religious insight was shot through with superstition, ignorance and fear.

The Church was now the sole dispenser of God's salvation or wrath, of his favour or displeasure. The individual believer was in no position to seek out Truth for himself. Every aspect of spiritual experience and revelation must be tested against the orthodox dogma. God was not to be found by the individual mind; he could be revealed only by the Church.

The challenge to authentic spirituality lay in the complete absence of mental freedom to develop spiritually by means of open search and genuine experiment. The medieval Church was not so much a skilful guide as an overbearing master. Faithfulness to the Church was not only valued above faithfulness to one's own truth; it was demanded at the expense of personal integrity. Whatever spirituality the Church could provide must be considered sufficient.

In the same way as Christ was the one Mediator between God and people, the medieval Church made itself the mediator between Christ and people. The life, grace and forgiveness offered in Christ could only be received through the Church. Only the Church could administer the sacraments of baptism, the Eucharist and penance. And these sacraments were taught as being indispensable to spiritual life, growth and salvation itself; the unbaptised could not be saved; without the Eucharist and Holy Communion the believer could not attain to union with Christ; without access to the sacrament of penance sins could not be forgiven. These spiritual gifts could be received only through the Church. Only a priest of the Church could administer them. If the Church chose to withhold them the believer was cut off from all spiritual succour.

The sacraments were now more than only external symbols of inner spiritual events. They were considered to be efficacious spiritual acts in themselves. Baptism was a real washing away of sin. The Eucharistic bread and wine were the transubstantiated Body and Blood of Christ. The priest's absolution was the only real forgiveness of sin. Spontaneous spiritual life had been concretized in these conventional symbols, and spiritual symbols had become the only effective spiritual means.

All of spirituality was explained, contained and practised within a relative pattern. For the ordinary believer in the medieval Church, God the Father was a Person with relative, even anthropomorphic attributes. Personal spiritual experience had become channeled and categorized in an array of sacraments, doctrines, liturgies, holy days, and so forth. At every step of the way the believer must depend on the Church for spiritual growth. It was as though the kingdom of God had been fully transplanted on earth and translated into a tangible set of rituals and formulas.

Of course this does not mean that the medieval Church was devoid of authentic spirituality. On both sides of the divide between clergy and laity there is much evidence of direct experience in Jesus Christ. Francis of Assisi is the notable example of a believer still walking in the simple path of Wisdom-Love taught by Jesus. But no one would dare to consider that the spiritual path could be walked outside of the church institution.

The Reformation

In many ways the Reformation, when it came after one and a half millennia of orthodoxy, was a reaction to the inescapable centrality of the church institution in Christian life. No doubt, ecclesiastical corruption made it easier to cast off the fear associated with breaking from the traditional Church with its emphasis on externals. Around these externalia a number of superstitious, magical and animist trends had developed among the laity. The simple Christian Gospel with its emphasis on direct communion with Christ and the love of Christ had all but vanished in a sea of superstition. Scantily educated priests and an illiterate laity could not access the original scriptures and traditional church writings. The teachings spread by the apostles were submerged beneath popular religious hocus-pocus. There was not much to encourage believers to seek out the truth for themselves.

The higher clergy, as well as the majority of monasteries and nunneries, were openly corrupt and riddled with worldliness. High office in the church establishment was often bought and sold as a means of financial and social advancement. The Papacy itself was little more than another political power, and its chief interests were with political intrigue and renaissance intellectualism. Popes were patrons of the great artists and craftsmen of the time. Their religious vision had more to do with the construction of grand cathedrals housing the highest expressions of renaissance creativity, with the magnification of Christianity in artistic works of genius, and with the expansion of the Church as God's kingdom on earth, than with selflessness and spiritual endeavour.

It is easy to see how the sale of indulgences came to stand as the pre-eminent symbol of the dull superstition, the departure from Christian Truth, the worldliness and corruption, as well as the conscious deception of its members, which had become the hallmarks of the late medieval Church. Indulgences were an ecclesiastical fraud perpetrated by the highest church leaders on the flock under their care. An indulgence was essentially a papal document which offered to Christians the remission of temporal punishments due for their sins, in exhange for money. By the purchase of indulgences Christians could liberate the suffering spirits of their departed loved-ones from the fires of purgatory. It was believed in the medieval Church that the spirits of the dead had to pass through the cleansing fires of purgatory before being admitted into the heavenly kingdom, and purgatorial suffering might endure for aeons. Christians convinced of this teaching could easily be persuaded to part with their money in order to free the tortured spirits of their dead children, parents or spouses. And it was an easy and efficient way for the papacy to obtain the funds needed to finance grandiose schemes such as the rebuilding of St Peter's Cathedral.

The new humanists, most notably Desiderius Erasmus, spoke into this corrupt and trivialized situation. In his writings Erasmus called the Church back to the original purity of Jesus' teaching, and that of the apostles. He sought to demonstrate that true Christian practice should be an interior search rather than a scramble for the multitude of external religious talismans. In his translation of the Gospels, he corrected the Vulgate mistranslation of the Greek *metanoia*, which Jerome had rendered as 'do penance' (*penitentiam fare*), into its actual sense: 'repent' or 'change your heart and mind.' Reconciliation with God should no longer be a matter of striving to win his approval by works of penance and self-mortification, but of opening one's mind to receive the truth of his grace, wisdom and love, expressed in Christ Jesus. It should be a fundamental reorientation of the deep mind from the mundane to the spiritual. Throughout Europe other eminent thinkers were admonishing the Church to return to the spiritual source. But the Papacy responded with arrogance and retribution.

This intransigent attitude of the Church hierarchy finally forced the hand of reform, in the person of Martin Luther (1453–1546), to go over into schism. Luther was an Augustinian monk who, through his own experiences of scrupulosity and self-condemnation, came to know how little relief could be found in the externalized Christianity of the Roman

Church. As a teacher of theology he came to see the gross discrepancies between the spiritual message of the Bible, and its corrupted formalized expression in the Church. Unlike Erasmus, Melancthon and other reform-minded intellectuals, Luther decided that the situation could only be fundamentally remedied by a break with the Roman Church, which so stubbornly continued to resist internal reform and revision of doctrine and practice.

Taking the abuse of indulgences as his starting point, he launched an attack on the Papacy. As the Church began to retaliate, using the lethal charge of heresy, he abandoned the controversy over indulgences and initiated a campaign against a variety of church doctrines and methods. For Luther the central focus of Christian life should be on faith in God and trust in the love of God made known in Christ. Reliance on self-redeeming activities such as pilgrimage, good works, veneration of relics and so forth, could do nothing to genuinely liberate suffering humanity. It was God's love and his saving work in Jesus which should be central to Christian experience.

In order to protect the rapidly growing reformist church from the power and reach of Rome, Luther cooperated with the political aspirations of the German princes who wished to throw off the Roman burden on their states and the restriction of their political power. Through his theological ability, spiritual sincerity and political acuity, Protestantism became an irreversible renewal of Christian spirituality.

For many Protestant thinkers, however, the Lutheran Church was not far enough distanced from the Church of Rome. Although it had given to its adherents a limited liberty to study and interpret the scriptures for themselves, a means for reviving inner spirituality, and a degree of independence from the church institution, it still maintained many orthodox practices and doctrines considered by the more liberal Protestants to have derived from a misguided, primitive and corrupt ecclesiastical tradition. They wanted even less externalization, symbolism, and reliance on sacrament. They wanted greater purity and simplicity and a more direct, individual experience between people and God in Christ: a spirituality freed from church trappings and intervention.

Although Luther had taken far-reaching steps in reform: retention of only the three sacraments of baptism, the Eucharist, and penance; a translation of the Bible into German; revised catechisms, and a new prayer-book, as well as returning a large degree of freedom to individual believers, the Lutheran Church still used Latin in the liturgy and held fast to a number of Roman traditions. In particular, Lutheranism continued to recognize the real presence of Christ under the species of bread and wine in the Eucharistic celebration.

The Swiss reformer, Huldreich Zwingli (1484–1531), introduced even more liberal measures. The Eucharist was to be understood as a symbolic remembrance of Jesus' sacrifice rather than as a real and spiritually efficacious re-enactment of it. Zwingli did away with the Catholic mass, celibacy of priests, legalistic fasting, saints' days, and church music. He encouraged open discussion of the scriptures between clergy and laity. He encouraged the liberty to reinterpret doctrine and practice.

Eventually his liberal stance brought him into conflict with Luther. The reformed groups, having broken with Rome, now became divided among themselves. Differences between the factions repeatedly erupted into violence. There were also ongoing battles with Catholic groups. In 1531 Zwingli was killed in a battle against the Catholic cantons of Switzerland.

The most influential and thoroughgoing reformer after Luther was John Calvin. By the time he came to Protestant Geneva in 1536, the Reformed churches were already well established. Also in 1536 Calvin published his 'Institutes of the Christian Religion' which he continued to enlarge throughout his lifetime as coherent system of Reformed belief.

Calvin's emphasis was on the absolute sovereignty of God, who foreordained all things, including which people were to be saved and which lost. People were mere enactors of God's predetermined plan. The most they could do to achieve salvation was to put their faith in Christ and live godly lives. To ensure godly living within the Christian community of Geneva, tight policing and spying were instituted. A church court (consistory) meted out punishments or excommunicated transgressors. In the Church there were pastors for preaching, teachers for maintaining doctrinal purity, lay elders to administer church discipline and deacons to carry out works of charity. Thus Geneva became the model of a dictatorially controlled Protestant city on whose citizens Christian simplicity and morality were enforced.

In 1534 the English Church under Henry VIII definitively broke with Rome. Although Protestant ideas had been circulating in England, the break with Rome was finally motivated by a papal refusal to allow Henry to divorce his wife, Catherine of Aragon, who had not produced a male heir. In response to the Pope's refusal Henry severed ties with the Roman Church and declared himself Head of the Church of England. The doctrines of the new Church were a mixture of Swiss Protestantism and Roman tenets. Thus, though Protestant, the English Church remained in many points, especially in liturgy and in episcopal structure, close to the Roman model.

From the new freedoms which Protestantism had gained, a number of communions, diverse in doctrine and practice, sprang up. On the whole they were motivated by a desire to move away from the growing formalism of Protestant religion itself. They were proponents of an even greater spiritual liberty than Protestantism had achieved. Some, like Michael Servetus, desired the liberty to reinterpret even the traditional doctrines of the Triune Godhead. These 'sects' were often persecuted by both Catholic and Protestant leaders. Servetus himself was eventually burned at the stake under Calvin's orders.

But the impetus for diversification introduced by the Reformation was irreversible. It would not be long before numerous schismatic Christian groups were established in Europe. Most of these embraced a spontaneous, prophetic and charismatic religious experience, and stressed holiness and simplicity of life.

The Counter-Reformation

From its side, the Roman Church now realized the pressing need for reform within its own institution. Challenged as it was by the growing exodus of its members to the Reformed churches, the only direction it could move in was towards some accommodation of Protestant principles. A Catholic fellowship known as the *Spirituali* wrote and circulated pamphlets whose doctrine closely resembled Calvinism. Other individuals, notably Caraffa, who later became Pope Paul IV, remained stubbornly unwilling to compromise, although they were agreed on ridding the Church of corruption and superstition.

The Council of Trent convened in 1545 and continued to address the question of internal reformation until 1562. In the end, while agreeing to purge the Church of corruption, the council reaffirmed most of the doctrines which Protestantism had rejected, and the Reformed churches were irrevocably alienated. The major reaffirmations of doctrine included transubantiation in the Eucharist, maintenance of all seven sacraments, purgatory, the real sacrifice occurring in the mass, granting of indulgences, and the invocation of the saints. The Church also continued to hold that salvation is attained by both grace and works, as opposed to the Protestant creed of salvation by grace and faith alone.

By the seventeenth century the Roman Church had recovered some of its former strength, and had become more centralized around the Pope. With the founding of the Jesuit order with its missionary and intellectual focus, the Church brought Christianity to the Americas and the Far East, and stopped the expansion of Protestantism in Europe. During this period there was a spiritual revival in many Catholic centres, and a new devotion and piety were evident. On the other hand, the Church carried out the infamous heretic hunts of the inquisition in which many non-conformists were tortured and put to death.

Protestantism

The Reformation was essentially a struggle to return to the simplicity and purity of New Testament teaching by purging religious practice of the many popular and superstitious accretions added to Catholicism in the course of some 1500 years. There was strong emphasis on the believer's direct access to God in Christ without the Church's mediumship. Every believer should have the same access to spiritual truth as was claimed exclusively by the clergy and religious orders, since Christ himself had not made such distinctions. At the same time, all believers, and especially the clergy, should show the fruits of Christ in holy living and charity.

Although the evolving Protestant orthodoxy was as keen as Rome to stamp out what it considered heresy, there was in Protestantism a much greater recognition of the believer's personal relationship with God and personal revelation of Truth. The role of the church was to guide and confirm believers in the Way rather than acting as an exclusive mediator to Christian Truth and the Divine.

The authority of church and clergy were made secondary to the authority of the scriptures or 'the Word of God.' The watchword was 'only by grace, only by faith, only by the scriptures.' All evolved tradition must be tested against the scriptures: whatever had no basis in scripture was to be rejected. The Bible therefore played a far greater role than in the Orthodox churches.

These shifts were reflected in all aspects of the Reformed churches. The church institution became a centre for ministry, teaching and solace rather than a monolithic altar of penance or formal vicar of Deity; the clerical hierarchy reflected function rather than authority or mediumship. The multifarious symbols of medieval Christianity were reduced to those directly derived from scripture, and sacraments became symbols only. Practice and piety became less formal and more personal, the emphasis being on the love of God rather than on his judgement. Spirituality in all its aspects was largely given back to the people.

Later Developments

The trend away from ecclesistical authoritarianism, centrality, and mediatorship was set to continue both in Protestantism amd Roman Catholicism, while the Eastern Orthodox churches remained faithful to the Byzantine tradition.

In Protestantism the new freedoms inevitably resulted in increasing splits as reform was taken further over the next 500 years. In the reforms of reformism two tendencies predominated: the search for a Christian path more conformed to that of the earliest Christians, and to the teachings of Jesus and the apostles; and the revival of holiness and authentic interior religion. From these tendencies arose such movements as Moravianism, Methodism, Pietism and Quietism.

Movements akin to these were also initiated in the Catholic Church, notably in Jansenism which accepted a form of predestination, strove for greater holiness in the Church and pressed for enforced exclusion of immoral Christians from the sacraments.

Although the Christian Church was no longer visibly united, there remained a core agreement on matters of faith and morals. The Apostles' and Nicaean Creeds were retained intact. For many the defining line between authentic and inauthentic Christianity was to be found in the 'invisible church': the true body of Christ consisting of faithful and holy believers in all the new denominations.

Mysticism, a tradition long present but sometimes disapproved of in Catholicism, became with time an established part of Protestantism as well. Mystics sought to move beyond scriptural literalism to rediscover in a vital and profound way the teachings and spiritual energies of their faith. They made use of contemplation, meditation and imagination to explore the deeper, non-cognitive revelations of their union with the Divine. Remaining content to conform outwardly to orthodox practices, they sought within themselves for the inner, transcendent meaning of these.

There were popular revivalist movements as well. These concentrated on the believers' inner experience of Christ, revealed in the inner person by the Holy Spirit. Such experiences sometimes involved a degree of emotionalism, but in their authentic form they engendered in the individual spirit a 'foretaste of God', a spiritual joy and peace which empowered believers to live out the teachings of Jesus and lent to them a genuine spiritual authority.

The seventeenth, eighteenth and nineteenth centuries witnessed a vast expansion of Christianity by the missionary work of both the Catholic and Protestant churches. The Jesuits took the Catholic Faith to the Americas together with the invasions of the Conquistadores. The Jesuit Francis Xavier led missions to Japan and China. There was also much missionary activity in africa. Many missionaries were martyred or died from local conditions. By the mid-nineteenth century martyrdom had come to take on a romantic appeal for many zealous priests and evangelists.

The settlement of North America provided a new impulse for the diversification of Protestantism. Puritans settled in Massachusetts and Connecticut to escape persecution in their home country. The Quakers settled in Pennsylvania for the same reason. By the late eighteenth century Puritan Congregationalism, Presbyterianism, the Baptist, Lutheran, Dutch Reformed and Roman Catholic churches were all present in the United States. All of these tended to establish themselves in relative independence from their European counterparts.

With the advent of revivalist preachers such as Wesley and, later, Finney and Moody, there was a new desire for personal religious experience, and this tendency eventually resulted in the formation of the Pentecostal and Charismatic movements, emphasising the experiences associated with spiritual rebirth in the Holy Spirit. In the twentieth century these groups expanded considerably, and penetrated even the conservative churches. They reflected, and continue to reflect, the desire among many modern Christians for a direct and personal experience of God in Christ in their daily lives.

Catholic renewal was accomplished by the Second Vatican Council (1962–64). Many rigid stances within the Church and towards non-Catholic groups were moderated. There was reconciliation with the

Eastern Orthodox Church and a sincere search for common ground with Protestantism, together with the formal acknowledgement that Protestants are 'brethren in Christ.' More than this, there was an admission that authentic spirituality could exist outside of Christianity. The Church also made a number of internal reforms aimed at making its teachings and offices more accessible to the laity and encouraging the laity to greater involvement in ecclestical affairs. The tone was reconciliatory, compassionate and open, and communicated a genuine move away from orthodox exclusivism. And there was a call to *redintegratio*: to the fraternal union of all Christians across denominational divides.

The Modern Church

The modern Church subsumes all the expressions of doctrine and practice resulting from these historical diversifications and schisms, but it excludes the sects which do not hold orthodox views about the nature of the Triune Godhead, of Christ and his salvific work, on the relation of God to people and people to God, and on the morality that is integral to Christian living.

The most important and recognizable communions can be listed as: Eastern Orthodox, Roman Catholic, Lutheran, Reformed, Evangelical, Anglican, Methodist, Baptist and Pentecostal. Between these there are differences in polity, theology, doctrine, practice, method, symbology, approach to personal religious experience, and interpretation of sacramental participation. These differences colour the religious paths of modern Christians but are no longer as sharply divisive as in previous centuries, except in the fundamentalist and exclusivist groups.

Generally, Christian spiritual development involves participation in the church institution, whatever its polity, as the body of Christ or body of believers; assent to the theology of the group, to the formal doctrines and to the preferred practices and methods. There is greater or lesser emphasis on religious experience and there are differing views on its manifestations and importance. Sacraments may be more or less central, and in some communions not at all necessary to spiritual growth.

CHRISTIAN DIVERSITY

As relative expressions of Absolute Truth generated by historical and developmental processes, the different Christian approaches demonstrate, by the variety of methods which they place at the disposal of Christians, the invalidity of exclusivism. Authentic Christians in all the diverse communions are seeking and finding the same salvation in Christ.

This says something about the ultimate necessity for diversity in itself. If we can accept that authentic Christians in all the communions are finding the same spiritual awakening in Christ, it follows that the differences in emphasis and interpretation, and in method and experience, are differences related only to the ordinary, provisional mind. They are not spiritual differences.

They are points of reference imposed on the ultimate nature of Truth by the ordinary mind, and they have no fundamental bearing on the ultimate personal experience of that Truth. When the Holy Spirit fills the believer with joy, grace, love, purity, wisdom and authority, all references to theology, doctrine, formal practice and method are secondary. Only in the aftermath of the real experience can the believer attempt to describe and define it in provisional formulas. Yet the real experience continues abundantly to exceed and even to contradict the formula. Thus ultimate liberation for the Christian implies liberation from these provisional formulations too.

The intention of this brief history of Christianity is to show how a spontaneous and authoritative initial spiritual impulse becomes gradually diminished, distorted and corrupted by protracted efforts at containing it in formulas and administering it through institutions. This view is upheld by the regular tendency of all Christian renewal movements to reach back to the original simplicity of the Gospel and the apostolic teachings.

Of course these teachings are themselves open to diverse interpretations, and it is these possibilities for diverse interpretation that lead to the striving for an increasingly precise orthodoxy with its complex formulations. The basic ground for a developing orthodoxy is the desire to avoid false and unskilful interpretations. In this regard Jesus taught that any interpretation is validated only by its fruits: the measure of spiritual attainment and its outflow in Wisdom-Love. It is the teachers of the Law who are condemned by Jesus: those who legislate the norms of spirituality and judge others on the basis of their adherence to these legalisms. At another level, doctrinalism can be judged by its tragic and self-defeating resort to exclusivism, excommunication and violence. A believer's fruits are not to be discerned in what exactly he believes, but in the degree to which his beliefs have conformed him to Christ. If this is so, the very notion of heresy must come under review.

No one assessing the history of Christianity can doubt that much of ecclesiastical development occurred far outside the Way revealed by Jesus. It is hard to see how any doctrinal step enforced by so much as the violent death of a single individual can be considered sacred. In many cases it is as though the Church and its leaders and reformers presumed themselves to be acting in defence of Truth. Yet true Truth does not need defending. In a specifically Christian sense, if God is the author of Truth, how can it need defending by any human institution? How can people presume to do anything more than propagate what they consider to be Truth, especially the Truth of God? To defend it, especially by harmful means, shows nothing so much as complete lack of faith in God.

That doctrines can be altered, refined, reformulated or formulated at all demonstrates their provisional nature. They are really nothing more than tools enabling the ordinary mind to channel itself towards Ultimate Truth. As tools they may need to be modified or even abandoned as the collective ordinary mind of people develops and reviews itself in the course of historical progress. Again, differing individual dispositions and capacities require different tools. When doctrine becomes inflexible, authentic spirtuality is restricted and decays. That is why constant renewal is inevitable. The tragedies of Christian history have always resulted from resistance to this dynamic. The spiritual energy of Jesus' teaching is shown in nothing so much as in its continued resurgence in spite of excessive doctrinal constraints.

But this does not mean that doctrine is bad or inherently destructive or divisive. Doctrine is neither good nor bad. It is only an attempt at articulating spiritual truth in relative language. It may do so more or less skilfully, or more or less effectively. It may reflect more or less accurately or it may distort the non-conceptual truth which it tries to reflect. But it is only valid when it engenders Wisdom-Love. Christian doctrine is wholesome when it reflects the Spirit of Christ and is applied as Christ would apply it. No matter how clearly it reflects Jesus, it can, however, never be enforced. And it must lead the believer to Christlikeness.

If a Christian communion is able to unite around a wholesome doctrine, that doctrine is of obvious benefit. But it is not better, truer or more beneficial than a different doctrine of equal spiritual efficacy. The same is true of polity, theology, method, symbol and sacrament. If Christ is attained by them, they are 'true'.

The sacraments, for instance, have been understood and administered in different ways at different times and by different communions. For Catholic and Orthodox Christians they are a *sine qua non* because they are believed to be effective from their own side, even without the operation of faith. For other communions they are more symbolic, and their efficacy is considered proportionate to the believer's faith in them. Yet other Christians regard them as ultimately superfluous.

In the final event, the very scriptures and traditions from which doctrines and practices are derived are undeniably provisional. The New Testament, largely if not completely a collection of letters, was written by the apostles and other early teachers as guidelines for understanding, practising and organizing the new faith. They represent the starting point of Christian doctrine, and their provisional nature is demonstrated by the variety of interpretations which they allow, by the diverse possibilities they offer for systematic elaboration, and by their boundless potential for furnishing allegorical derivations. They also reflect the peculiarities of thinking and socio-religious understanding of their time. Beyond this, they were selected on the basis of the extent of their usage by the early Church, and canonized by a council of bishops. Similar arguments would serve to demonstrate the provisional nature of the Old Testament scriptures, which were collected during the Babylonian captivity of the Jews, and many of which were considered by early Christian teachers as incompatible with the new faith. Yet none of these considerations make them less sacred or less useful if they are driving and informing authentic spiritual attainment.

So, while doctrine is necessary for definition of the beliefs, view, path and goal of a religious system, it is also inherently transient and mutable. If this were not so, doctrine could not be grasped or formulated by the transient, mutable ordinary mind. At the highest levels of spiritual attainment doctrine is transcended. In personal mysticism and in the experience of direct spiritual transformation and empowerment, doctrine is superseded. Like all tools, it must be laid aside at the point of completion.

But prescriptive doctrine and practice cannot be laid aside at the outset of the religious path. The spiritual journey begins at the level of the ordinary mind, and the ordinary mind is prone to scattering, excesses of imagination, misguided thinking, and emotionalism. Skilful doctrine helps to regulate such excesses and to preclude the lapse into unripe antinomianism.

Still, the limited nature of doctrine and formalism should not be disregarded. Adherence to doctrine at the expense of one's own authentic truth is an obvious stumbling block to spiritual growth, and the same is true of all provisional practices, methods and symbols. The Trinitarian formulation, for instance, says little or nothing about the directly experienced Truth of the Holy Trinity, for such Truth is beyond the capacity of ordinary verbalization. But understanding doctrine in this way, as provisional and relative, does not disallow conformity for the sake of visible unity and in order not to confuse believers who have not yet moved beyond the religious apprehensions of the ordinary mind.

A penetrative understanding of Christian history should lead to an unqualified acceptance of Christian diversity. There is nothing regrettable about it. What is regrettable is that uniformity was for so long enforced by the powerful and often vicious church-state institution. It resulted in a visible unity rendered inauthentic by frustrated currents of suppressed heterodoxy and non-conformism. The authentic spiritual progress of humanity as a whole is most truly reflected in visible diversity with a strongly emergent sense of the invisible spiritual unity of inner path and goal. This dynamic rightly reflects the provisional and variegated nature of relative expressions of the same Absolute Truth. It does not attempt misguidedly to make absolutes out of relative factors, a process which must always result in the concurrent relativization of the Absolute itself, a delusory diminishment which obstructs Wisdom-Love and deprives the ordinary mind of the insight into its potential for self-transcendence.

THE CHRISTIAN UNDERSTANDING OF HISTORY

The history of Christianity must also be considered in the light of the Christian understanding of history itself. God is understood by Christians as revealing himself, his will and his truth through direct intervention in history. The act of creation is the prime act of divine intervention by which the processes of history are begun. The creation of humankind in the image of God, the exodus of the Jews from slavery in Egypt, the inspiration of the kings and prophets, are all examples of divine intervention. The central point, the turning point of history, is reached by God's sending his Son into the world to accomplish the work of salvation. All of history can only be properly evaluated, from a Christian perspective, by referral to the work of God in Jesus Christ.

Outline Histories of Christianity and Buddhism

The sense of God's presence and activity in history also influences the Christian appreciation of dogma, practice, and its own historical progress. It is the history of unspiritual mankind striving against God's Kingdom, and of God intervening to bring people back to Truth. In the same way certain Christian communions believe that their scriptures, doctrines and methods have been divinely inspired and sanctified by the Holy Spirit so that, although the scriptures were written and selected by mere people, and the doctrines formulated by mere councils of people, these events were guided by divine intervention. One can see how this view renders doctrine inviolable. Christians holding the divine-historical view do not accept that any further revelations concerning the person and work of Jesus, the nature of the Trinity and other central doctrines which make up the *kerygma* will or can be made. By this assertion the Church is in possession of the full Truth, for in Jesus Christ Truth was revealed in its fulness. Thus all evolved and evolving church tradition can only be valid if it conforms to the teachings of the scriptures.

The history of humankind is seen also as the history of God establishing his kingdom among people. Although history is for the most part an expression in action of human free will, the progress of history in its entirety is ultimately in the hands of God. The full establishment of God's kingdom will be accomplished by the second coming of Jesus (*parousia*), for which all Christians wait. Until that event, the Christian's purpose is to labour with God to prepare the world in the Spirit of Christ, to work in Christ towards the redemption of the world, so that as few souls as possible will be lost when Jesus returns.

Between the advent of Jesus as Saviour and his return as Righteous Judge the Church is the living body in and through which God in Christ is revealed and expressed most clearly in the transient world. But the Church acknowledges with Paul that this Divine Treasure is contained in frail humanity, in 'vessels of clay.' This is the Christian admission of the relative, provisional nature of the body of Christ, and of its individual members in the world. And herein can be found sufficient grounds for justifying any impulse to self-revision and self-correction of the Church on earth, and the admission that it is, after all, a relative institution in a relative realm evolving by relative principles.

The Gospel for Buddhists and the Dharma for Christians
BRIEF HISTORY OF BUDDHISM

The Early Sects

After the death of the Buddha (c. 483 BC) and his passing into the *Mahaparinirvana*, the early Buddhist community soon began to diversify along sectarian lines. In the earliest period there were probably already more than twenty sects. Their differences in doctrine and polity arose from divergent elaborations of the Buddha's basic teachings. Since early Buddhism had no central authority and no unified, hierarchical structure of clergy, its sense of unity in diversity derived from a common adherence to the fundamental tenets of the Four Noble Truths.

The various sects were highly tolerant of one another. Members of the divergent communities remained in regular contact, keeping up a discussion of doctrinal problems. In some cases different sects shared the same monasteries in an attitude of mutual tolerance. They all had their original teaching and their refuge in the Buddha, and were more concerned with the development of an applied doctrine which would accurately express the nature of existence as a starting point for spiritual practice, than with enforcement of any one system of belief.

They were aware that their search must yield diverse and tentative answers because of the provisional conditions under which that search was being carried out. Among those tentative answers, however, there must be some which evinced greater internal consistency and yielded greater efficacy as a basis for spiritual practice. The striving for accurate formulations did result in some sharp criticism and even invective, but always in the spirit of keen intellectual debate and a genuine concern for achieving clarity.

There was no notion of an orthodoxy which could be abandoned only at the cost of excommunication. This could not be the case in a mental environment in which all Buddhist teachers realized from the outset, as the foundation of their understanding of existence, that there could be no absolutely true formulation of doctrine in a relative mental realm. The teachings of the Buddha posed for all of them alike the same problems of refinement and elaboration.

Early Buddhism was for the most part monastic. There was a sharp divide between monks and laity, with the latter gaining preparatory merit mainly through their support of the former. This sort of arrangement had for a long time been an established tradition in India. In the Indian religious mind the spiritual quest could only be conducted in an attitude of complete renunciation of and withdrawal from the world. The spiritual practitioner could no more be involved in worldly affairs; in the conduct of family life and livelihood, than the laity, preoccupied with these mundane activities, could successfully aspire to high spiritual attainment. For early Buddhism with its pessimistic view of the world order and its stress on the delusoriness of everything mundane, the only practical alternative was to opt for the seclusion and refuge provided by monastic life. In return for material support from the laity, the monks gave instruction in the teachings and performed religious offices.

The divide between monks and laity was a cause for differences and even conflict within the monastic system. Some viewed the religious life as being almost exclusively for the benefit of the meditatively evolved *Arhats* of high attainment. In this view it was the natural duty of the laity to cherish these spiritual masters who, through their spiritual powers, worked for the welfare of all beings. But there were also those monks who felt that the monasteries should be more concerned with bringing the Dharma to the laity and informing their environment with enlightened thinking. This introvert-extravert tension was also responsible for divergent approaches to monastic organization and rules.

The first scholastic splits were occasioned by these tensions, in the period roughly between 340 and 240 BC. The four representative schools which arose from them were the *Mahasangikas, Sthaviras, Pudgalavadins* and *Vibhajyavadins*. The doctrines of these schools formed the broad vision of the earlist Buddhist tradition, the Hinayana (Lesser Vehicle), but were also the seeds for the further elaborations of doctrine and method by the Mahayana, or Greater Vehicle, which were to be worked out around the beginning of the first century AD. The doctrines of the Mahayana, in their turn, were to give rise to the later tantric tradition, which arose around the year 500.

Monasticism

Before discussing the doctrinal differences of the early schools, it is useful to gain some idea of the developments in monasticism from the time of the Buddha's death to the period of the first Buddhist kingdom under Ashoka (ruled 274–236 BC). The monastic impulse, although it provided the benefits of seclusion and renunciate living, was rooted in a far more fundamental idea: that there were two distinct classes of human being: the spiritually ennobled (*Arya*) and the undeveloped ordinary class (*Bala-prthag-jana*). From the time of the Buddha those who were motivated to spiritual development separated themselves from the mundane class with its unspiritual aspirations.

The earliest communities of practitioners were not localised in a single place. They lived as wandering mendicants, teaching the Dharma as they travelled from town to town, and winning new renunciate adherents. This had been the common practice of all Indian ascetics from pre-Buddhist times. But the Buddhist Sangha was unique in its practice of gathering and living together during the three-month monsoon. The monastic rule evolved from the experience of these seasonal periods of communal living and in time the communities were permanently settled in monasteries.

The monastic order provided a stable, undistracting environment for religious practice. It brought with it the need for formal rules and a system of governance. It also changed the relationship between the monks and the laity. The wandering monk had a close involvement with the lay communities among which he travelled, dispensing spiritual wisdom and receiving material support in return, and living a visibly renunciate life to the extent that his very garments were made from rags collected in rubbish dumps. The conditions of settled monasticism, on the other hand, could resemble a life of privilege. It therefore brought the beginnings of estrangement from the laity on whose generosity the monasteries depended.

In later periods when the monasteries enjoyed royal patronage this dependence was lessened and even obviated, but in the long run alienation from the laity contributed heavily to the decline of Buddhism in India. Monastic introversion was in many ways a departure from the communally involved and missionary-minded spirituality of the Buddha himself. Concern for the spiritual development of the Arya was not balanced with spiritual concern for the worldling and tended to excessive self-involvement. This tendency was eventually to be corrected by the Mahayana. In the early Hinayana, however, the nurture of the Arhat, the being of high spiritual attainment, was the central concern.

Monastic rules had been formulated before the reign of Ashoka. The *Pratimoksha* deals with transgressions punishable by suspension or expulsion from the monastery, as well as lesser offences with their attendant punishments. Offences deserving expulsion are sexual intercourse, theft, killing and false claims to high spiritual attainments. Transgressions punishable by expulsion have to do with other sexual offences and, especially, with instigating dissent within the order. Lesser rules deal with the handling of money, misuse of gifts to the community, slander, giving high teaching to the uninitiated, wanton destruction of vegetation and the use of alcohol. By the fourth century BC these rules had been systematized in the *Skandhaka*. The collected rules in their comprehensive form came to be known as the *Vinaya*. The aim of the Vinaya was to ensure a secluded, peaceful and ordered environment, conducive to intensive study, meditation and other religious practices.

This formative period also saw the convening of four councils. According to Buddhist tradition the first council was convened at Rajagraha shortly after the Buddha's death. This council of 500 monks is considered to have completed the Vinaya as well as the *Sutras* (the Discourses of the Buddha) under the direction of Upali and Ananda. These were not, however, commited to writing, but were memorized and transmitted orally.

The second council at Vaisali was concerned with rebuking lax conduct and the relaxation of rules in certain monasteries. The third council was convoked by the Emperor Ashoka in Pataliputra around 250 BC. Some assert that the *Tripitaka* (Three Baskets) of Buddhist teaching, the official Buddhist canon, were completed at this council. A fourth council held at Jalandar under king Kaniska dealt with the composition of commentaries. Although some of these councils addressed sectarian controversies and rejected certain doctrinal positions, they had no intention or power to excommunicate dissenters. Their purpose was to establish an orthodox mean in doctrine and more especially in monastic discipline, monasticism being the normal vehicle for the practice of Buddhism. Sects whose positions were refuted by the councils were neither outlawed nor forbidden to practice.

Under Ashoka Buddhism enjoyed state patronage although the Sangha remained separate from the state institution. Ashoka purposed to administer his empire by Buddhist principles and to create conditions conducive to the welfare of his subjects in this life and the next. He saw himself as a compassionate father and his subjects as his children. All non-Buddhist religions were tolerated. After Ashoka's reign his dynasty, the Mauryan, declined, but Buddhism had grown into the religion of the people.

Under the Sunga dynasty Buddhism no longer had royal patronage, but popular Buddhism as well as the monastic form were thriving. The popular form tended to view the Buddha as a saving deity, an object of worship and supplication, to the extent that Hindu communities were able to reinterpret the Buddha as an incarnation of the god Shiva. At any rate, even orthodox Buddhism demanded less, in terms of both practice and insight, from the laity.

Lay adherents were exhorted to follow a basic moral code which would lead to a better rebirth. They were not greatly encouraged to the development of inner spirituality, and the profounder teachings were withheld from them. These conditions were a natural reflection of the notion of the two human classes, the spiritually ennobled and the lesser ordinary class, which also gave rise to two forms of teaching and understanding: the supramundane and the mundane. The supramundane teachings were relayed to the monks. The mundane teachings, more literal and less evolved, were intended to promote prosperity and a happy life for the laity in this world, it being understood that laypeople too would eventually achieve the auspicious rebirth allowing them opportunities to enter monastic life and to receive the higher teachings.

By the beginning of the first century AD the higher practices of settled monasticism and the rudimentary moral and ritual practices of the laity had become the established pattern of Buddhist religious life. By this time, too, Buddhism had been spread beyond the borders of India to Ceylon and Southeast Asia.

The First Scholastic Splits

The problem of the divide between monks and laity was the main cause of the first schisms in the early Hinayana. More specifically, the attainments of the Arhat (who was supposed to have attained Perfect Equipoise) became the object of controversy. The teacher Mahadeva argued that there were several obvious behavioural flaws which proved that Arhats were not yet perfected. They were at many points not essentially different from other people.

This view was a blow to Hinayana orthodoxy which considered the Arhat, secluded from and supported by the laity, and at the same time of enormous spiritual benefit to them, to be the ideal product of spiritual practice. The Arhat, abiding and working in transcendent mental realms, was seen as the highest fruit of Buddhist development, as representing that to which all people should aspire, whose presence and activity furthered the cause of illumining all beings, and who was worthy of all honour.

But Mahadeva pointed out their human frailty in areas such as sexuality, doubt, ignorance and dependence on others for teaching. The diminishment of the Arhat was not, however, an end in itself. The deeper motive was to shift attention away from the supposed chasm between ennobled and ordinary practitioners, and to focus more compassionately on the spiritual development of the laity.

Mahadeva's followers called themselves the *Mahasanghika*, and in time they developed their own theories concerning the person of the Buddha, the nature of the Pure Mind, and the value of conceptualized insights. They taught that the Buddha was completely transcendent, omniscient, omnipotent, infinite, eternally abiding in Perfect Mental Equipoise. He was more than only an example to aspirants: he was a Being in whom practitioners could put their faith. In their view the historical Buddha was really an emanation of this Perfect One, who also sent other spiritual helpers to humanity. From being an Enlightened Teacher, the Buddha was elevated by the Mahasanghikas to the status of a Saviour.

They taught that the ordinary mind was, from its own side and in its true nature, spotless, pure and luminous, and that it could not be essentially affected by mental impurity. They also asserted that all conceptualized insight, including formal doctrine, had no final value in this provisional, 'empty' realm. In these points they foreshadowed the Mahayana.

Those who did not hold with the new Mahasanghika teachings called themselves the *Sthaviras*, and separated themselves as holders of the original Dharma.

The next schism, between the Sthaviras and *Pudgalavadins*, occurred because of differing views on the nature of the person (*pudgala*) or 'self.' The orthodox view was that the person was devoid of anything that might be called 'real existence.' Self was nothing more than a delusory construct. The Pugalavadins held that there must be some way, albeit extremely subtle, in which an ineffable self actually exists. For one thing, there must be a subtly continuous self which bears its karmic traces from one rebirth to another. And there must be some entity, however subtle, which eventually attains to Buddhahood. These theories about self were later to be elaborated by the Mahayanists.

The third split was between the *Vibhajyavadins*, an orthodox Hinayana group, and the *Sarvastivadins* founded by Katyayaniputra. They contested the theory that only the present moment could be called real, while past and future moments have no existence. They sought to demonstrate, for instance, the inconsistency between the ideas of non-existent past moments and karmic cause and effect. If one's present condition is the result of past activity, and past moments are non-existent, then these present conditions must have arisen causelessly.

Although these splits are not in themselves significant to the casual student of Buddhist history, their general value is that they record the tendencies that led to the inception of the Mahayana. They show three preoccupations of the early Hinayana. First, there is the wish to bring monks and laypeople closer to each other and to make the Dharma more accessible to ordinary people. Second, there is the painstaking effort to elucidate and elaborate on the deeper aspects of the Buddha's teachings, and to answer the questions which logically derive from them. These efforts are made not so much in the interests of establishing a final dogma as to provide a basis for efficient spiritual practice. Third, there is the drive to define the real nature of Samsaric existence rather than turning away from it by simply dismissing all mundane phenomena, including self, as delusory and unworthy of further consideration.

All of these aspirations reveal an underlying desire to integrate Buddhist teaching and practice more skilfully into the patterns of the relative domain. In order to contend with Samsara it was necessary to gain insight into the ways in which relative domains and their phenomena existed and functioned. They were not simply to be ignored. These aspirations were to be fulfilled with the rise of the Mahayana. In the meantime, one important result of the new emphasis on philosophical theorizing was the composition of the *Abhidharma*, the third basket or *pitaka* of the Buddhist scriptures, which deals with the philosophical aspects of meditation.

Early Buddhist Practice

The early Hinayana period, with its concentration on the Arhat ideal and its emphasis on the distinctions between the Arya and the ordinary person, supramundane and mundane practice, and monks and laity, obviously resulted in sharp dichotomies in religious practice.

Outline Histories of Christianity and Buddhism

In the monastic environment, while study and practice might begin at the mundane level, the intention was to advance the practitioner to eventual supramundane attainment. The process would take place within the framework of study, conduct and meditation. Study would be directed at the acquisition of increasingly profound insight into the inner meaning of Dharma by leading the mind from conceptual to non-conceptual wisdom. Meditation would render the mind less distracted, more pliable, and able to find, and abide in, transcendent states. Disciplined and virtuous conduct would assist in stabilizing the mind and in removing impurities and obstructions.

The objects of study were the Four Noble Truths, the scriptures and commentaries, as well as the treatises of the sects. The methods of study would include oral teaching, discussion and debate. The aim was to gain an accurate view of the Way It Is, as opposed to the way it appears to be. Especially, the real nature of Mind, of self and of phenomena was to be understood.

The aim of meditation was to discover the transcendent modes of mental experience in which ultimate wisdom-insight could be attained. Beginning with the practice of mindfulness and advancing to higher meditative techniques, the meditator gradually arrived at the state of pure, undistracted awareness and penetrating insight into the emptiness of all provisional existence. From this dual basis the mind was trained towards the achievement of Full Enlightenment.

Conduct was rooted in harmlessness (*ahimsa*) and lovingkindness (*maitri*), and was mindfully scrutinized so that virtuous deeds could be made to arise spontaneously and carried out with an attitude of detachment and an awareness of karma. Study, contemplation and action were lifted to supramundane levels by meditative awareness. These practices were aimed at achieving complete liberation from the mundane in order to abide in the transcendence of Ultimate Truth. Such was the practice of the Arhat.

The laity, by means of their simpler observances, were supposed to gain merit rather than final wisdom. By accumulating merit, laypeople would ensure for themselves prosperity in this world, and rebirth into auspicious circumstances, especially rebirths allowing opportunities for monastic practice and the capacity for aspiring to Arhatship.

Merit was acquired by observing the five precepts: refraining from killing, stealing, sexual misconduct, lying and using intoxicants. The layperson must be devoted to the Three Jewels, must practise generosity and support the monastery, being particularly generous to evolved beings such as the sons of Shakyamuni and the Arhats, for greater merit was gained by giving to those of high attainment. Merit could also be gained by revering the relics of the Buddha, visiting holy places and constructing shrines and stupas as tokens of devotion.

Both the secular leaders and the populace considered the presence and activities of monks and Arhats to be beneficial to the community and to the country as a whole. By their teaching, example and spiritual practices they contributed to the harmony and virtue of the whole society. Indeed, it was believed that their presence could protect the country from wars, natural disasters and the like.

Early Missions

Under King Ashoka Buddhist missions were sent as far afield as Macedonia and Egypt, but the Dharma did not endure in these areas. In Ceylon, however, where the Dharma was first taught by Ashoka's son, Mahinda, around 240 BC, the teachings took root and flourished.

Ceylon also provided the first instance of Buddhism as a church-state religion. Monasteries were under perpetual state patronage and protection, and only Buddhists were allowed to be made king. Monastic institutions were richly endowed and supported, and the monks in their turn supported the king, even in times of battle. They accompanied king Dutta Gamani (101–77 BC) to the battlefield as 'a blessing and a protection.'

It was in Ceylon that the Theravada school was first so named. The entire canon of scripture and the commentaries were committed to writing there in the first century BC and, owing to the almost unbroken tradition of Buddhist practice in Ceylon (modern day Sri Lanka), all of these scriptures have been preserved

The Mahayana

In the first century AD the developments in early Hinayana thinking began to find expression in the Mahayana. The Arhat ideal had to a great extent disappointed the hopes of both the laity and the monks. It was becoming clearer that Arhats and monks were often as flawed as ordinary people. The laity also wanted greater access to the higher teachings. At the same time, a number of developments in philosophical thinking were compelling the Hinayana towards a more elaborate reworking of the basic teachings. It was felt that a new impulse and a new expression were needed to revitalize the transmission of Dharma and to adapt it to the changing needs of the time. A vast new literature was created over the ensuing five centuries.

Concurrent with the writing of these extensive scriptures a new religious vision of the Buddha arose. No longer was he to be understood only as a highly realized human teacher who had attained Liberation under the Bodhi Tree. He was now to be viewed as the manifestation in human form of Ultimate Truth itself. He had appeared as a man to convey as much truth as could be digested by people of his epoch but, as a living spiritual force of Truth, he would continue to impart profounder revelations to a more developed and receptive Sangha. What he was now revealing to Mahayanists was not a new truth, but a clearer exposition of the original Dharma. Thus new discourses (sutras) written by Mahayanists were put into the mouth of the Buddha himself. It was claimed that they had been spoken by him during his sojourn on earth and had been preserved by bodhisattvas in supramundane realms, to be relayed to the Sangha at the appropriate time.

The most fundamental shift of the Mahayana was the exchange of the Arhat ideal for that of the *bodhisattva* (a being of enlightened essence). Whereas the goal of the Arhat was the attainment of full supramundane wisdom, the bodhisattva's goal, generated by his compassionate concern for others, was the highest realization of wisdom and compassion as a unified expression of the Enlightened Mind. *Bodhicitta* (the Enlightenment Idea) is rooted in Wisdom-Compassion. While the efforts of the Arhat were concentrated on self-development, and therefore came to be seen as 'lesser' and 'self-centred', the bodhisattva was steeped in wise compassion for all living beings, desiring their welfare and spiritual wellbeing before his own. So great was the bodhisattva's compassion that he would sacrifice himself for the sake of sentient beings, and would delay his own entrance into Nirvana in order to save as many beings as possible.

This ideal led to the discovery of a pantheon of Bodhisattvas and Buddhas in transcendent realms, Enlightened Beings to whom the practitioner could turn in prayer and meditation for spiritual help. *Avalokiteshvara* was the Bodhisattva of Great Compassion, *Manjushri* helped the practitioner to realize emptiness, *Vajrasattva* removed spiritual obstacles, and so forth. Buddhas such as *Akshobya* and *Amitaba* generated their own realms or 'pure lands' into which the faithful could enter after death. These Enlightened Beings could manifest in a variety of forms in Samsaric realms to help those trapped in ignorance and suffering. By advanced practitioners these celestial beings were understood to exist very subtly, 'inseparable from the mind' of those who visualized them. But they were beneficial also to less advanced practitioners for whom they had an independent, objective reality.

A systematic description of the nature and activities of the celestial beings was elaborated. The Buddhas exist in three manifestations: as Absolute Enlightened Reality (*Dharmakaya*), as supramundane beings conveying Dharma in spiritual realms (*Samboghakaya*), and as emanations in the form realm (*Nirmanakaya*).

The bodhisattva has the same passions as ordinary people, but is not obscured or defiled by them. Although fully knowing the emptiness of all provisional beings, he nevertheless works to free them from suffering. His compassion, fused with wisdom, is boundless. On the way to Enlightenment the bodhisattva deals with self in two ways: he works self-sacrificially for the benefit of others, and he develops his mind to fully realize the emptiness of all phenomena.

The penetrative understanding of the real nature of existence is his wisdom. The fusion of wisdom and compassion is attained and practised in the Six Perfections: generosity, morality, patience, energy, meditation and wisdom. These *paramitas* are transcendent perfections, developed at the spiritual level: generosity is of a self-sacrificing nature; morality is spontaneous and utterly pure; patience implies also extreme endurance of difficult and fearful spiritual experiences; energy (or vigour) is dedicated and unfailing, drawing on transcendent wellsprings; meditation is perfected by the direct realization of emptiness, and wisdom is the stably abiding in The Way It Is.

The Bodhisattva Path has ten stages (*bhumis*) of increasing realization. The first six bhumis correspond to the Six Perfections (paramitas): one of these is fully attained at each successive stage. After the sixth bhumi, on which the paramita of wisdom is accomplished, and there is full insight into all ontological factors, the bodhisattva becomes a celestial being. On the last four bhumis the bodhisattva achieves control over the mundane realm and acquires miraculous powers. It is at this stage that he may become an object of faith. As a celestial Bodhisattva he may pass into

Nirvana, but he delays this passing in order to continue working for the unenlightened.

But the cultivation of Wisdom-Compassion is not sufficient to enable the bodhisattva to bring beings to liberation. To carry out his saving work he must develop the high wisdom of 'skilful means.' He must gain the insight to create liberating means appropriate to every kind of being and to every individual, skilful methods adapted to the karmic conditioning and capacity of each. The infinite variety of means used to lead beings to liberation arises spontaneously in the bodhisattva mind as the result of special insight. So skilful means might involve verbal transmissions, gestures, tests, special activities, and even some very eccentric behaviour.

In the Mahayana the Bodhisattva Path now became the highest goal of the practitioner, including some practitioners from the laity. Boundless loving concern for others coupled with supramundane wisdom changed the motivation of practitioners and the entire quality of Dharmic expression in the world. Aspiring bodhisattvas brought the teachings to laypeople with a fresh conviction and clarity. Their colourful and sometimes superhuman activities gave rise to popular movements and cults with a mythology growing up around their venerated *gurus* and saints.

Developments in Mahayana Doctrine

In the first 500 years of the Mahayana systematic treatises on the nature of ultimate reality were produced by a number of scholars and commentators, the most influential among whom were Nagarjuna, Vasubandhu and Asanga. Nagarjuna (c. 150) systematized the *Madhyamika* view. Vasubandhu and Asanga were responsible for the lucid formulation of the *Yogacharin* doctrine, a system which had been current at the time of Nagarjuna but was only set out definitively by the fourth century.

The Madhyamika school was mainly concerned with a logical formulation of the notion of 'emptiness' or 'suchness'. Its aim was to demonstrate clearly, by a number of logical propositions, that all phenomena, including self, were devoid of existence from their own side. Every perceptible object (*dharma*) exists only by imputation: a set of causes and conditions gives rise to an apparent entity whose 'existence' depends not only on the precursive causes and conditions, but also on the karmically conditioned and calibrated faculties of perception. But in and of themselves all phenomena are 'empty' of ultimate existence. In truth, they exist only 'such as they actually are'; that is as mere imputations. Suchness itself, although it can be logically described as 'emptiness' or 'voidness', is ultimately beyond all cognitive categories: indefinable. Its real nature can only be experienced in advanced meditative states, through ways of perception and knowing quite different to those of the ordinary discursive mind. In the void of non-conceptuality all objects dissolve into the One Silence of which nothing can be said. The self itself abandons self-identification and passes beyond duality.

The mind abiding in non-dualistic suchness is the fulfilment of wisdom. The perceived phenomenon is cognized simultaneously with its ultimately empty nature: the relative expression and its Absolute Basis are recognized as one and the same reality. Unconditioned and conditioned being are identical, as are Nirvana and Samsara. Tha relative path and the Absolute Goal are one. Thus supramundane insight is above both affirmation and negation of being: we cannot say of something either that it exists or that it does not exist because, although it exists insofar as we perceive it to exist, we can neither affirm nor negate its existence by thinking about how it exists or does not exist. The basis of existence or non-existence is beyond the reach of cognitive processes.

The Yogacharins took the leap of equating Unconditioned Ultimate Reality with Unconditioned Ultimate Mind. For them the goal of practice was to merge the individual mind with the ultimate state of pure, objectless awareness. Pure Being was pure awareness, undistracted, uncluttered by thoughts and feelings, unobscured by any motions or perceptions of the ordinary mind. Their view differed from that of the Madhyamikas in that it supposed all relative phenomena to arise from Absolute Awareness or, we might say, Primeval Mind. This seemed a logical candidate for the Uncaused First Cause. It is Mind that *just is*, that is the essence of all existence from 'beginningless time.'

For the Madhyamikas this was an unpermissible step. While the ordinary mind could be developed to attain to and abide in suchness, suchness itself could not be qualified. That the highest attainment of which the ordinary mind was capable was resting in pure awareness, did not constitute grounds for describing suchness itself as Pure Awareness. All that could validly be said was that the mind *experienced* suchness as pure, objectless awareness. The Yogacharins, however, found their formula useful enough to uphold. So the two main schools developed their divergent approaches without much reference to one another.

Outline Histories of Christianity and Buddhism

The Hinayana in the Same Period

The early Hinayana schools (who considered themselves the holders of orthodoxy) did not become absorbed into the growing Mahayana. Their response to the teachings of the Mahayana was more or less to ignore them. Their stance was that the Mahayana was indulging in unnecessary elaborations and speculations. To some extent, in any case, Mahayana teachings were only explicit statements of implicit Hinayana tenets, or secret teachings now being brought into the public domain.

During the formative period of the Mahayana, Hinayanists were chiefly occupied with reworking the *Jataka* Tales and systematizing the Abidharma. The Arhat ideal with its empirical inconsistencies was subjected to growing compromise and was more often being exchanged for lesser goals such as rebirth in the realms of the gods. By about 400 AD the early Hinayana had reached its full development, and some were bemoaning its compromised state. At the end of his elaboration of the Abidharma, Vasubandhu reflects on the sad possibility that the vitality of Dharma might soon be extinguished in a rising flood of ignorance.

The Jataka Tales were taken from Indian folklore and adapted to Buddhist ends. In the first phases of their adaptation they purported to be incidents in the Buddha's earthly life. Later they were harnessed to the bodhisattva ideal, becoming stories of the Buddha's previous lifetimes as a developing Bodhisattva. Through them the Bodhisattva Path was brought with lively anecdote into the popular mind. Other literature of a devotional kind included the *Buddhacarita*, written by Asvaghosa, a poet who also wrote dramas on Buddhist themes, and Matrceta's Hymn in 150 verses.

The Abidharma, part of the canon, was extended. It dealt with the number of dharmas that form the basis of perception, and examined the origins, nature and passing away of the universe. It dealt also with karma, the types of spiritual attainment and the various paths by which Enlightenment could be achieved. It treated of spiritual contemplation and meditation, and affirmed the fundamental view of the non-inherent existence of self. Although several treatments of the Abidharma were attempted, the most enduring and influential was that of Vasubandhu in his *Abidharmakosa*

Later Buddhist Missions

In the first 500 years after the Buddha's passing into the *Mahaparinirvana*, missionary activity was confined to the Indian subcontinent, Nepal,

Kashmir and Ceylon. In the first period of the Mahayana the spread of Dharma outside the Indian region began, with the Mahayana Path being the most frequently adopted by non-Indian cultures because of its greater flexibility and emphasis on the adaptive use of 'skilful means'.

The Buddha was born at Lumbini in Nepal, so it is probable that Buddhism existed there from earliest times, in the same form as that of Northern India. In Kashmir, Buddhism flourished during the reign of Ashoka, but there were periods of alternation between Buddhism and Hinduism, dependent on the religious preference of the king. Yet Kashmir remained an important centre of Buddhist learning. Kashmiri Buddhism was taken to Java by Gunavarman.

Although Ceylon remained stably Buddhist, the emphasis of practice was shifted from meditative realization to philosophy and other branches of learning, so that monks became proficient not only in Buddhist thinking, but also in such subjects as linguistics, history and medicine. Religious aesthetics were also stressed. But Ceylon was known for its holy practitioners too. In spite of some Mahayana incursions, notably by the exorcist Sanghamitra (who was later murdered), the Theravada school remained dominant.

By the silk route Buddhism spread to Central Asia, to such trade and cultural centres as Khotan, Kucha and Turfan. From there it was later conveyed to East Asia and China. The most influential schools in these transmissions were the Hinayanist Sarvastivada, and the Mahayana.

At first Buddhism was adopted by the non-Chinese inhabitants in the outlying areas of the Han empire. When this dynasty fell around 220 AD, the Dharma began to spread into China proper. By the third and fourth centuries Buddhism had become established as a major influence on the court, as well as on both the intellectual and popular Chinese mind. 1300 Buddhist writings in translation were available by the year 400.

During the first period of transmission into China, Buddhism was most often understood as complementing Taoism, or as a divergent method for attaining Taoist goals. This naturally resulted in a number of misinterpretations of certain aspects of the Dharma, especially in the cases of 'emptiness', which was equated with the Taoist 'void of potential existence', and of the non-inherent existence of self, where Chinese Buddhists tended to take a view similar to that of the Pudgalavadins (asserting the real existence of a subtle self), but with an unorthodox denial of the emptiness of self.

Outline Histories of Christianity and Buddhism

The scholar-monk Kumarajiva, brought as a war captive from Kucha to China, imparted a greater authority to the Dharma through his writings and teachings. One of his disciples, Chu Tao-Sheng (died c. 434) was the first to instill in Chinese Buddhism the notion of instantaneous Enlightenment. The central idea was of the utter 'otherness' of Nirvana. Since the Unconditioned was of an utterly different order, it could only be attained in its fulness in one instantaneous flash of insight. The gradual acquisition of insight taught by the Indian school seemed to him logically flawed. In fact, the Indian schools had always taught that the graduated path leads to instantaneous Enlightenment, but Tao-Sheng stressed that the preparatory practices were of the order of conditioned experience, discontinuous in the final analysis with the authentic Enlightenment Insight. This emphasis was to result in two streams of thought: the proponents of 'gradual' and those of 'instantaneous' Attainment. The latter was to find its fullest expression in Chinese *Ch'an* Buddhism, and in the Japanese *Zen*.

Popular Buddhism in China looked to rebirth in the realms of paradise. The main paradises to which the faithful could attain were the realms of the celestial Buddhas, Akshobhya and Amitaba, and of the Buddha-to-come, Maitreya. Adherents would be reborn in the 'Pure Lands' if they refrained from wrath and other harmful practices, and developed compassion for all beings. Although the cosmic Buddhas, Akshobhya and Amitaba, were discovered by the Mahayana, Maitreya, the Buddha who will appear in the world at a future time, was already known to the earlier Hinayana.

The Tantrayana

The third major development in Buddhism, the *Tantrayana*, having begun in the fourth century in India, was being spread abroad after 500 AD. Its doctrines and methods were richly infused with the use of ritual, symbol, religious objects and other devices for attaining quick spiritual realization. Spiritual energies were harnessed to the complexities of the imaginative faculties with their vast fund of conscious and unconscious symbolism. Its central characteristic was the determined and energetic use of all and any means to achieve the goal. It introduced *mantras, mudras, mandalas* and tutelary deities as helpful means on the path. These new devices were systematized by the *Vajrayana* (the Diamond Vehicle) after 750. The Tantrayana absorbed into itself many elements of the popular belief, including the variety of spirit beings, redefining them as helpers on the path.

The ideal now became the *Siddha*, the bodhisattva beyond the eighth stage, who has fully developed miraculous powers. The ideal of the bodhisattva has not been abandoned, but Wisdom-Compassion is now more strongly linked to skilful means expressed in supernatural powers and the use of spiritual energies. Meditative practice involves complex visualization techniques and the merging one's mind with the mind of a tutelary deity in the *Sadhana*. 'Magical' elements come into play, and the important teachings are kept secret because of the dangers they pose to the undeveloped mind, and to preserve them from misuse by practitioners not rooted in Wisdom-Compassion.

Thus the Tantrayana became the path for the capable few, its esoteric teachings and methods relayed orally from teacher to student. Whereas the Sutras and *Shastras* of the Mahayana were freely available to all who wished to study them, the tantric literature used allegorical and symbolic language which could only be understood by initiates. For the most part, this remains the case today.

The development of the Tantrayana may well have been based on the perceived need to unite the many gods and goddesses, the abundant symbols and rites and other occult practices of Indian religious life into one all-embracing, explosively energetic system. Tantric practitioners banded together in small groups around qualified teachers, and moved out among the laity to perform ritual acts for fulfilling a variety of needs and averting dangers. In these ways they provided an alternative to the old monastic tradition and kept Buddhism close to the people.

Mantras were recited for the protection of the mind, teachings were made more immediate by the use of evocative sacred gestures (mudras), mandalas were devised as energized visual fields describing the living qualities of particular deities, of the patterns of the human mind, and even of the entire cosmos. Deities could be evoked by the use of syllables of sound. Their reality was experienced in the course of profound meditation, and their minds could be merged with that of the practitioner. The so-called 'wrathful deities' (fearsome manifestations of compassionate spirit-beings) could be called upon as protectors of Dharma or of other sacred instances. A host of female deities was also discovered, the most popular of whom was *Tara*, the goddess of boundless compassion.

Outline Histories of Christianity and Buddhism

The belief in occult forces, in demonic and compassionate spirit beings, and in the miraculous, had always been accepted in Buddhism, although they did not enter into Buddhist practice. They were simply recognized as part of the cosmic order. But in the Tantrayana they began to be employed as a means for rapidly gaining spiritual realization in the course of a single lifetime rather than across aeons of rebirths.

Yet at the highest levels of practice these complex factors were recognized as aspects of the total human psyche and as innate mental tools for training the mind in Wisdom-Compassion. There would always be both a literal and a symbolic understanding of these beings, forces, visualizations and objects. In the end their own ultimate emptiness was to be affirmed.

A further important innovation of the Tantrayana was the notion that the passions and other mundane experiences, rather than being shunned or repressed, could be transmuted by the insightful mind into tools for advancing on the spiritual path. The energies of anger or lust, for instance, could be liberated and redirected for developmental use. In this way all experiences ordinarily considered to be obstructive to advancement could be turned into useful means, for it is the mind which determines whether something is obstructive or useful, and proper skill can penetrate to the spiritual usefulness of all experience and phenomena. Nothing is good or bad in itself, and all things share in the same suchness.

The Later Spread of Buddhism

In Nepal, Buddhism remained strong and had its own university: Patan. By the ninth century there was regular interaction with Tibet, and Tibetans visited Nepal to acquire the teachings. Padmasambhava, the great tantric teacher who was invited to establish Buddhism in Tibet, was met by Shankarakshita in Nepal and given the invitation of the Tibetan king.

Buddhism in Kashmir foundered after the Hun invasion under Mihirkula about 515 AD. Thereafter there was some revival of the teaching but it began increasingly to be subsumed into the Hindu sects.

The Buddhism of Ceylon also underwent changes and was challenged by the new schools. Both the Mahayana and the Tantrayana had a following and there were often sharp differences between the indigenous monks of the *Mahavihara* with its Mahayanist leanings, and the conservative *Abhayagiri*. A group calling themselves the *Pamsukulikas* reverted to earlier austerities, including wearing robes made from discarded rags.

As in Kashmir, Buddhism was influenced by Hindu practices from the eighth century onwards.

In Central Asia the Dharma flickered into life occasionally but did not take root. There are signs of Tibetan Buddhist influence in the eighth century, and the Uigurs were converted from Manicheanism in the ninth century. By the nineteenth century Buddhism was extinguished by Turkish Islam.

Buddhism gradually gained influence in Southeast Asia by the sixth century. In Burma a distorted version of the Mahayana and certain Tantric methods was practiced by a group of monks calling themselves *'aris'* (from *Arya*). In Cambodia a fusion of Shivaism and Mahayanism developed, a religious view and practice which was dominant in the Khmer kingdom and specifically at Angkor, built around the start of the ninth century. After 500, Buddhism gradually replaced Brahminism in Sumatra and Central Java. Under the Shailendra dynasty great temples were built, including the famous stupa of Borobudur, a stone mandala representing the graduated path to Enlightenment.

In Korea, Buddhism grew steadily from the time of the first transmissions in 372. By the seventh century it had become the state religion, with vast state expenditure being allocated to its upkeep, and to the erection of temples and other religious edifices. The Koreans were devoted Mahayanists, and it was through Korea that Buddhism travelled to Japan from China in the mid-sixth century.

Chinese Buddhism

Buddhism reached the high point of its creative expression in China between the sixth and ninth centuries. Several schools arose from the Mahayana. Among these were sects which concentrated on stricter observance of the *Vinaya* rules, and those which sought to bring Madhyamika and Yogacharin views into an expression more suited to the Chinese mind. There was much emphasis on the integration of the phenomenal world with Absolute Suchness: an encouragement to recognize the sameness of all provisional things reflected in the One Mind of Pure Awareness. Of these, the most enduring schools were the *Ching-tu* and the *Ch'an*.

The Ching-tu (Pure Land) school represented a formalization of the popular cult of Amitaba. It was a faith-based sect which believed in the Buddha Amitaba as a Saviour. All that was required of the practitioner was that he put his faith in the person and name of Amitaba and live a virtuous life to the best of his ability. When he died he would be taken to the Western Pure Land of Amitaba. The believer gained special merit by repeating the name of Amitaba, or by dwelling on it in meditation. The Amidists also worshipped a female version of Avalokiteshvara (the Buddha of Boundless Compassion), whom they named *Kuan-yin*.

Of more importance to the development and vital renewal of classical Buddhist practice was the Ch'an, whose approach would echo throughout Buddhism and eventually find enduring expression in Zen. Although Ch'an grew from the Mahayana and showed clear Tantric influence, it became an influential stream of thought and practice in its own right.

The Ch'an took two fundamental positions on which its further development was based: it decided that directly experienced realization was more important than philosophical understanding, and that sudden, instantaneous Enlightenment was truer to the Buddha's Dharma than the Indian method of graduated spiritual ascent. It was set on the short, direct, uncluttered path to the Ultimate.

In its preference for direct experience it shunned the use of intricate logic and elaborate doctrine. Its focus was on practical attainment: the shifting and awakening of the mind by immediate manipulation rather than by lengthy training. Meditation, not study, was its method. But even preparation of the mind by meditation was considered to be a provisional process having nothing in common with the moment of full realization which was of the order of the Absolute. The transmission from teacher to student must therefore rely on extraordinary methods—techniques that had much less to do with conveying cogent understanding than with breaking down conceptual barriers by a sort of shock-treatment: uttering odd sounds, yanking students' noses, and so forth.

Fixation on the Buddha was seen as obstructive to mental liberation. 'If you meet the Buddha on the way, kill him,' advises one Ch'an master. Another used a wooden statue of the Buddha as firewood. The idea, of course, was that the very objects of religious veneration could come to stand between the practitioner and his direct experience of the Way It Is.

Ch'an sought to demonstrate the simplicity of the state of pure awareness, the mental experience of suchness. It was something natural rather than a profoundly extraordinary condition: it could find full expression in everyday activities; talking, washing, sitting, walking, eating, lying down. The teacher P'ang-yun said, 'Spiritual understanding and practice is in carrying water and chopping wood.' The Dharma should not be regarded as something particularly marvellous. It is close to everyday experience, but most people lack the simplicity to perceive it. It should not be the object of energetic search and research. One should simply abide effortlessly in the pure, undistracted state. So also with the transmission from teacher to acolyte: it is Buddha-Mind communicating directly and simply with Buddha-Mind.

The practical orientation of Ch'an also showed itself in its monastic organization. It valued the austerity of the Vinaya but combined simplicity with the harmony of Confucian etiquette. And although its monks continued to use the begging bowl they were also required to work. 'A day of no work, a day of no eating' was the motto of Po-chang, the chief reviser of Ch'an monasticism.

Ch'an practice reflected a growing dissatisfaction with the bodhisattva ideal, and particularly with the notion that the ideal could be attained only after aeons of rebirths. In this it mirrored the impatience of the Tantrayana. While the classical Mahayanists were patiently working at their gradual ascent, Ch'an claimed to be producing Buddhas in the course of a single lifetime. Its ideal was the *Roshi*; one who had attained *wu* or 'insightful awareness' through the immediacy of Ch'an transmission

By the mid-ninth century Buddhism had become a dominant and prosperous, but unproductive part of Chinese social life. Its huge monasteries, richly adorned and continually consuming the country's economic resources to maintain themselves, began to rouse resentment. In 845 a persecution of Buddhists broke out and monastic assets were seized by the state.

Japan

The Mahayana, in its Chinese form, came to Japan from Korea around 550. At length it merged with the indigenous *Shinto*, which had opposed it at first. By the ninth century this fusion had been shaped into *Ryobu-Shinto*.

Several philosophical schools came into existence between 550 and 700, all of them founded on new expositions of earlier Buddhist writings by such teachers as Kumarajiva, Nagarjuna, Aryadeva and Vasubandhu. The *Kegon* school (founded about 730) endured for several centuries, its chief mark being its devotion to *Roshana*, the Japanese version of *Vairochana*.

In the Heian period (794–1186) *Tendai* and *Shingon* were established and became dominant. The founders of the later sects all emerged from the Tendai school. 3000 temples were built in the Tendai mountains near Kyoto. The Shingon sect, devoted to ritualistic practices, made its home on the mountain of Koyasan. Tendai followed the *T'ien-t'ai* Chinese school which adopted a syncretic Mahayanist view and meditation. Shingon was modelled on the *Mi-tsung* school with its leanings towards the mysteries of the Tantrayana, embodied in a great variety of symbols and rites. At the same time, the faith-based cult of Amitaba (Japanese: *Amida*) was taught mainly to the laity.

In the Heian period, too, there were often violent clashes between competing monasteries which had come to function as territorial feudal institutions. Mercenaries were hired to set fire to inimical monasteries and even to pressure government. The arts and literature were the chief preoccupations of monastic life at this time.

Tibet

Introduced into Tibet in the seventh century, Buddhism was at first violently opposed by the native *Bon* shamans who had great influence with the nobility and were feared by the people on account of their magical powers and control over supernatural beings. As the Buddhists enjoyed royal patronage, however, they were able to establish their first monastery in 787, and the first monks were ordained by Shankarakshita.

There followed a brief period of fruitful activity, including the translation of scriptures into Tibetan, and for a short while the monks had influence over the king. These gains were reversed in the reign of Longdarma (836–842), Buddhists were persecuted, and the Dharma disappeared from Tibet for the next 100 years.

In spite of this century-long interruption of Buddhist practice, the teachings absorbed before Longdarma's reign remained decisive for the characteristics of Tibetan Buddhism after its revival around the year 1000. These early transmissions came in four forms.

A powerful and abiding influence came in the person of the revered Tantric master Padmasambhava, who propounded a Vajrayana system and is said to have brought under control the demonic beings obstructing the advance of Dharma into Tibet. The *Nyingma* lineage of Tibetan Buddhism derives from the Tantric teachings of Padmasambhava (known affectionately to Tibetans as *Guru Rinpoche*, 'Precious Master'), who is considered by Nyingma adherents to be a Buddha.

Scholars from Magadha brought to Tibet the Pala Synthesis of the Mahayana, a fusion of the Perfection of Wisdom teachings and Tantra. The *Prajnaparamita* (Perfection of Wisdom) teachings were interpreted along Madhyamika and Yogacharin lines, the emphasis being on the realization of emptiness as equal to primordial Pure Awareness, with the preliminary or cognitive understanding attained by fine logical investigation.

The Hinayanist Sarvastivadins attempted to introduce their school into Tibet, but, in spite of having established a monastery there, did not endure. Still, through the translation of their literature, they left behind the only Hinayana writings included in the Tibetan canon.

A last influence, by default, came from the Chinese Ch'an school. When Tibetan Buddhism rejected Ch'an immediacy in favour of the Indian graduated path, the basis of its further development was set. After the Council of Samye (793-794) the Ch'an missionaries were expelled.

Buddhism After 1000 AD

In the first half of the eleventh century Buddhism disappeared in India. There were several reasons for its decline and eventual extinction here. Of these, the Muslim invasions, in the course of which Buddhist monasteries and universities were destroyed, was a major cause. The other factors were conditions obtaining within Indian Buddhism itself.

The distance between the monasteries and the laity has already been discussed. As a result of this gap there was really not much to keep ordinary people faithful to the Dharma in the face of Muslim persecution. They had little knowledge of the higher teachings and practices, and what little they had of doctrinal understanding and spiritual realization was not enough to cling to under pressure. And because of the alienation of the laity the monasteries had ultimately to rely on royal patronage. When it ceased under Muslim rule the monastic system could no longer sustain itself. Dedicated practitioners left India for other countries: Tibet, Nepal, and so forth.

In the popular mind there was not much to distinguish Buddhism from the overwhelmingly present Hindu systems. Much of Buddhism, including its deities, Bodhisattvas, and the Buddha himself, had been absorbed into various Hindu sects. Moreover, Buddhism had never insisted that laypeople abandon their traditional gods and devotional practices. They could simply integrate them into the Dharmic view. So Buddhism, for the laity, was not exclusively defined.

It could be argued also that the creative impulse had departed from Indian Buddhism. After the Vajrayana renewal there was no new vital impetus. It seems more likely, however, that Dharma practice had generally deteriorated so that the spiritual attainments were no longer the chief motive force in practice.

Buddhism in Nepal declined slowly but steadily between 1200 and the twentieth century. Again, it was mainly the case that Buddhist views were integrated into the broader Hindu religion. In the fourteenth century the monks disbanded and entered secular life as *banras* (honorable ones). The Gurkha conquest in 1768 was a further blow to Dharma. By the early nineteenth century, although there were still four distinct Buddhist schools, the Dharma was extinct among the laity. In recent times there has been a revival of Tibetan Buddhism owing to the presence of the many Tibetans living in exile in Nepal.

In Kashmir, Buddhism and Shivaism melded as the country fell into disorder from the ninth to the fourteenth centuries. In the mid-fourteenth, Kashmir came under Muslim rule, and from the beginning of the fifteenth century Buddhists were persecuted and finally forbidden to practise. The Dharma vanished. Popular Hinduism survived, together with a largely imposed Islam.

Indian invasions in the thirteenth century disrupted the Ceylonese state on which the monasteries depended for their survival. Large parts of Ceylon also came under Muslim and Chinese rule. In the sixteenth century Catholic Portugal persecuted Buddhists and forced conversions to Christianity. The periods of Dutch and English rule also had a negative impact on Buddhism. Between the seventeenth and nineteenth centuries the Sangha became so crippled that monks had to be brought in from Burma and Thailand. Under the influence of the Theosophical Society, Ceylonese Buddhism underwent a revival in the late nineteenth century. Since then the Sangha has been revitalized and has done much to preserve and spread the teachings.

Burma, Thailand, Cambodia and Laos show similar tendencies in the period under review. They all went through an initial period of Mahayanist and Tantric influence, and then turned to Ceylonese Theravadism. There were times when the Mahayana and Theravada flourished together, with the Tantrayana providing an eccentric minority.

State patronage, however, was given to the Theravadins with their orderliness, orthodox uniformity and strict adherence to the Vinaya. Monasteries in these countries were usually established within the lay community, and laypeople had free access to monk-teachers, temples and shrines. It became customary for them to undergo a novitiate in the monasteries, after which they would return to secular life. By this process they became literate, gained insight into Dharma and were educated in other fields. Thus monks and laity were not estranged from one another.

In spite of political changes and periods of oppression, especially under communism, these countries remain predominantly Buddhist, maintaining alongside the Dharma a belief in their indigenous gods and household deities. Severe blows were dealt to Buddhist life and culture by the American involvement in Vietnam, Burma and Cambodia. Yet the Dharma has persisted and shown signs of skilful adaptation to the modern lifestyle.

The two streams of faith-based Amidism and meditational Ch'an continued as the most characteristic expressions of Dharma in China. Ch'an diverged into five 'houses' which agreed in doctrine but differed in method. They agreed, fundamentally, that different types of people needed different techniques for awakening the Buddha within.

The two surviving Ch'an schools are the *Ts'ao-tung-tsung*, which practises contemplative meditation, and the *Lin-chi-tsung* which favours abrupt, direct transmission from master to acolyte. Both are proponents of sudden Enlightenment. In general the Ch'an schools are impatient of doctrinal intricacy and endless debate. Whether they prefer quietist or eccentrically active methods, they share the view that the quick achievement of direct insight into suchness is paramount. Other religious questions are secondary. That method is best which works quickest.

There were also influences on Chinese Buddhism from Tibetan systems. So-called Lamaism with its outward display of supernatural powers and the other colourful aspects of the Vajrayana impressed both the laity and the court. Attempts were made to amalgamate Chinese and Tibetan practices, to the extent that even Confucius was elevated to the position of a Bodhisattva. But Chinese Buddhism maintained its minimalist features.

Outline Histories of Christianity and Buddhism

Three waves of persecution have considerably weakened, but not eradicated, Dharma from Chinese life. The Christian Taiping rebellion (1850–65) destroyed thousands of temples and monasteries. Buddhism was again persecuted under the Kuomintang, and then suppressed under communism, especially during Mao's infamous cultural revolution.

The Chinese Buddhism of Taiwan is mainly of the Pure Land type, and has of course escaped the devastating impact of communist centralization of control and contempt for spirituality.

Buddhism was at its zenith in Korea between the twelfth and fifteenth centuries when it was vigorously supported by the Koryo dynasty. *Bonzes* (Buddhist priests) were regularly used as royal advisors and spiritual teachers to the king. They also worked among the laity, performing miraculous deeds and giving prophetic counsel. Great temples were built and Buddhist art flourished. Buddhism dominated the country to such an extent that monks were revered above all others, being exempted even from saluting the secular powers.

After 1392, with the change of dynasty, Confuciansim enjoyed privileged status at the expense of Dharma. The monks began to be suppressed, monastic property was confiscated, the twenty-three convents in Seoul were closed, and practice of Dharma was discouraged. Popular Buddhism, however, persisted in remote regions of the country. The doctrine was a mixture of Amidism and Ch'an, and incorporated local religious customs. By 1947 the Dharma had declined to the extent that only 7000 monks were counted. Since then religious life has been exposed to the violent struggles between communism and the democratic ideal. North Korea has suffered for years under a dictatorship. But Dharma does not play a pervasive role, even in the democratic south.

The Amidist schools grew in popularity in Japan during the twelfth century. The earliest sect, the *Yuzu Nembutsu*, was founded by Ryonin in 1124. He taught that the way to liberation was by repeating the Nembutsu (the mantra: *Namu Amida Butsu*) up to 60 000 times per day, and that it would be more beneficial for the aspirant if recited for the welfare of others.

Honen (1133–1212) founded the *Jodo* (Pure Land) sect which has continued to the present. He took the view that determined spiritual development was no longer effective in an age of decay: people should rely on the power of a saviour such as Amida (Amitaba). The practice involved ceaseless repetition of the name of Amida while 'walking, standing, sitting or lying down.' In the fourteenth century the patriarch Ryoyo Shogei reinterpreted the Pure land as meaning a transformation of mind rather than a celestial paradise. Thus the Nembutsu should be seen as a technique for attaining insightful awareness. Shinran, a disciple of Honen, further simplified the practice by teaching that it was necessary to call in faith on Amida only once. This was sufficient to ensure salvation. Furthermore, those who trusted least in their own merits would gain Amida's paradise. His sect, the *Shinshu,* is still one of the most popular.

Zen was introduced into Japan by Eisai (1141–1215) who drew on the Chinese *Lin-chi* teachings, which became known in Japan as the *Rinzai*. The Chinese *Ts'ao-tung* (Japanese *Soto*) was introduced by Dogen (1200–1233) and nurtured by Keizan Jokin (1268–1325).

The Zen teachings went even further than those of the Chinese Ch'an in that Zen supposes that Enlightenment is already present in humanity and needs only to be expressed in the simplicity of sitting in meditation, and in the carrying out of all activity and inactivity with an accompanying mental and physical elegance. The enlightened state is reflected in all things, 'in the donkey's chin or the horse's mouth.' It becomes perceptible to the undistracted mind in perfect harmony with its environment, and abiding effortlessly in it. But Zen also used specific techniques for generating *Satori* (Awakening).

Rinzai Zen was adopted by the Samurai and gave rise to the *Bushido* (Way of the Warrior). It informed with a new elegance the traditional social rituals of Japan, as well as the arts. Many artists adopted the motto that 'Zen and art are one.'

From the sixteenth century Japanese Buddhism went into decline, giving way to Confucianism and Shintoism. In the seventeenth century Rinzai Zen was revitalized by Hakuin. The *Obaku* Zen sect was derived from Chinese teaching in 1655.

By the late-nineteenth century Buddhism had all but died out in Japan, but by the early twentieth it was showing signs of revival. By 1950 it had been re-established throughout the population, with about two thirds of the nation showing Buddhist leanings. Japanese Amidism and Zen continue to be the main vehicles of that country's Buddhist expression

The Tibetan Lama-Ruler Phakspa of the *Sakya* Lineage first brought Buddhism to Mongolia in 1261. It flourished there for a century and, through the power of the Mongol Empire, established many monasteries of the Tibetan tradition in China. After 1368 the Dharma declined in Mongolia and the country reverted to its traditional shamanism.

Mongolian Buddhism was revived in 1577 by the Tibetan Dalai Lama, who impressed the Mongols by his ability to perform great supernatural feats. In this second period the Dharma was upheld with such zeal that around 45% of the male population entered monastic life, thousands of monasteries were established and the scriptures were translated into Mongolian. Buddhism had declined again by the beginning of the twentieth century and suffered further diminishment under the communist regime. In recent years the Dharma has gradually been reintroduced by teachers of Tibetan Buddhism.

Around the year 1000, Buddhism returned to Tibet, mainly under the authoritative teaching of the Indian guru Atisha, who came to Tibet in 1042 at the invitation of the king. He re-established the Mahayana teachings of the Pala school, and his coming led to the council of Tibetan lamas which took place in Tholing in 1076, during which Buddhism was confirmed as the religion of Tibet.

Over the ensuing 400 years the indigenous Tibetan schools were founded. The earliest of these was the *Kadampa*, founded about 1050. It adhered closely to the teachings of Atisha as set out in his commentaries, 'The Lamp Lighting the Path to Enlightenment.' It concentrated on virtuous living and monastic discipline, and practised celibacy.

The *Kagyu* Lineage was founded by Marpa, the teacher of the great Tibetan saint, Milarepa. Its emphasis was on spiritual realization rather than on theory. It was less monastically inclined, did not enforce celibacy and showed the more human face of Buddhism, accepting that even saintly practitioners might be flawed by human foibles.

The *Sakya* Lineage took its name from the Sakya Monastery founded in 1073. When Tibet's monarchy fell, the Sakya abbots assumed rule over the country. Phakspa, who took the Dharma to Mongolia, was one of these hereditary Sakya rulers. The monks of the great Sakya monasteries were for a time more concerned with secular power than with religion, and battles were fought between rival monasteries.

The *Nyingma* derived their tradition from the Vajrayana master Padmasambhava who had come to Tibet in the first Buddhist period, before the persecution of monks began. The Nyingma teachers asserted that Padmasambhava had hidden 'scriptural treasures' (*terma*) throughout Tibet. The masters who subsequently discovered these *terma* were known as *tertons*. Between 1150 and 1550 large numbers of these hidden writings were discovered, including the 'Tibetan Book of the Dead' (*Bardo Thodol*). Nyingma tradition was closely tantric and thus more earthy and eccentric than the strictly monastic schools. There was also much influence from the old shamanist Bon tradition. In the tradition of the tantric masters, the Nyingma Lineage practised the philosophy that even non-virtuous or simply mundane activities could be transformed into tools for gaining Enlightenment

Je Tsongkhapa (1327–1419), the great Tibetan Buddhist scholar, was the founder of the *Gelug* Lineage, the 'sect of the virtuous.' Basing his teachings on those of Atisha, he wrote a treatise on 'The Stages of the Path to Enlightenment.' Thus the Gelug method strongly propounds a systematic and graduated approach to spiritual development. The Gelug also paid close attention to monastic discipline, practice of the virtues, and celibacy. From the Gelug school has come all the Dalai Lamas down to the present, and it was this school which exercised political power in Tibet until the Communist Chinese invasion in 1950.

Until the Buddhist tradition was virtually annihilated by the Chinese in the 1960s and 1970s, Tibetans were the society most thoroughly and enduringly permeated by the principles of Dharma. Monasteries, monks and teachers were closely associated with the laity, not only in the area of religion but also in government, medicine and education. Religion was uppermost in the popular mindset, while in the monasteries there was both high spiritual attainment and a vast accumulation of scholarship.

Tibetan Buddhism has always been strongly tantric and has developed many of its own customs, rites and observances. These include the recogntion of reincarnate lamas (*tulkus*) and bodhisattvas, the use of prayer wheels, flags and other devotional aids, and pilgrimage to sacred sites in Tibet. And it has never completely disowned the old Bon religion, which remains present in such practices as the summoning of the *Nechung* Oracle and those practices associated with the *bardos* (intermediate states between dying and rebirth).

Since the Chinese occupation, Buddhism has been crippled inside Tibet by state oppression and persecution. But the exile community has, with heroic effort, re-established the traditions and lineages in India and elsewhere. Today Tibetan Buddhism is visible, vocal, and rapidly growing in the West

Outline Histories of Christianity and Buddhism

From the late nineteenth century, Buddhism gradually became an object of serious study in the West, but it remained for a long time largely misunderstood. Even when it was taken up by religious movements such as the Theosophical Society, its subtle teachings were only incompletely grasped. It was only in the latter half of the twentieth century that the Dharma began to be properly understood, and from that time it has been steadily growing as an alternative spiritual path among Westerners.

Today many Buddhist schools have found adherents in the West, and there is a tendency to eclecticism in practice. The schools most visibly represented are the Theravada, Zen, Tibetan and Amidist traditions. Much Buddhist literature has been translated and many teachers visit or reside in Western countries.

REVISION AND DIVERSITY

In reviewing the comparative histories of Christianity and Buddhism, most people stress the non-violent progress of Buddhism in contrast to the violence so ubiquitous in Christian history. This is a mistaken and unuseful approach. Firstly, there are traces of violence in Buddhist history, and these should not be played down. More importantly, the human failure evident in the development of any religion does not affect the spiritual impulse which is the unalterable Truth of that religion. It only contradicts it. In the history of Buddhism, as in that of Christianity, there is much to contradict the aboriginal spiritual Truth-Energy. This is true also of the way in which these religions are practised in the world today, because they are practised by conditioned humanity.

What is far more definitive in Buddhist history is its unashamed willingness to revise its doctrines and methods, and even to redefine its goal. Its practical character is what stands out. It remains subservient to the motto: 'There is no truth higher than Truth itself.' Thus its prime motivation is not so much to state its truth as to declare its determination to continually seek out Truth. For this reason it is devoid of chauvinism in its general stance, if not in that of all its adherents. It seeks out the highest spirituality to which all beings, and especially human beings, can attain; and it acknowledges attainment in all religious systems, on all spiritual paths.

But this does not make Buddhism an amorphous, open-ended, all-inclusive movement. Its subtly differentiated doctrines, methods and goals, though vast in extent, have their points of entry and exit. There are provisional factors by which Buddhists are clearly differentiated from non-Buddhists. But these factors, although definitive, have never constituted barriers between Buddhism and other religions, and especially not between Buddhists and non-Buddhist people. For Buddhism recognises emphatically that all people share the fundamental path of being human.

This is why Buddhists can say to all people of all religions, 'Take or borrow what is useful from our path, and discard what offends.' And it has shown itself quite willing to incorporate into itself useful elements from other paths. Its stress is not on what one believes but on whether what one believes or uses is spiritually beneficial. Some light is better than no light at all. More light is better than less. Whatever can liberate people from the suffering and ignorance of the ordinary mind is grist to the Buddhist mill.

This acceptance of diversity is implicit in the Buddhist understanding of historical processes, and particularly in its view of the history of a religion, and of the history of the Dharma itself. To Buddhists, the initial spiritual impulse, having been introduced into a relative world, must eventually decay. This mirrors the Christian view of the ever-increasing darkness of the world. It is not that the pure spiritual impulse is subject to decay, but that a relative realm growing increasingly complex and self-regardant gradually loses the ability to perceive and reflect the simple purity of Truth. Eventually that realm, having declined to such a degree of ultra-relativity that it can no longer express its Absolute Source, becomes extinct. It is extinguished at the exact point where it is completely divorced from the Absolute because complete separation from the Absolute is simple non-existence.

The Dharma itself does not decay: the Absolute cannot decay. What decays is the ability of the human mind to clearly and insightfully perceive Truth, and the capacity to be transformed by and conformed to Truth. Therefore diversity in method, doctrine and skilful means is always required to address effectively the ever-darkening collective mind. This mind, subject to growing complexities which increase provisional knowledge, is correspondingly darkened in its apprehension of the simple purity of spiritual wisdom. If diverse and complex methods are not in their turn devised to penetrate to the deep mind, it remains obscured. If new and vital religious means are not accepted, religion easily degenerates into merely another branch of provisional knowledge.

The study of a religion's history is the study of the progress of a spiritual impulse through the relative domain of time and activity, and through the changing capacities of the human mind. It is like the flow of pure water through a riverine system. The conditions of the relative system can be such as either to facilitate or to obstruct the flow, and to maintain or vitiate the original purity.

That is why it is imperative at every point in the history of the relative expression of the Absolute to reassess the authenticity and the authority of that expression. These can be measured in no other way than by the quality of the fruit which they are producing, both collectively and individually. A well-organized communion agreed in unity around a central dogma is not necessarily a spiritual communion. The individual who has a full cognitive grasp of his religion is not for that reason a spiritual person.

If doctrine and method are no longer effective, they have to be revised. If they have actually functioned to dry up or to vitiate the pure flow, they should be modified or abandoned. The danger is that doctrines and methods can themselves become ultra-relative, a condition of which the main qualification is that the relative mistakes itself for the Absolute. At that dire point the spiritual impulse is no longer present at all. And these same possibilities apply to the spiritual development of an individual.

HISTORY, DIVERSITY AND THE MEAN

In setting out to describe the paths and goals of Buddhism and Christianity, our understanding of these must now be qualified by our insights into their respective histories. Christianity has its historically developed variety of approaches to doctrine and method, as does Buddhism. Individual believers from divergent Christian communions will have their differences in emphasis, in understanding, and in practice. Buddhists of the various schools will differ in their approach too. Hopefully these differences, viewed in the light of history, will no longer be important enough to constitute barriers.

Where doctrines differ we must try to find the ways in which they are expressing the same fundamental Truth in various formulations. We need to penetrate beyond the inevitable obscurations of relative language to arrive back at the pure spiritual impulse.

As regards the varieties of method, we shall have to look beyond their apparent dissimilarities to the sameness of spiritual development which they set out to accomplish. And so far as the subtly differentiated goals are concerned, we can best consider them as constituting the variety of experiences of the same Ultimate Truth. In taking into account the variety of Christian and Buddhist approaches, then, we can proceed no more clearly than by penetrating to the mean of our common human experience of the spiritual domain. This means taking only a few small steps beyond the relatively superficial diversity of our religious systems.

Part 5

The Paths and the Goals

THE CHRISTIAN GOAL IN THE WORLD

Standing at the beginning of his path, the Christian has as his goal the attainment of Christlikeness. He wants to be conformed to the living pattern of Jesus because Jesus is both Ultimate Wisdom and Ultimate Love.

In his human life he has manifested as the perfect human expression of the Father's nature. In this manifestation he represents what all people can become. In his resurrected life, however, he is the Glorified Son, the Redeemer of all people. In his eternal nature he is the Word of God, the Divine Creative Principle. Thus Christlikeness can never mean becoming equal to Jesus in all his aspects. The Christian cannot aspire to be the Only Son of God or the Second Person of the Triune Godhead. Nor can the Christian ever become the Word of God. He can never become exactly what Christ is because Christ, while being the perfect expression of God, is also the very God whom he expresses.

Unlike Christ, also, the Christian cannot of himself become a perfected expression of the Father: he can only express the Father's nature in and through Jesus, just as he can only be indwelt by the Father in Christ Jesus. The Father in Christ is revealed in the Christian by the indwelling Presence of the Holy Spirit. The indwelling Christ is central. It is through Christ that the Holy Spirit abides to reveal Christ in the inner person, and it is through the indwelling Christ that the Father is inwardly manifested.

So Christlikeness comes by this inner revelation, and by submission to its imperatives. Of himself the Christian can do nothing to express the life of God. And the central teaching is, 'It is no longer I who live, but

Christ who lives within me.' This is the essence of Christlikeness both in this world and in the world to come.

Again, the Christian does not become Christlike by striving to be like Christ, but by dying to self in order that Christ can be made manifest through the exclusion of the worldly self. For Christ cannot be revealed in the worldly self of the believer. What then is meant by 'dying to self'?

Dying to self cannot mean the abandonment of all the processes of the human personality, for there would then remain no human person through which the nature of God could be expressed. By referring the question back to the fall of Adam we can see that the self which is to be put to death is the will-aspect of selfhood by whose agency the original fall into sin occurred. The will of the Christian must be placed in perfect submission to the will of God in Christ. Then the pure will of Christ, in perfect harmony with the will of the Father, can be expressed in the Christian. The Christian therefore must accomplish one perfect act of will, submitting the personal will to the Divine Imperative, which is Wisdom-love. This 'dying to self' is also 'dying to sin' and becoming 'alive in Christ.'

In addition to the personal will, there are those aspects of the ordinary personality which have no obvious connection with personal volition, but which nevertheless are obstructive to the expression of the Divine in Christ. These are habits of thought and feeling, the thought-feeling responses which arise spontaneously as a result of prolonged conditioning. Although they derive ultimately from the unsubmitted will, they have taken on an habitual life of their own. They are also connected to a deeper, subtler, unconscious will which we call the instinct.

Human instinct is usually described as part of the human condition rather than as something which arises in consequence of conditioning. But this is only because the processes of conditioning which determine our instincts are hidden even more deeply in the unconscious than the conditioning which determines the general nature of ordinary human volition. Yet human instinct can be directed by the personal will.

Thus, these three aspects of self (personal will, habits of mind, instinct) which constitute the sinful self are all conditioned by the mindstate of fallenness, which predisposes the person to sin. Their presence and activity in the total personality conditions that personality. Their removal from the total personality leaves the personality 'renewed', unconditioned, and able to accommodate the pure, unconditioned will of God in Christ, which permeates the renewed mind from its deepest centre, or spirit, to its outwardly expressive perimeters.

Defining 'dying to self' as we have done, we can immediately see the difficult challenge by which the repentant Christian neophyte is faced from the outset. It is the first and, usually, the lifelong spiritual battleground, and the battle is sometimes lost. It is of critical importance, therefore, to understand more closely what it is about the personal will, habits of mind and human instinct that render them obstructive to the pure expression of the Divine.

PERSONAL WILL, HABITS OF MIND, HUMAN INSTINCT

As mere functional aspects of the total human mind, personal will, habits of mind and human instinct are not spiritually obstructive in themselves. What makes them obstructive is that they are tainted by fallenness; they are unsubmitted and unsanctified. They are not set apart in the human mind for the purposes of God, to express through human awareness and activity the Wisdom-Love of God. In the unsubmitted carnal mind they can be used for good, bad or indifferent ends.

Since, in the carnal mind, they are not motivated by the Wisdom-Love Spirit-Energy of God, their motives, including good motives, are uninformed by the Spirit of God in Christ. They are always coloured by selfishness or self-interest. Because they are conditioned by the fallen mindstate their motions and acts are inevitably impure. There is nothing of the free, pure Mind of God in them.

The personal will was created by God to conform to his will, but its fallen nature makes it unable to conform. It functions only for the relative self, to defend its interests, fulfil its needs and gratify its desires. Its motives are determined by an ultra-relative conditioning which sees the self as self-existent and therefore inclines towards the *non-serviam*.

The conditioning of fallenness with all its aspects and pressures also has its roots in an act of will; not an act of the personal will, but of the collective adamic will. The fall of Adam, the act of Adam's will against the will of God, established a new set of conditions in and by which people must henceforth live. Together with Adam, all people fell into a coarsened milieu qualified by ultra-relativity. And the conditions obtaining in this domain have in their turn conditioned the collective human will. The only way out is by a new act of will which is for God and against fallenness. This new act of will has been accomplished by Jesus Christ and the Christian is saved from the power of adamic conditioning by a personal act of will for Christ: the act of submitting the unsanctified personal will to the holy will of Jesus. By this act the Christian is lifted above the reach of the conditioning imperatives of the fallen domain and is 'seated with Christ in heavenly realms.'

While it remains unsanctified, the personal will cannot exercise a sanctifying influence over the unsanctified habits of mind and instincts. The central characteristic of collective human mental habits is the habitual 'loving the world and the things of the world.' It is worldliness; a worldly way of approaching and interacting with the world. At an individual level habits of mind enforce selfish human preferences, judgements, opinions, and so forth. At both the collective and individual levels they predetermine people's reactions and responses to events and to other people (and other beings, including Divine Beings).

Although these mental habits and the reactions they engender seem unrelated to the direct functioning of the personal will, this non-relatedness is only apparent. Their actual relation to the will is seen in the fact that they can be checked even by the unsanctified will. And, once the will is sanctified, they can be transformed or eradicated by it.

While habits of mind in the collective sense are the result of adamic conditioning, individual mental habits stem directly from individual conditioning, and from the exercise or non-exercise of the personal will informed by such conditioning. But individual conditioning is itself informed in a general way by collective adamic conditioning. This twin stream of conditioning and its reinforcement by a conditioned worldly experience is what makes of people slaves to this world and to the prince of this world.

Human instinct, too, has been formed by adamic conditioning. With the fall of humanity into a coarsened personhood existing in a coarsened environment, a coarse set of survivalist conditions arose. Collectively, they condition the instincts of fallen humanity. Unless these instincts are sanctified by a submission of the personal to the Divine Will, they remain liable to be distorted into perverse, intensely selfish expressions of themselves.

Again, even the unsanctified personal will can to some extend prevail over the instincts. But by the sanctified will they can be brought to a spiritual expression, permeated and transformed by Widom-Love, so that their survivalist drives do not find outlet in sinful ways.

It is clear then that the sanctification of the personal will, its submission to the Divine Will, is the indispensable first, and ongoing, principle of Christian practice. It is the 'dying to self' and 'daily dying to self' by which the Christian is redeemed in Christ. To the extent to which the personal will is surrendered to God in Christ, the believer is being 'born anew' or 'born from above.'

THE BUDDHIST GOAL IN SAMSARA: WISDOM

At the beginning of his path the Buddhist practitioner has as his goal the attainment of Wisdom-Compassion. It does not matter much whether that goal is understood in relation to the *arhat, pratyekabuddha, roshi* or *bodhisattva*. All of these aim at the same wisdom, and although the compassionate ideal is more pronounced and pervasive in the Mahayanist bodhisattva aspiration, the generation and practice of spiritual love (*maitri*) are an integral part of all Buddhist paths.

The attainment of Wisdom-Compassion is also spoken of as the uncovering of the Buddha-Nature within the total mental domain of the practitioner. Thus the attainment of Wisdom-Compassion is not a process of adducing to the human mind a spiritual Truth-Energy that was not previously present, but of rediscovering what has always existed in the mind, but has been obscured by the karmic accretions of the ordinary (or 'fallen') mental condition.

At the same time, we cannot simply say that the Buddha-Nature *is* Wisdom-Compassion. In itself the Buddha-Nature simply is what it is; it remains beyond definition. But it expresses itself in the minds and activities of people as Wisdom-Compassion, and it is that spontaneous expression of the Buddha-Nature which the aspirant is seeking. If he attains to Wisdom-Compassion, the Buddha-Nature has been uncovered or 'awakened' in the practitioner. In order to clarify the route to this awakening we need to understand what is meant by both the wisdom component and the compassion component. And we need to know what, on this path, the obstructions are.

The search for wisdom is bound up with the search for a Right View: a mental transformation by which reality is known as it really is. It is a path which leads from ignorance to insight. The emphasis is on becoming liberated from ignorance rather than on being saved from sin. The right view, the Truth-View, once attained, must inevitably conform to itself the mind which has seen it, because the mind cannot but conform itself to its authentic understanding of what reality is. And right conduct in body, speech and mind inevitably proceeds from Right View.

This Wisdom of Right View is gained by fully understanding the emptiness of all provisional phenomena and beings on the one hand, and of the 'non-empty' or self-sufficient reality of the Absolute on the other. More specific to human experience, it is the full and direct understanding (in experience) of the emptiness of the ordinary mind and the ultimacy of the Absolute Nature of Mind.

It is only by gaining full insight into the emptiness of the ordinary mind that the practitioner is able to free himself of its delusional control because its control is exercised on the basis of ignorance. Only once the delusory nature in which the provisional self appears has been fully grasped, its emptiness established beyond doubt, will the practitioner be able to penetrate to the liberated experience of the not-self. But the not-self is not nothingness: it is not annihilation of self. It is the mental continuum abiding in Perfect Equipoise, unaffected by karma, in the pure awareness of the Absolute Nature of Mind.

As long as he abides in equipoise the practitioner is free from the afflictions of the conditioned mind. His actions and reactions are free from all conditioning. They are no longer determined by the self-preserving and self-serving habits of the deluded ordinary mind. If he evinces love, it is without the self-centred energy of conditioned love; if anger, it is without the self-satisfying energy of conditioned anger. For the practitioner abiding in equipoise is in full control of his mindstate. His responses and reactions are liberated in wisdom.

Attainment of the wisdom component is therefore indispensable to liberation from the ego-self. Only by the full realization of the emptiness of self can the obstructive workings of the self be completely eradicated. And this includes the obstructions posed by the selves of other beings, and even of supramundane beings such as deities, bodhisattvas, and Buddhas. If their emptiness is not recognized, they too can become obstacles. Belief in their inherent existence will make of them objects of faith or devotion external to the mind of the practitioner. Devotion will be directed at their persons rather than at the energies in the practitioner's own mind which their persons represent. And, as regards human and other mundane beings, a clear recognition of the emptiness of their conventional selves enables the practitioner to interact with them at a level much deeper and more authentic than that of their 'masks.' Their foibles and transgressions do not represent what they really are and therefore cannot elicit negative responses. For all beings are in true reality equalized in the Buddha-Nature which they have in common.

Likewise, a view holding to the emptiness of all mundane phenomena diminishes, and eventually eradicates, in the mind of the practitioner, the sense of their importance, their appeal, their desirability. It also diminishes the effects on the practitioner of their negative qualities, their irritating or dangerous sides. They lose their power as objects of attachment and aversion, and of hope and fear. And, of course, this principle extends also to other living beings with whom the practitioner interacts.

In order to be fully effective, the wisdom component must be understood or realized at two levels, or in two stages. The first stage of understanding is conceptual: the mind understanding emptiness through study, observation and logical inference. At the second stage, the 'realization stage', there is direct, non-conceptual insight into emptiness. It is no longer only understood, but directly experienced. This experience loosens all the bonds of grasping, including 'grasping at a self.' And, having attained this insight-experience, the practitioner is able to progress towards Full Enlightenment.

COMPASSION

Bodhicitta, 'the Enlightened Thought', is defined as 'the compassionate wish to liberate all sentient beings.' Compassion is boundless and all-inclusive. No sentient being is unworthy of it. This is the compassionate View to which the practitioner must attain.

True compassion cannot be discovered outside of wisdom (*vidya*), the insight into emptiness. If the wisdom of emptiness has not eradicated the delusory sense of an inherently existing self, the mind remains conditioned by the karmic biases of the ordinary sense of self. Compassion generated in such a mind must share in its conditioning, and therefore be conditional. It cannot be directed at all beings equally because the ordinary mind continues to falsely discriminate between those worthy, those less worthy and those unworthy of its compassion. Even if the pretense of equalized, boundless compassion is put forth, it will find no resonating conviction in the mind of its object.

If the emptiness of the object of compassion is not perceived as well, there will be a similarly conditioned result. One type of ordinary self seems to be more deserving or more needful of compassion than another. This arises from a false conviction of the inherent qualities of the other's ordinary self, the 'ordinary' object of compassion. An ordinary self which seems kind, humble or in some other way attractive, is deemed more lovable than an ordinary self emanating pride or malice. These false discriminations are made because the empty nature of the other's ordinary self is not penetratingly understood. The same Buddha-Nature present in all beings is not being fully recognized.

On the other hand, the understanding of emptiness should not be so confused as to conclude that there is in the other no self at all towards which compassion can be directed. There is a conventional self, and it is suffering. The provisional self of the other is ultimately real to the other who has not yet understood his own emptiness. In this sense there is a real object of compassion and the aim of that compassion is to help the other along the path to liberation from the conventional object of compassion, the ordinary self.

Whereas wisdom is the full understanding of the Way It Is, compassion is the expression of that understanding. Because the wisdom cognizing emptiness is at the same time the full recognition of not-self, the selfishness of self is overcome. In the absence of selfishness, compassion naturally arises.

In this way wisdom and compassion are intimately interrelated in the realization of emptiness. The view of not-self, so far from inhibiting the generation of compassion, enables compassion both to arise and to be applied with skill and insight. From its own side, compassion informs wisdom by intensifying the experiential understanding of the interdependence of all relative selves, of all sentient beings; and of their ultimate equality and oneness in the unconditioned Buddha-Nature.

COMPARATIVE COMMENT

In both the Christian and Buddhist goals three immediately noticeable similarities present themselves: there is need of an initial act of will, there is an imperative to deal with the carnal or mundane self, and there is an aspiration towards selfless Wisdom-Love or Wisdom-Compassion.

For the Christian, the initial act of will comes from the side of God, who lovingly wills that all people should be reconciled to himself in Christ. The act of will on the believer's part (that of submitting the personal will to the will of God in Christ) is always a response to the Father's love. And, actually, the Christian cannot make the initial act of will without being drawn by God, without God's Grace. For God is the initiator and finisher of the Christian's spiritual walk, and this is an obvious source of comfort and confidence for the believer on the path.

Some Christians believe that only those predestined by God for salvation are able to make the initial act of will; others believe that the person is able to come to God by his own initiative and free will. More to the point is the conclusion that no person would be able to turn to God if the capacity to turn to God were not inbuilt in people by God, their Creator.

The Buddhist believes that he is ready to make the initial act of will (the will to Enlightenment) on account of the karma he has himself accumulated. Over countless lifetimes he has acquired the wholesome karma which now enables his ordinary mind to see the truth and benefits of Dharma. A good deal of his confidence on the path is due to this self-view. He knows that he is ready to walk the path, or else he would not have come to it. So far from surrendering or abandoning his will, he can rely on his karmically prepared volition to confirm him on the path. Yet he knows that his will must be purified by spiritual practice because it will not escape its conditioned nature until the direct realization of emptiness is attained. So there is a need to submit his will to the example, wisdom-energy and Ultimate Truth of the Buddha, Dharma and Sangha.

For Buddhists and Christians alike, the central problem on the spiritual path is the problem of self. To be sure, the assessments of self, of the problems posed by self, and of the solution to the problem of self are very differently stated. For the Christian the self is a corrupt entity which can only be removed by 'death.' For the Buddhist it is a set of interdependent factors giving rise to something which only appears to be a self, and which has become corrupted by the delusion that it actually is what it appears to itself to be.

For the Christian, then, the removal of the problem of self amounts to a 'putting to death' of those central aspects of self which are unsubmitted to God's will, so that God in Christ can be revealed in the person. The

Buddhist, however, must remove the mistaken sense of a concrete self so that the interdependent processes which are mistaken for the self-entity can become the medium of expression for the Unconditioned Not-Self. It seems impossible that these two views can not have something to teach each other. Though they may be doctrinally incompatable, they both ring true intuitively.

It is the same with Wisdom-Love and Wisdom-Compassion. For the Christian they are found by identification with the person of Christ. The Buddhist must discover them by awakening the Buddha-Nature within his deep mind. In a parallel way, Christ is also to be found in the 'heart' of the believer, and the Kingdom of Heaven is 'within you.' There may be a way here for the Buddhist to arrive at a better understanding of Christ and to discover his own position in relation to the principle of an indwelling Christ. And for the Christian there may be a way to better understand how Jesus lives within and informs him inwardly.

CHRISTIAN PERSEVERANCE

The path to Christlikeness is likened in the Scriptures to the growth of the person from infancy to adulthood. There are two differing but complementary ways in which Christians can view the process of spiritual growth.

In the one view the person is actually being transformed from stage to stage by cooperating with the inner working of the indwelling Christ. The believer is working actively in submission to the guiding energy of the Christ within. The other view implies a more passive role on the believer's part: he is simply submitting to the unfolding expression of Christ in him. So long as he is passively submitted, expectant, faithful, Christ's living spirit will be actuated and manifested in and through him. In this view the believer's own exertions can only ever be an obstruction to the actuation of the inner Christ.

Whichever of these two views the believer holds, neither greatly influences or alters what the believer does: they are not much more than alternative interpretations of the same dynamic. But they have a bearing on the believer's view of self and of Christ, and on the value which a believer places on his own effort.

The first principle in both cases, that of active cooperation with, and that of passive submission to the Christ within, is perseverance. 'Those who persevere to the end will be saved.' The believer is called to persevere at each stage of growth and to stand firm in it. This is a sure indication that the path to Christlikeness is neither easy nor short. It is beset by difficulties and dangers. It is dogged by doubt, weakness, failure and fear. It is clouded by patches of ignorance and discouragement, and made dry by periods of drought when Christ seems to have departed from the heart. There may be harrowing struggles with spiritual evil. And there are times of despair.

Therefore, however much the believer may put his trust in being justified by his faith in Christ alone, he will not attain to Christlikeness without perseverance. Yet his perseverance is not generated by his own strength: he is being upheld by Christ. For he is 'in Christ' just as Christ is 'in him.' He abides in Christ and Christ in him. He rests in Christ while Christ works in him by the Holy Spirit, but he also works in Christ to make manifest the work of Christ in him. In this relationship of spiritual labour the believer perseveres. Otherwise he cannot reach the goal.

BUDDHIST DETERMINATION

The most easily intelligible and accessible model of the Buddhist Path is the graduated path of the bodhisattva. In any case, even if Enlightenment occurs instantaneously, there is still a gradual preparatory ascent to the moment of Enlightenment, just as there is a graduated acquisition of Wisdom-Compassion.

The Buddhist Path is one of activity and conformity. The practitioner acts with determination and effort to arrive at the attainment of his goal. At the same time he works to conform himself, and is spontaneously conformed, to the degree of insight which he has gained at any stage of the Path. His conduct in body, speech and mind are conformed to the achievement of a corresponding spiritual view.

The Buddhist practitioner does not submit himself to a Divinity, nor even to the Buddha. He submits himself only to the Truth of Dharma insofar as he is able to experience it for himself, and insofar as he has a genuine trust in those truths not yet made real in his own experience. To these he submits as a patient to a physician.

Certainly the practitioner will not get far without perseverance or strong determination. Buddhist practice requires sustained effort of mind, especially in the period before transcendent insights and energies arise spontaneously in the mental domain. Study and meditation require mental clarity and concentration. Body, speech and mind must be subjected to ongoing mindfulness, and must often be restrained from non-virtuous expression.

There are many obstacles to be overcome. There are doubt, weakness and failure. Like the Christian believer, the Buddhist practitioner also has to contend with negative spiritual energies, habitual ignorance, and despair. All that comes across his path, whether good, bad or indifferent, must be met with an acceptance qualified by equanimity. But he is helped to persevere by the 'hook of Dharma': the strong and deep attraction exercised on his mind by the truth and beauty of the Buddha's Dharma, the power of whose appeal is related to his wholesome karma; that wholesome condition of mind which binds him to Truth.

A NOTE ON THE STAGES OF THE PATH

Before moving on to describe the Christian and Buddhist Paths, we must make some a priori observations:

In this section we are dealing with the path which the believer and the practitioner must walk as human beings in the relative, mundane realm. For Christians there are paths to traverse when the human body has been laid aside in death. Some believe in the purifying path of purgatory. Most believe in the path between physical death and the resurrection of the body. All believe in the path of final judgement, when the 'sheep will be separated from the goats.' All believe in the path that leads to final and complete union with God in his Kingdom.

For Buddhists, too, there are paths after physical death. There is the path between death and rebirth into one of the samsaric realms. Tibetan Buddhists believe in the path of the *bardo*, on which liberation from cyclic existence can be achieved in the intermediate stages between death and rebirth. There is the path of entering into the Buddha's Nirvana, and the Bodhisattva's path of delaying entrance into Nirvana in order to work for the liberation of sentient beings. So we need to differentiate between these paths and the spiritual paths of human beings still in the world.

In setting out the stages of the Path we must remain aware that we are dealing with a construct, an ideal that often baffles practice, because a Way of the Spirit (or of Unconditioned Mind) is not bound by our constructs, and people on these Paths do not regularly conform in their practice to our regulated stages. Just as the Spirit of God in Christ can transform the believer in an instant, so Supreme Enlightenment can arrive in a flash. And people can advance more rapidly than our constructs permit, or they may never develop beyond the earliest stage. These are matters of capacity, of grace, or of karma.

Still, in here describing the stages of the Christian and Buddhist Paths, we are hopefully reflecting the general norm of aspiration, and the stages of that aspiration to which most Christians and Buddhists can relate through their own experience and spiritual expectations.

We must mention also the case of those Christians and Buddhists who are born into their religions. Their path may be a little different from that of people who, whatever their stage of life, have made a conscious choice for their spiritual way. Still, we proceed on the assumption that even people who are born and raised to a religious tradition eventually make a conscious, personal assent to devote themselves to its precepts.

We must also consider the difference between the 'religious' and the laity; those who practice within an institution such as a religious house, a monastery or a nunnery, or those whose lives are especially devoted to religion by their vocation, and those who have to practise their spirituality in the midst of worldly distractions and struggles. The stages of the paths described here are those which, in the highest traditions of Christianity and Buddhism, apply to both.

STAGES OF THE CHRISTIAN PATH

The stages of the Christian Path as set out here are not necessarily sequential. There may be overlap or simultaneity of some stages, regression from higher to lower stages, or even being stuck for a lifetime at one particular stage. Spiritual growth is a living path, and life is always much more unpredictable than system. To a large extent the systematization of spiritual development and experience is mere convenience: it hopes to express in an ordered way that which transcends order. Describing the path is different to walking it. The best hope must be that the description authentically conveys the sense of what walking the path is like.

The Christian model used here assumes that baptism represents an objectively accomplished fact which must then be subjectively actuated in the life of the individual Christian. At baptism the believer accepts that he is about to die to self in Christ, understands the meaning of this death, is put to death by immersion in water, is dead beneath the water, and rises from it resurrected to new life in Christ.

From an absolute vantage point, 'in heavenly realms' or 'in the Mind of God', all this is accomplished in the single act of baptism. But it remains to be manifested as an unfolding process of actuation in the relative life of the believer. He progresses gradually to realize in his own experience what is already accomplished as objective truth.

The stages of the Christian Path outlined here follow this pattern. They are divided into five developmental phases, each constituting an aspect of progress within the total Path. They are paths within a larger Path. They are: Renewal, Awareness, Dying, Death, and Resurrection.

FIRST STAGE: THE PATH OF RENEWAL

The Path of Renewal has actually begun before the baptism of the new believer takes place. As a catechumen (one being prepared for baptism), the new believer has become familiar with the basic teachings and has been given some instruction about the Path. He has also experienced the assurance of knowing that he is being drawn by God's Grace to a new life in Christ. He knows that he is loved by God.

At baptism his sins have been forgiven, his carnal self has been buried, and he has risen from the water as a new creation in Christ. The carnal mind is dead; the spirit is alive. For the newly baptized believer, however, these are statements of objective truth, mostly unconfirmed in subjective experience. Even though, in the first flush of renewal, he may have a strong sense of his newness, the habits of ordinary human experience soon assail the edified state. For renewal is a process in which the 'flesh struggles against the spirit.'

The flesh (the ordinary or carnal self) does not want to die. It does not want to abandon its desires and its self-centred appreciation of the worldly life. Even though, from the side of Spirit, the carnal person has already died in baptism, the flesh refuses to acknowledge this. It does not know what the spirit knows. So it has to be brought to know. This is the essence of the Path of Renewal.

On it the carnal mind will come to know and accept that it has been consigned to death, but will not yet die. Or, considered more profoundly; the carnal mind will be brought to realize that it has always been 'dead.' Its 'life' has never been more than a pseudo-life, an ultra-relative substitute for what life, in the spiritual sense, actually is. From this perspective its having been put to death in baptism is really a way of saying that, in objective truth, the pseudo-life of the carnal mind is seen for what it really is. At baptism, then, objective truth pronounces the flesh to be a dead thing.

The carnal mind is not relying on its own capacity to know these truths. It is not relying on its ordinary capacities which are able to accept, for instance, the fact of eventual physical death as inevitable in a relative realm. To such relative events the ordinary relative mind can directly relate. But, while it can know and accept spiritual inevitabilities conceptually, it cannot know them directly. It cannot trust in the fact of spiritual death as it does in that of physical death. So its direct knowledge and acceptance of self-death in Christ are being imparted by the indwelling Christ. And it is struggling against this imparted truth. It is suffering, angry and anxious.

Yet, while the carnal (or ordinary) mind is suffering, the spirit (or deep mind) is already tasting the consolations of the indwelling Christ. The sense of an awakening inner peace, joy, purity and security presents itself to the consciousness, even as the flesh suffers and struggles. Faith, hope and love are being awakened by the Spirit of Christ.

But they are at the same time being assailed by the protests of the carnal mind as it presents to consciousness its own habitual pleasures, achievements, desires, and so forth, in competition with the new and faintly experienced spiritual consolations. Doubt and anxiety arise, and with them temptations.

Doubts at this stage take on many forms, but they are always questions. Is the sense of consolation only imaginary? Is spiritual peace worth the sacrifice of worldly gratification? Is it possible to enjoy life at all without the full expression of the carnal mind? Is there not some way of compromise?

Essentially, though, these kinds of doubt have their root in the one fundamental Doubt: Is submission to Christ more rewarding than submission to carnality? For at this stage the believer is still far from unselfish service to Christ.

Anxieties, too, are self-related: What do I stand to lose in this transaction with the Divine? How will my mundane affairs be affected? What will other people think of me? But the root anxiety is fear of the loss of the carnal self. After all, it has been the only expression of self hitherto known to the believer.

Temptations are as various as human potential for self-gratification can be. The new believer will be faced by any and all of these. Sins of commission and omission, of body, speech and mind, will tempt the spiritual infant. And these temptations will extend to the urge to reject Christ himself. This is how frantic, in the face of its own extinction, the carnal mind can be.

In addition to mental doubts, anxieties and temptations, the neophyte must contend with the destructive distractions and negative demands posed by the external world, facing and resisting these at every turn as they arise moment by moment from the dynamics of the world and the activities of others. The believer is tempted from within and from without.

And there are spiritual forces of evil which attack the mind and circumstances of the believer. The principles and energies of spiritual evil are present in the world, in others, and in the believer's own flesh. They bring fear, bitterness, hatred, malice and a host of other negative energies into the struggle.

Of course, the believer has always been in this struggle. It is part of being human. But the carnal mind has always known how to rationalize and deny its errors, how to compromise with and how to justify itself. Now, in the grip of God's Grace and with the new sense of the Presence of the indwelling Christ, these rationalizations and compromises cannot be sustained. Their deceitfulness is revealed by the Holy Spirit. So the struggle is intensified. It is taking place now in the Light of Christ, and nothing can be hidden. The words of Paul the Apostle are now easy to grasp: 'Wretched man that I am! Who will save me from this body of death?'

The answer is: Jesus.

The qualities needed to stand in the struggle, and, if having fallen, to get up again, are all to be found in Christ. They are not qualities of the ordinary mind, but of the spirit. Qualities such as faith, hope, love, patience and fortitude are present in the ordinary mind, but only in a limited and conditioned mode. In the indwelling Christ they are pure, unconditioned and without limit. Therefore the new believer on the Path of Renewal must direct his mind as often and even as continuously as possible to mindfulness of his indwelling Lord.

Such mindfulness means ongoing communion with the Lord in the inner person. It may take the form of verbalized prayer, but should also be a simple abiding in his presence, as though sitting quietly in the presence of someone completely trustworthy. From time to time one might speak,

The Paths and the Goals

making known one's fears or needs. But there should also be openness to receive what the Lord is saying. This is the way of inner communion.

The neophyte also gains conceptual insight into the Mind of Christ by studying the Scriptures and other Christian writings, and by receiving teaching. These insights reinforce trust and faith in Christ and remove ignorance from the ordinary mind. The believer is able to contemplate the person of Jesus more meaningfully, and contemplation serves to increase mindfulness. At the same time, mindfulness of the indwelling Christ imbues the conceptual insights with a spiritual energy.

The precepts taught by Christ are also part of the weaponry in the struggle against the flesh. They displace worldly precepts, especially when they have been energized by communion with the Christ within. Their beauty and truth become more apparent and more intensely appealing. And once they have been energized, the carnal mind, although it may continue to resist them, can no longer simply refute them.

With persevering study, and by referring conceptual insight to the energizing Presence of the indwelling Christ, the precepts and teachings of Jesus gradually become spontaneously active in the believer's mind. They begin to work transformatively, and this process is reinforced by constant prayer, contemplation and inward communion.

A further and vital help is meeting in fellowship with the body of believers. In sharing teaching and experience with mature believers, the neophyte is comforted and encouraged. The sharing of the sacraments of the Holy Eucharist and Communion serves to confirm the believer in knowledge and in the sense of Christ's presence in the heart. And there is benefit in the spiritual energy present in the gathering of believers.

Through renewing his mind by these methods, with sincerity and perseverance, the believer becomes increasingly able to submit his personal will, habits of mind and human instinct to the informing and transforming power of the indwelling Christ. Though there will be failures, these will decrease if the believer perseveres.

But if there is failure, if the believer falls into sin, there is grace and forgiveness in Christ to help him up again. This grace is unmerited favour given the believer by God who sees the believer 'in Christ' and bestows on him the favour and blessing gained on his behalf by Jesus' meritorious work. Because of Christ's saving work the believer is not condemned, so long as he 'walks after the spirit' and not 'after the flesh.' God will not condemn the person who desires to follow Christ but stumbles an account of the carnal nature which has not yet realized its death in Christ.

Therefore, however discouraged he may be by his imperfect walk, the believer must get up every time he has fallen. He has fallen because of his imperfect communion with the indwelling Lord and because of his imperfect submission to the Spirit. Getting up again, he must restore communion and make an act of submission as he asks and receives forgiveness. Regaining his footing, he must be resolved not to sin again, trusting not in his own carnal strength (which is bound to fail him), but in Christ. Then he must walk on.

Just as he understands how God in Christ is indwelling him, the believer also has to understand how he is situated in God in Christ. For God is present not only in the believer's spirit but is also the Divine Milieu in whom all that exists has its being. All that exists proceeds from and is sustained in existence by God. There is nothing and no one beyond the reach of the power and love of God. To understand reality in this way is to see that nothing is random or meaningless. Everything is suffused by the wisdom and love of God.

The believer is situated in God in a special way. He is 'in Christ.' This means that he is included in Christ as Saviour and in Christ as Word of God, in Christ as Son of God and in Christ as Second Person of the Trinity. Thus he is especially close to the Father 'in Christ.'

Seeing how all things exist in God and are sustained by God, and how the Christian dwells in God in a special way, and is indwelt by God in Christ, the believer understands how he must relate to the world and to others in the world. He must love the world, even though it is a fallen world. But he must love the world as God loves it, and not as the carnal mind does.

The carnal mind's love of the world and of its beings, especially human beings, is an exploitative, self-serving love. God's love for the world is a redeeming love. So the believer should love the world and its creatures with a love that is spiritually concerned, and which sees the world as sustained in God. He should work to benefit the world, should pray for its redemption, endure patiently in it, and love and forgive others. For he, like Christ, is in but not of the world. He is 'of Christ in the world.' Therefore he should live to reveal Christ in the world in body, speech and mind.

The believer on the Path of Renewal should be familiar with and conformed in mind to the doctrines of his group. At this stage he is not

The Paths and the Goals

yet set free to practise authentically outside of the conceptual security of doctrine. He needs it as guidance, as a foothold, and as a mental refuge. It is still an aid to faith and understanding even though, at a later stage, it may become an obstacle.

By all these means the believer's carnal thoughts, emotions, personal volition, mental habits and instincts are being gradually conformed to the Mind of Christ. Their ordinary nature and modes of expression are being lifted to the spiritual level.

Thoughts, as they occur, are being referred to and 'taken captive' for Christ. Positive emotions are being spiritually energized and negative emotions surrendered to Christ. The personal will, habits of mind and instincts are more frequently and sustainedly examined in the Mind of Christ, whose insights the believer is gradually acquiring. Selfishness and harmfulness are being seen for what they are. The carnal mind is being trained to know and accept that it is being inevitably consigned to death in Christ.

When the Path of Renewal has been accomplished, the believer must be stabilized on it, or else he may regress. Stabilization comes by sustained practice in conditions both favourable and adverse. By the time of accomplishment, the insight that 'all things (including adverse things) work to the benefit of those who love God and are called according to his purposes' should be for the believer a spontaneous, living experience. For, if he has come to know this as a heart-truth, he will know both how to stand, and how to get up again if he falls.

One can see how many Christians can spend the whole of their earthly life on the Path of Renewal. Others do not even aspire to its level of practice. Yet others become discouraged and fall away completely. But those who accomplish it are being authentically 'transformed by the renewal of their minds.' Once stabilized on this path, the Christian seeking Christlikeness will be drawn by the Holy Spirit to the next stage.

SECOND STAGE: THE PATH OF AWARENESS

The Path of awareness is characterized by intense, continuous and spontaneous awareness of the indwelling Christ, which, for the sake of precision, can be defined as: awareness of God in Christ in the Holy Spirit, abiding in the deep mind or spirit of the believer.

This is the way of baptism in the Holy Spirit. It may come suddenly, overwhelmingly and dramatically, as it did to the apostles, and as it continues to come to many believers today. But it may also be experienced as a quiet, steadily growing sense of the spontaneous inner Presence of Christ.

The believer no longer has to awaken in himself by various methods, including prayer, contemplation, and study of the scriptures, the sense of the indwelling Lord. This does not mean that the believer now neglects these practices. But now, rather than being used to rouse or to stabilize the sense of inner Presence, they are carried out in the spontaneously arising awareness of Christ 'in the heart and mind.'

This new intensity of inner presence has come about because the believer no longer perceives it through the obscuring veil of the carnal mind. He no longer identifies himself with the carnal mind as being all that he is able to be. He has been loosened from this delusion by his experience on the Path of Renewal where, subjected to the alternating predominance of either the flesh or the Mind of Christ, he has tasted periods of liberation from carnal thinking.

But, at the same time, and owing to the same alternating experience, he does not perceive himself as being fully identified with the inner Christ either. He experiences his intrinsic awareness (or 'pure mind') as being something other than either the carnal mind or the indwelling Mind of Christ, although he senses its closeness to Christ. Thus, through feeling himself identical with neither the carnal mind nor with the Mind of Christ, his intrinsic awareness is able to observe both mindstates objectively.

At the same time, because of the intense and spontaneously arising sense of the indwelling Christ, the believer is more lucidly mindful of the activities of the carnal mind. They are being exposed and observed in the Light of Christ, in which the believer is able to see how the carnal mind arises and functions, and what its nature is. In this same Light, he is able to see the separation between his carnal mind and his intrinsic awareness, no longer wrongly perceiving the latter to be indentical with the former. Because of this realization, his intrinsic awareness is able to perceive the inner Christ directly, no longer obscured by the sense that it is identical with the carnal mind.

His intrinsic awareness now having been liberated from this mis-identification with the carnal mind, and not yet having been identified with the inner Mind of Christ, the believer is able to use his newly liberated 'pure mind' to simultaneously sense and distinguish between the spontaneously arising activity of the inner Lord and the conditionally arising activity of the carnal mind. And, having 'isolated' his intrinsic awareness, he can use it to concentrate either on the inner Christ or on the carnal mind.

When he concentrates steadily on the presence of the inner Christ, the sense of Presence is intensified. But even when distracted from such direct concentration, he remains aware, at a deeper mental level, of the abiding Presence. Christ is now alive within him outside of his own efforts to generate the sense of that life.

And Christ is spontaneously active in his spirit, communing with, teaching and transforming the inner person. And again, whether or not he concentrates on it, the activity is continuously sensed, like a light burden or an easy yoke.

Concentrating on the carnal mind while the sense of the inner Christ remains spontaneously present, the believer sees the carnal mind in the Light of Christ. He sees how it arises conditionally: arising only on condition that he looks steadfastly away from the inner Christ, and deliberately tries not to sense the inner Presence.

As soon as the believer deliberately looks away from Christ, those habits of mind and aspects of the personal will and instinct which have not yet been spiritualized by Christ (owing to an as yet incomplete submission to the inner Christ, because of not yet having died to self) give rise to a strong sense of the carnal mind's presence. This is what is meant by the conditional nature of the carnal mind's arising. It cannot arise of itself. It can present itself only in dependence on the activity of unrenewed (or unsubmitted) aspects of the ordinary mind.

But even when the believer allows the carnal mind to present itself, the presence of the inner Christ continues to arise spontaneously in his spirit. It, unlike the carnal mind, arises by its own power. It can obviously not be arising in dependence on unrenewed aspects of the ordinary mind. Nor can it be arising from those aspects which are renewed or submitted, because the Christ-Mind which is renewing the ordinary mind and bringing it into submission to itself cannot arise from the ordinary mind which is being renewed and submitted by it. Or else the ordinary mind would absurdly have to be renewed and submitted by the Christ-Mind before the Christ-Mind has become present in the believer at all. So the Mind of Christ, arising independently of any aspect of the ordinary mind, must be arising spontaneously.

Seeing how the carnal mind arises from the as yet incompletely renewed habits of mind and instinct, the believer sees also that carnal activity arises from an as yet incompletely submitted personal will. So the believer is able to recognize the conditional nature of carnal mind and activity. If unrenewed habits of mind and untransformed instinct were no longer functioning, the carnal mind would no longer present itself to his intrinsic awareness. Likewise, if his will were not still partially unsubmitted to Christ, no carnal activity could occur.

And, at this stage, the spontaneously arising presence and activity of the Christ-Mind are still, in one fundamental sense, conditional. They continue to arise spontaneously only because the believer's initial act of assent to Christ has been sustained. If it were to be withdrawn, as it still can be on the Path of Awareness, the believer would again become fully submitted to the carnal mind, and the presence and activity of the inner Christ would cease.

This is not to say that the Christ-Mind arises in dependence on the believer's sustained voluntary assent in the same way that flames arise in dependence on fuel. Human assent cannot bring the inner Christ into existence. Christ exists eternally, in and of himself. But the sustained act of voluntary assent allows the eternal, self-existent Christ to become manifest in the believer's subjective experience. Thus, if the assent is withdrawn, the experiential communion will cease, and the carnal dynamic will resume.

Severe spiritual regression can occur on the Path of Awareness because the carnal mind, having conditionally accepted that it has been consigned to death in Christ, has not yet actually died. Habits of mind are not yet fully renewed. Human instinct is not yet fully transformed. The personal will is not yet fully submitted. The believer might still regress to the early phase of the Path of Renewal or even fall away completely, doing extreme damage to his spiritual practice and leaving him in deep sorrow.

The most damaging risk on the Path of Awareness is the temptation simply to abide in the presence of the Christ-Mind as though this state were the highest point of spiritual attainment; to enjoy the consolations of the inner Presence without cooperating with Christ's inner activity. In order to avoid this passivity the believer should cultivate acute awareness of the inner spiritual activity, which is always drawing him towards higher ground, while abiding peacefully in the Christ-Mind. For the inner

Presence is not a final consolation. It is an encouragement to ever-increasing growth and deepening of communion.

If the believer, understanding these things, 'girds up his loins,' the accomplishments of the Path of Awareness will be brought to completion. Habits of mind will increasingly be renewed and spiritualized, worldly instinct will become more conformed to the love-instinct of the Christ-Mind, and the personal will to the will of God in Christ. Through all this the joy of Christ will sustain him.

Development of Self-View on the Path of Awareness

The basis for progress gained on the Path of Awareness consists in the believer having experienced his inner person as made up of three distinct 'minds': the mind of intrinsic awareness, of the inner Christ, and of the flesh.

Through his insight into how these minds (or mindstates) arise, he understands, firstly, that the carnal mind, arising conditionally, has no life in itself. He now knows, too, that his existence is not identical with that of the carnal mind, or else he could not observe the carnal mind by means of the intrinsic awareness. So, not being himself the carnal mind, he can be liberated from it without being annihilated. For, the carnal mind having been put to death in Christ, the believer's essential mind-life, the intrinsic awareness, will remain alive.

He sees that the intrinsic awareness is spontaneously present and active. Since it can objectify and observe the motions of his habits of mind, instinct and personal will as processes other than itself, it is not identifiable with them. It is controlling them and working to bring them to the inner Christ for renewal. If it were arising from their activity, it could be extinguished by an act of will.

So the intrinsic awareness, like the Christ-Mind, is spontaneouly present and active. It is the spontaneouly present eternal principle of his mind; the essential mental energy which can eventually be 'hidden in Christ' and infused by the Christ-Mind with the living energy of the Divine.

Although, at this stage, he continues to perceive three distinct 'minds' within his mental continuum, he knows that they are part of one and the same mental process, which is gradually unfolding towards his spiritual liberation.

The carnal mind, seeing what the intrinsic awareness sees about it in the Light of the indwelling Christ, knows that it has no life in itself. Having accepted that it must be consigned to death, it now realizes that its death is an inevitability, for, knowing how it arises conditionally, it knows, too, that it can have no claim to authentic life. It can only continue to exist as a coarse imitation of authentic personal life.

The intrinsic awareness, now clearly seeing its own spontaneous life, knows that it is the eternally living principle in the believer's mental continuum. It sees how, in its own pure nature, it is utterly other than the carnal mind, for it shares in the pure spontaneous life of the Christ-Mind. For its final liberation it needs only to be intimately fused with the spiritual Life-Energy of the indwelling Christ.

Being lucidly aware of all these things, the believer nearing the end of the Path of Awareness prepares himself, with clear insight, for the death of the carnal mind, and for fusing the intrinsic awareness with the Christ-Mind.

Knowing that it is still possible to fall away, the believer prepares himself with determination and single-mindedness. If he does not persevere single-mindedly the intrinsic awareness will lose lucidity and gradually relapse into ignorance of its true nature. Then, returned to ignorance, it must again identify itself with the carnal mind, allowing the flesh to rise again into pseudo-life. So the blessings of awareness must be used diligently for making progress, and its consolations enjoyed in the full realization that they do not represent the highest stage of Christian development.

Other Aspects of Growth

The lucid awareness and spontaneity of inner life attained on the Path of Awareness empower the believer to view and interact with the world at a spiritual level. Because he has been loosened from the direct influence of the carnal mind, the world can no longer tempt him directly. He sees the world through the Mind of Christ. Therefore his walk in the world is much purer, more loving, more peaceful, more detached.

He no longer strains himself to deal rightly with the world. The spontaneous arising of the Christ-Mind puts him at liberty to engage with it in spontaneous spirituality. Dealing with the world in holiness no longer demands the effort of the earlier stage. With spiritual spontaneity has come spiritual confidence. There is no need of striving to imitate Christ, for Christ is alive within him.

His dealings with others also reflect this spontaneous presence. As he views others through the Mind of Christ, the love of Christ goes effortlessly out to them. Knowing that the carnal mind of the other is not the other's essence, he loves and appeals to that in the other which is not the carnal mind. At the same time he sees how the other's suffering is caused by the carnal mind, and acts to illumine the other. And, knowing what the other really is, he loves the other in Christ and easily forgives transgressions.

Prayer, contemplation and communion with the inner Christ are unforced, flowing from the spontaneous to the spontaneous. The Scriptures yield their deeper revelations because they are studied in the Christ-Mind. The sacraments are vitalized and spiritually efficacious. In gathering with the fellowship of believers there is a deep sense of oneness in Christ, and in the Presence of Christ. Good works flow easily and evoke a sense of blessing. Virtue and purity are delightful; evil is detestable. Faith, hope and love arise effortlessly.

It is easy to understand why the believer would want to cling to the Path of Awareness and remain permanently on it. The whole mind is pacified: thoughts all turned to, and the emotions at rest, in Christ. The believer might think that he has attained all there is to attain.

Yet he should bear in mind, even as he enjoys these blessings, that he has not yet begun the process of dying, has not yet tasted death, and has not yet been resurrected in Christ. The consolations, insights and energies gained on this path have equipped him for the ensuing stages. They are not ends in themselves.

THIRD STAGE: THE PATH OF DYING

On the Path of Renewal the believer has undergone the initial struggle between flesh and spirit. If he has walked it with skill and perseverance, it will have led him to a stable surrender to Christ in which the carnal mind has accepted being consigned to death. But actual dying is still far off: there is still room for the flesh to manoeuvre and express itself. There is falling into carnality and getting up again.

On the Path of Awareness the carnal mind sees, by the Christ-enlightened intrinsic awareness, that it is a pseudo-life, and that its death is therefore inevitable. Still, it is not dead but dormant. It has opportunity to express itself only very rarely, if at all, because the intrinsic awareness is at peace in Christ. This phase is the 'Indian summer' of the Christian walk.

It is on the Path of Dying that the final and most severe battle takes place, and everything is brought to the fray. On this path the carnal mind is being led out to crucifixion. Although it has accepted being consigned to death in Christ, the process of dying is now upon it, and accepting death in reality is quite different from accepting it in principle. The carnal mind usually does not go quietly to the cross. It is desperate to avoid death. In the first two stages it has been 'imprisoned' and held in relative comfort to await its execution. Now its time has come. Owing to the lucid awareness attained on the second stage, the carnal mind now sees itself in the full Light of Christ. It knows there can be no compromise: it is condemned.

It will struggle and protest in various ways, bringing its pride, fear, selfishness and cunning to bear. It will try to prove to the intrinsic awareness that it is the believer's only true and cherished self; that it should be spared, as Barabbas was spared, and that the Christ-Mind should die in its stead. For this is the essence of its struggle: it wants to live instead of Christ because it knows that it cannot remain alive in Christ.

It will remind the intrinsic awareness of its mundane achievements, its intellect, its capacity for pleasure, its strength—or whatever it considers to be its most desirable qualities. And it will appeal for pity, for love, for forgiveness. It will promise to reform, and it will rise up in anger to fight for its survival.

And the carnal mind does not stand alone. The principles and energies of evil, of untruth and delusion, are on the carnal mind's side. It is because of the carnal mind that evil can exist and work in the world. Therefore evil attacks on its behalf.

For the believer this is a period of intense confusion and upheaval. Until now, even in the blissful stage of Awareness, he has, at least in principle, retained the option to revert to the carnal mind. Confronted now with the permanent loss of that option, he is forced to make a final decision. If he chooses for the carnal mind at this stage, it is unlikely that he will regain the grace to return to Christ. But if he chooses for Christ, the self-serving capacities of the carnal mind will be lost forever.

At the same time, he is being attacked from every angle in his intrinsic awareness. The carnal mind is appealing to it and threatening it by turns. Spiritual evil is assailing him with doubt and fear. The flesh and the

The Paths and the Goals

world are winking at him. Through all these bewildering distractions the presence of the indwelling Christ is only dimly sensed.

For the believer everything now hinges on pride. Only pride can still prevent him from completely submitting his habits of mind, natural instinct and personal will to the Christ-Mind. Pride in its essence is precisely this: the refusal to submit. There may be any number of reasons urged by the carnal mind to press its right to survival: doubt, fear, loss of worldly gratifications, and so forth. All of these can be used to justify an act of non-submission, but only pride can carry it out.

If the believer were being called upon to submit to something he neither knows nor trusts, the refusal to submit would be an act of wisdom, underpinned by fear and doubt. But by this stage of the Christian Path the believer has come to know and trust the indwelling Christ. If he now refuses to submit, it can only be because he prefers to exercise his personal will by the self-serving principles of the carnal mind. His own interests are given preference over the purposes of God in Christ. And if the carnal mind can persuade the intrinsic awareness to adopt this preference, it can only be adopted in an attitude of pride.

The way forward is to gaze steadfastly on the indwelling Christ, and not to be distracted. By the use of various skilful methods the believer must never lose sight of Christ. He should refuse to empathize with and admit no appeal from the carnal mind. Through prayer and communion, study of scripture, sacrament, fellowship, and perseverance in virtue, the believer must remain concentrated on Christ.

Abiding steadfastly in Christ and contemplating the carnal mind through the wisdom of the Christ-Mind, the believer judges and condemns the carnal mind to death in Christ. At this point, although the carnal mind continues to protest, the intrinsic awareness ceases from struggle. It begins to merge with the indwelling Mind of Christ.

It is in this process of merging that the carnal mind is put to death by depriving it of its sources of pseudo-vitality. These sources, as we have seen, are the unsubmitted and unrenewed aspects of the believer's habits of mind, natural instinct and personal will. In the course of the preceding two paths these have been gradually given over to Christ for increasing sanctification. But these have been only preparatory phases whose purpose has been to increase faith and trust in Christ.

Now, on the Path of Dying, this developed faith-trust is being asked to surrender the carnal mind to death in Christ. And this implies, of course, that its sources of pseudo-life are also to be surrendered in a final way.

On the preceding paths, habits of mind have been 'taken captive for Christ'; deliberately on the Path of Renewal, and spontaneously on the Path of Awareness. Negative or sinful thoughts and feelings, when they have arisen in the mind, have been repeatedly referred to the sanctifying work of the Christ-Mind.

Now, on the Path of Dying, habits of mind are being submitted to Christ in a final sense: in the sense that negative thoughts and feelings will no longer arise at all. There will no longer be any negative thoughts or feelings to be taken captive for Christ. The believer is surrendering his right to allow them to arise at all.

In the same way, he is surrendering his right to live by the dictates of the natural instincts, including the survival-instinct. Whereas he has, on the preceding paths, more or less willingly and spontaneously submitted them to Christ, he has not surrendered the right to choose which would be submitted and which not. Now he relinquishes this right too.

The final and complete surrender of habits of mind and instinct is accomplished by means of the complete submission to Christ of the personal will. Until now the believer has not surrendered the will-to-exercise-his-will. At the most fundamental level he has retained the right to allow Christ to abide in him, and has thus, by implication, not abandoned the right to disallow the Presence by withdrawing his voluntary assent. He has retained the right to submit his will to Christ to the extent that he has been willing or able to do so. Now he surrenders the right to any exercise of will at all. In so doing, his innate awareness becomes completely submitted to the Christ-Mind.

So the sources of the carnal mind's pseudo-life are cut off. The fuel from which the fires of the flesh have always arisen has been given over to Christ. The carnal mind is extinguished in the Holy Spirit, like a doused flame.

Falling Away on the Path of Dying

The believer remains on the Path of Dying for as long as it takes him to accomplish the final surrender of his will. Until that happens, he retains the right to return to the carnal way of life by withdrawing the voluntary

The Paths and the Goals

assent (the initial act of will) by virtue of which Christ still abides in the inner person. He retains the right to live in this sort of spiritual danger and, for as long as he retains it, the Path of Dying cannot be brought to completion. The possibility of falling away therefore remains.

He may spend a very long time on this path. While he remains on it he stays in the struggle, which is its condition, until final surrender is accomplished. And, although the struggle on the Path of Dying bears a resemblance to the struggle on the Path of Renewal, it is not at all the same. On the Renewal Path the struggle takes place before the experience of lucidity and bliss gained on the Path of Awareness. It is essentially the struggle to discover Christ in the inner person. If the believer falls away at that early stage it is because he has not yet fully discovered Christ, and his failure is ascribable largely to ignorance.

Falling away on the Path of Dying, however, is a conscious rejection, through an act of pride, of the inner Christ whom the believer has come to know intimately on the Path of Awareness. Such clear-sighted rejection is much more harmful to spiritual development. It is so harmful that the believer will probably not be able to recover the energies and insights needed to begin the path again.

Yet, even if he does fall away at this late stage, there can be no justification for despair. With Christ all things are possible, and the love and saving power of Christ are boundless. As long as the believer retains the slightest sense of yearning for the inner Christ, there is still hope. Nevertheless, the believer on the Path of Dying, recognizing its dangers, should determine in faith to bring it to completion at the right time.

Stability on the Path.

In the struggle on the Path of Dying all experience is intensified, and even exaggerated. The mind in struggle is more intensely alert and aware, and more intensely exposed to the various stimuli or influences arising in the dynamic of struggle. Thoughts, emotions, instinct and will are all active in a heightened mode. The activity of the carnal mind, in particular, is more insistent because it is in a state of resistance to death.

Worldly temptations are therefore all the more appealing, and the believer may be repeatedly and abruptly shifted from a spiritual to a carnal view of the world: from loving it as Christ does to loving it as the flesh does.

The same rapid and confusing shifts may also occur in his interaction with others, especially other people. When he views the other in the carnal mode, he interacts with the carnal mind of the other. When he sees the other through the Christ-Mind, he knows the other in spirit, sees the non-carnal other, and loves it in Christ.

Obviously these shifts can be damaging: they can prevent completion of the Path of Dying. The remedy is the cultivation of calm stability. Although it is a mindstate difficult to cultivate in the midst of struggle, the believer has had good training on the Path of Renewal and has to a great extent achieved stability on the Path of Awareness. From the former he has learnt how to awaken the sense of the indwelling Christ; from the latter, how to abide in the spontaneously arising Presence. These are invaluable lessons because the calm stability needed now is only to be discovered in the presence of Christ.

In this calm stability the believer can completely surrender his mental habits, instincts and personal will to Christ. As he does so his intrinsic awareness merges with the Christ-Mind. He is being 'buried' or 'hidden' in Christ. At this point the Path of Death commences.

FOURTH STAGE: THE PATH OF DEATH

It may seem strange at first to speak of a path rather than of a state of death because death seems to imply a final stasis. The spiritual mind knows, however, that death, like dying, is a process leading to rebirth or resurrection.

Although the Path of Death involves suffering and struggle, as all spiritual paths do, there is no possibility of regression or falling away on the authentic Path of Death because, at this stage, the carnal mind is no longer alive. The believer's intrinsic awareness is one with the Christ-Mind. His 'eye is single.'

Before explaining what this 'singleness' means, we should clarify what distinguishes the authentic Path of Death from its inauthentic forms. For the believer can deceive himself into thinking that he is on the Path of Death when he actually is not. So we must be clear about what specifically qualifies the authentic path.

The most obvious factor is that the carnal mind is no longer active. This being the case, the believer can no longer be tempted to sin. He cannot regress because the indwelling Christ is in control of his will to exercise his will. For this latter reason, he cannot even move forward on the Path of Death by his own volition. He is completely in the hands of Christ.

From this passivity in Christ he derives his 'singleness' of vision. He can no longer see as the carnal mind sees. He no longer interprets experience by its provisional principles. His perception of the nature of all things; of Truth, of the world, of himself and the other, can no longer be distorted by the self-interest and ignorance of the flesh. All that he sees is seen in the Mind of Christ: his eye is single. The duality between carnality and spirituality has been removed.

Purification

But even at this point the believer has not yet been perfected in Christ. He has died in Christ but has not yet been resurrected. Before he can be resurrected in Christ he must 'descend to the dead', as Jesus did. He must taste death in order to be finally purified in death.

The habits of mind, instinct, and personal will, which have been completely surrendered to Christ on the Path of Dying, must now be purified in Christ. Having been baptized in water and in the Holy Spirit, the believer must now be baptized 'with fire.' Fire is the archetypal symbol of purification. The believer is to be 'refined like gold.'

On the Path of Dying the carnal mind has been extinguished in Christ. It has been extinguished because there is no other way of dealing with it: it cannot be purified in Christ. Anything which depends for its existence on impure factors can ipso facto never be purified by any means. Once the impure factors which give rise to the carnal mind have been purified, the carnal mind must cease to exist. And this is exactly what has been accomplished.

What remains to be purified are the accretions of carnality in the record of the believer's life, the marks of the sins of body, speech and mind committed in the lifetime before the end of the Path of Dying. Although these have been forgiven in Christ, their 'traces' remain.

The results of the believer's erstwhile carnality are traceable in every sphere. They have marked those people whom he has harmed in one way or another. They have changed numerous sequences of events for the worse. They have left their mark on the world in general, and on the interdependent human community as a whole. They have given to evil a place in the world, and have reached into spiritual domains. These marks of sin are everywhere. No amount of restitution can eradicate them, even from the intrinsic awareness of the believer.

Precisely because the intrinsic awareness is now merged with the Christ-Mind, it undergoes this final purification. It has merged, we might say, with the purifying fire of Christ. The believer has been forgiven, but forgiveness is not purification. Indeed, it is only because he has been forgiven that the believer's intrinsic awareness can now be purified in Christ; otherwise it would be condemned.

As the precursor of purification, forgiveness has placed the believer in a state of grace, the only condition in which the believer is protected from judgement by the overwhelmingly purifying Presence of God. The intrinsic awareness cannot be dealt with by extinguishing it, as in the case of the carnal mind. Unlike the carnal mind, it does not depend for its arising on a set of impure factors. Nor is it impure in itself. Yet it must be cleansed of its history of association with the flesh.

This history elicits in the believer an abiding sense of regret, remorse and unworthiness. A similar sense experienced on the early paths by the immature believer is often put away out of sight, for he mistakes forgiveness for purification and convinces himself by any means that forgiveness in Christ is also cleansing in Christ. But the mature believer, having attained the end of the Path of Dying, sees himself as Christ sees him; as prepared by grace to 'descend to the dead' and be finally cleansed of every sinful mark.

The Path of Death is therefore a path of twofold suffering: on the one hand the believer suffers under the sense of his own unworthiness and uncleanness; on the other he suffers in the purifying fire of death in Christ.

His intrinsic awareness, merged with the Christ-Mind (or, with the intrinsic awareness of Christ, pure in its voidness of all historical sin), sees in the clear Light of Christ the marks of his past sinful activity, knows his unworthiness, and is torn by doubt. This is not the sinful doubt of the carnal mind which encourages doubts for its own selfish ends. It is the authentic agony of the intrinsic awareness, doubting its worthiness to be saved.

And this honest doubt is intensified because the Christ-Mind, until this point experienced as a Loving Presence, is now perceived in its purifying function, as a severe and painful energy. In the accompanying sense of desolation, the 'dark night of the soul', the believer may feel himself abandoned by his God, and thus confirmed in his unworthiness.

The Paths and the Goals

'These doubts, proper to the Path of Death, cannot, however, cause him to regress or to fall away. The carnal mind having been extinguished and the intrinsic awareness merged with the Mind of Christ, nothing can separate him from Christ. His sense of separation is only an affective aspect of the purifying process. His actual inseparability from Christ is made abundantly clear in that the believer, no matter how terrible his suffering and doubt on the Path of Death, does not abandon the Lord. This is also what distinguishes the authentic Path of Death from episodes resembling it. No believer on the authentic Path of Death can ever fall away or regress into sinfulness.

Completion

The Path of Death is completed when the work of purification in Christ is accomplished, and the cleansing Christ-Fire is again experienced as the Christ-Love. The believer rises from the dead into a fulfilled experience and vision of God in Christ in the Holy Spirit. He is now fully formed and passes on to the Path of Resurrection.

FIFTH STAGE: THE PATH OF RESURRECTION

On the Path of Resurrection 'all things have become new.' The believer's view of himself, others, and the world, is in full accord with the Christ-Mind. His vision is no longer in any way distorted by traces of impurity in the intrinsic awareness. Seeing himself fully formed in Christ, he lives and acts boldly in the spontaneous energy of the Spirit. He no longer condemns himself at any point, abiding in open friendship with the Divine. He has become a son of God born from above; a brother of Christ.

He therefore moves in the world with sureness and authority. Relying on the life, strength and wisdom of the indwelling Christ, he conducts himself with unself-conscious humility, yet with power. He walks in the world as Christ walked in it; unshakeable. And though life in the world may touch him with suffering, he can no longer be overcome.

He sees others as Christ sees him, not in the flesh, but in the spirit. He is beyond all respect of persons, judging and discerning only as Christ does. In dealing with people he is skilful, treating and counselling all according to their dispositions, capacities and needs. The love of Christ constrains him.

This fully formed believer, the Christlike person, is empowered in Christ. Because he does only what God in Christ reveals to him, he shares in the power of Christ. He has power to perform miracles, to heal, to speak a transforming word of faith to others. The gifts of the Spirit are fully entrusted to him by the One in whom he immoveably abides.

Besides living in the authority of Christ, he moves and acts in Christ's freedom. He is not bound by forms of doctrine, practice and even conduct. In Christ he is liberated from all legalism. His only guiding force is the Wisdom-Love of Christ in whom he has been resurrected. To him the words of Jesus to Nicodemus apply: 'The wind blows where it will. You hear its sound, but know neither where it is coming from nor where it is going to. That is how it is with all that are born of the Spirit.'

For this reason the Christlike person may sometimes be a cause of offence to immature believers still walking on the Paths of Renewal, Awareness and Dying. It is difficult for them to understand and accept the freedom of the Christlike person. His life is lived beyond the restrictions of doctrine, practice and conduct, which for them are necessary methods on the Path. His spiritual skills are beyond all formulas. He walks as Jesus walked, and as many Christlike believers walked in times when Christianity was so steeped in doctrine and institutional power that the ignorant were driven to put the Christlike to death as 'heretics.'

TWO APPROACHES TO THE CHRISTIAN PATH

The Christian Path outlined here favours the 'actuation' approach. As has been said, this approach views baptism as embodying in itself the whole of the completed path which then remains to be experientially unfolded or actuated in the believer's walk.

But this is not to say that baptism has brought into being a new event in the absolute domain. Nothing can be added to or taken away from the Absolute. Nothing new can occur in the Absolute. The right understanding is that baptism is the symbolic act which acknowledges and concurs with a Truth that has eternally existed in the Mind of God. Thus baptism is an initial act of faith. The believer, in being baptized, is confessing to an absolute Truth about himself, and putting his faith in it.

In the actuation approach the believer's faith in the Absolute Truth about himself (the truth that he has died and been resurrected in Christ) compels him to its unfolding in his own life. His faith in the Absolute

The Paths and the Goals

Truth initiates its unfolding in the relative domain. So long as he abides in faith the Eternal Truth about himself will continue to unfold until it is fulfilled in his life. He will undergo this Truth. In the process of faith-actuation, the Grace of God in Christ will strengthen him to persevere on the Path.

But besides the actuation approach, there is in Christianity also an approach based completely on faith. In this approach the believer has only to steadfastly believe the Eternal Truth about himself. On condition that he holds unswervingly to what has been eternally accomplished in Christ on his behalf, he can reckon on it having been fully accomplished in his own life. Christ has undergone the Path on his behalf. If only he believes this completely, he can reckon himself as having been 'born from above', and as being, therefore, a Christlike person.

A common error of the faith approach is to equate faith with simple belief, not understanding that Christian faith is not mere belief. It is also fidelity to the person and work of Christ. It is not only that these should be objects of belief. The believer is required to commit himself fully to the working of the inner Christ in the Holy Spirit, and to be fully surrendered to it. Christian faith is both belief and trust in, and committed adherence to, the person and work of Christ through all the vicissitudes of the Christian Path.

The path of faith does not exclude the possibility of the religious experience of the believer on the actuation path. But the faith approach does imply that any experience which falls short of fulfilled Christlikeness is the result of inadequate faith on the believer's part. If, for instance, he is still falling into doubt and sin, it is not because he has not yet undergone the Path of Death, but because he has not yet fully believed himself to have undergone it in Christ. His faith in Christ is incomplete.

On the path of faith, grace is seen to be that which enables the believer to attain to the perfection of his grace-given faith. By perfecting his faith in what Christ has already accomplished on his behalf, he himself is perfected. In this case he is empowered by grace to persevere on the Path until his faith is complete. Then, at the point of its completion, Christlikeness is accomplished.

These two approaches are usually not much more than a matter of emphasis. Most believers who achieve authentic Christlikeness are likely to have maintained a middle-way between the two. If the emphasis is placed on actuation at the expense of faith, the believer may fall into the error of striving to accomplish Christlikeness in his own strength. If, on the other hand, faith is emphasised at the expense of actuation, the believer may claim completion in Christ without the fruits of this state being evident in his presence-emanation and conduct.

OBSTACLES ON THE CHRISTIAN PATH

The believer has to contend with obstacles to progress until the completion of the Path of Dying. After entering the Path of Death there is no longer any possibility of regression. The anxiety and doubt experienced on the Path of Death do not present themselves as obstacles because they are elicited by Truth itself: they are reactions to the believer's self-view in Christ before final purification has occurred, and they are the result of the believer's full submission to the purifying work of Christ.

On all the preliminary paths which precede the Path of Death, obstacles can arise. The most common and dangerous among these are: carnal self-centredness, distraction, doubt, fear, temptation, sinful conduct, discouragement, presumption and despair. There is also the special category of spiritual evil. All of these obstruct or interrupt progress on the path and, if not overcome, may lead to regression and eventual falling away.

Carnal Self-Centredness

The self-centred carnal mind is the first cause of all sin and weakness on the Path. Firstly, owing to its fallen nature, it is incapable of pure perception and interpretation. For this reason it is liable to fall into many delusions. Second, it is caught in the habits of its attachments and aversions. It tends therefore to justify what it desires and to condemn what it wants to avoid, even if the former are bad for it and the latter good. It perceives, interprets and acts in every case by its own standards.

Its selfishness predisposes it to develop and express itself in an ultra-relative mode. This means that it sees itself as self-sufficient, existing in its own right, and entitled to live by its own norms. It is caught in this pride because of its distorted self-image. From ignorant carnal pride arises the baseless self-confidence which can become an attitude of wilfulness against God in Christ.

The carnal mind's attachments and aversions are the sources of the cardinal sins, those sins from which all other sins derive: pride, covetousness, lust, anger, greed, envy and indolence. The attachments and aversions themselves arise from the condition of original sin (the fall into the ultra-relative mode) which has shaped the carnal predispositions.

The carnal mind cannot be reformed or spiritualized. It must be extinguished. As long as it does not know this it can adopt spiritual postures, maintaining these by inward self-deception and outward hypocrisy. Its spiritual pose, however, cannot fool the authentically spiritual onlooker. But it can deceive the believer who attempts to spiritualize his carnal mind, and keep him in that state of self-delusion for a lifetime.

The carnal mind, in the sum total of its processes, is actually the only obstacle to spiritual growth on both Christian and non-Christian paths. The Christian Path constitutes a journey from the destructive influence of the flesh to the liberation of the sanctified awareness in Christ. On this journey the carnal mind functions not only as the prime Obstacle in itself, but as a channel for all the other obstacles. So until the carnal mind is extinguished in death, the believer on the Path will have to deal with constantly arising obstacles by a variety of skilful methods.

Distraction

Distractions on the Path are of two kinds: those which hinder mindfulness of the indwelling Christ, and the distractions of temptation which may lead to sins of body, speech and mind. The first kind, although seemingly less directly obstructive to spiritual growth, often allows temptation to enter by the fact that mindfulness of the inner Christ is disrupted. When distraction is so intense that temptation is able to enter the believer's mind, the possibility of sinful conduct is strong. Then, if the believer falls into actual sin, communion with the Christ-Mind is broken.

Thus the decline into sin always begins with distraction. The instances of distraction are as various as human experience, and are especially dangerous to the immature believer on the Path of Renewal. The sources of distraction are: the habit-patterns of the believer's own mind, pressures and opportunities arising in the mundane sphere, the activities of others, and the working of spiritual evil. All of these cooperate to distract the believer from the sense of Christ's inner presence, the very sense on which the intrinsic awareness depends for the attainment of the equipoise needed for spiritual growth.

This is an important point, because inexperienced believers are sometimes inclined to treat religious observances, objects and activities as spiritual ends in themselves. This sort of fixation on externals then distracts from the sense of the Presence of the indwelling Christ. When this happens, the believer is caught in an externalized religiosity which tends to sustain, rather than work towards the extinction of, the carnal mind.

Indeed, the carnal mind wants to be distracted. For it, the absence of distraction is ennui, and it can find its distractions even in the religious sphere. But, whether it is inviting distraction by coarse, sinful patterns, or by those generally considered moral or even religious, the crucial question is always whether or not the intrinsic awareness remains in communion with the Christ-Mind.

It is the same with the believer's interaction with the world: if it is sinful, communion with the Christ-Mind will be broken; but even if the interaction is motivated by a religiosity tending to charitable or virtuous activity, this can become an end in itself. In that case a self-congratulatory religious pride may develop, and the activies themselves will keep the believer unmindful of the inner Christ.

The believer can similarly be distracted by his dealings with others. Others should always be viewed and dealt with in the Christ-Mind, which is the only basis for spiritual authenticity, skill and authority in relationships. Otherwise the interaction is pseudo-religious, or simply carnal.

Distraction is most problematic for the believer on the Path of Renewal, where the sense of the indwelling Christ is still being cultivated or sought. External religiosity can be particularly troublesome at this stage. Instead of fellowship with the inner Christ, the believer may, for instance, prefer the activities and emotional consolations associated with group endeavours, so that fellowship with the group becomes a substitute for the sense of the Christ-Mind.

But distractions may also present themselves quite fiercely on the Paths of Awareness and Dying where the interior religious life is more intense and there is much inner struggle. It is probable that the distractions of spiritual evil will be strongest on these paths, where the carnal mind is being decisively dealt with. Spiritual evil always struggles to keep the carnal mind 'alive' because the carnal mind is the source of mind-energy for the existence of evil in the world. Whether by terror or enticement, spiritual evil seeks to prevent the extinction of the carnal dynamic by which it is sustained.

The only effective practice against distraction is ongoing mindfulness of and communion with the indwelling Christ. Mindfulness of religious activities is only useful insofar as it encourages and cultivates the knowledge of the Christ-Mind. So, whatever methods the believer is using to awaken and sustain the sense of inner Presence, mindfulness should also be exercised to prevent these methods themselves from degenerating into pseudo-religious distractions.

Doubt

There are many forms of doubt which arise to trouble the believer, and they all impact on his faith in and faithfulness to the presence and working of the Christ-Mind. When doubts arise, faith and fidelity are weakened: the believer's lucid perception and understanding of inner spiritual processes are dimmed. Looking inwards and outwards with a doubting mind, the treasures of Christ seem to be changed into fool's gold.

One of the main problems attached to doubt is that the believer may erroneously equate doubt with sin. Then, seeing doubt as sinful, he struggles against entertaining his doubt. He banishes it from his mind instead of examining it, discovering the questions it is posing, and answering them in the Mind of Christ. So, banished from mind and left unanswered, the same doubts repeatedly recur.

Sincere doubts are not sins. They only become sinful when they are encouraged for sinful ends. The believer must distinguish between sincere and sinful doubts. The former only become obstacles when repressed, left unanswered or answered incompletely; the latter are obstacles insofar as the carnal mind, using them for its own purposes, does not want to have them answered.

There are some fundamental doubts which must be answered to the believer's satisfaction if he is to make any progress, or even start out, on the spiritual path. He must answer the question: is the spiritual life real? For, if he concludes that it is an imagination, he must turn away from it. If he becomes convinced that it is real, he might go on to ask: is the spiritual life worth the renunciation of worldliness? If he decides that it is, he might consider: do I have the capacity for spiritual growth? And then: is salvation in Christ a Truth that can be relied on?

Although these might seem to be the sort of simpler questions that the believer will have addressed before assenting to baptism, they will return to afflict him on the Path until he has answered them conclusively. Only when they have been dealt with to the extent that they can no longer challenge his faith and fidelity can he progress beyond them. And even then, having grown beyond the reach of their coarser manifestations, they may recur in subtler forms corresponding to the increased subtlety of his spiritual insights. Again and again they will have to be convincingly answered rather than ignored 'in faith.'

Because faith cannot by itself dispel sincere doubts. They can only be dispelled finally by the informing wisdom of Christ. Faith and faithfulness are required to motivate perseverance in seeking answers in the Christ-Mind, and those answers will dispel all doubts. But doubts cannot simply be burned up in faith as wood is consumed by fire. If insight and understanding were not necessary to the skilful dispelling of doubts, no sincere doubts would arise to challenge them. They would arise only as factitious challenges to faith. So faith, rather than directly dispelling doubts, directs the believer's intrinsic awareness to the Christ-Mind, where the answers of wisdom are to be found.

Doubt, then, is an obstacle which can only be eradicated by understanding, and in the completion of understanding a large role is played by the intellect. Two points are important here. The first is that the extinction of the carnal mind in no way implies the progressive diminishment of the intellect, which is one of the most useful tools on the spiritual path. But - and this is the second point - the intellect is only useful to spiritual growth if it is being sanctified. Carnal habits of mind which distort intellectual apprehension of spiritual Truth must be displaced by the wisdom of the Christ-Mind. Then, as the intellect becomes increasingly immersed in spiritual wisdom, it grows in lucidity, keenness and discernment. It is by these qualities in the believer's intellect that doubts can be dispelled.

So, doubt acts to diminish faith; and the antidote to doubt is spiritual understanding. Indeed, much of spiritual growth is based on the progressive resolution of the variety of doubts and self-doubts that arise on the Path.

Fear

Fear diminishes resolve, and its antidote is perfect love. The Christian scriptures state unambiguously that 'perfect love drives out all fear.'

Fear is an obstacle on all spiritual paths. And because it is expressed far more powerfully in the emotions than, for instance, doubt, it requires a remedy that can overcome it in the area of emotional activity as well as in the faculties of understanding.

The Paths and the Goals

On his path the believer will have to contend with many fears, the more so as spiritual paths deliver up startling, profound and often incomprehensible revelations and experiences. Spiritual truths of the sort which the carnal mind habitually represses and avoids are brought into lucidity. In becoming increasingly open to spiritual energies, the human mind may often feel overwhelmed. In this dynamic two types of fundamental fear emerge: the fears of the carnal mind in relation to its own extinction, and the fears of the intrinsic awareness in relation to spiritual experiences.

The carnal mind fears its final death in Christ, and it fears the diminishment and loss of its own potentialities while it is being submitted to Christ's inner activity. The fear of these losses is intensified by the fact of its inevitable physical death. In Christ, it imagines, it is being consigned to death before its time. It therefore resists all the more vigorously any curtailment of its freedom to express itself.

Within the wider context of its fear of ultimate extinction in Christ, the carnal mind fears the surrender of its provisional rights and pleasures. Among its pleasures are not only the mundane enjoyments to which it has become accustomed, but also its sense of achievement, its knowledge, its worldly wisdom. In the light of these it has learnt to manage its own survival, and there is a natural anxiety associated with the loss of this kind of psychological control. The loss of the basic freedom to choose how far it will decline into ultra-relativity is the ground of its fears because its entire scope of options derives from this right.

These fears cause real suffering, which is not invalidated by merely pointing out the carnal mind's provisional nature and pseudo-life. Suffering is never alleviated by a resort to simple dismissal or rejection of the suffering mindstate. Even as it is being disciplined and illuminated into acceptance of its diminishment and ultimate extinction, the carnal mind should be viewed and treated with compassion. Loving it is not the same as indulging it. Indeed, it can only be extinguished in the Energy of love. Loving it means understanding with compassion how it has come to be the way it is and why it suffers, and presenting to it the only way out of these miseries.

This is how God in Christ loves the carnal mind, and there can be no reason why the believer should love it less, or in any other way. Harsh treatment of the carnal mind is likely to result in a harsh religiosity, including harsh treatment of others. And a harsh approach will actually serve to increase fear. Therefore the intrinsic awareness should deal gently with the carnal mind's fears, referring them always to the Love-Energy of the Christ-Mind.

The fears experienced by the intrinsic awareness on the spiritual path can only be stilled by the Wisdom-Love of God in Christ indwelling the believer. The most common and recurrent fear is that of failure, both as a possibility and when it has actually occurred. The fear of the possibility of failure is often the cause of failure. The certain knowledge of having failed, by having fallen into sin, for instance, rouses the fear that there may be no escaping failure, and that there may be no way back to the consolations of the indwelling Christ.

The potential for failure should not be feared because, except from the Path of Death onwards, it is always naturally present. And, although it is a negative potential, it is an inseparable part of progress. If there were no possibility of failure there could be no potential for progress, for progress is made on the same continuum along whose course the possibility of failure exists. The love of God in Christ takes into account the possibility of failure. If it were excluded from Christ's love no believer could be loved by Christ, for all may fail.

As long as failure is dealt with in the light, love and forgiveness of Christ, the believer can get up and walk on. If he is sincerely 'walking after the spirit', his failure is only an event occurring in the course of that walk. By re-establishing a love relationship with God in Christ whenever he has stumbled, he can prevent the recurrence of failure, even before the Path of Death is attained. To prevent its recurrence, at any rate, should be his aim.

Fear of Evil

The fear of spiritual evil is extremely problematic. It is a terrifying aspect of religious experience from which many believers may never fully recover, especially if the attacks occur on the Path of Renewal or during the early stages of the Path of Awareness, before they have developed an adequate sense of the protective power of God in Christ.

Christianity sees spiritual evil as personified in Satan and the hosts of fallen angels. These are all more or less powerful demonic beings endowed with evil energies, intelligence and will. They may oppress and, more rarely, possess the minds of people and even of believers who have somehow (perhaps through severe trauma or repeated sinful conduct) become open to the energies and influence of evil.

The Paths and the Goals

The demonic beings are described as 'powers and principalities' and 'evil in high places', and are ubiquitous. They are disposed to make use of people for their own evil purposes and are especially set against the work of Christ in people. In Christ they see their own defeat and the imminent end of their activities. For this reason they attack the children of God and strive to hinder the work of God in Christ.

Believers, especially new believers, experience great terror if the sense of the power and love of the Christ-Mind are not sufficienly developed to ward off the attacks. It is therefore especially important, in these cases, that the believer be familiar with Divine Love as protective power, and that he receive strong, patient and wise support from mature members of the communion. The experience of spiritual evil is a lonely and isolating trauma because the victim may feel himself beyond the reach of God's intervention, besides being unable to find fellow believers who can fully understand what has happened. There is a deep sense of helplessness and confusion.

Because such spiritual attacks bear close resemblance to neurotic or psychotic episodes there is a tendency, even within the Church, to view them exclusively as psychological disturbances requiring professional therapy. This is a mistaken view. While it is true that a percentage of these experiences is psychopathological in nature, demonic activity cannot simply be ruled out. These forces of evil exist and are active, even if they are not separable from the believer's own mind. While they are afflicting the believer they have, for him, and also for those who are supporting and counselling him, a very tangible objective existence.

Perfect Love as Antidote to Fear

While love of any kind can provide a degree of security in the face of fear, it is equally important to bring intelligence, understanding and confidence to bear. In Christian teaching it is 'perfect love', as distinct from the imperfect kind, which eradicates all fear.

As an antidote to fear, perfect love should be understood as love perfected in Christ. This kind of love is far more than only an emotional sense of security. It is a vast energy containing currents of wisdom, insight and purity. Perfect love can never be unwise or impure, and the believer whose awareness is merged with Perfect Love has, as a result, a capacity for insightful discernment, together with the courageous confidence that comes from inner purity. It is this kind of love which is the effective antidote to fear because it is established in authority. If the believer lacks this love and is afflicted by fear, especially fear of spiritual evil, counsel and support should be sought from someone who authentically possesses Perfect Love. Otherwise the problem may worsen.

Temptation

Temptation occurs when the intrinsic awareness is distracted by the carnal mind to the extent that unrenewed habits of mind, instinct and personal will become active in the field of distraction. If the energies of these unrenewed aspects of mind are allowed free play, temptation goes over into sinful expression in body, speech and mind.. Thus, the first defence against temptation is maintaining a mind undistracted from the presence and energy of the indwelling Christ.

Temptations arise initially from habits of mind and unrenewed instinct when these have entered the field of distraction. At this point it is still possible to quench them by a return of the intrinsic awareness to the Presence of the inner Christ. But, if the field of distraction is allowed to persist, temptations will begin to infect the personal will which is permitting the prolongation of distraction, for it is only by protractedly entertaining distractions that they become able to draw the personal will out of submission to the Christ-Mind. In the initial stage the personal will is already to some extent unsubmitted because the intrinsic awareness, having become aware of its distracted state, has by an act of will allowed distraction to continue, instead of immediately returning to the Christ-Mind. The personal will, now only partially submitted to Christ, is therefore more accessible to the energies of temptation. Ideally, distraction should be dispelled by a quick return to the inner Christ, for distraction results in a divided mind.

If temptation has been allowed to infect the will there is still an opportunity to return to full submission to the Christ-Mind, but it is very late in the process and must involve greater struggle.

Actual Sin

Sinful conduct is actuated when the personal will has been overwhelmingly infected by temptation. Whether it is a sin of body, speech or mind, it clouds, or, in extreme cases, breaks off communion between the intrinsic awareness and the inner Christ. The only remedy is the restoration of communion, and this should be done immediately because delay will invite increased distraction, further temptation and sinful conduct, and attendant discouragement.

Sinful conduct cannot be defined in merely legalistic terms. Any act on the believer's part which disturbs or breaks off communion with the Christ-Mind is a sinful act. Such factors as individual motivation or variations in sensitivity or maturity all serve to qualify sin. But this does not mean that sin is a purely subjective matter. The new believer has in some cases to learn by instruction what sin is and how deep it goes. Especially at the stages where the intrinsic awareness is still closely associated with the carnal mind, the new believer has to be sensitized to sin by wise and loving instruction.

Outside of its acquired mores, often very superficial, the carnal mind does not have much insight into the subtleties of sin. To these the growing believer becomes gradually more sensitive through increased awakening to the Presence of inner Christ. The cultivation of insight into the nature and consequences of sin depends, therefore, on instruction in the early stages and increasing awareness in the later. Ultimately, the spiritual understanding of sin is not a matter of subtle classification but of wisdom: direct experience of the nature of sinful energies and their consequences in the total spiritual environment. When these are understood by the energies of awakened wisdom, lapses into sinful conduct have graver consequences for the believer and, in these cases, it is more difficult to restore communion with the Christ-Mind.

Restoration of communion involves renewed submission of habits of mind, instinct and personal will to the inner Christ. Although there is forgiveness of sin through the accomplished sacrifice of Christ, there is no access to that forgiveness without concomitant submission to the Christ-Mind. Forgiveness is not God in Christ simply overlooking the believer's actual sin. It is a means for enabling the sinner to return to God. A believing sinner who has not returned to God would be unwise to consider himself forgiven. The proof that forgiveness has been obtained lies in the restoration of inner communion with God in Christ. Thus, forgiveness is essentially an invitation to renewed fellowship with God. There can be no forgiveness while God's invitation is being rejected.

Discouragement

When obstacles on the Path are not overcome the believer becomes discouraged. Discouragement signifies a lack of confidence on the believer's part in his ability to negotiate the spiritual Path, and in the saving grace and power of God in Christ. In this state the intrinsic awareness is more conscious of failure than of progress, and in many cases the strong sense of failure derives from scrupulosity. The believer may be setting unachievable standards for himself because he lacks accurate understanding of the tenacious nature of the carnal mind and of its guile. There is also the danger, on the other hand, of setting standards which are too low. In these latter cases there is not much to differentiate between the carnal and the spiritual mind, and the spiritual pursuit seems unrewarding.

The way to avoid discouragement is by not setting standards at all. The heart of the Christian Path is not a search for standards of conduct but for relationship with the inner Christ. It is the Mind-Energy of Christ which both determines and enables the believer to achieve the spiritual standards of God. The believer does not serve Christ for purposes of self-improvement. Christ is served for the sake of Truth and for the sake of others. It is only this degree of self-forgetfulness that will save the believer from discouragement—and if he tries to set standards of self-forgetfulness, this becomes in itself a self-interested exercise.

Therefore, discouragement is radically avoided only by a change of focus: the aim to serve Christ and to be useful in service to others, with no expectation of reward. When all thoughts of reward or loss are abandoned, discouragement is overcome by equilibrium and striving is pacified by confident relaxation in the love of Christ. While resting in Christ, the intrinsic awareness is always confident.

Presumption

Presumption arises from a believer's misguided notion that he has through his own merits deserved the salvation which comes through the merits of Christ alone, or that the merits of Christ will save the believer irrespective of whether or not he is living in submission to Christ. On the one hand it is a question of the believer placing too much value on his own efforts; on the other, it is a misguided reliance on the purely objective Truth of salvation in Christ.

The Paths and the Goals

It is really a matter of knowing the relation between faith and conduct (or, 'works'). Avoiding presumption is, however, not only a question of striking the right balance between faith and works, but of understanding how faith and works reinforce one another in the process of actuation in Christ. The right understanding is that, while the believer is indeed saved by faith in the objective Truth of his salvation in Christ, such faith has no value if it is not borne out in spiritual growth and its accompanying conduct. This is the understanding by which presumption is avoided.

Presumption leaning on works implies reliance on the carnal mind. The believer has not understood that the carnal mind cannot be sanctified, and that even its apparently good works cannot bear spiritual fruit (having spiritual consequences in spiritual realms) because these carnal works are never entirely free from self-interest. Since they do not originate in the Mind of Christ they are devoid of spiritual energy. The believer who relies on them is always infected by pride and essential lovelessness. The self-satisfied mind of the presumptuous believer is incompatible with the humble, loving Christ-Mind. So the path of presumption must always lead the believer away from authentic spirituality.

Presumption leaning on faith is always a misinterpretation of faith. It considers that mere belief in the finished work of Christ suffices to salvation. It does not take into account that faith also means faithfulness to the principle of the extinction of the carnal mind in the course of the subjective actuation of objective Truth. In this case also the carnal mind remains alive. Forgiveness of sin is taken for granted, even in the absence of real relationship with Christ, and there can be no progress towards Christlikeness.

In presumption leaning on works the believer is trying to reconcile the carnal mind with the Christ-Mind, in the conviction that the carnal mind can aspire to, express and ultimately achieve Christlikeness.

In presumption leaning on faith the believer is trying to reconcile the Christ-Mind with the carnal mind, believing that the sinfulness of the carnal mind will be overlooked by the loving forgivenesss of Christ. In neither case are habits of mind, instinct and personal will being submitted to Christ, with the result that the intrinsic awareness is prevented from merging with the Mind of Christ.

Despair

The despairing believer sees himself as beyond the reach of salvation in Christ: he has failed so profoundly that there can be no hope for him. Usually the condition of despair results from one of the two forms of presumption. A believer who has leaned on his own works for a long time, only to fall victim to the inevitable complete failure of the carnal mind, may despair or become a hypocrite. A believer leaning exclusively on faith will be faced with the same consequences when the cumulative burden of his sinful conduct reveals to him his failure.

But despair can arise from other causes: scrupulosity, trauma, ongoing suffering, and so forth. In every case, however, its source is misunderstanding and mismanagement of the spiritual Path. The remedy is cultivation of insight, usually with the help of wise counsel. The despairing believer needs to rediscover the full Truth of Christ in a lucid way. Especially, he must be brought to a clear understanding of the unfailing love of Christ.

Through seeing himself in relation to the boundless love of Christ, and as saved by that love from all judgement of himself, he can return to the initial act of will by which he invites God in Christ to be present and active in his spirit. From that point on he must resume walking the path to death of self.

SUMMARY: MIND ON THE CHRISTIAN PATH

The Christian scriptures exhort the believer to 'be transformed by the renewal of your mind.' As we have seen, renewal of the mind comes by death of the carnal mind, which arises from unrenewed habits of mind, instinct and personal will. These unregenerate sources of the carnal mind's pseudo-life, power and activity are themselves the result of 'original sin,' the sinful nature of humanity which came by the fall of Adam.

As the personal manifestation of original sin, the carnal mind, arising from unrenewed mental habits, instinct and personal will, is also the generator of ongoing sinful conduct in body, speech and mind. It acts out the mind of original sin.

But liberation from the carnal mind does not, in Christianity, come by a discovery or 'uncovering' of the believer's own innate pure mind. While it is true that the intrinsic awareness can be liberated from the control of the carnal mind, this liberation does not come by returning the intrinsic

The Paths and the Goals

awareness to the deepest pure energies of the believer's own mental continuum. That which liberates the intrinsic awareness is the Christ-Mind, and this Mind is not innate in the believer. It enters his mental continuum when he makes an initial act of will, inviting the Mind of Christ to enter his mental and spiritual domain and to remain there, carrying out the work of salvation. The Christ-Mind is not innately present in the nonbeliever, waiting, as it were, to be found in his deeper mind.

Although this is the generally held view, there are Christians who consider the Christ-Mind to be a latent spiritual potential within all people. In this view the Mind of Christ does not come to the believer from a spiritual domain outside of his own mental continuum: it has only to be discovered within by an act of faith and understanding. Jesus' parable of the treasure hidden in a field is sometimes used in support of this view.

These doctrinal points, however, do not represent a difference in the real religious experience. In experience the Path is a process during which mental habits, instinct and personal will are submitted to renewal in the Christ-Mind. Through their renewal the carnal mind is extinguished and the intrinsic awareness liberated in Christ.

It is clear that these same mental factors are the inner sources of obstacles, and that it is only by working with them that obstacles can finally be overcome. Whatever external factors might be at play in throwing up obstacles across the believer's path, the way to overcoming them is always by spiritual treatment of the sources of the carnal mind's arising: by examining how they are or are not submitted to the Energy of the Christ-Mind, and by assenting to their complete submission.

And, so far as the subtler spiritual obstacles are concerned, the mind of spiritual evil is also usually considered to exist outside of the believer's mental continuum. It gains access to his mind only if he allows it to do so by becoming open to evil influences. Again, there are Christians who hold that the demonic mind is not ultimately separable from the believer's own mind. Whatever the case, these manifestations of spiritual evil in the believer's experience can only be overcome by the Energy of the indwelling Christ.

Although Christians generally do not closely analyse the interplay of mental factors involved in their liberation in Christ, such an approach is not wholly alien to Christian understanding. It is present in Christian doctrine and method, but is usually veiled in religious symbolism and allegory. A systematic understanding of the mental factors and processes involved can, however, be very useful in preventing spiritual experience from declining into carnal expressions such as emotionalism or sentimentalism, or, at the other extreme, mere externalized moralism.

STAGES OF THE BUDDHIST PATH

At the beginning of his path the Buddhist practitioner has as his goal the attainment of bodhisattvahood: the perfection of Wisdom-Compassion. In order to move towards his goal he must cultivate a Truth-View of the nature of reality and of his own condition in reality. The view must be deepened, made more acute and stabilized in his mind through meditative practices. Then the stabilized View must be expressed in conduct of body, speech and mind, conformed to the Truth-View which has been cultivated. All progress is therefore based on the development of the interdependent View-Meditation-Conduct cycle, until these are finally unified in the spontaneous expression of Wisdom-Compassion.

Until spontaneous expression of Truth is achieved, the practitioner makes use of the two activities which enable spiritual growth: study and practice. Through close analysis of what reality actually is, and of what he himself actually is, he comes to understand in theory that his true nature is an Enlightened Nature (Buddha-Nature) and that the true nature of reality is spiritual Energy-Essence giving rise to 'empty' phenomena and beings.

While he makes efforts to understand these things through study, he simultaneously engages in meditative practice in order to bring these conceptually grasped theories of Truth into spontaneous expression in his mental continuum and conduct. So, the View-Meditation-Conduct system is driven by study on the one hand, and by practice on the other.

These methods are employed with increasing refinement and profundity on the five stages of the Buddhist Path. These stages are: Path of Accumulation, Preparation, Seeing, Meditation, and No More Learning. In our model we will interpret these Stages of the Path much more loosely than they are dealt with in the very precise presentations of the Way of the Bodhisattva devised by the great Buddhist scholar-practitioners. Yet, while our analysis is far less detailed, the presentation given here is a faithful rendering of overall spiritual development in Buddhism.

FIRST STAGE: THE PATH OF ACCUMULATION

On the Path of Accumulation the practitioner accumulates the merits and insights which will motivate him to seek Enlightenment. In the process

The Paths and the Goals

he becomes able to recognize the pervasive suffering of all life lived in the ordinary mind and experiences the wish to be liberated from it. This is the seed of the wish to attain wisdom. At the same time he recognizes the suffering of all others and wishes to set them free. This is the beginning of compassion. Thus, very near the start of the Path of Accumulation the practitioner generates the wish to attain Enlightenment for the sake of others. The Path is completed when this twofold wish, the Bodhisattva Wish, arises spontaneously and stably in the practitioner's mind.

The Path of Accumulation is attained not only by the wholesome karma generated in this lifetime but also by the accumulation of the wholesome karmic force generated in previous lifetimes. Indeed, if the practitioner has entered the Path, it is mainly owing to the weight of cumulative merit gained throughout countless previous lifetimes. The opportunity for entering on the Dharma Path has thus not been easily gained and should be regarded as exceedingly precious.

The obscurations and delusions of the ordinary mind are extremely dark and tenacious. One does not escape from them in a fingersnap. That the practitioner has gained access to the Path of Accumulation is proof also of insight gathered over many lifetimes and this hardwon understanding should not be wasted. The mere fact that the practitioner is able to see the suffering of the ordinary life and to feel compassion for others on the basis of this insight is a great karmic gain. That his karma has actually directed him to the Dharma-View is proof of much progress made in previous lifetimes: what he has gained thereby is of inestimable value.

Karmic forces do not determine only the external accidents of life. Much more importantly, they determine the readiness, pliability and acuity of the mind. The practitioner only recognizes the Truth of Dharma because he has prepared his mind throughout countless lifetimes. Otherwise he would not have come to Dharma in this lifetime. His mind now having been prepared by so much prior effort, he should practise Dharma with determination.

Now, on the Path in this lifetime, he studies and practises to strengthen the Bodhisattva Wish. His study is aimed at gaining preliminary insight into wisdom and compassion. His practice, not yet centred in meditation, is for the accumulation of greater merit through virtuous conduct of body, speech and mind. Such merit is gathered into a karmic energy which purifies his mind and brings about an external environment conducive to more advanced practices. His study and practice, working in tandem, will clarify and stabilize his Truth-View, causing the Bodhisattva Wish to arise continuously and effortlessly

He studies the Four Noble Truths in order to internalize them, if only in a preliminary way, without a fully developed grasp of their significance and power. He acquires increasing insight into the Truth of Suffering, of the Causes of Suffering, of the Cessation of Suffering, and of the Eightfold Path. In studying these, he achieves preliminary insight into the workings of karma and rebirth. He begins to grasp the Three Characteristics of Worldly Existence: to see that all phenomena and beings are suffering, transient and without inherently existing selves. He grows in understanding of cyclic existence; the endless repetition of the generation and exhaustion of wholesome and unwholesome karma by which he is caught in the cycle of birth, suffering, death and rebirth. He ponders the samsaric cycle with its principle of interdependent origination: how nothing and no one exists in and of themselves, but depend for their conventional existence on a multiplicity of causes and conditions. He discerns how all things and all beings in the conventional world arise from interrelated factors and remain trapped in their interplay. Then he begins to penetrate the truth of emptiness: the non-inherent existence of all phenomena. He begins to understand how his ordinary mind arises from the skandhas, and how this is the same for all sentient beings. So the sense of the fundamental sameness of all beings—sameness in their suffering and in their potential for liberation—becomes confirmed in his mind, and compassion is strengthened by this conviction.

He learns that others are more important than himself. As a group, others are clearly quantitatively greater than one self: their combined needs are greater than his own. In the case of the individual other, he knows that he can always be sure of acting rightly if he sacrifices his own interests for the sake of the other, whereas he can never be sure that acting to secure his own wellbeing at the expense of that of the other will have good karmic consequences. And he can always be sure that putting the other first will bring spiritual good both to the other and to himself.

So, understanding these preliminary principles pertaining to the real nature of himself, of other beings and of samsaric reality, he is enabled to act more righteously and to be less influenced by the ordinary mind's habitual tendencies and desires. In all this he is advancing in skill and accumulating further merit.

The Paths and the Goals

Knowing that the Path to Enlightenment is a path of the mind, the practitioner prepares himself for meditation by the practice of mindfulness. He trains his mind in awareness of the ordinary mind's workings. Instead of allowing thoughts, feelings, desires and aversions to arise unguardedly, he observes their motions, seeing how they come and go in endless succession. By mindfulness he becomes increasingly adept at objectifying the motions of his mental continuum, and is able to separate the observing wisdom-consciousness from the observed ordinary mind which he has hitherto habitually identified as 'I.' By increasingly taking distance from the ordinary mind he becomes increasingly able to control it, for it is not 'himself.' The habitual discursive mental activity which arises and disappears spontaneously need have no influence over him if he simply lets go of it.

In the same way he increases mindfulness of the emotions. If he becomes angry at someone he observes his own anger; how it arises spontaneously, habitually, in the self-centred ordinary mind, and how it dissipates again. He sees that the other person, the object of his anger, cannot be the cause of his anger. No thing or being extraneous to his own mind can generate anger within his mental continuum; only he himself can do this. Then, observing his anger, he knows that he himself cannot be that anger, because he cannot be the very aspect of mental activity which the wisdom-consciousness is observing. He can no longer say with any conviction, 'I am angry.' He can only acknowledge that anger is arising in his mental continuum. If he 'is angry', he would always have to remain angry. But he does not. He can furthermore discern that 'anger' is only a designation for a certain negative emotional energy. If he ceases from labelling it 'anger', what is it in itself? It is only a selfish energy. He can let it go. The other person cannot cause it to remain. Similarly, he can let go of any negative emotion habitually arising because he discerns that emotions are conditioned responses, reactions of the karmically conditioned ordinary mind. Observing them, watching them arise and dissolve, not holding onto them, not coming under their control, he is transforming not only his mind but also his karma, undoing the karmic conditioning of the ego-mind.

In practising mindfulness of the body, of the way it feels, moves, functions and reacts, he becomes aware that his body also is not 'I.' When there is pain, he observes it. He observes pleasurable sensations and neutral repose. He observes the beating of his heart and his breathing. When he walks, stands, sits or lies down, he cultivates mindfulness of these actions. Through these practices he grows more able to control the body and to stand apart from its urges and passivities.

The practitioner also undertakes some preparatory meditative practices. Sitting in a comfortable position, grounded and alert, he observes his breathing: the inbreath and the outbreath. As he tries gently to settle his mind on these, he becomes aware of mental distraction: thoughts and feelings arising and dissipating. If he grasps at them he loses awareness of his breathing. If he lets them go, he is able to return to watching only the breath.

With time he becomes proficient at leaving the distractions to come and go of their own accord while he watches exclusively his breathing. He is becoming more alert and more relaxed, not straining against distractions as though in a struggle. He simply allows them to arise and dissolve naturally, while he watches the breathing with a gentle attention. He is training his mind to be still and calmly focused, while cultivating deep inner relaxation. He is becoming gentler with himself and with others as he increasingly develops a relaxed control over his ordinary mind which, after all, is not 'I.' Practising daily in this way, he becomes more detached from his hopes and fears. He is no longer straining to defend and maintain an 'I' which is more and more revealing itself to be 'not-I.'

Concurrent with the practices of mindfulness and preparatory meditation he practices, with mindful detachment, the moral aspects of the Eightfold Path: Right Action, Right Speech and Right Living. They are easier to practice once the mind has been a little trained in meditation. Since he is now to some extent able to control his thoughts and feelings, his actions and reactions are no longer tightly conditioned. Less controlled by the selfish habits of the ordinary mind, his actions, speech and labour become less aggressive and less harmful because he is more detached from those events to which he would normally react defensively. And, in being less harmful to others, he is less harmful to himself.

Thus, on the Path of Accumulation, he is beginning to practise the perfections (*paramitas*) of generosity, morality, patience and vigour. He is not yet practising them in their spontaneous transcendent energy, but is beginning to grasp that, in giving, there is no giver that is 'I' and no recipient that is the receiving 'I.' Giving is not a transaction between two concrete selves. It is the conscious and detached removal of an energy from one locus to another. In this awareness the practitioner can give

The Paths and the Goals

generously to the 'undeserving' and the 'deserving' alike. He can give of his goods, time or labour without a sense of loss or of being used. His mind, now less informed by the ordinary mental patterns, also becomes more generous and spacious. He is less likely to condemn others or even to dislike them out of all sorts of habitually instilled biases. He is being liberated from ungenerous prejudices and preferences.

Growing increasingly detached from his ordinary mind, the practitioner exercises greater patience. He is more patient with events confronting him in this world, with others, with himself, and with his practice. So harmlessness grows and, with it, virtue. Becoming mentally more at ease, he is naturally more vigorous: his energies are not being squandered through negative emotions, thoughts and actions, and are therefore more available to him for positive uses.

Through all these developments he is becoming less at home in the ordinary mind and more reliant on the wisdom-consciousness. This wisdom-consciousness should not be thought of as a separate mental faculty or entity: it is a mode of awareness which is being uncovered and developed on the Path. It is not an 'I'. The wisdom-consciousness observing the ordinary ego-mind is not a real 'I' observing a deluded 'I'. It is just a developed quality in the total mental continuum, in which no 'I' can be discerned. For even the subtlest expressions of self are not ultimately 'I'.

But, being more at home in the wisdom-consciousness, and having become stabler, more at ease and more acute mentally, the practitioner is able to contemplate more keenly the truths of Dharma. He considers the Four Noble Truths from every angle and plumbs to some extent their spiritual depth. They are present to him no longer as theories only but, being quickened as wisdom-energy, are applied to everyday life.

By the quickening of these energies through the determined practices of mindfulness, study and meditation, he is slowly advancing in the growth of Wisdom-Compassion. On the wisdom side, he already knows that the habitually designated 'I' is not really 'I'. So, no longer upholding and defending 'I' and 'mine', he is more spacious and vulnerable. And it is from this open and vulnerable experience that compassion arises. Compassion flows from all the areas previously guarded by the self-regardant ego-mind.

To further help the process of gradual liberation from the false sense of 'I', and to encourage growth in compassion, the practitioner may carry out certain formal rites. He can formalize his preparatory meditative practices so that these include rituals which imbue the mind with the sense of openness and sacrifice.

The form of such practices might be as follows: he begins by making offerings of water to the Three Jewels, to Enlightened Beings, and to Dharma. Water is used as a symbol of the pure mind and because it can be offered with unhampered generosity, without the influence of the ordinary mind's meanness. Then he takes formal refuge in the Buddha, Dharma and Sangha. After this he might recite a mantra to steady his mind. Then he performs the preparatory meditations: watching the breath. When he feels that his meditation is going well, he sustains it for a little longer and then stops before becoming distracted. Then he sits quietly for some time in the relaxed mind of post-meditation. Finally, he dedicates any merit gained by this practice to the welfare of all sentient beings.

In order to generate greater compassion, the practitioner may employ his imagination to visualize an Enlightened Being, whose body is made of clear light, facing him at a small distance. From the heart-centre of this Being a shaft of warm golden light streams out and enters the practitioner's heart-centre. He feels the light entering and gathering there. As it accumulates in energy and luminosity, he visualizes countless sentient beings and sends the light in streams from his heart-centre to theirs. He continues this visualized cycle of giving and receiving light until a strong sense of warm compassion is generated. Having sustained this practice without distraction for some time, he visualizes the Enlightened Being as coming to hover above his head and dissolving into pure light which enters at his crown and sinks down to his heart-centre, where it remains. He sits for a while, experiencing the light. Then he stops the meditation and dedicates the merit for the benefit of all beings.

By these sorts of meditative practice both the wisdom and compassion aspects of spiritual growth are made more lucid. There is a preliminary advance towards the understanding of the empty (*shunya*) nature of self, all beings, and all phenomena. Even though he cannot yet clearly see emptiness (*shunyata*), he is slowly training his mind to discriminate between how things exist in their conventional and in their ultimate modes. The conditioned view of 'I' is receding. At the same time, he is advancing towards the spontaneous generation of Great Compassion (*Mahakaruna*). In all this he is removing the obscurations which hide the Buddha-Nature from his awareness.

The Paths and the Goals

There are also techniques for dealing with failure. Negative karmic conditioning is the cause of which failure is the effect. The impure mind of ignorance is generated by impure karma. When the practitioner fails by non-virtuous or unwholesome or ignorant conduct of body, speech and mind, he must take steps to purify his karma. Even when failure is not immediately experienced, he should continually purify his karma. In so doing he brings purity and lucidity to his mind, enabling him to advance on the path of wisdom. And, in purifiying his own karma, he is also purifying his contribution to the collective karma of his immediate environment and, ultimately, of all sentient beings. Thus, purification of his individual karma contributes to the wellbeing of all beings, and is therefore a compassionate act.

Purification is accomplished by four steps called 'powers,' for each has the power to influence karma. The first power deals with the harmful consequences of unwholesome conduct. The practitioner recognizes that his indulgence in non-virtuous conduct has been as though he has imbibed a potent poison. The negative consequences he is experiencing are the effects of having been poisoned. He generates the intense regret of one who realizes that he has foolishly taken poison and is now ill and in danger of death. Seeing his folly and its consequences, he determines never again to experiment with poison. It is a strong determination, arising from the anxious reflections implicit in his regret. This resolve to stay away from poison is the second power. By the third power the practitioner refreshes his insight into the benefits of spiritual practice by placing them in sharp contrast to the dire consequences of imbibing the poison of non-virtue. In the fourth power he renews his refuge in the Buddha, Dharma and Sangha in whose energies he can find the security and encouragement to continue practising with optimism and dedication.

He also establishes his mind in the Four Exhortations to Enlightenment. First, he acknowledges the obvious preciousness of human life as a special opportunity for gaining liberation from Samsara, and the particular good fortune of being able to practice Dharma. Second, he contemplates the inevitability of death, and how it may come suddenly and without warning. Third, he understands that the way to freedom is by transcending the forces of karma. Fourth, he considers the intensity and inevitability of suffering in Samsara. By internalizing these insights he generates the motivation to renounce the mundane life and to concentrate on the spiritual Path.

By these means he is strengthened to overcome failure and even to use failure, if it arises, as a means for establishing his mind in Dharma. His experience of the painful and obstructive consequences of failure lead him to establish the mind of renunciation: renunciation of his habitual, karmically conditioned interaction with Samsara and with others in Samsara.

So the practitioner accumulates those merits and insights which cause the Bodhisattva Wish to arise spontaneously in his mental continuum. In all his practice this wish—to attain Enlightenment for the sake of others—colours his endeavour. All his spiritual application is for the sake of others in the first place. Abiding in this attitude, he is freed from all self-centredness in his practice, and from the strain of achieving something for his own sake. He can relax in his endeavours because they are motivated by compassion.

On account of having established this attitude he also makes progress in the cultivation of Right Effort: the effort to generate and maintain wholesome thoughts and feelings, and to prevent or dispel unwholesome arisings.

Through his preparatory meditative practice he is also growing in mindfulness and Right Concentration. So, in addition to developing the aspects of the Eightfold Path relating to morality—Right Action, Right Speech and Right Living—he is also cultivating those aspects which have to do with mental development: Right Mindfulness and Concentration. Besides these, he is also becoming established in the wisdom components of Right Thinking and Right Understanding, at least in a preliminary way. His thinking is against malice, desire and harmfulness. His understanding is bent on the search for the real nature of existence. On the Path of Accumulation, then, the practitioner is already to some extent engaged in the complete practice of the Eightfold Path.

And, with regard to the first Six Perfections of the Bodhisattva Way, he has made some progress in the aspects of generosity, morality, patience and vigour (or, energy). But, through his preparatory studies and meditations, he is also becoming acquainted with the aspects of the perfection of meditation and the wisdom of perceiving emptiness. At this stage he is far from an energized or 'spiritualized' experience of these *paramitas*, but their paths are being developed in his mind.

The Path of Accumulation may take a lifetime or many lifetimes to complete. It is up to the determination and skill of the practitioner. And

The Paths and the Goals

it is necessary to become connected with an accomplished teacher. The teacher plays a central role in Buddhist practice. There can be no progress beyond a certain point without the skilled guidance of the guru. Realizing this, the practitioner should work to create the causes and conditions which will bring the teacher to him.

If he practises with perseverance, and especially if he has adequate guidance, he can complete the Path of Accumulation relatively quickly, the more so if much of it has been completed during previous lifetimes. Driven by the beauty and energy of the Bodhisattva Wish, he is bound to advance rapidly if he practises without distraction. At the end of the accumulation stage he enters on the Path of Preparation.

SECOND STAGE: THE PATH OF PREPARATION

On the Path of Preparation the practitioner prepares his mind for the profound meditations on emptiness (*shunyata*)—the insight into how all provisional phenomena, including the self, exist conventionally while being void or empty of ultimate entityhood—which will eventuate in the direct non-cognitive experience of Truth about himself and all reality.

On this path he is not yet actually meditating on *shunyata*. He is occupied in refining and honing the mental tools which will put him in a position to meditate with skill on the Ultimate Nature of Mind, and of being. The preparation involves both study and practice.

The practitioner will study more closely the implications of karma, rebirth, interdependent origination, the three characteristics of samsaric existence and the five aggregates or skandhas. He will consider them more profoundly and in ways that will increase his conceptual understanding of emptiness. On the Path of Preparation he must form a very lucid conception of the empty nature of conventional phenomena and self. At the same time he must deepen his insights into the function of compassion, for compassion is not only subjective sensibility: it is a practice intimately bound up with wisdom. So the practitioner studies to clarify how wisdom and compassion are integrated in the bodhisattva mind.

To clarify what is meant by the wisdom component he must learn what exactly is meant by emptiness as the final condition of existence in Samsara, because final wisdom is final insight into emptiness. The direct realization of emptiness is the liberating insight-energy towards which all his study and practice in the wisdom aspect are directed. In order to be liberated from the habitual, conditioned sense of 'I' he must know exactly how 'I' exists and does not exist. Only by seeing the emptiness of 'I' as a conventional entity can he fully escape from 'I.'

Thus, the understanding of emptiness is not a mere philosophical exercise. There is a crucially practical reason for eventually attaining direct cognition of emptiness: it is the only way to full liberation from the delusory sense of 'I' and 'mine.' If he fails to realize his own emptiness he will forfeit both wisdom and compassion. When he studies to understand his own emptiness he therefore states his motivation: 'I am studying emptiness in order to gain liberation for the sake of all sentient beings.'

First, he understands that the conditioned and habitual sense of 'I' is continuously arising in dependence on the five skandhas: form, sentience, perception, mental formation, and consciousness. None of these skandhas, taken singly, can be 'I' because 'I' would then have to be either form, sentience, consciousness and so forth. Clearly, none of these is 'I.' Neither can 'I' be the composite of the skandhas because the parts would then have to be indistinguishable from the composite 'I', but they are not; and 'I' would have to be indistinguishable from its parts, but is not. By these and other investigations the practitioner comes to see that 'I' arises from the skandhas without being identifiable with them. 'I' is an idea brought on by skandhic activity.

And, even as an ideal continuum, 'I' depends for its ongoing arising on a sequence of before- and after-moments. Nowhere in this ongoing sequence of experiential moments between birth and dying is an inherently existing 'I' to be found. The 'I' of twenty years ago and the 'I' of this present moment are equally evanescent. It is a flux which becomes 'I' only when it is grasped at and designated 'I' on the basis of conventional experience. Otherwise it simply flows on.

There are many analyses or reasonings, some very acute and complicated, which the practitioner can use to establish in his mind the non-inherent existence of 'I'. These are not to be valued in the first place as philosophical statements of truth. Their central purpose is to free the mind from grasping at an 'I' that is only a conventional construct, does not exist in and of itself, and is therefore not a final 'I.' The practitioner is not forced by the Absolute Nature of Mind to clothe himself in 'I.' This 'I' need not inevitably control him. It is not his self-entity.

But this does not mean that the conventionally experienced 'I' simply does not exist. It has a conventional, relative existence as a depen-

The Paths and the Goals

dent arising. So the practitioner does not seek to negate the conventional existence of 'I.' He is only negating its inherent existence, its unimputed existence from its own side. It is important to be very clear what it is about the 'I' that is being negated. Having negated the inherent but not the conventional existence of 'I', the practitioner avoids simple nihilism. He consciously expresses himself through the conventional 'I', and can enjoy self-confidence in it. But he is no longer under the delusion that he *is* in any ultimate sense 'I.'

It is the deluded conventional 'I' that has been caught up in the ignorance generated by its karma. Over countless lifetimes it has accumulated the karmic traces—the mental traces of cause and effect—that have dragged it down towards ultra-relativity: a false view of itself as self-sufficient. The way back to the pure state of Equipoise is by undoing this chain of unwholesome karma. The practitioner must use the laws of karma to eventually transcend karma, just as he must use his relative mental states and energies to find his way back to the Nature of Mind, the Buddha-Nature. He must use these to arrive at the subtle 'self-experience' which is not an entity but a mindstate: the state of Enlightenment.

As he grows in conceptual insight into the empty nature of 'I', the practitioner sees how, despite its emptiness, it suffers in its conventional nature through ignorance, attachment and aversion. He sees the suffering caused by its conditioning and its transience and understands how great is the suffering of all beings clinging to an 'I' which can bring them no lasting inner contentment. Seeing the frustration caused by their captivity in delusion, his compassion grows, and the wish arises to set them all at liberty.

Meditative Preparation

In order to meditate effectively, the practitioner should choose a location conducive to contemplation and concentration. Ideally, there should not be too much disturbance such as barking of dogs, loud chatter and so forth. A place should be set aside for meditation. It should be peaceful and not associated with unwholesome activity.

The practitioner should be disciplined in body, speech and mind, and should withhold himself from all non-virtuous conduct. He should not be distracted by mundane considerations such as the quality of food, clothing, comforts or accommodation. His mind should be fully set on what he aims to achieve in meditation.

It is best if he has with him a few Dharma friends; not more than three. These should be good practitioners whose company encourages practice and who are able to offer skilful advice. But there should be no chatter, brash conversation or humorous commotion. Yet the atmosphere should not be stern, rigid and devoid of laughter.

The meditator must guard against laziness, inattention and the thought, 'I cannot do this.' He should meditate with the insight that meditation is a vital task, leading to his liberation. He should remain mindful between sessions and should keep in mind that all his practice is ultimately for the benefit of others.

First Step: Cultivating Non-Distraction

On the Path of Accumulation the practitioner has learned to concentrate non-distractedly on the breathing. This non-distracted meditation must now be stabilized in preparation for the ensuing, more difficult and demanding meditative practices.

In cultivating non-distracted meditation the meditator begins the session by simply allowing the mind to relax. He observes with increasing detachment the flux of thoughts and feelings in his mental continuum. Then, when his mind is collected, he states his intention: 'I am meditating in order to achieve Final Liberation for the sake of all sentient beings.'

He then concentrates his attention on the in- and outbreaths. Though still aware of discursive mental arisings, he desists from grasping at them. If he does grasp at a thought and becomes distracted, he gently returns his attention to the breath. He should not become irritated or frustrated. He should not struggle with discursiveness. He simply recognizes that he has been distracted, and returns to the breath.

His concentration should not involve effort which is tense. If he becomes tense, emotion will enter into his meditation. He should remain calmly alert, gently returning his attention to the breath whenever discursiveness distracts him, and treating his mind with kind firmness. Practising in this way, he will reach the meditative state where thoughts arise and dissolve spontaneously, like clouds in the sky. When they arise he is aware of them without grasping at them, and keeps a calm concentration on the breathing.

As he becomes more proficient at keeping his mind tethered to the breathing, the arising of discursiveness becomes less distracting, leaving

The Paths and the Goals

him able, eventually, to concentrate exclusively on the breath. Thoughts and feelings are perceived without attention, like birds passing overhead very high up in the sky. The breath, however, is like a quiet flow of water on which the meditator's awareness is fully concentrated.

What is being achieved here is a preliminary calming down and light concentration of the mind. Mental energies are being calmly but firmly brought under control and enabled to remain undistractedly in one place. The whole endeavour is infused with kindness and patience. Harsh and forceful treatment of the mind will cause mental rebellion and intensified distraction. So a compassionate mind must be maintained.

The meditator should not manipulate the breathing by, for instance, prolonging the in- and outbreaths. Breathing should be normal and relaxed. If there is difficulty in remaining focused he may use some technique to help maintain concentration. He may count 'one' on the inbreath and 'two' on the outbreath, until his mind is steadily concentrated; then he returns to watching the breath.

After some months he will have attained a degree of fusion of calm and non-distraction in meditation. His mind will have become restful, alert and serviceable. With the ordinary consciousness in submission to the wisdom-consciousness, the practitioner is no longer flung about or dragged along by the flow of distraction. His mind is being made into a keen instrument for carefully investigating inner Truth.

At the conclusion of each session he dedicates any merit gained for the welfare of all beings. Then he abides for a while in the calm clarity or 'luminosity' of the post-meditation mindstate. He should try to keep this mindstate as he returns to his ordinary activities.

Second Step: Identifying the Wrongly Perceived 'I'

In the preceding meditations the practitioner has become more familiar with his inner mental 'space.' He is able to move about in it instead of being aware only at its superficial periphery. He is also able to objectify many mental processes and constructs, to observe them from a detached distance.

In this second step he searches for the habitual experience of the ordinary 'I' and, having identified it, he observes it 'from a corner of his mind.' He already knows conceptually that 'I' is empty of inherent existence. He wants now to observe how it habitually arises and appears to the consciousness perceiving it. He wants to identify exactly what it is that he is being liberated from.

Sitting in the correct posture, he allows his mind to become calm and clear, meditating on the breath. Then he waits for the sense of 'I' to manifest. He must wait calmly, not concentrating his mode of apprehension too much. If the sense of 'I' does not manifest spontaneously under his observation he can cause it to arise by remembering instances when the 'I' was badly treated or embarrassed. As he does so the 'I' will manifest in the energy of self-defence, and he can observe it.

The 'I' should be observed as it is ordinarily experienced by the habitual mind: as a self-sufficient, self-existent entity. Sometimes it seems to be a physical entity, at other times a mental one. Or it may seem to be situated in a part of the body which is experiencing pain or discomfort. The observing consciousness should think 'I', and when the intuitive energy of 'I' appears to the mind it should be continuously watched. On thinking 'I' or 'mine' a certain presence manifests separately from the concept of 'I.' It is this presence rather than the idea of 'I' that is to be watched. It is this experience of 'I' that is keeping the practitioner bound in Samsara.

This meditation should be repeatedly practised for several weeks until the appearance of 'I' is easy to evoke, is always findable and observable for a sustained session. In this way the meditator becomes thoroughly familiar with the 'I' whose inherent existence is to be directly negated.

Third Step: Reasoned Negation of the Inherent Existence of 'I'

In this step the practitioner resorts to analytical meditation. Using his developed clarity of mind he establishes a set of reasoned arguments for the emptiness of the 'I' with which he has now become thoroughly familiar.

First, he identifies the object to be negated. He does not want to negate the conventional existence of 'I', but its inherent existence or 'self-existence from its own side.' He wants to demonstrate by reasoned analysis this ultimately non-inherent mode of its being.

He may use any number of reasonings for this purpose. If he understands clearly the reasoning of dependent arising he can affirm: 'Since the habitually arising sense of 'I' arises in dependence on the skandhas, it must be empty of inherent existence, because no thing which arises in dependence on causes and conditions other than itself has inherent existence, or 'Since the habitually perceived 'I' arises from causes, it must

The Paths and the Goals

be empty of inherent existence, because that which exists inherently must also exist causelessly.'

To complete this step the meditator must generate a clear and accurate view of how the 'I' is empty of inherent existence. Not only must his intellect lucidly perceive the flawless sequence of his reasonings, but they should remain in the mind as an energy of conviction. He should be thoroughly convinced by the analyses he has carried out.

By carefully investigating in this way the meditator arrives at the sense of the complete absence of an inherently existing 'I.' It is as if a cow standing in a field has suddenly been removed and the practitioner is suddenly aware of the complete absence of what was formerly a cow.

Fourth Step: Cultivating Calm Abiding (Shamatha)

In *shamatha* meditation the meditator trains his mind to concentrate exclusively on a single mental object. In the course of this practice he will achieve great meditative stability and mental stillness. He will attain meditative states free from all distraction, in which even the arising of discursive thoughts completely ceases. He will discover the vast spaciousness of mind and gain the ability to sustain undistracted meditation for long periods. Meditation itself will become easy, effortless and fulfilling.

There are many mental objects which a meditator may choose, but the most auspicious is said by Buddhists to be the body of a Buddha. The meditator studies a picture or statue of a Buddha-body and then internalizes it. He carefully memorizes its features, colours and so forth, transforming the form representation into an object of the mind.

Sitting in the meditation posture, he visualizes the Buddha-body, about one fingerlength in size, as spontaneously arising in space, at the level of his eyes, at a distance of about three armlengths. He concentrates until it is more or less visible to the mind's eye, and then attempts to apprehend it to the exclusion of all other mental arisings.

The aim is to place the entire attention of the mind on the object. At first this is extremely difficult to do. The perceiving consciousness can apprehend the object only fleetingly and without much definition, and may frequently be interrupted by distracting thoughts, feelings or images. The meditator has now to train the consciousness to the point where apprehension of the object is both stable and clear. In the course of this training he will pass through several stages until full calm abiding is achieved.

As he repeatedly practises the meditation with perseverance, the initial instability and vagueness of the mental object will decrease. In the early phases some mental force is needed to gain apprehension of the object and to return to it when distractions occur. If the meditator has adequately prepared his mind in the breathing meditation this difficulty is more easily overcome.

Gradually the period of undistracted apprehension is lengthened. Still, the periods of distraction are generally longer than those of uninterrupted apprehension. By firmly and repeatedly re-engaging with the object, the observing consciousness becomes more familiar with it and the problem of vague apprehension is overcome, although instability of apprehension remains.

So the consciousness should be engaged in two ways: primarily it is concentrated on the mental object, but it is involved secondarily in the introspective acts regulating distraction and returning to the object. By the repeated use of the secondary, introspective aspect, distractions are lessened and eventually exhausted.

While the mental object is being closely apprehended, the introspective function is dealing with such mental obstacles as lethargy, discomfort, discouragement and so forth. Through sustained practice these are diminished and gradually abandoned, so that the object is held by the consciousness with ever-increasing lucidity and stability.

With the right amount of effort intermittent apprehension is changed into a fluid, continuous and clear observation of the object. The meditator can hold to it exclusively for an entire session and is able to do this even when he is not meditating. His mind can be continuously and effortlessly fixed to the lucid and stable appearance of the Buddha-body. And when he returns to formal meditation the object arises spontaneously and lucidly with very little effort.

Tight apprehension is used to dispel laxity: when, for instance, the object seems to fade from the mind's eye. Then apprehension is tightened in order to regain clarity and prevent distraction from arising. Should the mind become tense, tightness of apprehension is relaxed to prevent the object from going lost through over-exertion.

Eventually the introspective function dealing with obstacles such as distraction, laxity, tension and over-extertion is increasingly relaxed as the object is more easily and spontaneously held in a stable and lucid way. At this time the mind experiences great calm, immoveability and

The Paths and the Goals

luminousness. There is a sense of inner expansiveness, giving the meditator a taste of the vastness of mind, as well as of its essential purity. It is in this limitless mind-space, pure from beginningless time, that there is room to accommodate the suffering of all sentient beings and to generate Boundless Compassion.

With the achievement of calm abiding comes a sense of wellbeing of both body and mind. Physical and mental tasks can be performed with little effort, and the inner environment is one of cool, clear light. These qualities are carried over into everyday life, lending ease to all the practitioner's endeavours.

As with all meditations, the shamatha exercises are preceded by a statement of intent: 'I am preparing my mind to achieve Full Enlightenment for the sake of all sentient beings,' and is concluded with a dedication of merit for the welfare of others.

Fifth Step: Single-Pointedness (Vipashyana)

In this step the consciousness observing the object, the Buddha-body, is trained to hold to it more tightly. Not only must the object be apprehended with increased clarity but should be held so firmly that it can be penetrated. The object should be undistractedly and keenly observed for long periods, so that it appears in great detail and definition, and is seen 'in the round.' Once it is seen this sharply, the observing consciousness should penetrate it as the eye might penetrate into the centre of a sphere of light.

Then the observing consciousness, having achieved well-defined and penetrative apprehension, is held undistractedly and single-pointedly in this mode of observation. The penetrative quality of observation is not allowed to diminish in intensity nor the object to lose clear definition. Thus the consciousness is kept stably, lucidly and penetratively in one place. It does not detach.

Again a middle-way must be found between laxity and tension. If the mode of concentration becomes lax the object will lose lucidity and will not be penetrated. Concentration will become unstable. If too tense, the concentrated consciousness will simply lose the object through excess effort. Calm, firm fixity is sought.

The Gospel for Buddhists and the Dharma for Christians

Purpose

In these meditative practices the mind is being trained in stability and sharpness so that it can eventually meditate effectively on the extremely difficult qualities of emptiness. In these meditations very refined and intricate analyses will have to be performed; so the mind is being prepared to investigate these complex propositions with clarity and penetration. At the same time concentration is being stabilized in order to deal with non-conceptual insights; to remain undistracted as it transcends ordinary consciousness.

Mind and Modes of Consciousness

At this stage of his mental development the practitioner may experience confusion with regard to his conceptual understanding of mind, personal mind, ordinary mind and other aspects of consciousness such as ordinary consciousness, wisdom-consciousness, consciousness apprehending the object, and so forth.

The cardinal error would be to regard any of these as disparate, delineable entities: regarding the ordinary mind, for instance, as one entity being observed by another, the wisdom-consciousness; or viewing the consciousness apprehending the object as one entity observing another.

Mind is a continuum of pure awareness. The skandhas themselves are relative aspects of mind rather than entities, and by these skandhic aspects the personal mind arises and finds its conventional expression as ordinary consciousness. Once the ordinary mind becomes somewhat displaced by a preliminary understanding of emptiness other 'minds' or modes of consciousness are revealed. The point is that all these 'minds' are seamless modes of awareness and not separate mental faculties.

Just as a happy state of mind is not an entity but a mental state, so a wise state of mind (or, wisdom-consciousness) is also a mindstate, a much profounder state than ordinary consciousness. The consciousness apprehending the object is also a mental condition: a particular activity arising in the mental continuum.

Any mode of consciousness which has been developed and is maintained in the mind suffuses and influences the condition of the whole mental continuum. If an ordinary consciousness is maintained, the delusions of the ordinary mind will persist. If wisdom-consciousness is developed and upheld, the entire mental continuum reflects that wisdom. And

The Paths and the Goals

this mental continuum is also not an entity: it is sequence of discontinuous mental moments following one another *ad infinitum*.

The meditator will experience many states of consciousness, right up to the final state of Enlightenment. None of these states are entities in themselves or disparate mental faculties. There is no faculty of enlightenment, only an Enlightened Mindstate. The principle is perhaps analogous to that of the diffusion, focusing, refraction and reflection of light. None of these ways of using light creates an entity of light separable from light itself, or separable within the context of light. All of them represent only ways in which the original light source has been manipulated. In the same way, by manipulation of the mind mental states are created, but none of these is separable from the total mind. None of them is an entity.

General growth on the Path of Preparation

On this path the practitioner's mind has been trained, disciplined and much expanded. It has been made into a pliable instrument for discovering wisdom and generating compassion. Moreover, it has become open, spacious, peaceful, confident and spontaneous. Through the penetrating clarity of its developed insight into particulars it is able to discriminate with detachment rather then being carried along by what it observes. It is controlling its own experiences rather than being controlled by them.

At the completion of this stage the practitioner is walking the Eightfold Path with greater spontaneity. Because of the strong enhancement of mindfulness, concentration and effort, Right Action, Speech and Living are seldom diminished through distraction. But even if distraction arises, the practitioner is able to revert rapidly to mindfulness, and in this way to prevent the arising of desire and aversion. Stability and lucidity of mind, together with compassionate openness, make virtuous conduct effortless.

Throughout the Path of Preparation many obscurations, affllictions and defilements of the mental continuum are removed by intensified mindfulness. The same lucid consciousness which now sees to some extent the emptiness of the ordinary 'self' has to the same extent liberated the practitioner from captivity to his delusory 'selfness': the sense of self from which mental afflictions and impurities arise. Ignorance is giving way to clear understanding, and this clarity is spontaneously expressed in conduct of body, speech and mind.

The Gospel for Buddhists and the Dharma for Christians

By means of clear and stable mindfulness Right Thinking is established. Thoughts and attitudes all tend towards harmlessness, turning aside from deluded views of self, others and the world. Although insight into the emptiness of 'I' is not yet complete, it is sufficiently developed to have formed a wholesome preliminary Right Understanding: understanding how all transient phenomena, including self and others, exist conventionally, without possessing ultimate entityhood. Seeing through these provisional appearances, the mind of preliminary Right Understanding interacts with them in spiritual insight. So, by Mindfulness and Understanding, the root afflictions are controlled if not yet fully eradicated.

These root afflictions are: desire, anger, pride, ignorance, doubt and deluded seeing. They give rise to a range of secondary afflictions: aggression, resentment, concealment, malice, jealousy, miserliness, deceit, dissimulation, haughtiness, harmfulness, lack of shame, lack of embarrassment, sloth, excitement, lack of faith, laziness, lack of conscientiousness, forgetfulness, lack of introspection, and distraction.

The root affliction of desire arises when an impure consciousness perceives some mental or physical object, in its mere appearance, as something conducive to pleasure. Discriminating neither the true nature of the object nor of the consciousness perceiving it, the impure consciousness is caught in desire for the wrongly perceived object. Then the result of nurturing such desire is suffering.

Anger wants to inflict harm on beings, phenomena and mental arisings, which are perceived to be the cause of some form of suffering. Thus anger can be directed either outwards or inwards. It is a result of the wrong view of 'I' leading to a defensive stance in relation to 'I' and 'mine'. It even wants to defend 'I' from 'I'. It is a completely useless response whose result is separation from happiness.

Pride also arises from a deluded sense of 'I' and 'mine', including 'my possessions', 'my achievements', and so forth. The simple but unwholesome act of thinking 'this is I' is an act of pride. And from such thinking arise all the inappropriate and disrespectful modes of pride, such as: 'I am superior', 'I am only a little lower than that great person', 'I have much spiritual attainment', 'my good fortune is a reflection of my achievements', and so on. The consequences of maintaining a proud mind are denseness of spiritual perception and general harmfulness to oneself and others.

Ignorance is evidenced in the afflicted view of the modes of existence of self, other beings and phenomena in general. It takes for granted

The Paths and the Goals

that the immediate experience of these corresponds exactly with their final reality. Thus it precipitates every form of unskilful and non-virtuous conduct. Its result is ongoing entrapment in the realm of conventional appearance with all its concomitant suffering.

Doubt is an unstable mind, incapable of holding to the right view. It obstructs practice by reintroducing the energies of the other root afflictions into the mental continuum. If not remedied through mental training it leads to the abandonment of practice.

Deluded seeing is the ordinary mind's habitual view of self, others and the world. It is the product of ignorance but, more specifically, arises from the sense that 'I' is more important than others, and has the right to dispose of phenomena as it sees fit. It is the self-centred view. Its results are everywhere to be seen.

On the Path of Preparation the arising of the root afflictions is controlled by stable, lucid mindfulness and by a developed understanding. As soon as an afflicted impulse arises mindfulness detects it, understands, recognizes and disarms it, and its energy is depleted.

Through the capacity to quell the root afflictions, the secondary afflictions are also prevented from gaining access to the mind. The resultant mental purity impels spontaneous growth in the Six *Paramitas*. Generosity becomes spontaneous because the view of the emptiness of self is established, and because of openness and spaciousness of mind. Morality is guarded by mindfulness and understanding. Patience is increased because of inner calm, confidence and non-distraction. Vigour is applied in correct measure because of non-distraction. Meditation becomes spontaneous and effective because of being correctly motivated and applied. Wisdom is dawning because of growth in the ability to understand emptiness.

All of these factors are amassing merit and wholesome karma for the practitioner. Because his mind is not separable from the collective mind of all beings, the merit gained by him benefits all. And because individual karma is part of the collective karma of all beings, his wholesome karma benefits all. Conscious of this, and impelled by his increased purity, openness and spaciousness, the practitioner generates a strong energy of compassion. Having made these important advances, he is ready to enter onto the Path of Seeing.

THIRD STAGE: THE PATH OF SEEING

This path marks the beginning of actual meditation on emptiness. Using the qualities acquired on the Path of Preparation the practitioner will practise two forms of meditation: he will alternate between analytical meditation which seeks to cognize with lucid precision the logical grounds for asserting the emptiness of all conventional selves and phenomena, and meditation which confirms him in stability of mind. On the one hand he will be penetratingly analysing verbal propositions and, on the other, holding the mind firmly in non-distraction.

These two types of meditation will be practised alternately in order to prevent the mental tension which may arise in analytical meditation from going over into distraction, and to prevent mere calm abiding in *shamatha*, which may cause aversion to the intense mental activity involved in penetrative analysis.

Analytical Meditation on Emptiness

The meditator now takes as his object for meditation one of the reasonings affirming emptiness as the final nature of conventional beings and things. He meditates penetratively on each step of the reasoning until he understands it clearly and thoroughly. If he is using the reasoning of dependent arising he may reason as follows:

'A chariot does not inherently exist because it arises in dependence on certain causes and conditions. When the parts (wheels, axles, platform and so forth) are arranged in a given manner, the appearance of a chariot arises. As this appearance (phenomenon) arises, the consciousness perceiving it labels it 'chariot.' But outside of the collection and assembly of these parts the appearance of a chariot cannot be discerned. It arises and exists conventionally only once the parts have been assembled and the chariot discerned and labeled.

'However, a chariot does not exist inherently (has no existence from its own side) because it is not discernible as an entity separable from its causes. If it existed inherently, it would have to exist (absurdly) before the causes and conditions, which give rise to its appearance, have been established. But since a chariot cannot be discerned apart from its causes, nor before its causes appear, nor before it has been designated and labeled, it does not inherently exist.

The Paths and the Goals

'In the same manner, the conventional self does not inherently exist. It cannot be discerned apart from its causes and conditions (the parts of the body and the skandhas), neither does it exist before the establishment of the causes and conditions in dependence on which it arises and is designated "self." Therefore self does not exist from its own side.'

The meditator carefully investigates such arguments—or any other reasonings which will help him to perceive the emptiness of conventional things—until a lucid apprehension of emptiness is achieved.

Alternating Meditation

In the first meditative mode the meditator fixes the mind until calm abiding is established. He then analyzes the reasoning which he has selected as his argument for asserting emptiness. He carefully, clearly and penetratively scrutinizes the reasoning until he arrives at a lucid concept of emptiness: of exactly how and why a conventional phenomenon (including self) is empty of inherent existence.

During the analytical phase the mind will become excited or overwrought in consequence of the close and intense mental effort. When such excitement arises the meditator switches to the second phase: he stops the analysis and takes the mere *sense of emptiness*, as apart from his conceptual understanding of emptiness, as the single object of meditation. This sense of emptiness is held as the object in the same way in which the Buddha-body was previously held. He now keeps his mind gently but firmly fixed to the sense of emptiness, avoiding, through concurrent introspection, any lapse into laxity or excitement. When he has established a state of stable apprehension of the object he abides in it for some time, holding exclusively to the non-conceptual sense of emptiness.

Then, when the mind is calmly and lucidly resting on this object and abiding stably in one place, the meditator returns to the first meditative phase, resuming meditative analysis of the reasoning.

These alternating meditations are the first stage of meditative practice on the Path of Seeing. The meditator continues to practise in this way until a clear non-conceptual sense of emptiness has been generated and is established as the single object of further meditation.

Meditation on Emptiness

In the second stage the meditator concentrates only on the non-conceptual sense of emptiness. Having gained, through analysis in a state of calm abiding, a clear and precise apprehension of emptiness, he no longer needs to resort to repeated analytical meditation to awaken the sense. Concentrating his wisdom-consciousness on it, he abides stably in meditation, holding firmly to this inner intuition of emptiness.

At first the object (non-conceptual sense of emptiness) will seem strongly differentiated from the perceiving subject, the wisdom-consciousness. The observed object and the observing mind will be distinctly sensed as duality. Gradually, though, through repeated practice, this dualism of perception will lessen, as though the wisdom-consciousness were merging with the object.

This phase marks the beginning of the attainment of 'penetrative insight' (*vipashyana*) because the wisdom-consciousness is so penetratingly apprehending the object that some dissolution of the subject-object divide is experienced. One might say that the wisdom-consciousness is entering into the sense of emptiness and becoming diffused in it. Still, at this stage, a subtle sense of differentiation remains.

The meditator continues repeatedly to engage the wisdom-consciousness with the sense of emptiness until, at the point of attainment of Seeing, the two are fully merged 'like water being poured into water.' At this point subject and object become one, and the direct realization of emptiness is achieved.

With this realization the practitioner is freed from all reliance on conceptual modes of apprehending and understanding the emptiness of phenomena, self and others. His insight is direct and experiential. It is like the difference between one who has only heard about the ocean and one who is swimming in it. Having attained this state, the practitioner has become one who 'sees', without conceptual intervention, the Truth of existence, and the Path of Seeing is completed.

Attainments of Seeing

The Path of Seeing may take a lifetime or several lifetimes to complete, depending on the motivation, capacity and determination of the practitioner. Once it has been completed he becomes a bodhisattva on the first level (*bhumi*) of attainment.

The Paths and the Goals

With the direct realization of emptiness comes the preliminary knowledge of selflessness. It is called preliminary because only the non-innate false self-views have been abandoned: those self-views which have been inculcated through conditioning occurring in the course of everyday life, and which have resulted in a stronger habitual thinking 'I' and 'mine.' The innate false view of self, the result of karmic conditioning over countless lifetimes from beginningless time, has not yet been eradicated. Even so, the bodhisattva has gained a powerful and spontaneous insight into emptiness, and clinging to self has been abandoned.

The root afflictions are all but extinguished. Their activity is weak. They no longer have the energy to distract the bodhisattva from the spontaneously generated energies of the Eightfold Path and the Way of the Six Perfections. He is therefore radiant with virtue and Great Compassion.

The attainment of Seeing is also the point at which wisdom and compassion are inseparably fused into one spiritual energy. Discerning with great clarity the truth of emptiness as the path out of suffering, which leads to transcendence of karma, to cessation, to Final Enlightenment; and seeing the ignorance and suffering of beings who have not yet attained to Truth, the bodhisattva maintains spontaneous compassion, boundless and undiscriminating, for all sentient beings.

With the attainment of Seeing, the Inner Teacher is awakened. By experientially realizing Truth, the bodhisattva has uncovered the wellsprings of the Buddha-Nature. Its Light illumines all his consciousness, thinking and understanding. He is continually able to assess the real nature of all beings, events, tendencies and so forth. He receives clear guidance not only when awake but also during sleep. He experiences many pure dreams and appearances. The Inner Teacher emanates from him, so that others recognize his wisdom and authority.

All the components of the Eightfold Path arise spontaneously as one continuum in his mind and conduct. They now function as a living principle beyond mere moral systems. The slightest deviation from them is instantly noticed and quelled at the source. Right Understanding, in particular, has now been fully attained, so that all the other components, Right Action, Speech, Living, Mindfulness, Concentration, Effort and Thinking, are arising as virtuous energies having their origins in understanding. They are being spontaneously generated by Wisdom-Compassion.

On this first bhumi the full Perfection of Generosity is attained. Although the bodhisattva is practising and developing the other perfections, and although they are near to completion, generosity is fully perfected on the Path of Seeing, owing to the full realization of emptiness and the sense of selflessness which arises when the wisdom-consciousness merges non-dualistically with the sense of emptiness.

On the next path the bodhisattva will bring to perfection the qualities of morality, patience, vigour, meditation and wisdom. In addition, four remaining perfections will be completed: the perfections of method, wishes, power and exalted wisdom.

Meditation and Post-Meditation

At the attainment of Seeing the bodhisattva has developed a great capacity for meditative practices and for maintaining mindfulness during periods when he is functioning outside of meditation. In all his daily activities his mindfulness does not falter. He walks in the Truth which he has directly seen, informed by the energies of Wisdom-Compassion, infused with the Buddha-Nature, and guided by the Inner Teacher.

He has not yet, however, achieved complete transcendence over duality. Although his mindstate is replete with the understanding of emptiness he can not yet perceive phenomena and their emptiness simultaneously. When he perceives another person, for instance, he can with full understanding impute to that person the emptiness which he has directly seen, but cannot experientially realize the person and the person's emptiness in one act of apprehension. And, when he sees emptiness in meditation he cannot simultaneously see phenomena. In order to achieve simultaneous apprehension he must abandon the karmically generated innate false view, the conventional miscalibration which precludes simultaneity of the cognition of phenomena and emptiness. This is the one remaining obstruction to full clarity of seeing. When it is removed the bodhisattva can deal in perfected skill with the needs of sentient beings. The removal of this obstruction, therefore, now becomes his great motivation.

The unobstructed view of emptiness is the completion of selflessness. When the wisdom-consciousness perceives simultaneously and thoroughly both the conventional self and its emptiness, the way to deathlessness is attained, for only the conventional self dies. It is also the way to the completion of Great Compassion and spiritual love, for thoroughgoing selflessness liberates the energies of these. And it is the way to Final Enlightenment because liberation from the false and constraining

The Paths and the Goals

view of self sets free the wise modes of consciousness which can realize the Buddha-Nature.

FOURTH STAGE: THE PATH OF MEDITATION

Having attained the direct, non-dualistic cognition of emptiness, the bodhisattva on the Path of Meditation familiarizes himself with this experience by returning to it repeatedly in meditation. Again and again taking the sense of emptiness as his object, he enters into the state of direct cognition.

Through carrying out this practice with determination he gradually removes all the innate false views of conventional existence. He is like a person who, having been born with certain visual defects, practises with skill to correct them. Whereas on the Path of Seeing he has removed those distortions artificially produced by wearing badly designed lenses, he now applies himself to the innate optical defects.

The repeated experience of blissful union of the wisdom-consciousness and *shunyata*, merged in a non-dualistic suchness, affords great energy, calm and mental spaciousness. It is a selfless abiding in pure mind, lending power to the completion of the remaining perfections.

He brings morality (or, virtue) to perfection as both virtuous view and virtuous conduct. Tracing the relative expressions of virtue back to their Absolute Source, he recognizes that virtue and wisdom are inseparable. So virtuous motivations arise spontaneously and continually.

He brings patience to perfection with regard to its aspects of compassion, endurance and fearlessness. Self having been thoroughly abandoned, all hopes and fears that have to do with self are stilled. Great stability and clarity of mind having been established, there is no fear in the face of the deep experience of emptiness. All the appearances on whose false basis impatience arises have been penetrated by wisdom, leaving no negative emotions to limit the expression of compassion and endurance.

Completion of the Perfection of Vigour is attained when, through the energies of wisdom, and through thorough mindfulness, the bodhisattva engages easily in spiritual conduct of body, speech and mind. Because his empowering energies are arising from the Nature of Mind itself he walks the *Arya* Path with ease. He is neither toppled by achievements nor overcome by obstacles. His energies are balanced and his path is sure.

Meditation (or, concentration) is perfected by him in skilful meditative practice. He is stably and lucidly mindful at all times, remaining detached and undistracted. His equilibrium is never disturbed, even by events usually considered catastrophic.

The bodhisattva attains the Perfection of Wisdom when both the artificial and innate false views have been abandoned in the direct realization of emptiness. He now knows all things in their essence. His understanding of the Four Noble Truths is immaculate to the extent that insight and conduct are never inconsistent with each other.

Having brought the Six Perfections to completion on the first six bhumis of bodhisattvahood, he goes on to complete, on the remaining four bhumis, the additional perfections of Method, Wishes, Power and Exalted Wisdom. Whereas the six already completed are primarily qualities of the bodhisattva's own nature (although they also have an altruistic function), the additional perfections are brought to completion for the specific purpose of leading other beings to liberation.

Thus the Perfection of Method (or, skilful means) is the complete ability to devise approaches and teachings for sentient beings of varying capacity, disposition and circumstance. By this perfection the bodhisattva can reach into the conditions of every kind of karmic outcome pertaining to beings, in order to set them free.

The Perfection of Wishes is the ability to ensure that skilful means are not futilely employed: they will have the outcome which the bodhisattva intends.

Through the Perfection of Power the bodhisattva is able to engage authoritatively and authentically with all beings. His work among them is spontaneous, effective and effortless, for his power is indissolubly conjoined with Wisdom-Compassion.

The Perfection of Exalted Wisdom is the ability to understand completely the states of development and mental attitudes of all beings. It is an intuitive and penetrating insight into the conventional mind and karmic conditioning of all those with whom the bodhisattva engages.

By the attainment of the additional perfections the bodhisattva is able to discern the full extent and qualities of the conditioning of the objects of his compassion, devise skilful appropriate methods for dealing with them, ensure that the methods are effectively employed, and transmit the authentically liberating wisdom.

The Paths and the Goals

Wisdom-Compassion and The Perfections

All the *paramitas* are generated and brought to completion by wisdom. This means that the transcendent nature of the perfections derives from penetrative and immediate insight into emptiness. When the bodhisattva attains the direct non-dualistic realization of emptiness, the paramitas are infused with the wisdom-energy of that insight: they are manifested and practised in the full understanding of emptiness, with its concomitant detachment.

Thus the bodhisattva practises generosity knowing that there is no inherently existing giver, no inherently existing gift, and no inherently existing recipient. His virtuous conduct has no inherent value: it is a matter of an empty person performing empty deeds, neither good nor bad in themselves, except in conventional terms. The virtues are being acted out for the sake of others, to bring them to freedom.

One might therefore wonder how wisdom, arising as it does from the realization of emptiness, and infusing all the perfections with the detachment arising from insight into emptiness, is at all compatable with Great Compassion. It begins to seem like a form of moral play acting. But such an interpretation would be the result of a wrong understanding of detachment.

What is meant by a detached application of Great Compassion and the Perfections can best be illustrated by the following sorts of analogy:

The bodhisattva is like a person who returns willingly to an insane asylum with the compassionate wish to liberate the patients from their mental delusions. Their insanity is a cause of great suffering inasmuch as it compels them to act harmfully towards themselves and their fellow patients, and keeps them captive to a gruesome mental experience rooted in fundamental ignorance and congenital deludedness.

The bodhisattva in their midst is sane and, therefore, necessarily detached from their deluded views and conduct. He has no share in their deluded mindstate. Moreover, he recognizes that mindstate as unreal: as having no connection with sane existence, and as devoid of ultimate validity in the face of the real.

Yet, in order to liberate these beings, he must live among them and partake of their mindstate in order to engage skilfully with them. If he immediately spoke to them from his profound sanity they would regard him as the insane one among the sane many. So he remains fully detached from their views and self-views, yet fully engaged with the truth of their ultimate nature; the healthy nature of sanity.

In the same way, the perfections which he manifests and practises among them have the single purpose of rousing them to sanity, even while they resist him, misunderstand him and are, perhaps, even inclined to harm him. His gifts are designed to remedy their delusion, his virtue to dispel it, his patience to labour gently for their liberation, and so forth. Thus one can see why Great Compassion is needful.

A second analogy is that of a room full of drugged, sleeping people who are constantly experiencing nightmares. Among them the bodhisattva alone is awake. Although he knows that they are suffering only in their dreams, he knows also that their miseries are no less distressing for that. He therefore finds skilful means to enter their dreamworld and to manifest in it his skills for bringing them to wakefulness. For they cannot be woken by any word spoken outside of their dreams.

By these analogies can be seen how great is the compassion and courage of the bodhisattva. It is also clear from them how needful the Perfections are. And it is clear also that no effective liberating work can be carried out without fully realizing the emptiness of the dream or nightmare world in which these unfortunate sleepers are kept in ignorance. One can easily see that compassion uninformed by the wisdom cognizing emptiness would result in a case of the blind leading the blind.

FIFTH STAGE: NO MORE LEARNING

Having fully attained the Wisdom-Compassion by means of whose light and energy all sentient beings can be liberated, the bodhisattva enters the Path of No More learning. So far as the components of Wisdom-Compassion are concerned, he has nothing more to learn.

But this does not mean that he has come to the end of spiritual growth. He has not yet achieved Final Enlightenment, and he will walk many paths among sentient beings as he works for their benefit. There is still much room for spiritual enlargement through his ongoing experiences in samsaric realms. But he will never be mistaken or at a loss, nor will he ever fail or fall away.

Even so, as he moves along countless paths of bodhisattva activity, both inward and outward, he will be growing, becoming richer and increasingly replete with spiritual endowments, and all of this is, of course, a

The Paths and the Goals

kind of learning. So there is a sense in which this path might better be described as one of 'no more unlearning.' On it there are no more false views, distorted interpretations and karmic habits which have to be unlearned. This is why the bodhisattva is now fully qualified not only to teach but to carry out countless activities for the welfare of all beings. His teaching and conduct will always be free from error and from wrong motives.

He has unlearned the artificial innate conditioning that keeps people restricted in relative pathways. He has used the relative path with all its relative methods, references, allegories and practices to escape from relative conditioning. He has skilfully employed relative factors and means as a method for transcending relativism. In this he has acted rather like a prisoner who, having carefully studied every aspect of the prison and the experiences of his imprisonment, has gone on to use the very features of the prison environment to effect his escape.

Thus, though he continues to teach and use method and technique, he himself is beyond them. Although he continues to walk the path, he has already arrived at the goal. For him the Path and the Goal are one. Samsara and Nirvana are one. Even as he continues to make use of the myriad devices of conventional experience he is never caught in or used by them. They are at his disposal, not he at theirs.

Because he is able to walk on all paths, discerning simultaneously their varieties of method and their sameness of essence, and abiding in the Goal as he walks, he is ready to devise countless paths for sentient beings, liberating each according to his needs.

He is also liberated from all convention. Although he may respect the conventions of ordinary people he is not bound by them if they do not serve the interests of Truth and Compassion. While he is bound by no doctrine, system, tradition or collective habits, he may decide to use these for his purposes.

In his mind countless Pure Realms and Paths are generated, and in them he can abide in perfect inner Equipoise. But he is not yet entirely free from the general limitations of the body in space, time and his specific environment. Although he is capable of supernatural feats, of influencing matter, including his own body, by the power of his mind, he will not be completely liberated from bodily needs and constraints until the time of physical death. While he remains in the body it is, however, radiant, controlled, and emanating wholesome energies. To him the famous words of Shantideva apply: 'The selfish work for their own interests; the Buddhas work for the benefit of others: just look at the difference between them!'

OBSTACLES ON THE EIGHTFOLD PATH

The Fourth Arya Truth is the Truth of the Eightfold Path. Its eight components when integrated, reinforcing one another, and functioning interdependently, are the Path to Enlightenment and, in our model, the Path to the Wisdom-Compassion ideal of the bodhisattva.

Obstacles to spiritual growth are therefore those which hinder development on the Eightfold Path. More accurately put, they are those obstacles which arise when the Eightfold Path is not walked in an integrative way. When certain of the components are not used to reinforce or maintain other components the result is an incomplete system, a broken chain of causality and conditions from whose unefficacious incompleteness obstacles arise.

If, for instance, effort is not adduced to mindfulness, mindfulness degenerates, resulting in non-virtuous conduct. If action, speech and living are non-virtuous, the causes and conditions for cultivating understanding cannot be generated. Without understanding the Path cannot be walked.

Obstacles are essentially the products of wrong views and wrong attitudes, which are related, respectively, to an absence of Right Understanding and an absence of Right Mindfulness. Obstacles arising from wrong view have to do with the ways in which a practitioner wrongly interprets reality: the dharma of self, others, phenomena, events, and the Dharma itself. Obstacles arising from wrong attitude have to do with expression or reaction: wrong conduct of body, speech and mind in relation to self, others, phenomena, events, and the Teachings.

Wrong View of the Self

Wrong view of self is of two kinds: the view that self exists autonomously and ultimately, which leads to thinking 'I' and 'mine', and the view that the notion of self is so delusory that self can be said not to exist at all. The right view is that self exists conventionally but non-inherently and is therefore not in any final sense an 'I am This.'

The wrong view of self as ultimately existent, and the concomitant thinking 'I' and 'mine', lead to self-centredness, possessiveness, self-defence and pride. These and other egocentric energies are causes of suffering to self

The Paths and the Goals

and others, and keep the person in ignorance. There can be no progress on the Path until the mind clinging to 'I' begins to loosen its grip.

The right view of self cannot quickly be attained because emptiness is a difficult teaching. Moreover, the mind thinking 'I' does not want to hear this teaching. Therefore emptiness is traditionally not taught to beginners. On the preliminary paths other methods may be used to loosen the congenital mental grip on 'I.'

Without frustratingly struggling against 'I', the practitioner can come to recognize the looming obstacle of 'I' by mindfully noting how 'I' causes suffering to itself and others; how it leaps to its own defence, deceives itself, puffs itself up and so forth. Such mindfulness creates a very real suspicion of 'I', can generate much laughter at the expense of 'I', and generally tends to make 'I' seem much less important.

Then by persevering in unselfish conduct the practitioner begins to experience the benefits of altruism: a more peaceful mind, less general harmfulness, less strife, and the growth of inner contentedness. By adopting a less defensive stance, by not always acting to avoid or preempt difficult or trying circumstances and occurrences, an attitude of acceptance and spaciousness is engendered, and with these comes decrease in anxiety.

By rudimentary practices in meditative mindfulness, such as simply looking inwardly at anger, noting how it arises and dissipates, the sense of 'I' becomes separated from the sense of anger (and whichever other negative emotions are being watched). By always focusing on the negative emotions themselves instead of on their objects—the people at whom 'I' am angry, disgusted and so forth—they can be stilled without struggle or self-judgement.

These simple techniques have the effect of freeing the practitioner from the tight, habitual control of 'I'. The world and others in the world become less threatening. In these ways, long before effective insight into emptiness is achieved, the wilful monkey 'I' can to some extent be tamed and trained.

Wrong View of Others

Before gaining adequate understanding of the emptiness of persons, the practitioner may mistakenly view the other or others as 'You', 'He', 'She', or 'They'. Then, not discerning the non-inherent existence of 'You', he interacts with 'You' as though 'You' were the final definition of 'You.' The self of the other is dealt with at face value.

If the other acts unpleasantly the practitioner thinks, 'He is unpleasant.' If the other seems threatening, 'He is a threat', and so forth. On the other hand 'he' or 'she' or 'they' may be 'kind', 'clever' or 'helpful.' This sort of view is mistaken in that neither the other's self nor the qualities manifested by it are being recognized as provisionally existent. They have become fixed definitions of fixed selves. And it is the same with 'He has done this harm to me' or 'She has disappointed me' or 'Tomorrow he may harm me.' The other has been misidentified as a concrete self intending to harm 'me' and 'mine.' The practitioner is thinking about and reacting to a conventional construct misconstrued as a real entity in its own right.

It is as though, during a drama being acted on the stage, one of the actors were to take the wrong view that the other actor is really the character he is playing, and ultimately responsible for that character's actions. If the other actor, following the script, were then to insult him or to slap his face, he would respond as though the stage character were real. And, of course, by responding in this wrong way, he too would suddenly be 'real.'

Of course the other's self is never completely 'unreal' in the same way that a character in a play is unreal. But the other person is never ultimately real. What is ultimately real about the other is not the conventional self being expressed, but the Buddha-Nature in the deep mind. The other is first and foremost a sentient being with the potential for achieving Final Enlightenment, and with the present need to be liberated. Thus the other must always be an object of respect and compassion: respect for the latent Buddha-Nature and compassion for the as yet unliberated self.

So the right view of the other's self is that it is conventionally but non-inherently existent, transient and suffering. What is to be discerned in the other is the 'not-self.'

Wrong View of Phenomena

The essential nature of all phenomena is also to be understood as not-self. The world as a whole is to be discerned in this way. With regard to inanimate things, not-self is the absence of the quality of self-existence, of being inherently existent. No worldly things exist inherently. By the reasoning of dependent origination all mundane phenomena are recognized as constructs, the results of causes, conditions and subjective mental ac-

The Paths and the Goals

tivity. As such they are transient, decaying and unattainable in any final sense. They are all part of the passing show.

Viewed rightly, the transience and illusoriness of worldly things engender a mindset of renunciation. They can never be seen as ends in themselves. If wrongly viewed they easily become objects of attachment or aversion. Of course, the wrong view of phenomena is connected to the wrong view of 'I', and clinging to this twofold ignorance makes all interaction with the world of things harmful and futile: the mind thinking 'I' and 'mine' interacting with the things 'I' want and do not want.

Wrong View of Events

Wrong view of events is related primarily to ignorance of karmic forces, coloured by a wrong view of self, others and phenomena. Without insight into the karmic origins of events they can easily exert a disproportionate influence on the practitioner's mind. He is left without the understanding by which all events can be used as spurs and means to spiritual growth. He is controlled by what happens rather than empowered to shape every occurrence to beneficial ends

Without insight into the law of action, of becoming, of cause and effect and conditionality, events appear random and meaningless. They seem to have no other relation than to the brief episodes of a mundane lifetime. They are only the struggles or fortunes of this life. So all their meaning can have to do only with mundane living and self-preservation. Their spiritual energy is neither understood nor utilized. They loom large in this world because their provisional nature and their control by karmic forces are not discerned. They seem of small value to the spiritual life because their deep wellsprings in the mental continuum and in the karmic shaping of that continuum are not seen.

Where there is a wrong view of self, others and phenomena, coupled with a lack of insight into the operations of karma, events are ascribed only to their apparently immediate agents. The mind thinks, 'He, she or it is doing this to me'; 'They are wrongfully taking what is mine'; 'I have been undone by bad luck'—or, 'I have done a very good thing and deserve to be rewarded.'

So, unless an understanding of karma and emptiness is acquired, events can neither be traced to their ultimate source nor analyzed as to their real meaning and value. The practitioner stands helpless before them and is tossed about on the waves they create. His practice is jeopardized by the very events which should be used to encourage it.

Wrong View of Dharma

The Dharma, understood as the Teaching of the Enlightened One, is, for the practitioner, the royal road to Enlightenment. Having come to this Teaching through his own karma he should seize the opportunity to grow beyond the cycle of suffering. But he should not view the Buddha's Dharma as the only way to Truth. It is indeed beneficial for him, but it is not for those who are not yet ready to accept it.

Neither should the Dharma be viewed as a means for adding 'spiritual' qualities to the ego-mind. Spiritual development takes place beyond the ego in the mindstate which clearly knows the emptiness of ego. As the Diamond Sutra says: 'There is no self that can be brought to Enlightenment.'

On the other hand, the Dharma cannot be understood as leading to mere nihilism, as though there were no conventionally existing self. Therefore it is crucially important to know what it is about self that is to be negated by the practice of Dharma.

In short, just as the Buddha taught the avoidance of all extremes, so the Dharma itself should not be viewed from an extremist vantage point. The Dharma is neither very easy nor impossible to practice. It is neither incomplete nor final. It is in no way absolute. It is a relative Path walked by a relative being in a relative realm.

Wrong Attitude to Self

The mind thinking 'I' and 'mine' cannot attain to Wisdom-Compassion because 'I' is a closed system. It guards its entrances and nurses its vulnerabilities. It shuts the door through which wisdom must enter and from which compassion and lovingkindness (*maitri*) flow outward to other beings. For bodhicitta to develop in the mental continuum the most vulnerable part of the ego-mind must be laid bare, but the mind thinking 'I' naturally resists such self-exposure.

The self-protecting 'I' is a mind afflicted by ignorance, desire, anger, doubt and pride. All of these afflictions are closely related to the refusal to open the mind, to make it spacious and to expose its weaknesses. And the

The Paths and the Goals

closed, self-preserving ego-mind, subjected to the afflictions, is naturally prone to outward-looking fear and inward-looking anxiety.

Despite its innate ignorance it sees itself as the measure of all things. Therefore it justifies the indulgence of its desires and its clinging to 'mine'. It defends its terrain with multiple forms of aggression, withdrawal and stubbornness. It asserts itself with pride. Yet, because of its deluded vision, it is filled with doubt: 'Can this be trusted?'; 'Can I achieve this?' and so forth.

These afflictions are not only turned outwardly but are brought to bear on the wrongly viewed self. The self itself becomes the object of desire, pride, anger, doubt and fear. It may well be treated quite harshly. It can even become the object of hatred and disgust. Instead of attending to the aspects of the mental continuum that are causing his problems, the ignorant person chastises the self. So, itself becoming the object of unwisdom and harshness, it cannot but project these negative energies into the external evironment.

So the self must be trained to let go, to cease from clinging to 'I' and 'mine'. And it must be trained in an atmosphere of compassion. Harsh treatment of the ego-mind can have no good result. Just as all relative beings suffer, the 'I' also suffers, and harshness is not the remedy for suffering. With patience, compassion and intelligent firmness 'I' must gradually be opened to Truth.

Wrong Attitude to Others

Others fall into the three conventional categories of friends, neutrals and enemies. Because we label them differently we react to them in different ways. We cannot bear in an enemy what we easily tolerate in a friend, and to neutrals we are simply indifferent. Our attitudes towards each are determined at face value. This is an ignorant approach.

The practitioner should know that his reactions can never be determined by the behaviour of the other. The other cannot make me angry. The other cannot reach into my mind to arouse either hatred or love, nor can he leave me indifferent. These reactions occur as a result of my conditioning and are my own responsibility. Anger arises not because of the other but because of myself. When I stop thinking 'I', when I cease from clinging to 'mine', anger dissolves, love is liberated from the aspect of attachment to the other, and indifference is not possible. So the practitioner's attitude towards friends, enemies and neutrals is determined exclusively by himself, by his own mindset, and by the extent of his control over his mind.

Towards friends the wrong attitude is one of attachment, of clinging to and placing expectations upon friends. Such an attitude is transactional: it expects a return on the friendship it gives. It makes friendship conditional on what the friend renders and is therefore not wholly determined by the freedom of the practitioner's own mind. In making claims upon friends and in being attached to friends it makes possessions of friends. Then, instead of remaining (in freedom) *a friend*, the friend becomes *my friend* and, being *mine*, is made subservient to *me*.

An enemy is one who has harmed, is harming, will harm, or is inclined to harm me. He may also threaten me by threatening those I love. He may threaten me in a variety of ways, if only by not agreeing with or conforming to my way of being. But in every case, from the most harmful and threatening to the most subtly disagreeable; aggression and malice, anger and the like, are wrong attitudes towards an enemy. By wrongly imagining that an enemy is arousing negative emotions in my own mental continuum I immediately weaken myself in two ways: I allow an enemy a delusive control over my own reactions, and my real capacity to react in freedom is paralysed. And because I believe my enemy to be the cause of my negative emotional responses I remain unliberated from him: I am allowing him to determine my behaviour. Then, even when I try to view him compassionately, I must first enter into struggle with the negative feelings which I believe him to have aroused in me. So the first step in dealing correctly with an enemy is to be liberated from the wrong notion that he can in any way directly influence my emotional responses to him.

Then, acting in liberty, not thinking 'I' and 'mine', and perceiving the non-inherent existence of the enemy, while knowing that he cannot influence my reactions, and bearing in mind the infallible operations of karma, I can transform my enemy into my benefactor. For an enemy is a greater teacher than a friend, for whom it is much easier to feel compassion, patience and the other positive emotions. And in the enemy's deep mind, as much as in my own, there is the Buddha-Nature.

But this approach does not mean that the practitioner should allow malice and violence in the enemy to go unopposed. These should be opposed, but only by their proper opposites: truth, beneficence and compassion. The practitioner's central concern should be for the welfare and liberation of the other, even if the other is the 'enemy'.

The Paths and the Goals

If attachment to friends and aversion towards enemies are overcome it will not be possible to feel indifferent towards neutrals. They will assume, for the developing bodhisattva, their rightful place of 'important others.' For the equalizing wisdom beyond attachment and aversion sees all others as objects of active compassion.

Wrong Attitude to Phenomena

Exploitation, in a word, is the wrong attitude towards phenomena. The things in our realm, the resources in our world, are for our needs and not for our greeds. In exceeding our needs we do violence to the needs of others and, of course, we harm our world.

Wrongly viewing phenomena as ultimately existent, we desire them without reference to their spiritual meaning and value. This kind of desire, rooted in ignorance, prevents the awakening of renunciation without which there can be no genuine spiritual growth.

But renunciation should not be understood as a simple and final turning one's back on the world. Right renunciation is fostered by taking an intelligent view of mundane objects: discerning how they exist, at what points they meet our needs and are useful for spiritual development, and at what point they become obstacles. We should moderate our relation to things, not clinging to them by subjecting them to the sense of 'I' and 'mine.' The practitioner at all stages of development can live very comfortably in the world without being wracked by feelings of loss and gain. Here again, detachment is crucial.

The right attitude is that there is no inherently existing 'I' gaining or losing an inherently existing 'something.' Like mental phenomena; like thoughts, feelings and imaginations, worldly phenomena come and go, are established and decay, enter into and pass from our possession. None of this should be cause for the excitement and stress of clinging, hoping and fearing. We can enjoy things without longing to keep them; we can lose them without longing to have them restored to us. To the awakened mind both gain and loss are equally important in their role as spiritual teaching.

Because they are transient and only conventionally present, all desirable things disappear in the very grip of the hand which seeks to grasp them permanently. Undesirable things present themselves again and again to the experience which seeks to avoid them permanently. Good things are to be used wisely, bad things are to be wisely avoided or opposed, without allowing the mind to become distressed. No thing is good or bad in itself.

Wrong Attitude to Events

It is clear that wrong views lead to wrong attitudes and wrong attitudes to wrong actions and reactions. The same causal chain applies to the practitioner's attitude and reactions to events.

Events are never random. They are karmic expressions in the realm of action. Moreover, they are an outflow of the collective karma of the group of beings, especially the human beings, who initiate and are affected by them. And these beings have no inherent existence. Therefore events have no ultimate reality. Without the interpolation of the minds influenced by karma no event could arise. This is true even of events which seem to have no connection with apparent mental agents, such as natural processes and occurrences, or disasters. They all come by the individual and collective karma of the beings inhabiting a realm.

Understanding karma, emptiness, and the centrality of mind, the practitioner's attitude to events will be wise, open and detached. Neither good nor bad events will cause inordinate excitement or distress. The mind that is not overly impressed by events can respond to them in liberty. The practitioner's mental liberty is always the key to right attitude. A mind free from fear, desire and blame cannot be trapped by events.

For a mind developing in this way all occurrences are opportunities for the practice of Wisdom-Compassion and teachings on the Eightfold Path. Whatever may happen to him, the practitioner can grow by it

Wrong Attitude to Dharma

Doubt and complacency are wrong attitudes to Dharma. The doubting mind thinks, 'This Dharma is an insufficient path' or, 'I am not able to walk this path.' Then, doubting either the sufficiency of Dharma or its own capacity to practice, such a mind becomes discouraged. Discouragement in its turn acts to diminish effort, and progress is stymied, leading to increased doubt.

The complacent mind thinks, 'This Dharma is easy.' It overestimates its own capacity and underestimates the profundity of the Teaching. Therefore it mistakes small accomplishments for big and fails to eradicate

The Paths and the Goals

the real obstacles to the attainment of bodhisattvahood. Its hallmarks are pride and lack of insight.

Confidence and determination, proceeding from a right assessment of one's capacity, are the right attitude to Dharma. The practitioner can draw confidence from the recognition that his own karma has brought him to the Path. Were he not ready, he would not have found it. But he should realize, too, that the opportunity to practice Dharma is precious. He cannot know how many times he might have to pass through Samsara before this opportunity is again offered. Bearing in mind his own suffering and that of all sentient beings, he should walk the Eightfold Path with strong determination.

DISTRACTION AS SOURCE OF OBSTACLES ON THE CHRISTIAN AND BUDDHIST PATHS

As on the Christian Path, distraction is the chief source of obstacles on the Eightfold Path. The practitioner becomes distracted when mindfulness is not maintained; in other words, when Right Effort is not adduced to the practice of mindfulness.

Right Mindfulness, as has been said, is of four kinds: mindfulness of the body, of feelings, of the mind, and of objects of the mind. Practised in this way, mindfulness functions to clarify, purify and concentrate the practitioner's awareness. The result is stabilization of the mind in wholesome states, and such stabilization is increased by the concurrent practice of meditation.

The ongoing practice of mindfulness, during which the wisdom-consciousness is continually observing the ego-mind, checks and gradually weakens the ignorant tendencies of self. The ego-mind cannot be overcome by struggle. Struggling against it is only another way of asserting its ultimate reality. It needs only to be watched, to discover how its activities arise and vanish so that its ultimate unreality becomes apparent and, in the process, its ignorance, attachment and aversion are dispelled as influences on the mental continuum.

But mindfulness does not watch only the unreal aspects of mind. It is also continually aware of the energy of the Buddha-Nature. While remaining aware of the shallowest mental energies at one end of the continuum, it reaches ever deeper into the Enlightened Mindstate, not only becoming increasingly aware of its luminous energy but actually merging with it. In this dynamic the Energy of the Buddha-Nature itself becomes the source of mindfulness as the wisdom-consciousness is increasingly steeped in and dissolves itself in it. The effort hitherto adduced to mindfulness then becomes spontaneous or 'effortless'.

Without this growth in Right Mindfulness, Right Understanding can neither be generated nor maintained because, until Right Understanding itself arises and persists spontaneously, it must continually be renewed and upheld by mindfulness. And the same applies to the other wisdom component of the Eightfold Path, Right Thinking.

Understanding this, we can see how Right Mindfulness, Right Effort and Right Meditation function interdependently to establish and maintain Right Understanding and Right Thinking, and how these five components of mental development and wisdom bring Right Action, Speech and Living into spontaneous life as expressions of the Energy of the Buddha-Nature.

We can see, too, how crucial non-distractedness is to spiritual growth. When distraction occurs, mindfulness and understanding are suppressed. Then wrong views and attitudes arise to spread afflictions in the practitioner's mind.

So, just as the Christian must maintain mindfulness of the inner Christ on the one hand, and of the tricky carnal mind on the other (guarding the gates of the mind), so the Buddhist is mindful of the Buddha-Nature while not neglecting to watch the activities of the ego-mind. In both cases this practice involves watching the body, too, for it is not separable from mind.

OVERCOMING AFFLICTIONS (OBSTACLES ON THE CHRISTIAN PATH IN BUDDHIST PERSPECTIVE)

When the wisdom-consciousness of the Buddhist or the innate awareness of the Christian are obscured by prolonged distraction, doubt, fear, temptation, sin and discouragement are given the opportunity to manifest. In the Christian experience the remedy for these always comes by referring them to the inner Christ. For the Buddhist these negative manifestations must be liberated in the Enlightened Mindstate of the Buddha-Nature. But these ultimate remedies do not preclude the need to deal with such obstacles by other methods, especially during those phases of the Path where the sense of the inner Energy is not strongly developed or spontaneously present and active.

For Christians and Buddhists alike these are matters involving mindfulness and understanding. Doubts are resolved by an honest cultivation of Right View, based not on hearsay but on experience and on an authentic insight.

Fear can be an obstacle for Buddhists as much as for Christians. The teaching of emptiness with its implied loss of the habitual self can be a source of fear. There are fears related to failure on the Path, fear occurring during profound meditations and in some cases fear of evil beings. These can only be radically calmed by the Wisdom-Compassion which derives from the Buddha-Nature. On the wisdom side the remedy lies in detachment from the feared objects by the cultivation of insight into their empty and transient nature. Such detachment also implies letting go of unrealistic hopes because the ignorant mind fears disappointment. On the side of compassion, fear is counteracted by compassionate wishes and conduct, even towards evil beings. Lastly, as an inevitable product of Wisdom-Compassion, purity of mind naturally dispels fear.

The Buddhist dispels temptation by mindfulness and purifies his karma when non-virtuous deeds have been committed. Mindfulness and purification are practised so that the wisdom-consciousness can be returned to undistracted communion with the Buddha-Nature.

In the case of discouragement views and attitudes must be revised and renewed: Right Mindfulness and Right Understanding must be re-established, together with all the other components of the Eightfold Path. These, as we have seen, are to be maintained by the stabilization of mind which comes from a merging of the mental continuum with the Buddha-Nature in meditation.

Presumption and despair in Buddhism have to do with pride, over-confidence, lack of confidence and laziness. The mind thinking, 'I cannot do this', is viewed in Buddhism as one result of laziness. The remedy in all cases lies in the calming and equalizing wisdom of the inner Energy and, once again, the way back to it is by Right Effort applied to Right Mindfulness. These, while undistractedly maintained, generate a balanced and realistic confidence in the Dharma and in one's capacity to follow it.

WRONG VIEWS AND ATTITUDES (OBSTACLES ON THE BUDDHIST PATH IN CHRISTIAN PERSPECTIVE)

For Christians, wrong views and attitudes proceed from a mind out of communion with the inner Christ; for a mind in that condition of distraction is incapable of Christlike understanding and Christ-informed mindfulness. In short, wrong views and attitudes are generated by the carnal mind.

For the believer the wrong view of self is that it has any right to autonomous life. The Christ-Mind knows that it has never possessed such a right because it has never been ultimately alive. Jesus said, 'Let the dead bury their own dead', and Paul, 'Reckon yourselves dead to sin but alive in Christ.' Such reckoning is not a mere act of the imagination. It is an acknowledgement of the spiritual truth that the carnal mind only appears to possess life in itself until it encounters the inner Christ. From then on it is destined to perish and to be resurrected in Christ. Seen in this way, Christianity clearly admits the provisional nature of the 'life' of the ego-mind, its emptiness, transience and suffering.

The wrong view of others follows from the failure to reckon the carnal mind dead in Christ, by which failure the believer cannot but see other carnal minds as having life in themselves and interacts with them on that ignorant basis. And, viewing them as self-existent entities, he cannot see through the other's carnal mind to the inner Christ by which it is obscured. The carnal mind cannot see others as Jesus does or as Paul does when he says, 'Henceforth I know no person after the flesh.' If the believer knows the other 'after the flesh' (by the conditions and conditioning of the carnal mind) he cannot love others in spirit.

(At this point we come up against the problem inherent in the doctrine that Christ is not present in all people but only in those who believe in him and have accepted his salvation. It is a tenet that predominates in Christian doctrine, but we must at least make the point here that the possibility of Christ's universally indwelling all people, even when his presence in them is obscured by the ignorance, sin and unbelief of most of them, is by no means ruled out either by the Scriptures or by all Christians).

In Christianity, the wrong view of phenomena is the view which fails to recognize that they are passing and 'of this world'; subject to all the dynamics of relative existence. The Christ-Mind, however, sees them in their essential nature and renounces them on the grounds that they are

The Paths and the Goals

unenduring and incapable of rendering genuine contentment, whether in the enjoying or in the possessing of them.

Events and eventualities are wrongly viewed when the will of God is not discerned. Again, it is the carnal mind which cannot discern the wisdom of God's will in all that occurs. Only in the Mind of Christ can the meaning and Divine intention of all events be discovered, because their spiritual purposes are revealed in Christ. In Christ the believer knows that all events and circumstances, including episodes of suffering, work ultimately to the good of those who love God and are fulfilling his purposes.

The karmic principle is not absent from the Christian view of events. It is embodied in Christ's teaching, 'as you sow, so shall you reap.' The spiritual law of cause and effect operates within the context of God's will. By dying to self and becoming one with the inner Christ the believer transcends the ordinary dynamic of cause and effect by coming into conformity with the Divine Imperative, so that everything that happens to him is transformed into means for spiritual growth in Christ.

The carnal mind is responsible for all wrong views of Christ's Teaching because it can only experience the teaching as a legalistic formula, devoid of spiritual energy. If the carnal mind were to know the Teaching as Energy, it would be extinguished in that energy. Therefore it is restricted to making of spiritual Truth a set of precepts which it cannot practise without some tendency to self-interest and hypocrisy. Just as the Buddhist cannot practise Dharma without overcoming the ego-mind, so the carnal mind cannot authentically walk the Christian Path. As Jesus taught, 'What is of the flesh is flesh; what is of the spirit is spirit. My words are spirit, and they are Life.'

We see, then, how, as in Buddhism, wrong views in Christian spirituality spring from lack of understanding and of mindfulness. For the Christian, spiritual understanding comes through mindfulness of the inner Christ. Then that mindfulness, by which the intrinsic awareness is merged with the Christ-Mind, is transformed into the spontaneous Presence of Christ in the inner person, directing, teaching and consoling the believer.

And, as in Buddhism, wrong views lead to wrong attitudes. These have already been discussed as obstacles on the Buddhist Path and need not be re-examined from the Christian perspective since their characteristics can easily be extrapolated from the nature of the wrong views outlined above. We can note, however, that their unspiritual nature closely resembles that of their Buddhist counterparts. In essence they proceed from a view which wrongly interprets the 'life' of self, which lacks insight into the laws of cause and effect and the transcending of these laws, does not penetrate to the final understanding of transience and relativity and, through lack of spiritualized energies, does not attain to unity with the spontaneous inner Energy, whether this Energy is understood as the inner Christ or as the Buddha-Nature.

SELF AND THE INNER ENERGY

We have seen how the practice of the Eightfold Path traces an essential line from the experience of selfhood in the ignorant ordinary mind to experiential Truth as a merging of the wisdom-consciousness with the Buddha-Nature. In this process the ordinary self is put out of play by a wisdom-recognition of its emptiness. This line seems to be mirrored on the Christian Path where the carnal self is 'put to death' or 'reckoned as dead' so that the intrinsic awareness can be liberated to merge with the Christ-Mind. The obvious question must be whether the Christ-Mind and the Buddha-Nature are actually one and the same Enlightened Energy.

Before attempting to answer this question we can pause to determine whether the self, the ordinary or carnal mind, is defined and experienced similarly by Buddhists and Christians. Is the self that is put to death in Christ the same self which Buddhists merge with the Wisdom-Energy of the Buddha-Nature? Is the non-inherently existing Buddhist self the same as the spiritually dead Christian self? Are Buddhists and Christians engaged in becoming liberated from the same unspiritual mental construct?

Both certainly see the self as exercising a delusory and unwholesome control, centred in desire and ignorance, over the total individual mental continuum. Both see the ego-self as expressing itself in the afflictions: anger, pride, greed, and so forth. Both recognize its self-serving and self-preserving bias. They also agree that, as the fundamental obstacle to spiritual living, it cannot be transformed into something spiritually alive: it must be transcended, overcome, abolished.

Both conceive of the self as 'dead'; as lacking inherent existence or life in itself. In Christ, the Christian puts to death a self which, as a mental aggregate, has never in truth been alive. The Buddhist accomplishes essentially the same thing when he attains the direct realization of emptiness.

The Paths and the Goals

With regard to the sinful or ignorant nature of self, the Christian considers fallen habits of mind, mundane human instinct, and personal will to be adamically predetermined and as operating, therefore, under the 'law of sin and death.' This law can with much justification be considered a Christian interpretation or model of the law of karma. The decline into ultra-relativity which has formed the Buddhist ego-self has formed the Christian carnal self also. It is responsible for the universal human condition of conventional selfhood. The factors on whose basis the phenomenon of self is considered by Buddhists to arise, the five skandhas, cannot be argued out of the Christian self. Logic and empirical investigation easily confirm the skandhic construct and, in the final analysis, it is used only to confirm what Buddhists and Christians already agree upon; that the carnal self is devoid of life from its own side.

If we can accept without further investigation that the same self is being dealt with on both paths, we must go on to ask whether the methods used by these paths lead to the same result. Are the Christlike person and the bodhisattva both completely liberated from self? At least ideally? For we know that, in practice, the fully liberated saint is a precious rarity on any religious path.

The Christian says of his liberation in Christ, 'It is no longer I, but Christ that lives within me.' The Buddhist describes his experience of liberation as being 'like water being poured into water.' In both cases the idea is that of profound unity with a vital inner Energy.

Whether or not this idea adds up to the same religious experience is another question. Studies of religious experience provide us with a variety of experiences even within a single religious system. The Christian mystic has an experience of Christ which differs from that of the literalist or the charismatic. The arhat experience is not the same as that of the bodhisattva. Yet, in their diversity, these are generally accepted as multiple experiences of the same essential Truth-Energy. By the same token, there are varieties of spiritual conduct which are acknowledged as deriving from the same convictions regarding wisdom, love and purity.

Taking all this into account, it seems unwise to dogmatically reject the proposition that the inner Christ, experienced through the Holy Spirit, and the Buddha-Nature, experienced in the Nature of Mind, are two expressions of the same spiritual Energy.

For most Christians and for many Buddhists, however, such a position would be untenable. Christians would see in it a radical departure from belief in the uniqueness of Christ. And then, as has been said, most Christians do not accept that Christ is inherently present in all people, including non-Christians. The position also raises difficulties with regard to the accepted doctrines of the Holy Trinity, the more so as Buddhists do not accept the idea of a personal Godhead.

In their turn, Buddhists would certainly argue against the understanding of the inner Energy as an indwelling Person. For them the Buddha-Nature is an Enlightened Mindstate, devoid of all personal attributes. It can only be personalized insofar as it finds expression in and through the person experiencing it.

Of course, doctrinal systems can be devised to advance either view: the essential sameness and accidental difference, or the essential difference and accidental sameness, or even the utter difference or sameness of the Christ-Energy and the Buddha-Energy. So there can be no profit in taking that direction.

The real test can only be made by means of dialogue, communion, and the sharing of experience. Only by these means can people move beyond doctrinal theories and sticking points. Only by coming into relationship with one another will Christians and Buddhists be in a position to assess directly their respective spiritual fruits.

METHOD

Whether or not we agree that the Christ-Mind and the Buddha-Mind are the same inner Energy, we can hardly disagree with the proposition that Christianity and Buddhism see the essential spiritual Path in the same terms: as a Path in which the ignorant view and experience of self are led to extinction in that inner Energy.

And, beyond their agreement on the need for self-transcendence, they are agreed that there is a spiritual aspect of the mental continuum (which we have called 'intrinsic awareness' and 'wisdom-consciousness') which merges with the inner Energy to generate a transcendent or spiritual life experience.

To achieve this a variety of methods are used, and there are details of difference within the Buddhist and Christian communions themselves. Between Christians and Buddhists there are more definite differences, reflecting the divergence in their respective understanding of relative and

The Paths and the Goals

absolute factors: of the natures of the ordinary mind, of conventional existence, and of the Divine.

Still, we can discern some essential similarities. The most obvious of these is the practice of mindfulness or contemplation with its function of maintaining an awareness that is spiritually centred, observant, introspective and circumspect. In Buddhist practice mindfulness, refined and intensified through meditation, is the prime method for the uncovering of the Buddha-Nature. In Christian practice mindfulness is intensified by prayer and contemplation, especially in the profounder practice of these, where prayer and inner communion are continuous and non-verbal. In both cases the wisdom-consciousness is made to concentrate increasingly on the inner Energy, until the two are merged.

Mindfulness is used by both as the means to growth in right understanding, until spiritual Truth arises spontaneously and directly in union with the inner Light. In both cases there is some form of alternation of study and practice. For Christians, as for Buddhists, the analytical study of scriptures and commentaries should move from the merely cognitive to the revelatory; the point at which the wisdom-meaning of sacred literature and oral teaching is revealed to the opened mind, where the letter comes to life and becomes part of the energy of mindfulness.

Other aspects of mental training show sameness of purpose even where the methods differ. The cultivation of right views and attitudes to self, others and mundane things is one example. Emphasis on purification of the mind is another, together with the uncovering and stabilization of love and compassion.

At supposedly more superficial levels there are similarities of intent found in devotional practices such as the making of offerings and the transfer of merit for the benefit of others. Similarities are also evident in the recitation of formal prayers and the use of external aids such as rosaries and icons. Even tantric methods involving visualization and other forms of harnessing the energies of the imagination are not alien to classical forms of Christian practice.

At every level of internal and external practice the varieties of method reveal themselves as techniques for achieving fundamentally similar goals. If this is admitted, the failure of Christians and Buddhists to investigate each other's methods seems not only unprofitable, but remiss.

EMPOWERMENTS

Neither Buddhists nor Christians walk their paths in unempowered human weakness. From the moment they make a decision for Truth, an inner strength and comfort are awakened. There is a new courage, warmth of heart, and lucidity of mind; a sense of inner Presence that is entirely absent from the ordinary mind with its mundane concerns and intentions. Then, as they grow in Truth, this sense waxes in intensity, adding faith and consolation to their quest.

These are empowerments discovered in refuge; the Buddhist refuge in Buddha, Dharma and Sangha, and the Christian refuge in Christ, his Teaching and his Church. What these aspects of refuge provide, in addition to spiritual empowerment, is a secure spiritual space, a circumscribed well of spiritual energy which protects and upholds the adherent.

For Buddhist and Christian adherents alike the Teacher is both an example and an immanence; that which points to Illumination and is at the same time the Energy of Illumination. The Teaching, at first a refuge of right precepts for the conceptual mind, becomes a refuge of Truth-Energy as wisdom is revealed beyond all concepts. The communion of practitioners or believers, from the least to the greatest, and including those no longer alive in the material realm, encourage, exhort and comfort the one on the Path. They walk before and with him.

This is the common experience or, at least, the common view.

THE GOAL

In assessing the commonality of goals we have of course to ask again whether Christlikeness and bodhisattvahood amount to the same type and degree of spiritual transcendence. A large part of our answer to this question will have been determined by our views on the sameness or difference of the Christ-Mind and the Buddha-Mind. If we agree that they are the same, it follows that the Christian and Buddhist goals, both as ideals and as actual attainments, must be the same also.

We can, however, approach the question from another angle: that of the definitions of the goals as Wisdom-Compassion and Wisdom-Love. In this approach we must decide whether or not the Buddhist and Christian understanding of these is the same. Then we can go on to consider their fruits as ideals of experience and conduct.

The Paths and the Goals

In Buddhism wisdom is understood to be the full insight into and direct realization of the empty (*shunya*) nature of all conventional beings and things, and the corollary that Ultimate Truth can only be known to minds which have transcended emptiness and are therefore able to perceive Truth, emptiness and conventional reality simultaneously. The wise mind sees through all appearances to discern their empty essence.

Christian wisdom is seeing all things, conventional and ultimate, in the Mind of Christ. The Christ-Mind sees all conventional reality as 'passing away' and as 'dead in sin.' It sees them as devoid of any permanence and, hence, of inherent existence. For that which exists inherently is qualified by its permanence. The experience of Truth, in Christianity, occurs beyond these 'passing' states, in the Life-Mind which Christ himself *is*. Seeing Truth in Christ, the Christian sees the delusory nature of all conventional phenomena and beings. More than this, he knows himself to be in intimate union with the Christ-Mind, which is the 'I am that (which) I am': the indefinable Absolute.

The sameness of the essential interpretation of wisdom is clear: wisdom is seen as penetrating to the provisional nature of all mundane appearances (or, in Christian parlance, 'all created things'), concluding that Truth cannot be discovered or experienced in these. It finds Truth in transcendent mindstates, in the Mind-Energy of the inner Christ or the Buddha-Nature, and it acknowledges that the ordinary or carnal mind must be overcome if Truth is to be seen directly.

With regard to love and compassion, the bodhisattva's experience of these is described respectively as 'the wish to liberate all sentient beings from the cycle of samsaric suffering' and 'the wish to attain Enlightenment for the benefit of all beings.' From the outset the ideal is utterly altruistic. The bodhisattva walks his Path for the sake of others. He cultivates his mind in countless skilful means in order to be effective in leading others to Truth. Moreover, he is prepared to sacrifice all he has, including his life, for the sake of others.

The Christlike mind is self-sacrificial in exactly the same way. It lives and dies for the sake of establishing others in Christ. The outstanding example of the Christlike mind is found in the life of Paul who, centred in Christ, worked ceaselessly to bring others to Christ. His practice of skilful means is evident from his statement, 'I have become all things for all men so that some may be saved.'

The ideal of conduct, in both cases, can be defined as activity which aims at alleviating the other's provisional suffering while pursuing his final liberation. 'Doing unto others as you would have them do unto you' is the provisional ideal, but is not an end in itself. Refraining from harming others and actively doing good to others are ideals of conduct which find their highest fulfilment as means to guiding others to Truth.

Thus spiritual love means dying to self for the sake of others. As Jesus said, 'Greater love has no man, but that he lay down his life for his friends.' The Christlike and the bodhisattva both understand that all beings, especially human beings, are friends.

BEYOND PHYSICAL DEATH

Although it is outside the intention of this book to investigate what Buddhists and Christians believe about the afterlife, it is worth briefly considering this question here. Of course, it is a question whose answer must rely completely on doctrine, whether that doctrine rests mainly on faith or on logical extrapolation from other insights. We can in no way refer to reported experience except insofar as we can accept what the Teachers have told us.

The Christian View

Christianity does not accept the principle of rebirth into various relative realms, except in the case of the realm, or condition, of purgatory; the place where souls are purified before entrance into God's Heaven. But even this transitional realm is not entered by rebirth. It is a transitory phase of the eternal soul's progress towards the Divine. Furthermore, it is a tenet of faith rejected by Protestantism.

The believer is faced ultimately with only two possibilities: ascent to God's Heaven or descent into Hell—and these are both eternal states.

Hell is the realm reserved for those who have rejected Christ's salvation, preferring to abide in sinfulness. It is described as a place or condition of infinite and eternal suffering in complete separation from God. Hell is the abode of Satan and the fallen angels, and of all unredeemed beings. 'Lower' beings, such as animals, can experience neither Heaven nor Hell because they are without eternal souls.

This horrible domain continues to be understood in a variety of ways by Christians. Some accept a very literal interpretation: Hell is a realm of

The Paths and the Goals

fire and torment where the spirits of evildoers suffer everlasting punishment and regret. Others see it as an eternal mindstate of separation from God. Yet others hold that, while Christians must believe that Hell exists, they are not obliged to believe that any person has ever been put there. And, in other attempts to reconcile the existence of Hell with the love of God, some assert that evildoers are cast into Hell outside of the Divine Will, by the force of their own wicked mindsets. And others hold that Hell is not an eternal state.

The Christian idea of eternal paradise, into which the Christlike will enter, is also subject to various interpretations. Probably the most useful route to a general and consistent view starts with a consideration of the mindstate (or, spiritual condition) of the Christlike person.

The Christlike person has 'died to self' and been 'resurrected' in Christ. According to these spiritual symbols, the redeemed person henceforth abides fully 'in Christ', or merged with the Christ-Mind. The Christ-Mind, in which the believer fully abides, is intimately united with the other two Persons of the Trinity; the Father and the Holy Spirit. Thus the believer, too, is united in the fulness of Godhead, and it is this dynamic of being which enters Heaven. How it does so and how it is expressed in Heaven remains a mystery.

There are views in which Heaven is anticipated as a kingdom in which Godhead reigns as Infinite Light, surrounded by angelic hosts and the spirits of the faithful, or Heaven is understood as an eternal condition of joy and peace, as an unutterable mystical union with the Divine, and so forth.

This mystery is deepened by the doctrine of the resurrection of the body, whose literal interpretation is that the dead will rise again in spiritually transformed bodies, like that of the resurrected body of Christ. This teaching is rendered the more mysterious in that the physical body of Jesus is believed not to have experienced decay, whereas the bodies of the Christlike obviously return to dust. So here again there is room for many doctrinal explanations, often bound up with eschatological teachings.

At best the Christian accepts these doctrines in simple faith, as mysteries yet to be revealed. He knows that, however limited his understanding of these things must be, he will abide after death in the Presence of God, in Christ and through the Holy Spirit, in boundless peace and glory.

The Gospel for Buddhists and the Dharma for Christians

The Buddhist View

Buddhist views of the eternal Enlightened Mindstate also vary with reference to Theravadin and Mahayanist systems and their differing ideals of the arhat, pratyekabuddha, and bodhisattva. As regards the samsaric realms into which the unenlightened are repeatedly reborn, however, there is general consistency.

Buddhists speak, in the main, of six cyclic realms into which beings may be reborn and from which they must be liberated into Enlightenment. These are: realms of gods, demigods, human beings, animals, hungry ghosts and hell-beings, associated respectively with the predominating vices of pride, envy, desire, ignorance, greed and hatred. These are all relative realms, into which sentient beings are driven to take birth by the forces of their own karma, and from which they can be liberated by Truth. So there is no notion of an eternal Hell, although the Buddhist hell-realm corresponds in other ways with its Christian counterpart.

The samsaric realms, as 'afterlife states' into which beings are reborn, are in the relative category. The sentient being moves from one episode of conventional existence to another. Between death and rebirth there is an intermediate state in which the mental continuum is driven by karmic forces towards the appropriate realm of rebirth. According to some tantric systems it is possible to achieve Final Liberation by performing certain practices during the course of this intermediate (*bardo*) process.

The other, and final, category of the afterlife is the attainment of Buddhahood: the final liberation of the enlightened mental continuum from all samsaric realms. At this point it is the Mindstate of Enlightenment itself that becomes a Buddha-Being. We might say that the total mental experience of Enlightenment, occurring in the last lifetime of the bodhisattva, is the Energy which *is* Buddha.

For many lifetimes the bodhisattva has returned to samsaric realms to work for the benefit of beings. In his last lifetime he passes beyond rebirth. In the cessation from all becoming the Enlightened Mindstate of Perfect Equipoise is established.

This Mindstate is not in any way a personal self as we ordinarily understand selfhood. There is no question of a personality being uplifted into Buddhahood. The sources of ordinary personhood; karmic and skandhic factors, have been transcended. The Buddha is the Enlightened Mindstate itself having become a *kaya* or 'body.' But this body is not to be

The Paths and the Goals

misunderstood as something concrete. It is a mode of manifestation involving Mind and mental mobility; a discrete, compound mental energy abiding in Equipoise.

As such, a Buddha remains a non-inherently existent, relative being, but the quality of his relative nature is so subtle as to have escaped all relative forces and influences. So there is in this manifestation a quality of absoluteness. For one thing, the Buddha-Being is not caused by the creation of a new mindstate in the bodhisattva's mental continuum, but is a return to the aboriginal state of Enlightenment that has existed from beginningless time. This state is uncaused in that it proceeds directly from the Absolute Nature of Mind without the interpolation of karmic activity. Its causes are therefore not to be discovered in any relative factors. Therefore it does not rely on any relative factors, including consciousness of itself, as causes for its continuous arising. It spontaneously and simultaneously cognizes both its relative existence and its ultimate emptiness. And, because it does not depend for its arising on consciousness of itself, it abides in non-duality, and is able to perceive simultaneously all conventional phenomena and beings, and their emptiness.

Because this aboriginal Enlightened Mindstate has existed, albeit non-inherently, from beginningless time, it neither relies on nor is conditioned by karmic forces. Being unconditioned, it abides beyond all conditioned limitations and is therefore omniscient. And, being unconditioned, it manifests spontaneously without any departure from Equipoise.

In its spontaneously arising nature it effortlessly generates emanations of itself, without departing from Equipoise. In generating these expressions of what it *essentially is*, it partakes of the nature of the relative realm, for its perceptible manifestations could not otherwise be perceived. The Absolute cannot be perceived except in its relative manifestations.

Finally, because of its partaking in the natures of both the relative and the Absolute, because of its being uncaused, unconditioned and yet present and active in relative ways, it is beyond the duality of existence and non-existence. It is neither absolutely existent nor relatively non-existent.

Common Ground

Although such descriptions of Buddhahood are not easily understood by those not trained in Buddhist thinking, it should be clear that both Buddhism and Christianity agree that what lives on after death (understood as a state of final release) is the indestructible aspect of the individual mental continuum which has merged with the Wisdom-Compassion-Love-Energy of the First Principle of Mind.

This mental dynamic, however articulately it may be described in conventional terms, must ultimately remain a mystery to Christians and Buddhists alike. The only religious experience of which we can speak authentically is that which we experience between birth and dying.

The opportunities for sharing knowledge and insight are, at any rate, only to be discovered and used in this lifetime. It seems perverse to wait for the common insights that might come to us after physical death. That sort of attitude would be a tragic denial of our present common humanity, the deepest common ground on which we walk right now.

Part 6

Conclusion: An Invitation to Spaciousness

A SPACIOUS MIND ALWAYS has room for more than it presently contains. Yet, while it is open to continuous, open-ended growth in Truth, it is obviously not lax or undiscerning. Its spaciousness derives from centredness and balance, and it is centred in Wisdom-Love. It is the Christlike or the Bodhisattva Mind. Whatever is being added to its central knowledge and experience of Truth can be accommodated, but there is no room for untruth.

Even the most spacious Christian mind cannot make room for any tenet or experience which diminishes the person and teaching of Jesus Christ, yet it can refine its insights. Likewise, the bodhisattva can accommodate all paths which do not diminish the energies of Wisdom-Compassion.

Christians and Buddhists on their respective paths, knowing that these must inevitably lead them beyond provisional doctrines, have no reason to restrict the natural, luminous spaciousness that is their true nature, and the ultimate nature of their paths. However much each might consider their own path to be complete in itself, there is no reason why gifts of wisdom and love should not be exchanged. A good gift, even if it does not fulfil a necessity, must always be an enrichment. And there are occasions when needs themselves are not recognized until they are suddenly met. The unspacious mind must forego such gifts of growth.

The mind becomes more spacious as it separates what is essential from what is adventitious. The spiritual mind starts from the essential and brings in other mental objects to clarify, enhance and beautify the essential.

We can attempt to make room in our Christian or Buddhist minds by considering our paths both as essence and as systematic developments of that essence: their Truth, and their means of attaining and defining

Truth. In doing so the intention cannot be to predetermine precisely what we can and cannot share with one another. A prescriptive approach would be a denial of the free, vital and spacious nature of individual spiritual growth. It is up to all spiritual people in every new situation to discover in it what is helpful for progress.

THE ESSENTIAL PATH

All spiritual people have spent a portion of their lives in initial ignorance; a time of worldliness, unwisdom and spiritual darkness. This period is followed by a phase of self-searching and reassessment when it becomes clear that the mundane life is ultimately frustrating, unfulfilling and incomplete. Then a spiritual path is sought. When it is found, its teachings are absorbed in a process of intellectual learning. Next comes direct experience and inner knowledge of the Path. Finally, there is growth into conformity with Truth.

During the initial period of ignorance life is lived at the most superficial levels. Spiritual questions, if they occur at all, are brushed aside, or attempts are made to rationalize and reformulate them in the context of ordinary life. All effort is spent on managing life in the world, with varying degrees of success or failure, enthusiasm and boredom, and so forth. It is a process necessarily involving much compromise. Morality, knowledge, wisdom and relationships are all subjected to worldly norms. The fundamental goal is comfortable survival in the various systems set up by the world order. Periods of strain are offset by periods of recreation and escapism. The cycle is bounded in time by birth and death. The central focus of all activity is 'I' and 'mine'. For most people this is all there is to life.

Many, however, are brought in one way or another to a place of frustration where the cycle ceases to satisfy. The details of the mundane life become tedious and overwhelming. What the survivalist struggle delivers, both materially and psychologically, fails either to satisfy or to pacify the mind. When this sting is felt, the person has reached a crisis. There can never be a return to blind happiness in the world. The only ways out are forward towards meaning or downwards into mundane escapism. Either way, worldly complacency has gone over into search: the mind seeking a way out of suffering.

This search is for a new way of knowing and experiencing life. The old ways can no longer yield contentment. The material world of loss and

Conclusion: An Invitation to Spaciousness

gain cannot bring inner peace. Therefore the answers must be found in the mental-spiritual realm. Because the material cycle cannot be transformed, the mind must encounter it, regard it, know it, and experience it in a transformed way. This insight is the beginning of the spiritual Path. It acknowledges the need for a mental life that is liberated, joyful and at peace.

When a spiritual path is discovered, it naturally commences with a process of learning. The person goes through the doctrinal phase, absorbing and clarifiying the teachings. But these teachings are not the final objective of the search. They are only a means of crossing the divide between the mundane and the spiritual mind. They are a set of precepts which, while they prepare the mind for the experience of Truth, provide a foretaste of spiritual life. They cannot by themselves satisfy the mind in search of Truth for they are not Truth, even though they are true. Truth is the transformation of doctrine into Energy. On a spiritual path it can be no other way because the doctrine is always leading the person to the overcoming of self.

Then, as self dies, spiritual Energy begins to operate. Learning is going over into knowing. And what is becoming known is not an increasing field of doctrinal truths but an increasing power of Wisdom-Compassion; of joy, love, insight and peace. It is a knowledge which both informs and transforms the mind. It brings the person into conformity with itself and, in so doing, leads beyond the limitations of formal creeds and systems. It outshines all legalism.

Then, in the transformed person, the Path and the Goal become one. The liberated mind extends its Energy of Wisdom-Love beyond the reach of religious quibbles. It is as generous as it is powerful, as authoritative as it is unrestricted. It 'blows where it will.'

The essential spiritual Path is universal. All purified minds in which self has been overcome experience the absolute Truth-Energy, however differently it may be expressed as doctrine or even as conduct. There is one essential source and one result.

DOCTRINE

Although varying in allegory and symbol, all authentic religious doctrines express a universal Truth. They lead beings beyond the liberation from self, and on to the experience of their true nature. Beyond the restricting experience of the ordinary mind there is the same Enlightened

Mindstate. Otherwise people on differing religious paths would have to be fundamentally different in their very humanness, and would be unable to communicate with one another.

And, indeed, when doctrine is given the upper hand over Truth, the particulars over the essential, communication does fail. It fails because doctrines are not penetrated to the level of their radical sameness. It is as though, examining the drawings of a tree made by a number of people of differing backgrounds, only one expression is admitted to represent a tree. The inadequacy of such an exclusivist subjectivity is easy to see, not to mention its tragic limitations.

In what may be called their 'ideal essence,' however, all authentic religious doctrines describe paths of mental transformation whose goal is the discovery of Truth-Energy beyond the obscurations of ego. They point to a 'Kingdom of Heaven within' or to the 'Luminous Nature of Mind.'

They speak of similar aspects of spiritual growth, involving moral purification, mental development and the attainment of wisdom. Whether they view the person as made up of body, soul and spirit, or of body, ego-mind and wisdom-consciousness, is ultimately irrelevant. These too are constructs imposed upon an infinite mental potential within the human being. And they speak of a similar experience of the human mind, referring in differering ways to the same physical, personal and infinite aspects.

To closely unravel the intricate threads of Christian and Buddhist doctrine in an attempt to place the corresponding elements of each upon a vast table, like pieces of a puzzle, and then to show how each locks in with the other, has not been the intention of this book. Any work which sets out to accomplish this would be aiming at a Christian-Buddhist syncretism in which both paths would have to go lost. That would be an act against natural diversity, tending to diminish the ever-developing enrichment of diversity, an enrichment which is most fully gained, not by means of unimaginitive amalgamation, but by genuine, open sharing.

Amalgamation also robs the person of the opportunity for sharing. If people were all made to share the same hybridized fruit, what would be left to enrich and diversify religious practice? What would be left for mental spaciousness to take in and give out, or of the need for discernment in the acts of giving and receiving?

Actually the accidents of doctrine are most helpful to one another precisely when they do not seem compatible, inclusible and absorbable. That is the point at which new energies of insight are coerced into being

Conclusion: An Invitation to Spaciousness

and where, through fearless generosity, old ideas about Truth come under revision. This is always a task for individuals because it takes place on the path of individual spiritual growth.

It is a truism about doctrinal formulations and the allegories and symbols on which they are based, that they can be manipulated to mean even the opposite of what they apparently say. That is why religion can so easily be used to justify the most unspiritual of human actions. But if doctrines can be put to use to divide people, how much more can they be used to achieve a fuller human communion. And why should it be less fearful when doctrines are used to justify harmful and divisive conduct than when they are used to bring spiritual people closer to one another?

SPACIOUSNESS

If we are able to mindfully distinguish between relative and absolute, non-essential and essential, individual and universal, we can discover a new roominess in our minds. We can see a unity of endeavour beneath the surface of apparent disunity, and take the first steps out of the restrictive atmosphere of religious fixation into the spaciousness of spiritual liberty.

We do not have to abandon the orthodoxy of our own paths to achieve this freedom. All we need to understand is that our orthodox paths are not absolute. They are good for us who walk in them, and they can lead us to Truth. The paths to Truth, however, are manifold. If we can only acknowledge this, our own paths become suddenly so much more precious because we can see how they carry us to Truth along a way of universal wisdom.

Only at the level of spiritual essence can we genuinely perceive the spiritual nature of all others. When we walk in our essential Truth and uphold it, there is no need to defend it. Truth defends itself by being Truth. We can therefore relax with all Truth, and with all people who are sincerely seeking Truth.

In examining the doctrines and traditions of Christianity and Buddhism, in looking at their historical diversification and their variegated expression in the world, we find ourselves faced with two alternatives: either Truth is truly expressed in many different ways, or there is only one true way among the many. If we adopt the latter position we are forced to choose what we believe to be the right path, not only for ourselves, but for everyone. We must choose on behalf of all humanity. In doing so we cannot but exclude from spiritual communion all people who cannot choose our own path.

That is the essence of our dilemma, and the answer cannot be to try to draw or force all people into one path. The dynamics of relative minds in a relative realm will not allow it. Only when we can accept this are we able to begin to conceive of the real beauty of Truth in our world. For we can then see how Truth expresses itself in a myriad outward forms, corresponding to the inherent diversity of all aspects of this conventional realm and making sense both of its own nature and the nature of all its relative expressions.

END

May this book bring benefit to many.

www.ingramcontent.com/pod-product-compliance
Lightning Source LLC
Chambersburg PA
CBHW050616300426
44112CB00012B/1522